20/07

£5-0

TINY

EPIC LAND BATTLES

EPIC LAND BATTLES

RICHARD HOLMES
EDITOR: S.L. MAYER

Bounty
Books

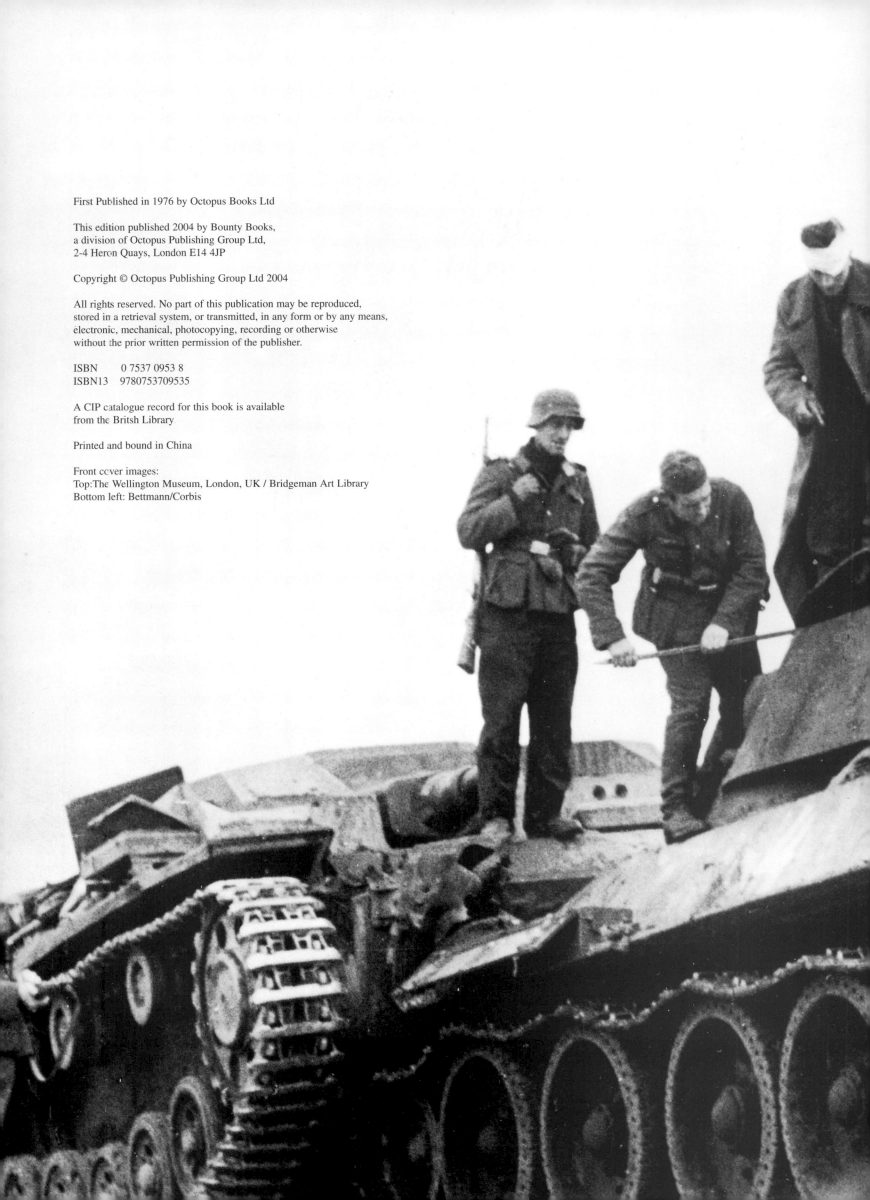

First Published in 1976 by Octopus Books Ltd

This edition published 2004 by Bounty Books,
a division of Octopus Publishing Group Ltd,
2-4 Heron Quays, London E14 4JP

Copyright © Octopus Publishing Group Ltd 2004

ISBN   0 7537 0953 8
ISBN13   9780753709535

A CIP catalogue record for this book is available
from the Britsh Library

Printed and bound in China

Front cover images:
Top: The Wellington Museum, London, UK / Bridgeman Art Library
Bottom left: Bettmann/Corbis

Contents

Introduction

Edited by S L Mayer

There are many myths in military history, often created out of the feeling, engendered in both the camps of the victor and the vanquished after a war, that the next conflict will be similar to the last. France expected that the *élan* which had brought them victory under Napoleon I would be sufficient under Napoleon III. Their belief in this myth was shattered at Sedan in 1870. The German breakthrough at Sedan led the French to believe, in 1914, that a German thrust would take place in the northeast of France, and French military strategists devised Plan XVII on this basis, to plunge into German-controlled Alsace before the breakthrough came. They were shocked when Germany invaded France via Belgium, forcing the armies of Pau and Castelnau to move thousands of men west to the Marne to defend Paris. In 1940 France's eastern flank was defended by the Maginot Line, and she hoped to counter Hitler's expected offensive in the west by moving her forces into Belgium at once, so rendering a revival of the Schlieffen Plan impossible. The result was a breakthrough at Sedan which effectively trapped both British and French forces behind German lines when the *Wehrmacht* swept to the Channel. The escape from Dunkirk saved their lives, if not their equipment. In short, history may repeat itself, but it is wiser to look for parallels well into the past, for it is unlikely that any nation will attempt the same strategic plan twice in succession.

An even greater myth, running throughout the whole course of military history, is that seafaring nations cannot fight land wars; only Continental armies, with their long tradition of large standing armies, can mount great offensives which win wars. If one examines the history of two great sea powers, Great Britain and the United States, who in this century have maintained the largest navies on earth and who have fought the most decisive sea battles, one finds that quite the opposite is true. In 1914 Britain had a small army: some 200,000 men, half of whom were policing the Empire. Germany, on the other hand, had a standing army of well over a million men and reserves numbering several millions more. Germany had applied the principle of conscription for decades while Britain depended entirely on volunteers. Yet the British Expeditionary Force was the best-trained body of men at the Battle of the Marne. Their drive between Germany's First and Second Armies turned the tide of battle in favour of the Allies. By 1916 Britain, who had by now introduced conscription, had millions in the field and held the Germans to a draw at the Somme when the élite of both nations were pitted against each other. At Waterloo Napoleon was defeated, not by the great land armies of Russia and Austria, but by the British under Wellington, with the help of the Prussion Army under Blücher. Wellington had fought many exciting tactical battles in the Peninsula, but no British Army had faced the forces of Napoleon in a set-piece battle on the grand scale in the entire 25-year war between Britain and France. The result was a British victory.

In the War of the American Revolution, the British won victory after victory over the American Republic on land—from Quebec and Bunker Hill to the Southern campaign. When they finally lost at Yorktown in 1781, it was due to the failure of the Navy, not the incompetence of Cornwallis or his men. The retreating British were thought to be no match for the cunning and power of Rommel's *Afrika Korps* in the Desert War of 1941–3. Yet, with their backs to the wall, Montgomery's Eighth Army overwhelmed the Desert Fox and forced him to begin his long retreat to Tunisia and defeat at El Alamein. The American armies of the Second World War, though vastly inexperienced compared with the *Wehrmacht*, were caught by surprise in December 1944 at the Ardennes Offensive; but the German breakthrough was stopped in its tracks, and thanks to hard fighting and superior air power, the Americans forced the Germans to retreat to the Rhine within a month. Despite all the naval strength that the United States was to muster against the Japanese in World War Two, it was land-based forces from both the Marines and Army who had to take Iwo Jima and Okinawa prior to the dropping of the atomic bomb, which made it unnecessary for a five-million-man land force to invade the four home islands of Japan.

A third myth, or rather a debate about the myth, centers around the efficacy of conscripted troops. In the 18th century conscripted troops were hardly considered by military and political strategists. Although Washington attempted to enforce conscription on a state-by-state basis during the American Revolution, these efforts were something less than a success. The *levée en masse* decree of 1792 during the French Revolution attempted to pit untrained recruits against professional armies at the Battle of Valmy, and the amateurs won. Napoleon proved that initially untrained personnel could be quickly hardened to battle-readiness, and his victory over the Austrians and Russians at Austerlitz was perhaps the most outstanding example of the ability of non-regular forces to overwhelm an entirely professional regular army. After several campaigns, Napoleon's *parvenu* general staff and soldiery was more than a match for the opposition.

But the debate continued throughout the 19th century. After Waterloo the French distrusted a conscripted force, while the Prussians learned that not only was a massive reserve necessary in modern warfare but that it was only possible through conscription from the civilian population. General Helmuth von Moltke proved his point conclusively at Königgrätz, when the Prussians routed the Austrians, making the unification of Germany under Prussian leadership possible. The Prussian victory only half-convinced the French that they too ought to begin conscription, and in a half-hearted way the military law of 1868 took steps to redress the military balance. But the French reserves were a paper army, and many of them had never held a rifle in their hands. They were unready, and Moltke exhibited the lack of French preparation by his crushing victory over the forces of Napoleon III at Sedan two years later. In the two world wars it was largely conscripted troops that faced each other throughout the conflicts. Since 1945 the tendency of Western armies to return to the principle of smaller, professional forces has accelerated. Both Britain and America have abandoned conscription, and it is thought that combat effectiveness has been increased, not weakened. It remains to be seen if they are right, but there can be little doubt that combat experience is the essential quality required of armies, professional or otherwise. Once conscripts have faced an enemy in action, their skills are learned quickly or the men simply do not survive.

The last and perhaps the greatest myth of military history in the past two centuries has emerged from the Second World War. It has been a constant criticism of the efforts in Korea and Vietnam that these wars, unlike wars in the past, were political in character, and therefore the politicians restrained the hand of the professional soldiers who could have won these wars outright had it not been for political interference from above. It was as if all prior wars had been in some way placed outside the political context and that Clausewitz's definition of war as a continuation of diplomacy by other means had never been written two centuries ago. What were the Napoleonic Wars if not politically motivated? His attempt to extend French power as well as the ideas of the French Revolution, liberalism, democracy and nationalism, created as much opposition from the reactionary forces which opposed him as enthusiasm among those who rallied to his cause. The American Civil War was a war between opposing economies as much as it was a fight between two distinct political ideologies within the United States. Lincoln's conduct of the war was masterful because he knew the political limitations to his course of action. Only in 1863 did he dare to attempt conscription. Only in that year, two years after the war had begun, did he dare to free the slaves, hesitating previously in order to avoid alienating the four slave states which still adhered to the Union cause. In 1863, the great victories of Vicksburg and Gettysburg in the same week of July ended Southern hopes of retaining the independence of the Confederate States from the American Union. The epic struggle between Nazi Germany and Communist Russia was as much a conflict between two rival totalitarian ideologies as it was a fight for hegemony in Europe. If Hitler had not mistreated the Slavic minorities of the Soviet Union when 'Operation Barbarossa' was launched in 1941, he might have gained their support and not have faced the massive defeats at Stalingrad and Kursk which effectively put an end to the terror of the Third Reich. The struggle against Hitler by the Western democracies was equally ideological and equally controlled by political forces from above.

No war is total war. Wars in the 20th century have indeed been borne by whole populations who shared in the suffering endured by the men at the front. But war aims, insofar as they are actively defined, are never total. If Britain and America were fighting the Second World War to rid the world of totalitarian dictatorship, why did they stop at the Elbe? General George S. Patton, for one, was prepared to continue his drive eastwards beyond Czechoslovakia into the Soviet Union itself. He was restrained by Eisenhower who, in his turn, was restrained by Truman, who ordered Ike to withdraw all his forces from their positions close to Berlin, Vienna and Prague back across the lines drawn by Roosevelt, Churchill and Stalin at the Yalta Conference. Korea and Vietnam were limited wars—limited in weapons employed, limited in the aims they hoped to achieve—in consonance with every war ever fought in modern history. Political leaders called the tune there as they had done in the past. The inter-relationship between political decision and military action and the continuity of the development of strategy and tactics in all periods of history was maintained, for no war is uniquely different.

In his discussion of the twelve epic land battles of the past two centuries, Richard Holmes has masterfully dealt with the myths and realities of modern military history from Washington to Montgomery. Strategy, tactics and leadership in military campaigns have been dealt with in all their subtlety. Warfare has been endemic in human history. An understanding of how and why wars are fought is essential to an understanding of history and human nature itself. The richness and complexity of the inter-relationship between political decisions and military command is handled with unique adroitness by Richard Holmes in this account which captures the heroism of Pickett at Gettysburg, the insanely cool aplomb of Haig at the Somme, the daring of the *Waffen SS* at Kursk and the Ardennes, the courage of Rommel in the Western Desert and the brilliance of Napoleon at Austerlitz, presented in all their drama and color in this analysis of the epic land battles which altered the course of the history of the world.

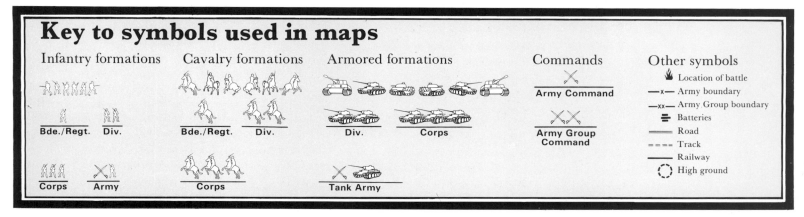

Key to symbols used in maps

Infantry formations	Cavalry formations	Armored formations	Commands	Other symbols

Yorktown

1781

At the end of the Seven Years War (1756–63) Britain was the unchallenged master of the seas. The colonial empire of France was largely won and what some historians have called the First British Empire was at its zenith. A peace conference was convened in Paris to divide the spoils of France and Spain. Twenty years later another Paris peace conference was held; but this time it was the British Empire which was being partitioned. Within the space of one generation the 'world had been turned upside down'; a new revolutionary nation had been born out of the wreckage of the First British Empire, the United States of America. The War of the American Revolution was the first colonial war in modern history won by the colonists. It was also the first modern guerrilla war won by a revolutionary state against a European great power. The Battle of Yorktown was its decisive conflict which broke the British will to carry on against the Americans. It was another Dien Bien Phu, another Tet

Offensive in Vietnamese terms. Although the British could have continued the war, they lost their will to do so. Yorktown was one of the most important battles of the last two centuries. It created the United States as an independent country.

The Treaty of Paris in 1763 recognized the world-wide achievements of British arms in the Seven Years War, but it was less of a triumph for British diplomacy. Britain's former allies thought

Far left: General John Burgoyne presents his sword to Horatio Gates after the Americans had defeated the British at Saratoga in 1777. This victory convinced the French that the United States was worthy of support. **Near left:** 'Gathering of the Mountain Men', by Lloyd Branson. The guerrilla activities of American irregulars in the South and West hampered British supply lines and harassed the armies of Cornwallis marching northward to Virginia. **Below:** Storming of the Redoubt at Yorktown.

themselves betrayed by her sudden withdrawal and her enemies considered the peace terms excessively harsh. On both sides resentment was increased by the fear of British domination in Europe and envy of her colonial wealth. No major European nation would regret any future British difficulties or raise a finger to help her. The Peace of Paris inaugurated no *Pax Britannica* but was rather the prelude to one of the greatest blows British pride ever suffered. Moreover, this discomfiture was to occur in America, where Britain's most conspicuous successes had been won.

Even before peace was achieved there were prophets who foresaw the dangers of total victory. In 1761 the Duke of Bedford told the Duke of Newcastle, then Prime Minister, that he did not know 'whether the neighbourhood of the French to our American colonies was not the greatest security for their dependence on the mother country, which I feel will be slighted by them when their apprehension of the French is removed'. The security which the British had achieved in North America also brought to the fore a fundamental disagreement on the role and status of colonies. For the British government, and indeed for most Britons, colonies were still significant only as a source of wealth for the mother country. North America in this period could not compete with the riches to be obtained elsewhere, and other colonies such as the West Indian islands were easier to defend and to govern.

A Costly Triumph

It is scarcely surprising that after the war Lord North's government, faced with the perennial need for economy, wanted to reduce their colonial overheads to the minimum and to maximize their receipts. They therefore wanted the Americans to pay more for the garrisons which defended them from the original inhabitants of their country, and if they could not directly match the value of other colonies to at least provide markets and not competition to the mother country. Using the 17th-century Navigation Acts the Government tried to ensure that the Americans traded only with Britain or her colonies and with newer legislation, such as the Stamp Act of 1764, they hoped to defray the cost of the garrisons in the colonies. Unfortunately the Government had not appreciated the difference between the American colonists and those in Asia and the West Indies. The Americans were settlers, who did not intend to return to the home country as soon as they had made their fortunes. They considered that America had interests of its own, independent of the welfare of Britain and they increasingly sought political recognition of this. But these interests could not be properly represented at a Parliament on the other side of the Atlantic, and at Westminster there was little support for a surrender of sovereignty to a colonial administration.

By 1774 the quarrel had passed beyond the realm of political philosophies. Lord North underestimated the seriousness of the situation when he told the King that as 'the New England Governments are in a state of rebellion, blows must decide whether they are to be subject to this country or independent'. The British leaders continued to trust in the comparative loyalty of the southern colonies throughout the war, and to shape their strategy accordingly. At first they tried to hold the line at the Hudson River to isolate the more actively rebellious New England colonies. This policy fell apart with the surrender of Sir John Burgoyne's army at Saratoga—an event of more than local significance, for it convinced the European powers that the Americans seriously threatened British supremacy. France made an alliance with the United States in February 1778 and soon after was at war with Great Britain. In the following year Spain also declared war and in 1780 the Northern Powers (Sweden, Russia, Prussia and Denmark) plus Portugal formed an Armed Neutrality to break the British blockade of France and Spain. In 1781 the Dutch joined the other European powers, widening the war still further. Britain was completely isolated, and home defense became more important than securing the American colonies.

Below: The city of Savannah, Georgia in 1779, with the French encampment in the foreground. The British policy of clearing the South was prompted by the opposition they encountered in their earlier Northern campaigns from the population, who they felt would be less hostile to British interests in the tobacco economy of the South, which depended on Britain for most of its manufactured goods. The latter part of the war was largely conducted in the South, where regular American forces, French troops and American irregulars attempted to block the British seizure of the ports and the interior.

The Armed Neutrality's blockade of Britain's Baltic trade cut off the supply of wood for shipbuilding which had formerly come almost exclusively from Scandinavia and America. But despite agitation by radical politicians like John Wilkes, George III resisted attempts to abandon the American colonies, arguing that if America were lost, the West Indies would also become independent. Without her Empire's trade, he argued, Britain would be so poor that she would inevitably fall to her European enemies. He therefore insisted that his Ministers accept the expense and unpopularity of a long world war.

The One-Crop Economy

Because of the fact that the South was largely a one-crop economy based on tobacco, many Southerners could not see the advantage of independence from a Britain which provided them with most of their finished goods in exchange for tobacco. Northern manufacturers were in competition with the mother country and it was not surprising that the most highly industrialized colony, Massachusetts, was the most revolutionary. The rural South, at least along the coast if not in the interior, was probably the least revolutionary. Thus the British sought to secure a large territorial base in the South and drive northwards to encircle the Americans.

In America, Saratoga meant that the British effort in the North became increasingly defensive and confined within their great base at New York. Pursuing the dangerous will-o'-the-wisp of Southern good-will, a small expedition captured Savannah on 29 December, 1778 and the rest of Georgia was soon cleared. French attempts to restore the situation failed and in 1780 the British Commander-in-Chief, Sir Henry Clinton, was ready to extend his grasp of the Southern colonies. In May he captured Charleston but his success sowed the seeds of disaster. Clinton left 4000 men under Lieutenant-General Cornwallis to complete the conquest of South Carolina. Although Cornwallis quickly destroyed the remaining American regulars in the province and defeated an incursion from North Carolina, he found that his attempts to establish a civil administration and a flourishing economy were sabotaged by the guerrillas who infested the country. Cornwallis was convinced that these forces were only kept in the field by the encouragement they received from the North. An attempt to invade North Corolina in the autumn of 1780 failed and Cornwallis fell back to Winnsborough. He remained there until January 1781, gathering his strength for his next campaign. He was sure that this should be in North Carolina and Virginia, where he could identify a real enemy, General Greene's force of the Continental Army. He was prepared to pursue Greene even deeper into unfriendly territory, though South Carolina was still not properly secured at his rear.

In New York Sir Henry Clinton had other plans for the new year. His first priority was the defense of New York, 'as I must ever regard this post to be of the utmost Consequence, whilst it is thought necessary to hold Canada, with which, and the Northern Indians, it is so materially connected'. He held to this conviction despite the

urgings of Cornwallis and of Lord George Germain, the Secretary of State and another keen supporter of a Virginian campaign. However, Clinton did think it worthwhile to establish 'a station for the protection of the King's ships' on the coast of Virginia and he considered 'no place so proper as York Town'. From this base he intended to fight a war of coastal raids, using columns such as that already operating under Arnold, in the hope that this would be enough to divert the Continental forces in Virginia and relieve the pressure on the Carolinas. He even thought that Cornwallis might be able to detach a large proportion of his army to strengthen the garrison of New York against Washington's army.

If Clinton could have been at Washington's headquarters in early 1781 he might not have been so convinced of the need for defense. Mutinies in the Pennsylvania and the Jersey lines were the most conspicuous expressions of discontent in the Continental Army. The army's pay was usually in arrears and in any case was almost worthless in an inflated economy. Besides the financial exhaustion of the American cause, Washington was only too aware of the disillusion and fatigue which affected all sides in this long-stalemated war. He knew that a new initiative was necessary if anything decisive was to be achieved and that this initiative must come from Europe. He told an officer he sent to France: 'Next to a loan of money, a constant naval superiority on these coasts is the object most interesting. This would instantly reduce the enemy to a difficult defen-

Above: General Cornwallis, the leader of the Southern campaign, who marched to Virginia for the winter in 1781 only to be cornered at Yorktown.

Right: The Count de Rochambeau, whose French armies combined with those of Washington to close in on Cornwallis at Yorktown. **Far right:** The Marquis de Lafayette, who unlike Rochambeau, was a volunteer at the age of 24 to fight with Washington. His force joined the other two to pin Cornwallis against the York River in 1781. **Below:** The siege of Charleston, when the French tried to retake this major Southern port after the British landed there in 1779. Retention of Charleston was vital for the British, whose supplies entered South Carolina through the port.

sive, and, by removing all prospect of extending their acquisitions, would take away the motives for prosecuting the war. Indeed it is not to be conceived how they could subsist a large force in this country, if we had command of the seas, to interrupt the regular transmission of supplies from Europe'.

Thus Washington clearly appreciated that it was sea power which enabled Britain to continue the war, safeguarding her communications across the Atlantic and giving the British Army strategic mobility along the coast of North America. Moreover, British troops knew that however hostile the countryside in which they operated might be, there was a line of retreat open to them on the coast. But if the French could be persuaded to make a major naval effort on the American coast the stalemate on land might be broken.

Unfortunately France was also seized by war-weariness. Operations in Europe had brought no real successes to restore French pride and there was a growing dissatisfaction with the maneuvers of Spain, whose only apparent concern was to recapture Gibraltar, Minorca and Jamaica. Once again the French treasury could not meet the demands of war and the Comte de Vergennes, the French Foreign Minister declared, 'This war has gone too slowly; it is a war of hard cash, and if we drag it out the last penny may not be ours'. By February 1781 Vergennes was looking for a way out of the war and he hoped to find it in mediation by Austria and Russia between the powers. He was prepared to leave the Americans to their fate if necessary, and the news of the mutinies in Washington's army helped to convince him that in any case the final collapse of his allies would not be long delayed. However, he was prepared to continue the struggle while the machinery of mediation was established, especially if he might win a new bargaining point. During the early months of 1781 a fleet was prepared under the command of Admiral de Grasse to take advantage of whatever opportunities

in the harshest of winter weather. Sick, stragglers and deserters dropped from his army like autumn leaves, but for all his speed Cornwallis could not trap the rebels before they crossed the River Dan into Virginia. When he reached the border he was at the end of his resources, and still he had not fought his battle. He fell back to Hillsborough, rested until the end of February, and then marched out to meet an incursion by Greene's reinforced army. Though outnumbered by two to one, Cornwallis routed the American militia and dislodged the Continentals from their positions. But he lost 532 men, more than a quarter of his force, and he had no reserves with which to pursue his beaten enemy. An indecisive victory was worse than no battle at all and Cornwallis, obeying the first instincts of a British general, fell back toward the security of the coast at Wilmington. Greene made no attempt to follow, but moved to South Carolina. In three months Cornwallis had lost two-thirds of his effective troops and all the gains of the last two years were now in jeopardy.

Cornwallis might have moved by sea to Charleston and continued a defensive campaign in the hope that time would prove to be on the British side. The alliance between his enemies might not have survived for another year. But such ideas were far from Cornwallis's mind; on 10 April he wrote to General Philips, who had reinforced Arnold in Virginia:

'Now, my dear friend, what is our plan? Without one we cannot succeed, and I assure you that I am quite tired of marching about the country in quest of adventures. If we mean an offensive war in America, we must abandon New York, and our whole force in Virginia... If our plan is defensive, mixed with desultory expeditions, let us quit the Carolinas (which cannot be held defensively while Virginia can so easily be armed against us) and stick to our salt pork at New York, sending now and then a detachment to steal tobacco.'

Virginia had become an obsession with Cornwallis who could not see the strategic significance of New York as a base for the Navy and for Loyalist action in the North and Canada. Moreover, his Commander-in-Chief clearly had no intention of abandoning New York. In fact Clinton even hoped that he could draw reinforcements from Cornwallis and operate in the Delmarva Peninsula himself. When the remains of the Southern army emerged from the backwoods of North Carolina Clinton realized the impossibility of this, but he believed he could maintain his existing conquests. His greatest fear was that Cornwallis would disappear into Virginia, exposing South Carolina and even Georgia. The ideas of Sir Henry Clinton and his deputy were now so totally different that even allowing for the problems of communication it is difficult to believe that Clinton was trying to control the conduct of the war in his theater. He had issued no clear directives to his subordinates, generally preferring to criticize the plans of others. It is not surprising, therefore, that Cornwallis, knowing that Germain trusted him more than Clinton, took matters into his own hands and marched into Virginia, joining the forces already at Richmond

Above: General Nathaniel Greene, called by many the best American soldier of the Revolutionary War, who successfully harassed Cornwallis' march northward through the Carolinas.

Opposite top: Lord Cornwallis, whose disgrace at Yorktown did not end his career. He went on to a successful tour in India after the Revolution. **Opposite bottom:** Colonel William Washington at the Battle of Cowpens, January 1781. In this battle Daniel Morgan's men forced the surrender of Tarleton's forces, which weakened British power in the Carolinas. At this point it was impossible for Cornwallis to consider a retreat southward, so he headed for the coast, where he hoped the British Navy would effect an escape by sea if the going got rough.

might arise across the Atlantic. De Grasse was to sail in March and go first to the West Indies, where he would assist the Spaniards if they began any serious operations. In the hot season he was to sail north; he might have to rescue the French forces in America if the colonists' army had collapsed, or he might have the chance of a more positive success. The final outcome of the campaign of 1781 in America, and hence also of the entire war, rested with de Grasse's fleet from the time it left Brest until the moment it met the small British army operating in the South.

On 7 January Cornwallis advanced from Winnsborough with 4000 men in search of the decisive battle which would destroy Greene's army. However, Greene did not intend to risk a stand-up fight. Instead he divided his army and began raising the guerrillas on Cornwallis's flanks. Cornwallis had to split his own force and at Cowpens, a column under Tarleton, his ablest subordinate, was almost completely destroyed. Cornwallis, abandoning his baggage, made a forced march to cut off the victors, often covering thirty miles a day through atrocious country and under Arnold on 20 May.

Clinton was at last stung into action. He ordered Cornwallis to fortify a defensive post at either Williamsburg or Yorktown and, keeping only enough troops for seaborne raids, return as many men as possible to New York. Cornwallis prepared to follow his superior's strategy, although he decided to fortify neither Williamsburg nor Yorktown, but Portsmouth which could be held by the small force which would remain after his detachments to New York. Meanwhile Clinton had changed his mind. He wanted a base for ships of the line in the York River or at Hampton Roads and this meant holding the Williamsburg Peninsula. He therefore authorized Cornwallis to retain all his troops and ordered him to fortify Old Point Comfort at the tip of the peninsula. Old Point Comfort was surveyed by engineers and naval officers and found unsuitable both as an anchorage and a defensive position. Instead Cornwallis moved to Yorktown and his army began to fortify the town, although neither Cornwallis nor Clinton seems to have had any clear idea why the place should become a naval base. He also established a post on the far side of the York River, at Gloucester. But the plans of these two officers were increasingly irrelevant, for as the troops labored in the August sun, the power to influence affairs was slipping away from their commanders. The decisive moves in the campaign at Yorktown were to be made at sea.

De Grasse and the French fleet had arrived in Martinique near the end of May, avoiding the British squadron posted to intercept them. Wasting no time de Grasse sailed for St Lucia and Tobago, capturing the latter two days before the arrival of Admiral Rodney and the British fleet on 4 June. Rodney had an opportunity to attack the French fleet on the following afternoon, but preferred not to take the risk of a night battle

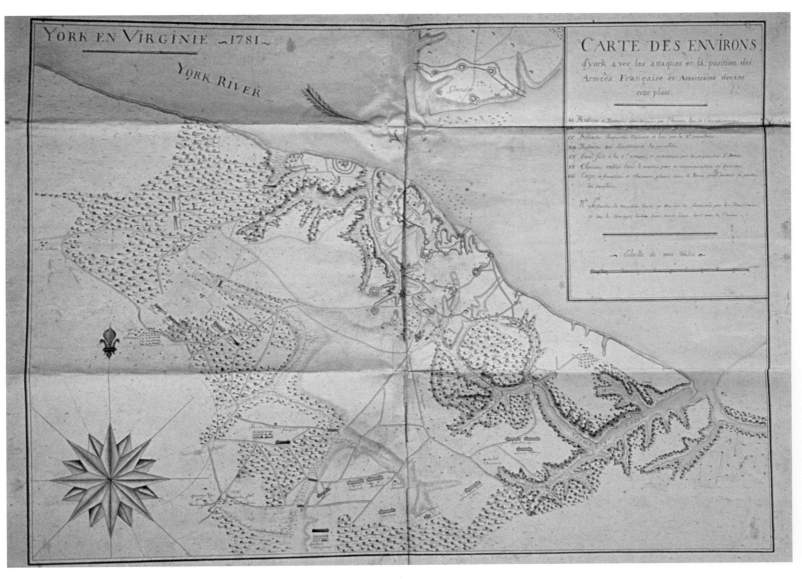

YORK EN VIRGINIE ~1781~

YORK RIVER

CARTE DES ENVIRONS
dyork avec les attaques et la position des
Armées Francaise et Americaine devant
cette place.

Above: An original French battle map of Yorktown.

among the islands. The British had lost two early opportunities of crippling de Grasse's ambitions and they scarcely deserved a third. The Spaniards revealed that they were preparing a winter campaign against Florida and planned nothing before then. De Grasse was therefore free to listen to the pleas which reached him from Washington and the Comte de Rochambeau, commander of the French troops in America.

In May the two commanders had decided to attack New York, believing that without command of the sea they could not operate further south. However, Washington was prepared to keep an open mind; on 13 June he wrote to Rochambeau that:

'Your Excellency will be pleased to recollect that New York was looked upon by us as the only practicable object under present circumstances; but should we be able to secure a *naval superiority*, we may perhaps find others more practicable and equally advisable. If the frigate should not have sailed, I wish you to explain this matter to the *Count of Grasse*.'

Washington was well aware of the options open to the British and at the back of his mind he prepared alternative schemes. If Clinton reinforced Cornwallis he would attack New York; if Cornwallis moved to support Clinton then he would attack Virginia. If the French could gain the upper hand at sea after the British had committed themselves to one plan or the other, Washington would concentrate against the weak-

er force. Deprived of the ability to move reinforcements rapidly by sea, or even to evacuate their endangered army the British would have to stand and fight. If he could obtain French money as well as a French fleet, Washington was sure that he could gain decisive superiority on land. Rochambeau needed no urging to put these views to de Grasse, for they coincided exactly with his own.

'I must not conceal from you, Monsieur,' he told the Admiral, 'that the Americans are at the end of their resources, that Washington will not have half the troops he is reckoned to have, and that I believe, though he is silent on that, that at present he does not have six thousand men; that M. de La Fayette does not have a thousand regulars with militia to defend Virginia, and nearly as many on the march to join him; that General Greene has pushed a small force far in advance of Camden where he was repulsed, and that I do not know how and when he will rejoin M. de La Fayette; that it is therefore of the greatest consequence that you will take on board as many troops as possible; that four or five thousand men will not be too many . . . . . I am quite persuaded that you will bring us naval superiority, but I cannot too often repeat to you to bring also the troops and the money.'

De Grasse's decision was not an easy one; North America was a secondary objective as far as his government was concerned, and he had promised to support the Spaniards before the end of the year. However, having made up his mind to intervene in the north, he concentrated all his strength for the blow. There was a vast

Far left: Revolutionary cannon on the battlefield of Yorktown today, which is preserved as a National Park. **Left:** The naval battle of the Chesapeake was tactically indecisive, but it was the most important naval victory of the war. The French under de Grasse prevented the British Navy from springing Cornwallis from the Yorktown trap making his capitulation inevitable.

convoy waiting to go to France; that had to wait for the rest of the year because no ships were spared to escort it. In view of France's financial state this was a particularly brave decision. Ten of his ships were long overdue for a refit and had been ordered home, but de Grasse kept them with his fleet. From Santo Domingo he took 3000 French troops, also promised to the Spaniards for the winter, and from the private citizens of Havana he raised a loan of over a million livres. To charter transports for the army's artillery and stores de Grasse spent his own fortune. On 5 August the whole armament, 27 ships of the line and a 50-gun ship left Santo Domingo to join the eight French ships of the line in America, where the British fleet numbered seven. To avoid detection the fleet took the dangerous, and therefore little used Bahama Channel between Cuba and the Bahamas, and

on 29 August anchored off Chesapeake Bay.

It was no surprise to Rodney that the French fleet should go to America but he had never considered the possibility that de Grasse would take every available ship. His own assessment was that about fourteen ships of the line would go north and that de Grasse himself would return to Europe, escorting the year's trade. This was what he proposed to do himself and at the beginning of August six of the twenty British ships of the line in the West Indies were dispersed on convoy duties. Admiral Rodney returned to England to recover his health, confident, as he told Germain, that 'His Majesty's Fleet will be superior on the coast and prevent the enemy's designs, provided the officers who command will do their duty'. The fourteen ships of the line which remained sailed on 10 August under the command of Rear Admiral Hood. Taking the

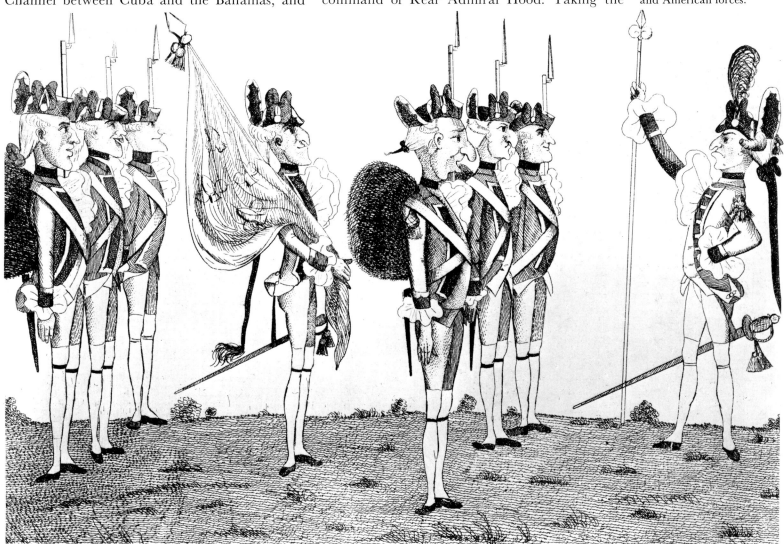

convoy waiting to go to France; that had to wait for the rest of the year because no ships were spared to escort it. In view of France's financial state this was a particularly brave decision. Ten of his ships were long overdue for a refit and had been ordered home, but de Grasse kept them with his fleet. From Santo Domingo he took 3000 French troops, also promised to the Spaniards for the winter, and from the private citizens of Havana he raised a loan of over a million livres. To charter transports for the army's artillery and stores de Grasse spent his own fortune. On 5 August the whole armament, 27 ships of the line and a 50-gun ship left Santo Domingo to join the eight French ships of the line in America, where the British fleet numbered seven. To avoid detection the fleet took the dangerous, and therefore little used Bahama Channel between Cuba and the Bahamas, and

Below: A British caricature of Rochambeau leading the French troops. The presence of the French proved to be no laughing matter to Cornwallis, who was heavily outnumbered at Yorktown by a combination of French and American forces.

direct route, and sailing faster than the French, Hood arrived off Sandy Hook on 28 August and came under the command of Thomas Graves.

Washington learned of de Grasse's plans in a letter which he received on 14 August, while both fleets were at sea. By then he had abandoned the idea of attacking New York. Another 2400 German mercenaries had joined Clinton there and the garrison outnumbered the Allied army. Instead Washington decided to move to Virginia, where Lafayette had scarcely a thousand men to oppose Cornwallis's designs. Admiral Barras, who commanded the small French squadron at Rhode Island, was persuaded to take the siege-train, which could only be moved by sea, to the Chesapeake. Only 2500 American troops were left to watch Clinton and protect the Piedmont region; the remaining 7000 French and American troops marched south on 16 August. It was an anxious journey; the northern regiments disliked moving so far from home, but were reconciled by an issue of pay. Furthermore, Washington could not be sure that the British fleet would not forestall de Grasse and occupy the Chesapeake first. South of Philadelphia Washington's mind was set at rest; de Grasse was within the Capes of Virginia and the British fleet had not appeared.

But on the day that this news reached Washington, 5 September, the two fleets at last came in sight of each other. Graves had been encouraged by Hood to come south at once. They knew that Washington was on the march, and they soon learned that Barras had sailed. Graves hoped to catch Barras at sea, but it was not until he sighted the Capes, that he realized that de Grasse had brought his whole fleet north.

The British were outnumbered by 24 ships to nineteen, but the French had to beat out of their anchorage in Lynnhaven Roads, which somewhat disordered them. Graves might have exploited this disorder, and the wind, which was in his favor, by making a pell-mell attack before the French could form a line of battle. But Graves did not know how much stronger his enemy was, and he no doubt remembered the fate of Admiral Byron, who had encountered a French fleet coming out of Georgetown harbor in Granada two years earlier. Byron had risked a general *mêlée* and had been severely handled, only escaping great loss by good fortune. Graves preferred to arrange the battle so that he could control his weaker fleet, rather than commit his ships beyond recall. He therefore occupied himself in complicated maneuvers until the French had formed a line of battle and then tried to bring on a closer action. Unfortunately most of his fleet were not used to working under his command; his signals were misunderstood, and only the van of his fleet got near the French. Night ended the action and the two fleets spent the 6th refitting. The French, having the wind, could have engaged on the next two days if they

Below: A view of Yorktown from the York River, taken from a sketch drawn by a British officer around 1754.

20

had wished, but Graves's ships were too damaged to force an action on an unwilling enemy. On the 9th the French withdrew altogether and when Graves found them again in Chesapeake Bay they had been joined by Barras and were overwhelmingly superior. Graves could only return to New York in the hope of finding reinforcements and some means of rescuing Cornwallis.

Chesapeake Bay might be called the Valmy of the American War for, although it was tactically only an indecisive cannonade, it ensured the survival of the American Revolution just as Valmy would ensure the survival of the revolution in France. In Yorktown the situation of the British Army grew worse each day. De Grasse had brought 3000 French regulars and they had joined perhaps another 5000 Continentals and militia in front of Cornwallis's works. In theory Cornwallis had 6000 men with him, but barely 5000 were present and fit for duty. Deprived of his expected escape route, Cornwallis began to consider breaking out of Yorktown before the odds against him could be increased. However letters from Clinton, who expected naval reinforcements from England and assured him that he had 4000 men ready to sail to his relief as soon as these arrived, convinced Cornwallis that the best course was to hold on in Yorktown. His supplies would last until the end of October and so he wrote to Clinton that, 'If I had no hopes of relief I would rather risk an action than defend my half-finished works. But as you say Admiral Digby is hourly expected, and promises every exertion to assist me, I do not think myself justifiable in putting the fate of the war on so desperate an attempt'. By 26 September all of Washington's troops had reached Williamsburg and it was too late to think of breaking out of Yorktown.

Yorktown in 1781 was a town of less than 3000 inhabitants, standing on a bluff overlooking the York River. Along the river bank, partially protected by the bluff, were the warehouses and jetties on which the prosperity of the town depended. Yorktown was not a fortress, nor even well-protected by nature, except the western side of town which was encircled by the Yorktown creek which ran through a deep ravine and a marsh to the coast. However, on the eastern side there was a broad expanse between Yorktown and Wormley Creek. It was big enough for a besieging army to deploy and it was obvious that any engineer would approach the town from that side. Cornwallis was too experienced an officer to believe that anywhere could be made proof against a regular siege. A well-fortified position could only buy time for its defenders; Cornwallis must delay the inexorable approach of the Franco-American trenches until relief came. Unfortunately the whole plan of defense rested on the false premise that the Royal Navy would command the sea. Cornwallis assumed that the Navy would not only rescue his army but delay the work of the besiegers by forcing them

Below: Lafayette at the head of his troops.

The Siege of Yorktown, 1781

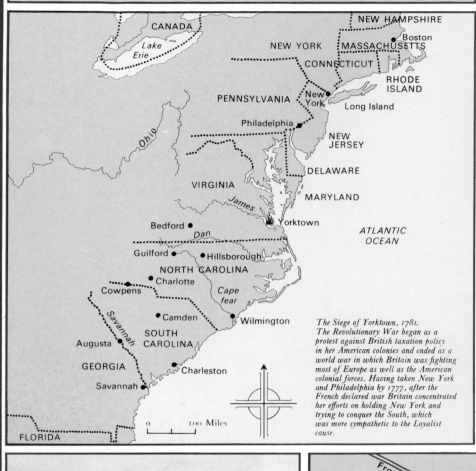

France made an alliance with the United States in February 1778 and soon after was at war with Britain. In the following year Spain joined France and in 1780 Sweden, Russia, Prussia, Denmark and Portugal formed an Armed Neutrality to break the British blockade of France and Spain. In 1781 the Dutch joined the other European powers. Britain was completely isolated and home defense became more important than securing the American colonies.

Because the Southern States' one-crop economy based on tobacco depended on Britain which provided them with most of their finished goods, many Southerners could not see the advantage of an independant administration. Thus the British sought to secure a large base in the south and drive northwards to encircle the Americans.

A small expedition captured Savannah on 29 December, 1778 and the rest of Georgia was soon cleared. In 1780 Sir Henry Clinton captured Charleston and left a force of 4000 men under Lieutenant-General Cornwallis to complete the conquest of South Carolina.

The Siege of Yorktown, 1781.
The Revolutionary War began as a protest against British taxation policy in her American colonies and ended as a world war in which Britain was fighting most of Europe as well as the American colonial forces. Having taken New York and Philadelphia by 1777, after the French declared war Britain concentrated her efforts on holding New York and trying to conquer the South, which was more sympathetic to the Loyalist cause.

Greene did not intend to risk a stand-up fight. Instead he divided his army and began raising the guerrillas on Cornwallis's flanks. Cornwallis had to split his force and at Cowpens a column under Tarleton was almost destroyed.

An attempt to invade North Carolina in the autumn of 1780 failed and Cornwallis fell back to Winnsborough. He remained there until 7 January, 1781 when he advanced with 4000 men in search of the decisive battle.

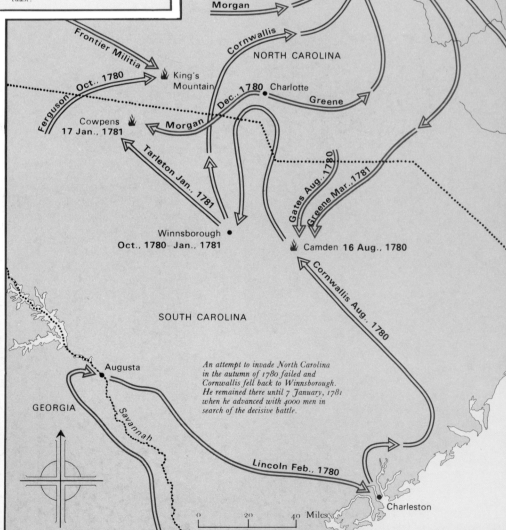

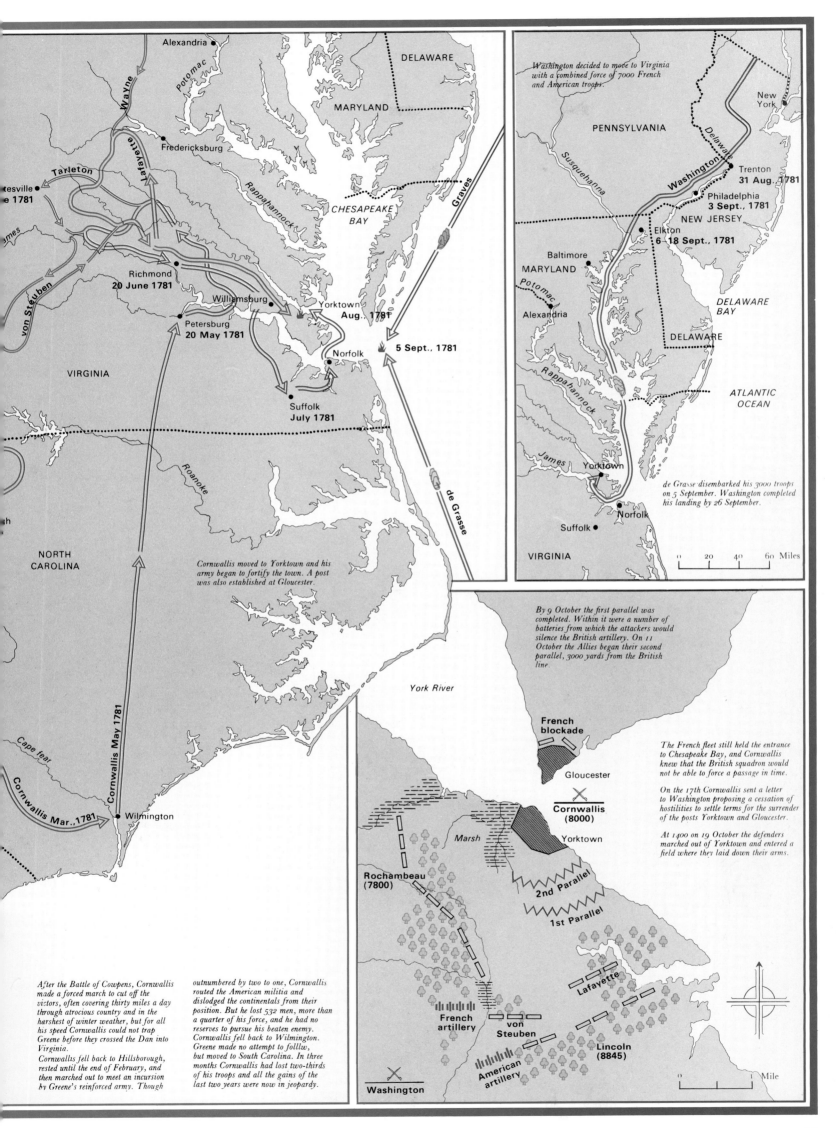

Alexandria

DELAWARE

MARYLAND

Potomac

Fredericksburg

Wayne

Lafayette

Tarleton

...tesville
...e 1781

...es

von Steuben

Richmond
20 June 1781

Williamsburg

Petersburg
20 May 1781

Rappahannock

CHESAPEAKE
BAY

Graves

Yorktown
Aug., 1781

Norfolk

5 Sept., 1781

VIRGINIA

Suffolk
July 1781

de Grasse

Roanoke

NORTH
CAROLINA

Cornwallis May 1781

Cape fear

Cornwallis Mar., 1781

Wilmington

Cornwallis moved to Yorktown and his army began to fortify the town. A post was also established at Gloucester.

Washington decided to move to Virginia with a combined force of 7000 French and American troops.

New York

PENNSYLVANIA

Delaware

Washington

Trenton
31 Aug., 1781

Philadelphia
3 Sept., 1781

NEW JERSEY

Elkton
6–18 Sept., 1781

Baltimore

MARYLAND

Potomac

Alexandria

DELAWARE
BAY

DELAWARE

Rappahannock

ATLANTIC
OCEAN

James

Yorktown

Norfolk

Suffolk

VIRGINIA

de Grasse disembarked his 3000 troops on 5 September. Washington completed his landing by 26 September.

0   20   40   60 Miles

By 9 October the first parallel was completed. Within it were a number of batteries from which the attackers would silence the British artillery. On 11 October the Allies began their second parallel, 3000 yards from the British line.

York River

French
blockade

Gloucester

✕
**Cornwallis
(8000)**

Marsh

Yorktown

2nd Parallel

1st Parallel

Rochambeau
(7800)

French
artillery

von Steuben

Lafayette

Lincoln
(8845)

American
artillery

✕
Washington

The French fleet still held the entrance to Chesapeake Bay, and Cornwallis knew that the British squadron would not be able to force a passage in time.

On the 17th Cornwallis sent a letter to Washington proposing a cessation of hostilities to settle terms for the surrender of the posts Yorktown and Gloucester.

At 1400 on 19 October the defenders marched out of Yorktown and entered a field where they laid down their arms.

0   1 Mile

After the Battle of Cowpens, Cornwallis made a forced march to cut off the victors, often covering thirty miles a day through atrocious country and in the harshest of winter weather, but for all his speed Cornwallis could not trap Greene before they crossed the Dan into Virginia.

Cornwallis fell back to Hillsborough, rested until the end of February, and then marched out to meet an incursion by Greene's reinforced army. Though

outnumbered by two to one, Cornwallis routed the American militia and dislodged the continentals from their position. But he lost 532 men, more than a quarter of his force, and he had no reserves to pursue his beaten enemy. Cornwallis fell back to Wilmington. Greene made no attempt to folllw, but moved to South Carolina. In three months Cornwallis had lost two-thirds of his troops and all the gains of the last two years were now in jeopardy.

to move their artillery train by land. To defend the town Cornwallis therefore constructed two lines of fieldworks. The outer ring consisted of unconnected redoubts. One, the Fusilier Redoubt, was in the west, almost on the river bank. The others covered the approach between the ravine and Wormley Creek and were intended to delay the enemy's occupation of this key ground. The inner defenses were composed of ten linked redoubts. Again the main emphasis was on the eastern side of the town where the defenses were given greater depth by Redoubts 9 and 10, placed two or three hundred yards in advance of the main works. If the besiegers could bring their artillery to this position, they would be in point-blank range, and Cornwallis realized that his newly-dug defenses, lacking the inert massiveness of European fortifications, could not long survive the battering of heavy artillery.

Time is the essence of all sieges, and never more so than at Yorktown. Washington was as oppressed by its influence as Cornwallis was. When Graves appeared at the mouth of the Chesapeake on 5 September the transfer of his army across the bay from Baltimore and Elkton to Williamsburg was suspended. De Grasse was due to leave for the West Indies on 15 October, and if command of the sea passed to the British, Cornwallis might yet be saved and all the maneuvers of the year wasted. On 17 September Washington won the battle for time by persuading de Grasse to stay on the coast until Yorktown was captured. On 28 September the combined army marched from Williamsburg and the next day encamped before the British outworks.

On 29 September Cornwallis decided to abandon most of his outer defenses, with the exception of the Fusilier Redoubt. He has been criticized for this decision, because it gave the Allies early access to the eastern plain where they could dig their own trenches and sap towards the town. However, time was not the only factor with which Cornwallis had to deal; there was also the question of manpower. When Clinton's relieving army arrived a battle might have to be fought and Cornwallis's assistance would be vital; he must preserve every available man for that moment. On 29 September he received a letter from Clinton, who hoped to leave New York on 5 October and might be expected to reach the Chesapeake within a week. The outworks could not be held against a determined assault. If Clinton kept to his timetable the time which Cornwallis would buy would not be worth the lives he would have to spend.

South of the river, Cornwallis was trying to disturb the measured approach of the Americans and the French. The bulk of the siege-train was still en route and making very slow progress. So great was the shortage of draft animals that Washington sent his own baggage-horses and asked that other officers follow his example. In the meantime Cornwallis was superior in artillery; on 2 October one Virginia militiaman described the consequences:

'The Firing from the Enemies' works was continued during the whole night at the distance of fifteen or twenty minutes between every shot—by these means

our works were interrupted altho' no Execution was done—Since Sunrise this morning the firing has been much more frequent, the intermissions seldom exceeding five minutes and often not more than one or two minutes.'

Washington's casualties were not high but the work of preparing 'gabions' (baskets filled with earth) and 'fascines' (bundles of brushwood) levelling approaches for the heavy guns was seriously slowed by the need to dive for cover every few minutes. However, by 6 October his artillery parks were full and he was ready to begin the siege proper. During the night a line of infantrymen approached to within 800 yards of the British defenses and under the direction of the engineers began to dig a long trench. This was the 'first parallel', and it followed the line of the British works for 2000 yards from a point opposite their center to the York River. Attempts by British artillery to disrupt this work were hindered by the overcast sky, which made it impossible for the gunners to guess exactly where the Americans were digging. Cornwallis might also have tried to delay his enemies by sorties to drive off the pioneers, but he was still more concerned with preserving his manpower.

By 9 October the first parallel was completed. Within it were a number of batteries from which the attackers would try to silence the British artillery. Having gained the upper hand they would then sap forward to a second parallel from which they could batter the defenses themselves and launch the final assault. The French had constructed more batteries on the other side of of Yorktown and the combined weight of fire that poured into the town was immediately effective. Washington reported on their success in the first 24 hours:

'The fire now became so excessively heavy, that the enemy withdrew their cannon from their embrasures, placed them behind the 'merlins' (the part of the parapet between two embrasures), and scarcely fired a shot during the whole day. In the evening the Charon frigate of 44 guns was set on fire by a hot ball from the French battery on the left, and entirely consumed. By the report of a deserter, our shells, which were thrown with the utmost degree of precision, did much mischief in the course of the day.'

The extent of this 'mischief' can be judged from the account of one of the German mercenaries:

'The enemy threw bombs, one hundred, one hundred fifty, two hundred pounders. We could find no refuge in or out of town. The people fled to the waterside and hid in harshly contrived shelters on the banks, but many of them were killed by bursting bombs. More than eighty were thus lost, besides many wounded, and their houses utterly destroyed.'

Within the town the only glimmer of hope for the British was a new despatch from Sir Henry Clinton. It was taking longer than he had expected to assemble enough shipping for the relief force and the naval reinforcement from England had been only three ships. Nevertheless, Clinton confided that 'Your Lordship may be assured that I am doing everything in my power to relieve you by a direct move', and he hoped to leave New York on 12 October.

On 11 October the besieging armies began their second parallel, which was scarcely 300 yards from the British line. Here the ground nearest the river was still dominated by Redoubts 9 and 10, which also outflanked the second parallel. The Allies sapped closer to the forts and prepared an assault for the night of 14 October. They were garrisoned by less than 200 men, but the approaches were entangled by sharpened stakes and *abatis* (trees felled with their branches pointing towards the enemy and entangled). Each strongpoint was attacked by 400 men, Number 10 by the Americans and Number 9 by the French. The Americans, charging with fixed bayonets, surprised the defenders and captured their objective before much resistance could be made. The approach of the French was detected earlier and they had a fierce struggle to pass the abatis. However, they eventually overran the parapet and the outnumbered garrison surrendered. At once the Allies began to incorporate the redoubts into their

second parallel and to establish breaching batteries. There was good reason for Cornwallis to be pessimistic when he reported to Clinton on 15 October:

'My situation here becomes very critical; we dare not show a gun to their old batteries, and I expect their new ones will open tomorrow morning. Experience has shown that our fresh earthen works do not resist their powerful artillery, so that we shall soon be exposed to an assault in ruined works, in a bad position, and with weakened numbers. The safety of the place is therefore so precarious, that I cannot recommend that the fleet and army should run great risks in endeavouring to save us.'

But the British commander was determined to make one last effort to delay the end. Early on the morning of 16 October 350 men under Lieutenant Colonel Robert Abercrombie slipped through one of the British lines. Entering the second parallel they found a French battery and by claiming to be Americans took the sentry off-guard and overran the sleeping gunners. The guns were spiked with bayonets and Abercrom-

Below: The American encampment before Yorktown. Washington (center) is being shown a battle map, as Rochambeau issues orders (left). Lafayette is to the right of Washington and just behind him.

Right: Cornwallis asks Washington for a cessation of hostilities. Lord North, hearing of the loss of Yorktown, shouted, 'It is all over!' It was. **Below:** John Trumbull's painting of the surrender of Cornwallis at Yorktown, which hangs in the US Capitol in Washington. The band played the tune 'The World Turned Upside Down'. A new nation was born and the British had lost their First Empire in America, although they retained Canada and some Caribbean islands in the Peace of Paris of 1783 which brought the war to its official close.

York. Virginia 17ᵗʰ Octr. 1781

Sir

I propose a Cessation of Hostilities for Twenty four hours, and that two Officers may be appointed by each side to meet at Mr. Moore's house to settle terms for the surrender of the posts of York & Gloucester. I have the honour to be

Sir

Your most obedient & most humble Servant

Cornwallis

*His Excellency
General Washington
&ᶜ. &ᶜ. &ᶜ.*

Above: A letter from Cornwallis to Washington asking for surrender terms after the battle was hopelessly lost.

Opposite top: The fight to take the last British redoubts was particularly fierce. **Opposite bottom:** The return of Cornwallis' army to Britain at the end of the war. Cornwallis was not considered to have fought badly. His reputation emerged from the carnage of Yorktown unscathed.

bie's force pressed on toward an American battery. This time Abercrombie claimed to be French and then sent his men into the battery with the order 'Push on, my brave boys and skin the bastards'. Although three more guns were spiked the noise was noticed by a French piquet, which recaptured the battery and drove the British off. Abercrombie's gallant exploit made little difference to the course of events; Washington's artificers soon removed the makeshift spikes and throughout the rest of the day nearly a hundred guns pounded the British position.

All Hope Gone

Cornwallis now gave up all hope of relief by Clinton. The French fleet still held the entrance to Chesapeake Bay and Cornwallis knew that the British squadron would not be able to force a passage in time. However, he was not yet ready to surrender everything. He would take every able-bodied man across the river to Gloucester and break through the weak lines there. His troops were used to hard marching in hostile territory and something might yet be saved. Unfortunately he did not have enough boats to ferry his whole force at once. It would be necessary for them to make three trips during the night of the 16th. The first group crossed successfully, but while the second was in midstream a sudden storm blew up. The fates were undoubtedly against the British. When the weather improved there was no time to complete the operation before first light. Cornwallis recalled those troops

across the river and waited for the dawn to break.

The morning brought no miracles and as the Franco-American bombardment started Cornwallis inspected the defenses with his technical officers. This was only a matter of form, for their decision was inevitable. 'Our works', Cornwallis reported, 'were going to ruin, and not having been able to strengthen them by an abatis, nor in any other manner but by a slight fraizing, which the enemy's artillery were demolishing wherever they fired, my opinion entirely coincided with that of the engineer and principal officers of the army, that they were in many places assailable in the forenoon, and that by continuance of the same fire for a few hours longer, they would be in such a state as to render it desperate, with our numbers, to attempt to maintain them. We at that time could not fire a single gun; only one eight-inch and little more than 100 Cohorn shells remained'. No garrison was expected to resist after a practicable breach had appeared in their works. The defenders who made their opponents risk an assault ignored the usages of civilized warfare and could expect no mercy in the final attack. It was no surprise to Washington when, at 1000 hours on the 17th, a drummer mounted the ramparts of Yorktown. Even if his drum could not be heard over the cannonade the invitation to parley was unmistakable. As the guns checked their fire, an officer with a white flag crossed over to the American lines; he carried a letter from Cornwallis to Washington, proposing 'a cessation of hostilities for twenty-four hours, and that two officers may be appointed by each side, to meet at Mr Moore's house, to settle terms for the surrender of the posts of York and Gloucester'.

After the first peaceful night in Yorktown for over two weeks the commissioners met to settle the articles of capitulation. There was some haggling over details. Washington was prepared to allow the garrison most of the honors of war, but insisted on avenging an insult inflicted on the Americans at Charleston by Sir Henry Clinton. The regiments must march out with their colors cased. Cornwallis tried to protect the American loyalists in Yorktown, but Washington was not prepared to accept them as prisoners of war. Cornwallis therefore packed as many of them as possible into the sloop he was allowed to send to New York with despatches. He was in no position to argue about the terms, but he did develop a fever which confined him to bed and left the task of surrendering the army to his second-in-command, Brigadier General Charles O'Hara. At 1400 on 19 October the defenders marched out of Yorktown, passed through the French and American works, and, their route lined by the two armies, entered the field where they were to lay down their arms. Those fifes and drums which exercised their privilege of playing chose the song *The World Turned Upside Down* to express their feelings.

'If ponies rode men, and if grass ate the cows
And cats should be chased into holes by the mouse...
If summer were spring, and the other way 'round,
Then all the world would be upside down.'

Austerlitz
1805

On 2 December, 1805 the French *Grande Armée* met the combined armies of Russia and Austria near the Moravian village of Austerlitz. The French were ostensibly at a disadvantage. They were deep inside hostile territory, heavily outnumbered and faced by an aggressive and confident enemy. Yet within the space of a few hours the *Grande Armée* had won its most spectacular victory, routing the Allied armies, forcing Austria out of the war and sending a thrill of horror throughout Europe.

The dramatic and far-reaching consequences of Austerlitz should not be permitted to obscure its equally significant background. Few battles can usefully be studied outside their diplomatic and military context, and Austerlitz, the culmination of a campaign of movement and a war of alliances, is certainly not one of them. The diverse elements which brought about Austerlitz account, in themselves, for much of the battle's course and character. The midwinter clash in Moravia was not simply one of a series of battles; it was the focal point of a campaign and was to leave its stamp on Europe for the next decade.

From 1792 to 1797 Revolutionary France had been at war with the 'First Coalition', a tenuous alliance between England, Prussia, Russia, Austria and Spain. By 1797 only England continued the struggle. A French expedition to Egypt in 1798 met with success on land, though the destruction of the French fleet in Aboukir Bay (Battle of the Nile) ensured the expedition's ultimate failure. The leader of the abortive descent on Egypt was the young General Napoleon Bonaparte.

Born at Ajaccio in Corsica in 1769, Bonaparte had been commissioned into the French artillery in 1785. The upheavals following the Revolution of 1789 facilitated his rapid promotion; in 1793 he distinguished himself at the siege of Toulon and, three years later, commanded the French army in Italy. Bonaparte's Italian campaign of 1796 established him as a commander of the first order, raised him to eminence within France and brought him to the notice of Europe at large. Undaunted by his failure in Egypt Bonaparte, on his return to France, was instrumental in removing the Directory and replacing it by the

Consulate, with himself as First Consul. After some six months of frenzied political and administrative work, Bonaparte took the field once more.

His adversaries were now the members of the 'Second Coalition', formed in 1798, which was to meet with as little success as the first. A Russian army under Marshal Suvorov reached Zurich, only to be defeated by General André Massena in September 1799. Austrian successes in northern Italy, however, compelled Bonaparte's personal intervention, and on 14 June 1800 he defeated General Melas at Marengo. In February 1801 France and Austria made peace at Lunéville and, the following month, Spain, who had already been giving France naval support, made a formal alliance with her. A series of fruitless military and diplomatic maneuvers failed to produce any result in the Anglo-French struggle, and March 1802 saw peace concluded at Amiens.

Much as it was welcomed on both sides of the Channel, peace did not survive for long. French moves in Europe and the West Indies, matched by a marked reluctance on the part of Britain to relinquish Malta, brought about a renewal of war in May 1803. The British at once blockaded France and began to seize French overseas colonies. Bonaparte responded by closing European ports to English trade and concentrating an army of invasion on the channel coast. Britain set about the formation of a 'Third Coalition'; Russia joined eagerly enough, followed in August 1805 by Austria and subsequently by Sweden and Naples. Prussia, deluded by French diplomacy, decided, for a while at least, to remain neutral, but Spain, Bavaria and Württemberg adhered to France.

The Coalition's plan involved five major armies. An Austro-Russian force of some 94,000 men was forming under the Archduke Charles in

AUSTERLITZ.

northern Italy. These forces were to be linked by a smaller Austrian army, commanded by the Archduke John, in the Tyrol. To the south a small Anglo-Russian force was to sail from Corfu to Naples, and, aided by the Neapolitans, was to march into northern Italy. In the Baltic a tripartite English, Russian and Swedish force was to move from Stralsund to Hanover, threatening Holland and putting pressure on the Prussians. The main blow was to be delivered by the Austro-Russian army in the center which, when fully concentrated, was to invade France by way of Strasbourg. The Archdukes would accompany this move by advancing through Switzerland into France. If the main force incurred a reverse, the Archduke Charles was to defend the line of the River Mincio and send reinforcements to the north. The plan relied heavily on British gold financing continental manpower, backed by the British fleet; it was, inevitably, fraught with the problems which so often attend alliances.

One of the most serious difficulties was that of command. The Austrian Aulic Council remained preoccupied with northern Italy, home of the Archduke Charles' disproportionately powerful army. The Austrian element of the central army was commanded by the Archduke Ferdinand, but the Emperor Francis had instructed him to obey the orders of the Chief-of-Staff, General Mack. Francis himself proposed to take personal command of the central army once the Russians had armed. The leading Russian force, under the eccentric veteran Marshal Kutusov was due to arrive in Bavaria toward the end of October, closely followed by another army under General Buxhowden, with a third army under Marshal Bennigsen operating to its north. Kutusov had been instructed by the

Tsar to obey the orders of the Emperor Francis or one of the Archdukes, but not those of any other Austrian general. These arrangements made chaos an integral part of the Allied command, chaos which was to worsen with a series of violent personal disagreements between commanders. The tottering edifice was crowned with supremely bad staff-work which failed to take into account the fact that the Austrian and Russian calendars differed by ten days. This oversight was to result in the Austrian force under the divided command of Ferdinand and Mack remaining dangerously isolated in the Ulm-Augsburg area.

Napoleon Crowns Himself Emperor

While Allied machinations went on, Bonaparte, elevated in December 1804 to the dignity of Napoleon I, Emperor of the French, concentrated his army on the Channel coast with the apparent intention of invading England. A descent on England was certainly not a viable proposition unless the combined French and Spanish fleets could destroy the British fleet and thus guarantee free passage for the invasion force. It is, indeed, open to discussion as to how seriously Napoleon took the planned invasion. Nevertheless, if the Emperor had any doubts he kept them to himself, and the summer of 1805 saw the *Grande Armée* massed in the area of Boulogne, with detachments in Holland, Hanover and Brittany.

After assessing the various Allied threats, Napoleon adopted a strategic plan which, in contrast to that of the Allies, was as brilliant and incisive as it was hazardous. The invasion of England was postponed—a postponement which was to be turned into cancellation with the defeat of the French fleet at Trafalgar on 21 October, 1805. The *Grande Armée* was to march to

the Danube with all possible speed, collecting the Bavarians *en route* with the intention of encircling Ferdinand and Mack, before moving eastwards to deal with the advancing Russians. The envelopment of Mack depended upon the French advance being carried out in secrecy and with great rapidity. The accomplishment of a swift and secure maneuver over such distances, with an army of over 200,000 men was in itself a strategic novelty. Marlborough had accomplished it for the Blenheim campaign of 1704, but the problems facing Napoleon, in terms of supply and transport, were infinitely greater.

Napoleon's task was facilitated by the composition and organization of the *Grande Armée*. The French army of 1805 was the result of the fusion of many disparate elements into a cohesive and vibrant whole. The wars of the Revolution had not only put an unprecedentedly large number of Frenchmen into uniform but they had also allowed the creation of an army in which rank was no longer the prerogative of an aristocratic minority. Most of Napoleon's senior commanders in 1805 had risen from the ranks by merit; only two of them, Marshals Augereau and Bernadotte, were over forty years of age. The organizational basis of the *Grande Armée* was the corps, a large all-arms group formed of several divisions. The corps of the *Grande Armée* differed in size according to their role; they were, however, flexible formations, well-suited to overcoming the logistic problems posed by Napoleon's strategic plan.

Napoleon dictated his orders to Count Daru, Intendant General of the *Grande Armée*, on 13 August. He decreed the simultaneous advance of what he termed 'my seven streams'. Bernadotte, with 17,000 men of 1st Corps, was to march from

Hanover to Bavaria by way of Würzburg—13,000 men were to remain in Hanover in case of an Allied landing in north Germany. Marshal Marmont's 2nd Corps, 20,000 strong, was to join Bernadotte at Würzburg, having marched by way of Mainz and Frankfurt. The most able of Napoleon's marshals, the level-headed Davout, was to lead the 26,000 men of his 3rd Corps from its camp at Ambleteuse, on the Channel coast, to Mannheim. Marshal Soult was to take the 4th Corps, 40,000 men, from Boulogne to Spires, where a division would be detached to strengthen 5th Corps under Marshal Lannes. The red-headed Marshal Ney—'bravest of the brave'—would link up with Lannes at Strasbourg with the 24,000 men of 6th Corps, having marched from Montreur on the Channel coast. Marshal Augereau's 7th Corps was to march from Brittany to the Rhine, bringing up the rear.

The advancing infantry were preceded by the cavalry of the *Grande Armée*, 22,000 horsemen under the flamboyant Marshal Joachim Murat. Part of Murat's force was employed with 5th Corps in the Black Forest, drawing Mack westward and distracting him from the danger looming to the northwest. Napoleon himself was accompanied by the Imperial Guard under Marshal Bessières, 7000 strong.

Its itineraries laid down by meticulous staff-work, the *Grande Armée* surged eastward in September and early October, and the jaws of the trap closed about the unwary Mack. The latter, hindered by bad relations with Ferdinand and his divisional commanders, concentrated on

Ulm. On 13 October Lannes took Elchingen and its half-demolished bridge after a brisk engagement. Ferdinand, following yet another dispute with Mack, broke out of the Ulm position on the night of 14/15 October, but, pursued hard by Murat, only a very small proportion of his force actually managed to escape. On the 17th Mack agreed to surrender if Russian help had not materialized by the 26th. However, for reasons which remain unclear, he capitulated early, on 20 October, with nearly 30,000 men.

Kutusov had indeed been making for Ulm, but was too far away to be of any assistance to Mack. He reached Braunau on the River Inn on the 20th, but even though he had assimilated a stray Austrian division, he had only 40,000 men immediately available. He heard of the Ulm capitulation on 23 October, and at once fell back over the Inn, burning its bridges behind him.

The second phase of the campaign began on 26 October, when the *Grande Armée* set along the Danube. The French crossed the Inn on 29/30 October, but the pace of the advance was slowed down by bad weather. Ney had been sent to contain the Austrians in the Tyrol, while Marmont, in the Salzburg area, checked any threat from the Archdukes Charles and John.

The bulk of the *Grande Armée*—Soult, Lannes, Bernadotte and Murat—moved along the right bank of the Danube. Davout's troops linked the main body with Marmont, while Marshall Mortier, with Gazan's and Dupont's divisions, followed the left bank of the Danube.

Kutusov fell back with the stubbornness and

The Battle of Austerlitz, 1805

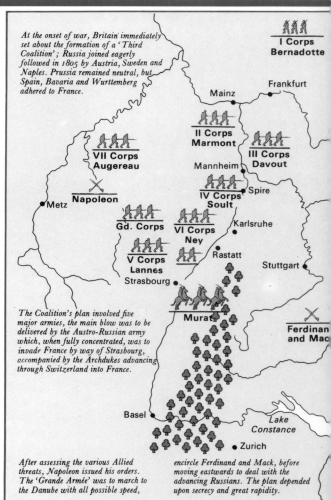

At the onset of war, Britain immediately set about the formation of a 'Third Coalition'; Russia joined eagerly followed in 1805 by Austria, Sweden and Naples. Prussia remained neutral, but Spain, Bavaria and Wurttemberg adhered to France.

The Coalition's plan involved five major armies, the main blow was to be delivered by the Austro-Russian army which, when fully concentrated, was to invade France by way of Strasbourg, accompanied by the Archdukes advancing through Switzerland into France.

After assessing the various Allied threats, Napoleon issued his orders. The 'Grande Armée' was to march to the Danube with all possible speed, encircle Ferdinand and Mack, before moving eastwards to deal with the advancing Russians. The plan depended upon secrecy and great rapidity.

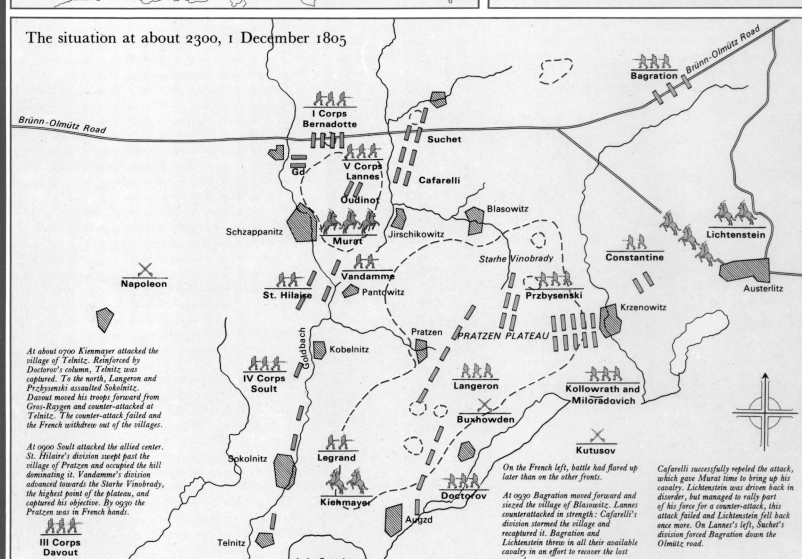

The situation at about 2300, 1 December 1805

At about 0700 Kienmayer attacked the village of Telnitz. Reinforced by Doctorov's column, Telnitz was captured. To the north, Langeron and Przbysenski assaulted Sokolnitz. Davout moved his troops forward from Gros-Raygen and counter-attacked at Telnitz. The counter-attack failed and the French withdrew out of the villages.

At 0900 Soult attacked the allied center. St. Hilaire's division swept past the village of Pratzen and occupied the hill dominating it. Vandamme's division advanced towards the Starhe Vinobrady, the highest point of the plateau, and captured his objective. By 0930 the Pratzen was in French hands.

On the French left, battle had flared up later than on the other fronts.

At 0930 Bagration moved forward and siezed the village of Blasowitz. Lannes counterattacked in strength: Cafarelli's division stormed the village and recaptured it. Bagration and Lichtenstein threw in all their available cavalry in an effort to recover the lost ground.

Cafarelli successfully repeled the attack, which gave Murat time to bring up his cavalry. Lichtenstein was driven back in disorder, but managed to rally part of his force for a counter-attack, this attack failed and Lichtenstein fell back once more. On Lannes's left, Suchet's division forced Bagration down the Olmütz road.

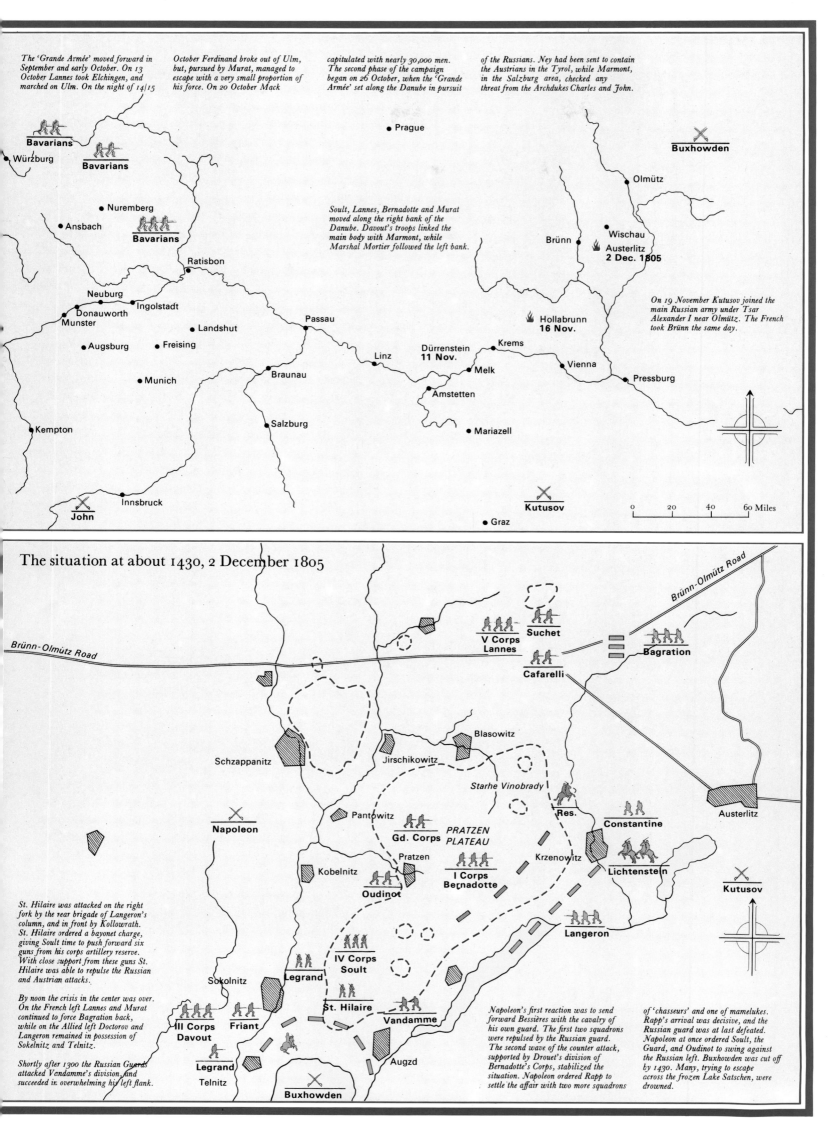

The 'Grande Armée' moved forward in September and early October. On 13 October Lannes took Elchingen, and marched on Ulm. On the night of 14/15 October Ferdinand broke out of Ulm, but, pursued by Murat, managed to escape with a very small proportion of his force. On 20 October Mack capitulated with nearly 30,000 men. The second phase of the campaign began on 26 October, when the 'Grande Armée' set along the Danube in pursuit of the Russians. Ney had been sent to contain the Austrians in the Tyrol, while Marmont, in the Salzburg area, checked any threat from the Archdukes Charles and John.

Soult, Lannes, Bernadotte and Murat moved along the right bank of the Danube. Davout's troops linked the main body with Marmont, while Marshal Mortier followed the left bank.

On 19 November Kutusov joined the main Russian army under Tsar Alexander I near Olmütz. The French took Brünn the same day.

Bavarians
Würzburg
Bavarians
Nuremberg
Ansbach
Bavarians
Ratisbon
Neuburg
Ingolstadt
Donauworth
Munster
Landshut
Passau
Augsburg
Freising
Munich
Braunau
Linz
Salzburg
Kempton
Innsbruck
John
Graz
Mariazell
Amstetten
Melk
Vienna
Pressburg
Krems
Dürrenstein **11 Nov.**
Hollabrunn **16 Nov.**
Brünn
Wischau
Austerlitz **2 Dec. 1805**
Olmütz
Prague
Buxhowden
Kutusov

0   20   40   60 Miles

The situation at about 1430, 2 December 1805

Brünn–Olmütz Road
V Corps **Lannes**
Suchet
Bagration
Cafarelli
Schzappanitz
Jirschikowitz
Blasowitz
Starhe Vinobrady
Res.
Austerlitz
Pantowitz
Napoleon
Gd. Corps
PRATZEN PLATEAU
Constantine
Krzenowitz
Kobelnitz
Pratzen
I Corps **Bernadotte**
Lichtenstein
Oudinot
Kutusov
Langeron
Sokolnitz
Legrand
IV Corps **Soult**
St. Hilaire
Vandamme
III Corps **Davout**
Friant
Legrand
Telnitz
Augzd
Buxhowden

St. Hilaire was attacked on the right fork by the rear brigade of Langeron's column, and in front by Kollowrath. St. Hilaire ordered a bayonet charge, giving Soult time to push forward six guns from his corps artillery reserve. With close support from these guns St. Hilaire was able to repulse the Russian and Austrian attacks.

By noon the crisis in the center was over. On the French left Lannes and Murat continued to force Bagration back, while on the Allied left Doctorov and Langeron remained in possession of Sokelnitz and Telnitz.

Shortly after 1300 the Russian Guards attacked Vandamme's division, and succeeded in overwhelming his left flank.

Napoleon's first reaction was to send forward Bessières with the cavalry of his own guard. The first two squadrons were repulsed by the Russian guard. The second wave of the counter attack, supported by Drouet's division of Bernadotte's Corps, stabilized the situation. Napoleon ordered Rapp to settle the affair with two more squadrons of 'chasseurs' and one of mamelukes. Rapp's arrival was decisive, and the Russian guard was at last defeated. Napoleon at once ordered Soult, the Guard, and Oudinot to swing against the Russian left. Buxhowden was cut off by 1430. Many, trying to escape across the frozen Lake Satschen, were drowned.

Above: Marshal Joachim Murat, who commanded the advance guard, failed to follow the Russians and made straight for Vienna. Kutusov's forces made good their escape, forcing Napoleon to follow him northward to Austerlitz.

The Russians suffered severely in the confused and bloody action at Hollabrunn, but managed to slip away under cover of darkness. Bagration's steadfastness enabled Kutusov to continue his retreat unmolested, and on 19 November he joined the main Russian army, under Tsar Alexander I, near Olmütz. The French took Brünn the same day, but the *Grande Armée* had reached such a peak of exhaustion that, on 23 November, Napoleon was forced to suspend operations for the time being.

The overall strategic picture was now one of some peril for the French. The Archduke Charles, in a campaign which reflects unfavorably upon this otherwise capable general, had withdrawn from Italy under pressure from Massena, but was joined in Carinthia by John, who had marched via the Brenner Pass. The end of November saw the Archdukes in the Marburg area, watched by a part of Marmont's corps around Graz to the north. The main Austro-Russian army was strongly posted in the area of Olmütz, with secure lines of communication with Russia and Silesia. There was a very real danger that the *Grande Armée* would find itself cracked like a nut between the Archdukes from the south and the Austro-Russians from the northeast. Napoleon's danger was magnified by his logistic problems, which were largely responsible for keeping his army sprawled over a wide area from Brünn to Vienna, and then westwards along the Danube. There were few ways out of the situation. A retreat toward Ulm was, perhaps, the safest, but such a maneuver was an open admission of defeat.

Napoleon's solution to the problem was as dramatic as had been his original strategic plan. He decided to snap the mainspring of the Allied threat by persuading the Austro-Russian army around Olmütz to attack his concentrated forces between Brünn and Vienna. His first priority was to secure his southern flank. Marmont was ordered to remain on the defensive, and to avoid, at all costs, a pitched battle with the Archdukes. If necessary, he could be supported by Davout and Mortier, who were around Vienna. The second part of the plan was more hazardous. Soult and Lannes, with the guard and three cavalry divisions, were concentrated around Brünn, while a hussar brigade was sent forward to Wischau on the Olmütz road. As soon as the Allies had taken the bait and moved forward, Napoleon would summon Davout from Vienna and Bernadotte from Iglau. This assembled army would then be only slightly weaker than that of the Allies—75,000 against 88,000. Finally, the Allies would be induced to attack the deceptively weak French right; while this attack was in progress Napoleon would turn the Allied right, severing its lines of communication and inflicting a defeat on the Austro-Russian armies which would change the complexion of the war.

The plan depended very heavily upon the deception. If the Allied commanders realized what was afoot and declined to attack, Napoleon's position would worsen by the day, and he would probably be forced to retreat via Brünn, to the northwest, into Bohemia and thence to Württemberg. The French were aided, as they had been at

determination he was famed for. The French, impeded by atrocious roads, were unable to encircle him as Napoleon had hoped. On 8 November Kutusov slipped across the Danube at Krens. Murat, commanding the French advance guard, failed to pursue the Russians, but made instead for the Austrian capital of Vienna, now lying open before him. He was within a few miles of the city when, on 11 November, he received a stern rebuke from Napoleon, informing him that 'there is no glory except where there is danger. There is none in entering a defenseless capital'. On the same day Mortier, on the left bank of the Danube, collided with the Russians at Dürrenstein. He had with him only Gazon's division, and lost heavily in a desperate action, being saved only by the timely arrival of Dupont.

The Austrians had declared Vienna an open city, but held the nearby Danube bridges in strength. On 12 November Murat and Lannes seized the bridges by a brilliant ruse, and at once moved in pursuit of Kutusov. Napoleon entered the capital the same day, well pleased with Murat's stratagem. The dashing Murat was not, however, destined to remain in favor for long, for on 13 November he was duped into accepting a brief armistice which enabled Kutusov's main body to make good the escape. Napoleon furiously repudiated the armistice as soon as he heard of it, and on 16 November Lannes threw General Oudinot's grenadiers at the Russian rear-guard, commanded by the staunch Prince Peter Bagration.

earlier stages of the campaign, by the confusion and the bad feeling so prevalent in the Allied command. The reputation of the Austrian armies was low, in Russian eyes, following Ulm, and relations between the armies were not aided by the looting carried out by the Russians around Olmütz in what was, after all, Austrian territory. Efforts to persuade Prussia to join the Coalition had met with some success, but, although Prussian troops were on the move, the Prussian Foreign Minister, Count Haugwitz was—unbeknown to the Allies—negotiating with Napoleon.

The mood in the Allied camp was particularly bellicose. The Emperor Francis and his Chief-of-Staff, the pedantic General Weirother, favored a counteroffensive with the aim of recovering Vienna. The gay Russian firebrands surrounding Alexander were also loud in their demands for immediate attack upon the insolent French. There were, it is true, leveller heads in both armies; the Austrian Prince Karl Schwarzenburg joined Kutusov in demanding caution.

Napoleon's stratagems, however, poured fuel on the fires of Russian temerity. On 28 November he sent General Savary to negotiate with the Tsar, a mission the Allies instantly interpreted as a sign of weakness. Why would he negotiate if he were not in difficulties? Further credence was given to this viewpoint by a meeting between Napoleon and Count Dolgoruki, at which Napoleon appeared to ask for terms. Dolgoruki returned to the Allied camp convinced that the French were trying to buy time; his evidence simply confirmed the Allied leaders in their belief that they were dealing with a beaten man.

Napoleon had chosen his battlefield as early as 21 November, long before the Allies had taken the bait. He had ridden over Moravia for several days, and on the 21st he pointed to a stubby hill, the Santon, north of the Brünn-Olmütz road near the village of Austerlitz, and remarked to his staff, 'Gentlemen, examine this ground carefully, it is going to be a battlefield; you will have a part to play upon it'. The main road from Vienna to Olmütz ran north to Brünn, where it

turned sharp right and ran northeast toward Olmütz. It was a straight, tree-lined highway, and was to mark the northern limit of the battlefield. To its north lay the wooded foothills of the mountains of Moravia.

The village of Austerlitz—a group of houses clustered around the residence of Count Kaunitz —lay just south of the road, about fifteen miles from Brünn. Two miles west of Austerlitz the ground rose rapidly into the Pratzen Plateau, just under 1000 feet high at the Starhe Vinobrady, its highest point. The village of Pratzen lay in the neck of a small valley on the western edge of the plateau, with the Goldbach stream running north-south about a mile west of the village. Parallel with the northern edge of the Pratzen, the Goldbach forked around another piece of high ground, just south of the Brünn-Olmütz road. The village of Puntowitz lay near the fork, with Kobelnitz, Sokolnitz and Telnitz further downstream. The Goldbach itself was a shallow marshy stream, easily fordable. South of Telnitz it was fed by two lakes which, naturally enough in December, were ice-covered.

The French Move Into Position

The French army began to slide into position west of the Goldbach on 29 November. Lannes held the northern sector, around the Santon, with the divisions of General Suchet and Cafarelli; the field defenses were placed on the Santon itself, the cornerstone of the French left. On Lannes' right, Murat's cavalry and horse artillery bivouacked around Schzappanitz, with Oudinot's grenadiers to their north. Bernadotte's corps, still on the march, were to take position behind Oudinot on arrival. Soult's 4th Corps was more widely extended. Generals Vandamme and St Hilaire were along the line of the Goldbach north of Puntowitz—south of this village General Legrand's division held Kobelnitz, Sokolnitz and Telnitz with small detachments. Davout's corps, when it arrived, would strengthen the dangerously over-extended Legrand.

Across the Goldbach the ponderous Allied army moved into position on 1 December. Alexander and Francis set up their headquarters in the village of Krzenowitz where, in the fatal tradition of the Allied command, the inevitable Council of War took place on the afternoon of 1 December. Kutusov was nominally Commander-in-Chief, but naturally his authority did not extend to the monarchs, whose adherents at once resumed their squabbles. Kutusov himself, seated in his traveling armchair, dozed intermittently throughout the Council, well fortified by several bottles of his favorite wine. Francis was by now less enthusiastic about an immediate advance on Vienna, but the young Alexander was carried away by the advice of hotheads surrounding him.

The Allied plan was the work of Weirother, who arrived at Kutusov's quarters just after midnight, bringing with him a vast map of the area. He then proceeded to read out the dispersions in what General Langeron, an *emigré* Frenchman in Russian service, called 'an elevated tone and with an air of boastfulness that proclaimed his ultimate conviction of his merit and our incapacity'. Kutusov was by now asleep, and

Left: Marshal Bessières, commander of the 7000 men of the Imperial Guard, which remained under the personal control of Napoleon.

Leuthen: Oblique Order

On 5 December, 1757 Frederick the Great of Prussia attacked an Austrian army under Field-Marshal Daun and Charles of Lorraine at Leuthen in Silesia. The odds were heavily against the Prussians, who were outnumbered by nearly three to one. The Austrian position was, furthermore, a strong one, running from Sagschütz in the south to Nippern in the North, squarely blocking the Breslau road, Frederick's main line of advance. The Prussian plan was simple enough. Frederick intended to make a feint against the Austrian right while the main weight of his army, swinging south of the Breslau road, struck the Austrian left around Sagschütz. The Prussian advance guard ejected an Austrian detachment from the village of Borne at first light, and Frederick sent a small force to threaten the Austrian right while the remainder of his army, in two huge columns, marched southeast, hidden from the Austrians by rising ground west of Leuthen.

The blow fell on Sagschütz at about midday. The Austrian commander in this sector, General Nadasti, was overwhelmed, and the battle swept on to Leuthen itself which, stoutly held by infantry sent forward by Charles of Lorraine, was finally carried by a brilliant charge by the Prussian Guard. Frederick's progress now became more difficult, for the Austrian troops around Frobelwitz had time to change front to meet the threat. Nevertheless, by late afternoon General Lucchessi's last cavalry counterattack was repulsed, and the position had collapsed completely by nightfall. The Austrian army was routed, with heavy losses in men and equipment, and Breslau fell two weeks later.

Napoleon called Leuthen 'a masterpiece of movements, maneuvers and resolution'. The tactics which Frederick employed were, however, far from new. The Theban general Epaminondas pioneered oblique order at Leuctra in 371 BC, when his force of 6000 defeated 10,000 Spartans. As Sir Basil Liddell Hart puts it, 'the oblique order which Frederick made famous was only a slight elaboration of the method of Epaminondas'. Furthermore, Frederick's oblique order was not universally successful. At Prague in 1757 the Austrians had time to change front to meet the attack, and at Kolin in the same year the Prussian attack was fatally disorganized by the fire of Austrian light troops.

Frederick pointed out that oblique order had three major advantages. It permitted a small force to defeat a larger, it attacked the enemy at a decisive point, and, if the attacker suffered a reverse, it enabled him to retain unengaged troops to cover his withdrawal. The benefits of oblique order have not escaped more recent military commanders. The Austro-Russian plan for Austerlitz was a variation on oblique order, as was Napoleon's own counter-plan. Subsequent use of oblique order has often been directed towards 'single envelopment', outflanking the enemy rather than 'rolling up' his exposed flank. The special conditions of desert warfare are ideally suited for such maneuvers; Allenby forced the

Turks from the Gaza line by thrusting to Beersheba in 1917, and Rommel employed similar tactics with great success in the Western Desert in 1941–42. Although oblique order and outflanking attacks have produced an impressive list of victories—Leuctra, Leuthen, Chancellorsville and Gazala, to name but a few—they have similarly resulted in disastrous failures. Napoleon's outflanking attack at Leipzig, the Battle of the Nations, in 1813 proved abortive, as did a similar Union attempt at the First Battle of Bull Run in 1861. The success of oblique order depends, as Frederick himself realized, upon mobility and deception; the enemy must remain fixed in his defensive position while the attacking force carries out its outflanking move. To employ such tactics against an enemy who retains the liberty to maneuver as he pleases is, as generations of soldiers have discovered to their peril, disastrous.

The oblique order tactic was used to perfection by Frederick the Great at Leuthen in 1757, but both the Austro-Russian forces and Napoleon attempted to use a variation of this tactic at Austerlitz in 1805. The outflanking of the enemy by a single envelopment approach is itself a variation on the double envelopment tactic used at Canne. It is best used when one flank is inoperable because of difficult terrain, or if, as in the case of the Desert War of 1941–42, one flank is covered by water.

Nippern

Feint attack

Borne

Frobelwitz

Charles of Lorraine

Leuthen

Scheuberg Hill

Frederick

Radaxdorf

Lobetnitz

Sagschütz

Left: Frederick the Great.

of the assembled Allied commanders, Langeron noted that only the conscientious little General Doctorov actually appeared to pay attention.

Weirother's plan was to turn the French right by crossing the Goldbach between Telnitz and Sokolnitz, exploiting the crossing by swinging north and cutting the French to pieces as they fell back on Brünn. General Kienmayer, with the Austrian cavalry on the Allied left, was to swing left once across the Goldbach, and sever the Brünn-Vienna road. On the Allied right, Bagration was to launch an attack along the Brünn-Olmütz road, taking the Santon and unhinging the French left.

The crossing of the Goldbach was to be accomplished by General Buxhowden's corps. Doctorov would storm Telnitz with his 13,500 men, while Langeron, with just under 1200 men, would take Sokolnitz. General Przbysenski, on Langeron's right, would offer assistance as necessary. Once his initial objectives were taken, Buxhowden was to move against the French center around Kobelnitz. Simultaneously, a powerful corps of Austrians and Russians under Generals Kollowrath and Miloradovich, would move over the Pratzen Plateau and complete the French defeat. The Russian Imperial Guard, under the Grand Duke Constantine, was to remain in reserve, and the 4500 cavalry of Prince John of Lichtenstein were to link Bagration and Kollowrath.

Such, then, was Weirother's scheme. It looked attractive enough on the map, but was subject to severe practical limitations. Firstly, the Russian center would be uncovered at the crucial moment of the battle. Langeron pithily inquired what would happen if the French attacked the Pratzen, but the assembled commanders envisaged little possibility of such a move. Secondly,

Weirother's plan was not produced until the early morning of 2 December, and the first attacks were to go in at dawn. The remainder of the night would thus have to be spent moving into assault positions; it would be difficult to maintain secrecy, the troops would be unable to get any rest, and there was every chance that bad map-reading coupled with poor staff-work would produce serious delays. Finally, the task of unified central control was matched by divided command at lower levels.

Napoleon spent 1 December in inspections, waiting anxiously for news of the approach of the 3rd Corps. Without Davout the French right would be desperately weak, and there was some chance of Weirother's bookish plan succeeding. As news of the Allied movements reached Napoleon during the day, so his confidence grew. At last, at about 1600 hours, a staff officer arrived from 3rd Corps announcing that Davout was

Above: Napoleon dining on his favorite pre-battle supper of potatoes and onions fried in olive oil on the eve of the Battle of Austerlitz.

Below: Napoleon gives the order to advance as the battle begins.

Above: Napoleon inspects his Imperial Guard by torchlight on the eve of the battle.

close, and his leading division was at Gros Raygern, southwest of Telnitz. Napoleon issued his orders at about 2030. Lannes was to hold the Santon, backed by Murat's cavalry. Bernadotte was to deploy between Puntowitz and Jirschikowitz in preparation for an attack on Blasowitz. On the right, Legrand was to contain the attack across the Goldbach until Davout came up in support. In the center, meanwhile, Soult was to assault the Pratzen with the divisions of Vandamme and St Hilaire. Oudinot's grenadiers and the Imperial Guard were held in reserve; they could be used to bolster the southern flank or to reinforce a successful attack in the center.

Napoleon's customary pre-battle proclamation was distributed to his army. 'Soldiers!' it thundered, 'The Russian army is presenting itself before you in order to avenge the Austrian army of Ulm. These are the same battalions which you defeated at Hollabrunn, and which since then you have pursued steadily to this point ... This victory will end the campaign, and we shall be able to resume our winter quarters, where we shall be joined by the new armies that are forming in France, and then the peace I shall make will be worthy of my people, of you and of me.' This proclamation sent a shiver of excitement through the *Grande Armée*; morale rose with a bound. After dining gaily with his staff, on his favorite dish of potatoes and onions fried in oil, Napoleon visited his lines on a last inspection. He returned to his tent, and slept for less than an hour before being awakened with news of skirmishing in the area of Telnitz. Savary was sent off to investigate, and returned with the information that Legrand had brushed with a detachment of Austrian Hussars, and that there were unmistakable signs of enemy movement in the Augezd area. Napoleon rose again, and set off on reconnaissance, accompanied by Soult and a small group of staff officers. He satisfied himself that the Allies were in fact making against his right, clashed with a Cossack picket, narrowly avoiding capture, and returned to his own lines. He dismounted in the safety of the French camp, and was greeted by a tremendous display of

confidence and enthusiasm; soldiers leapt to their feet to light his way with blazing wisps of straw, and frenzied shouts of 'Vive L'Empereur!' split the frosty night.

The Allied commanders were unaware of the cause of the blaze of light across the Goldbach. They failed to profit by the fleeting target it offered to their guns, and the massive troop movement went on. Napoleon, meanwhile, returned to his headquarters and dictated orders slightly modifying his dispositions. St Hilaire was to attack through Puntowitz rather than to follow Vandamme further north, and 3000 men of the 4th Corps were detailed to support the weak right wing until Davout reached the field in strength. His orders issued, Napoleon snatched some more sleep as his army moved forward into its final positions.

The adversaries completed their deployment in thick mist between 0400 and 0700 on 2 December. Despite the presence of a large part of the 3rd Corps at Gros-Raygen, the French were outnumbered by about three to one. Of the 73,000 French in the area, about 12,000 were too exhausted or too ill-equipped to fight. The Allies, on the other hand, expected reinforcements from Olmütz to raise their strength to 90,000 during the course of the day. They also had a comfortable artillery superiority, 178 guns as opposed to 139. The Allied deployment was predictably confused. Lichtenstein's cavalry was badly placed, three miles too far south near the foot of the Pratzen. The Allied left was in some disorder, as was the central force of Kollowrath and Miloradovich.

At about 0700 Doctorov's advance guard under Kienmayer clashed with the French 3rd of the Line in the village of Telnitz. After a short period of bitter hand-to-hand fighting, Kienmayer was reinforced by the bulk of Doctorov's column, and Telnitz was stormed. To the north, Langeron and Przbysenski assaulted Sokolnitz, falling on the French 26th Light Infantry, and carrying the village after a sharp fight. The 3rd fell back from Telnitz, screened by some of Davout's light cavalry, and rallied behind the Goldbach. Davout, moving with his customary energy, brought his tired troops forward from Gros-Raygen and counterattacked Telnitz with General Heudelet's brigade. Unfortunately one of Heudelet's regiments, the 108th of the Line, became disordered crossing a ditch and was cut up by some Austrian Hussars. The counterattack failed, and the subsequent French withdrawal was marred by an accidental engagement between the 108th and the 26th Light, retreating from Sokolnitz.

While the French right fought desperately against the advancing Allied columns, the French center prepared to assault. Napoleon, clad in his grey greatcoat sat his little Arab horse west of Puntowitz, surrounded by his marshals. The fog and the dense smoke of the campfires obscured the divisions of Vandamme and St Hiliare, but the Russian columns could be seen on the higher ground, moving continually southward. Soult was eager to unleash his attack.

'I beg Your Majesty to hold me back no longer,' he urged, 'I have 20,000 men to set in motion.'

'How long will it take you to climb the Pratzen?' inquired the Emperor.

Left: Napoleon orders his troops forward into the Austro-Russian lines at the start of battle.

'Less than twenty minutes, Sire,' replied Soult.
'In that case,' concluded Napoleon, 'we will wait for another quarter of an hour.'

Soult's attack went in at 0900. His men, fortified by a triple ration of brandy, advanced with determination, urged on by the shouts of their officers and the hammering of the *pas de charge*. Vandamme and St Hilaire both advanced in the same formation, battalion columns preceded by lines of skirmishes. St Hilaire swept easily past the village of Pratzen and occupied the hill dominating it. Vandamme, advancing towards the Starhe Vinobrady, the highest point of the plateau, was held up briefly, but went on to capture his objective.

Soult's advance had been partially shielded by the mist, and his attack was well under way before the Allied commanders could take counter-measures. Kutusov, accompanying Milorado-vich's force, realized the danger as soon as the French appeared on the plateau, but the two battalions he sent forward were quickly brushed aside. By 0930 the Pratzen was in French hands. At the same time, there was a brief lull in the south as the Allies reorganized in the captured villages of Sokolnitz and Telnitz. A French cavalry charge had delayed the Allied advance, and at about 1000 General Friant's division of the 3rd Corps counterattacked. General Lochet's brigade went boiling through Sokolnitz, only to be attacked in its turn by Langeron and the Kursk Regiment. The fighting eventually stabilized with the French in possession of the southern end of the village, which was by now crammed with the casualties of both sides. Doctorov remained secure in Telnitz, with fresh reserves at hand. Once

Left: Napoleon, on a bluff above the battle, directs operations as the French make for the Pratzen Plateau.

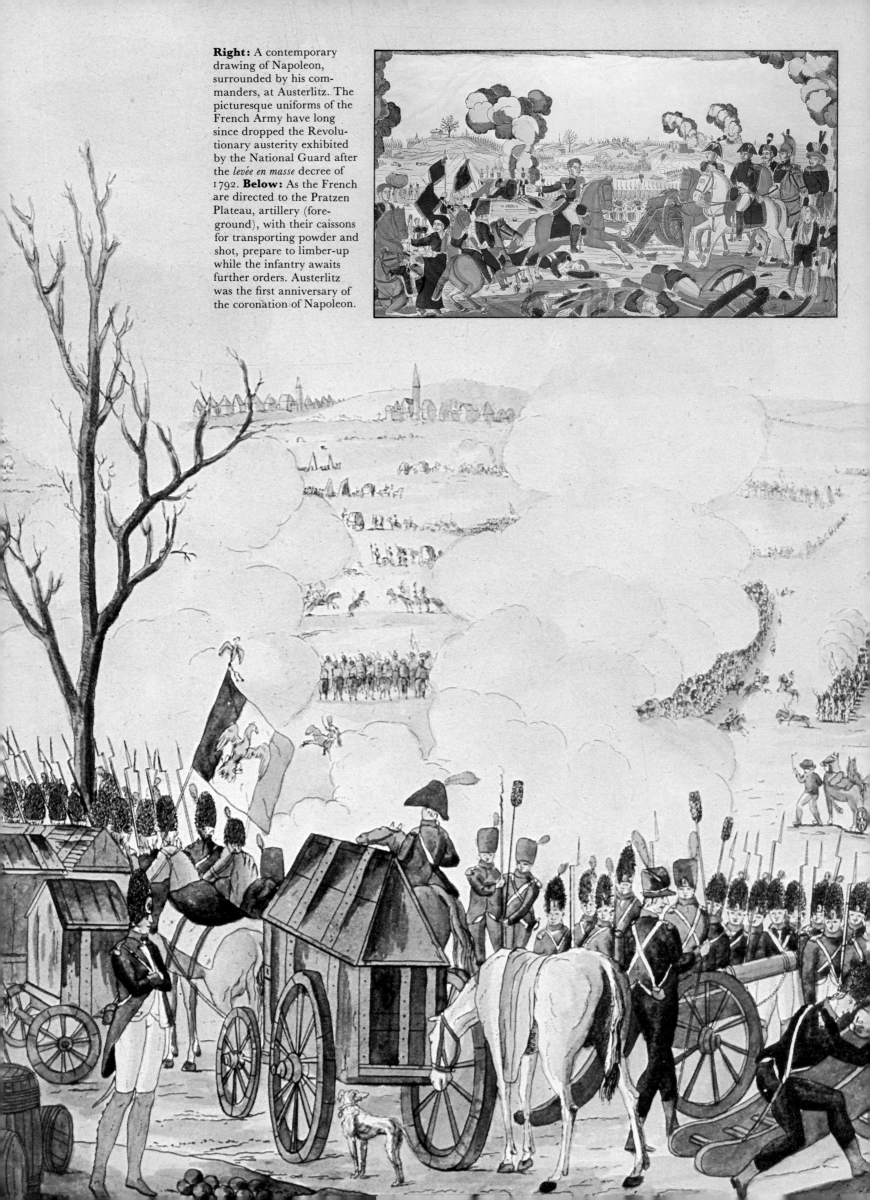

Right: A contemporary drawing of Napoleon, surrounded by his commanders, at Austerlitz. The picturesque uniforms of the French Army have long since dropped the Revolutionary austerity exhibited by the National Guard after the *levée en masse* decree of 1792. **Below:** As the French are directed to the Pratzen Plateau, artillery (foreground), with their caissons for transporting powder and shot, prepare to limber-up while the infantry awaits further orders. Austerlitz was the first anniversary of the coronation of Napoleon.

again, however, the defective Allied command took its toll. There was no attempt to launch a cohesive attack through Sokolnitz and Telnitz since the man who should have organized it, General Buxhowden, the overall commander in this sector, was incapably drunk.

By mid-morning, then, the picture was one of French success in the center, but a more desperate contest in the south. Away on the French left, battle had flared up later than on the other fronts. Lannes' task was to hold the Santon, and to prevent Bagration from swinging south against the Pratzen. To his right was Murat, whose cavalry were to be used to exploit the eventual French breakthrough. This plan was dislocated when, at about 0930, Bagration moved forward, seizing Blasowitz with two battalions of the

Russian Imperial Guard. Lannes, aware of the significance of the sound of gunfire from the Pratzen, counterattacked in strength. Cafarelli's advancing division, supported by General Keller-man's light cavalry, was charged by a mass of Russian horse. Kellerman waited until the Russian attack had spent its energy against the volleys of Cafarelli's infantry, and then swept forward and drove the Russians off. Lannes continued his advance, but was now heavily engaged by Bagration's 40 guns, and, though Lannes replied

with his own artillery, his corps ground to a halt. After an unproductive exchange of fire, both commanders lunged forward on their right. Bagration's attack on the Santon was thwarted by the tenacity of the 17th of the Line, but Lannes' assault on Blasowitz was successful, though at a very heavy cost.

Murat Cuts Off Buxhowden

The fall of Blasowitz gave Murat the opportunity of cutting Bagration off from the Allied center. Before Murat's attack got under way, Bagration and Lichtenstein—who had at last arrived in the right place—threw in all their available cavalry in an effort to recover the lost ground. Cafarelli, emerging from Blasowitz, was assailed by 40 squadrons of cavalry, but drove them off by sustained fire. Cafarelli's steadfastness gave Murat time to bring up the cavalry of Generals Nansouty and D'Hautpoul, huge *cuirassiers* with steel breastplates and sweeping horse-

hair plumes. They trotted forward in immaculate order and collided with Lichtenstein's horsemen with a crash which could be heard all over the battlefield. Lichtenstein was driven back in disorder, but managed to rally part of his force for a counterstroke against the over-extended French. This move was itself counterattacked by the 2nd *Cuirrassiers*, and Lichtenstein fell back once more. On Lannes' left, Suchet's division made progress in the face of heavy fire, slowly forcing Bagration down the Olmütz road. The engagement in the north prevented Bagration from intervening in the center, where the battle was nearing its climax.

The Allied center was by no means as denuded of troops as Napoleon had believed. Many Allied infantry had been detained behind the center as a result of the traffic jam caused by Lichtenstein's erroneous early morning deployment, and were thus in a position to engage Soult. Vandamme's division, on the high ground at the northern end of the Pratzen, was better placed to resist a

VENI
VIDI
VICI

. BERGER ET. INV. F.   1806 .

Left: Napoleon, who viewed himself as a reincarnation of Julius Caesar and the French Empire as a revival of the Roman, is portrayed in classical Empire style leading a Roman triumphal march. *Imperator* was the Roman title given to Caesar as the conquering hero of Gaul. The Emperor Napoleon, leading the latter-day Gauls to victory, came to Austerlitz, saw the Austrians and Russians, and conquered them.

counterattack than was St Hilaire, around the village of Pratzen. St Hilaire was attacked on the right flank by General Kamenski commanding the rear brigade of Langeron's column, and in front by Kollowrath's Austrians. Even the dogged St Hilaire was briefly nonplussed, but he recovered in time to order a desperate bayonet charge, giving Soult time to push forward six guns from his corps artillery reserve. With close support from these cannon St Hilaire was able to repulse the Russian and Austrian attacks. Vandamme consolidated his position on the northern end of the Pratzen with little difficulty for Miloradovich, although personally able, spent the morning making theatrical gestures and, like his tippling colleague Buxhowden, failed to organize a general counterattack.

By noon the crisis in the center was over. On the French left Lannes and Murat continued to force Bagration back, while on the Allied left Doctorov and Langeron remained in possession of Sokolnitz and Telnitz, but were unable to advance further due to pressure from Davout, now supported by Oudinot's grenadiers, dispatched by Napoleon from his left. The Russian commanders in this sector were by now seriously preoccupied with events on their right, and perturbed by the absence of orders from Buxhowden.

Bagration was more fortunate in the latter respect for, in the early afternoon, he received intelligence of the collapse of the Allied center, and was ordered to hold open the Olmütz road as a line of retreat for the army. He responded by attacking Lannes' left to keep him engaged. Lannes at once swung his right wing forward, threatening to swing Bagration back against the mountains of Moravia. Bagration quickly realized what was afoot and straightened his line at right angles to the road. Under heavy pressure from Cafarelli, Suchet and Murat, the Russians were driven back, with heavy losses, beyond the point where the Austerlitz fork joins the Olmütz road.

Murat, possibly smarting under the reprimands which he received earlier in the campaign, decided not to launch his forces in an all out attack on the retreating Bagration. The Allied right thus managed to limp off the field, and the vital road remained open.

Napoleon and his entourage had ridden to the Starhe Vinobrady soon after midday. The Emperor had ordered the guard to cross the Goldbach, and had ensured that Bernadotte did not become seriously engaged against Bagration. At about this time he made the decision which was to result in the destruction of the Allied left. The French army was to swing to the right, and encircle Buxhowden in the Telnitz-Augezd area. Before this maneuver could be executed, the French center had to sustain the last major Allied effort; the charge of the Russian Imperial Guard.

Four battalions of the Semionovski and Preobrajenski regiments attacked Vandamme's division, but were forced back after causing heavy casualties. This determined attack was followed by a charge by the cavalry of the Russian guard, led by the swarthy Grand-Duke Constantine in person. The horsemen, fifteen squadrons of the finest youth in Russia, swirled over the 4th of the Line, took its eagle, and went on to maul the 24th Light. Vandamme had swung these two regiments around to cover his threatened flank and now, with the footguard renewing its attack on his front, he was in a desperate situation.

Napoleon ordered Bessières to support Vandamme with the cavalry of his own guard. Bessières sent forward two squadrons of *chasseurs*, only to see them driven back. He then pushed three squadrons of horse grenadiers and two more of *chasseurs* together with the horse artillery of the guard, into the fray. Bernadotte, to the northwest, had seen the dangerous plight of Vandamme, and, on his own initiative, ordered General Drouet D'Erlon's infantry division to intervene. A frightful *mêlée* was already in progress when Napoleon ordered one of his *aides de camp*, General Rapp, to settle the affair with two more squadrons of *chasseurs* and one of Mamelukes. Rapp's arrival was decisive, and the Russian guard was at last defeated. Prince Repnine, commander of the Tsar's chevalier guard, was captured with 200 of his men. All the artillery of the Russian guard fell into French hands. Napoleon looked on the scene with satisfaction, remarking that many fine ladies would weep in St Petersburg the next day.

The defeat of the Russian guard at last permitted Napoleon to carry out the great right-wheel which was to destroy Buxhowden. Bernadotte was directed to occupy the Pratzen, while Soult, the Guard, and Oudinot, swung against the Russian left. Buxhowden was cut off by 1430; an order sent by Kutusov some three hours earlier, telling him to retreat, did not arrive until the time for safe withdrawal was long past. As the French closed in, the Allied troops in the southern pocket fought desperately. Some managed to break out to the east before the ring was closed; many, trying to escape across the frozen Lake Satschen, were drowned. Przbysenski was captured and his column destroyed. Both Langeron and Doctorov got away, though the majority of their men were killed or captured.

The battle was over by 1700. To the north, Bagration was in full retreat, though Lannes and Murat failed to press him closely. In the center and south the French collected a rich body of prisoners and trophies. About 12,000 Allied troops were captured, with 180 guns and 50 colors. The Russians had lost some 11,000 men killed and the Austrians perhaps 4000. French casualties were altogether less heavy, and in killed, wounded and captured did not much exceed 10,000, most of whom were wounded.

Austerlitz was certainly no ordinary victory; it was the decisive battle upon which Napoleon had counted. Francis asked for an armistice the following day, and brought Austria out of the war; Alexander took his troops back to their Russian homeland. The news of Austerlitz broke William Pitt's heart; he died soon afterwards. Prussia, who had vacillated for rather too long, was forced to make a humiliating treaty. Finally, in the summer of 1806, goaded beyond endurance, she broke with France, only to suffer total defeat at Jena.

The campaign and battle of Austerlitz were triumphs of the Napoleonic system of central command. This was, in fact, the first occasion on which Napoleon had enjoyed undisputed command of the French army, unmolested by restive political masters or the bickering of other army commanders. The campaign represents the triumph of an overall strategic plan, differing radically from the piecemeal strategy employed by the Allies. Napoleon later wrote that 'the victory of Austerlitz was only the natural outcome of the Moravian plan of campaign. In an art as difficult as that of war, the system campaign often reveals the plan of battle.'

Napoleon's conduct of the battle shows the same qualities as his plan of campaign. The Allies were already off-balance before the first shot was fired; they were lured into launching an attack on an enemy they believed to be on the verge of collapse. To this masterly scheme of deception Napoleon added a sound tactical plan, based on concentration of force at the decisive point, which speedily threw the Allied machine into disorder. The Weirother plan was an altogether more risky venture. Its essential premise was that the French were already half-defeated. It contained no safeguard against a French attack across the Pratzen, and the southern striking force compromised more men than could effectively be employed in the marshy and broken ground around Sokolnitz and Telnitz. Perhaps the most dramatic point of comparison between the adversaries is that of command. Strong central control, with energetic subordinates characterized the *Grande Armée*; a disordered high command, with corps commanders of uncertain quality, was the hallmark of the Allied army.

Austerlitz was fought on the anniversary of Napoleon's coronation. His Moravian victory ensured the survival of the French Empire and earned the *Grande Armée* a role it was to retain for the next decade, that of the predominant weight in the balance of power. The Parvenu Empire came of age on the Pratzen Plateau on the morning of 2 December, 1805; as the sun of Austerlitz broke through the mist it heralded the birth of a new force in European politics.

Opposite: The meeting of Napoleon and the Habsburg Emperor Francis II after the battle.

49

Waterloo 1815

The invasion of Russia in 1812 proved a disaster for Napoleon. In an attempt to dominate all of Europe rather than merely most of it, the French Empire came crashing down around his ears after the Battle of Leipzig in 1813. By 1814 Russian troops were in Paris and Napoleon was forced into exile on the island of Elba just off the Italian coast.

The Congress of Vienna met to reconstruct the map of Europe, while Napoleon, unhappy and restless, plotted to regain France. His lightning return and reconquest of France sent the Bourbon King Louis XVIII scurrying back to England. Men sent to capture the Emperor fell in line behind him. Napoleon was master of France within

days. But could he once more become master of Europe? The Battle of Waterloo put paid to Napoleon's ambitions forever and saved Europe from another series of debilitating wars to prevent French hegemony on the Continent.

Napoleon's escape from the island of Elba brought unanimity and speedy decision to the hitherto dilatory and bickering Congress of Vienna. Within hours of receiving the news the Powers had reformed their Alliance and decided on war against their old enemy. The dispersal of their armies was halted and for the second time in just over a year France was threatened with invasion. Napoleon had landed in France with scarcely more than a battalion of troops, but the magic of his name was enough to destroy the stronger forces sent against him. The attitude of the French nation was well summarized by a Paris journalist:

'The Tiger has broken out of his den
The Ogre has been three days at sea
The Wretch has landed at Fréjus

The Buzzard has reached Antibes
The Invader has arrived in Grenoble
The General has entered Lyons
Napoleon slept at Fontainebleau last night
The Emperor will proceed to the Tuileries today
His Imperial Majesty will address his loyal subjects tomorrow.'

The author of this lampoon went to the heart of Napoleon's renewed popularity, which was based on his success and not on any deep loyalty to his person. Apart from the hard core of Bonapartists, most Frenchmen hated the thought of more years of war. In particular they dreaded the return of conscription. Napoleon may have claimed that he wanted peace, but the Congress Powers were soon massing a million men against him. Five armies were preparing to invade France. The Duke of Wellington had an army of British, German, Dutch and Belgian troops in the Low Countries, with Marshal Blücher's Prussians on his left flank. An Austrian Army was forming in the Black Forest, with more Austrians and Italians threatening

Below: Entry of the Allied sovereigns into Paris, 1814. Alexander I of Russia had Europe at his feet when Napoleon abdicated and left France for the Isle of Elba.

to the borders of France and there were also strong Bonapartist factions in Belgium and Holland. The Emperor's decision was made in early May and in the first days of June his army began a carefully screened concentration on the Belgian frontier.

The Grande Armée Reassembled

From all over France 132,000 men were assembled, leaving the fortresses in the hands of the National Guard. Napoleon naturally assumed the supreme command, but he could no longer count on his old team of subordinates. Marshal Berthier, his matchless chief of staff, was dead, Marshal Murat he considered a traitor, and several other Marshals refused to serve because of age or their oaths of allegiance to Louis XVIII. Napoleon's appointments in 1815 have often been criticized by historians, and many of them were far from suitable. Marshal Soult, an able independent commander, became Chief-of-Staff although he had no training in staff work. Marshal Grouchy was originally selected to command the cavalry, for which he was well qualified, but was later given command of the right wing of the army despite the fact he had never commanded even a corps. The left wing was entrusted to Marshal Ney, whose defection to Napoleon's cause had been a vital factor in the triumphal progress to Paris; he was known to be a fighting, not a thinking, machine. Marshal Davout, the ablest of the Marshals, was left to hold Paris for the Emperor.

But if Napoleon's subordinates were unsuitable the plan he laid before them was worthy of the Emperor at his best. From French sympathizers in the Netherlands he had a very clear picture of his enemies' dispositions. The two armies were dispersed in loose corps groupings. The Prussians (105,000 infantry, 12,000 horse and 296 guns) lay within the area Liège-Dinant-Charleroi-Tirlemont, and Wellington's army (79,000 infantry, 14,000 cavalry and 196 guns) covered the area Brussels-Ghent-Leuze-Mons-Nivelles. It would take some days to concentrate the Allied forces and if he struck quickly Napoleon might prevent this movement altogether. The lines of communication of the two armies diverged; Wellington's running north from Brussels to Ostend and the Channel and Blücher's westwards into Germany from Liège. If surprised and forced to retreat the Allies would tend to fall back along these lines, wanting to get nearer the security of home, and making it easier for Napoleon to concentrate undisturbed on one army or the other. Napoleon's own deployment was ideally framed to assist such a move. Two wings under Ney and Grouchy were to lead the army and Napoleon and the main body would follow in a central position ready to throw their weight on one flank or the other. Moreover, the axis of advance was to be along the boundary between the two armies, a proverbially weak spot with all composite forces.

In Belgium the Allied commanders had little idea of Napoleon's preparations. Wellington had always laid great stress on intelligence, on knowing what was happening on 'the other side of the hill', but he was not allowed to send his scouts beyond the frontier and was misled by reports from the Prussians. He relaxed his guard, making only

the Riviera; behind them a Russian Army was marching to the Central Rhine.

Faced with these forces, Napoleon abandoned the pretence that war could be avoided. To the Bourbon army of 200,000 he added 80,000 volunteers, most of them veterans, and he hoped to raise a further 150,000 by re-conscripting the Class of 1815, the so-called Marie-Louises who had been pressed into service to defend 'la patrie en danger' once before. Every available weapon was refurbished and the factories poured out new uniforms to clothe them. But time was not on Napoleon's side; he could only mobilize a proportion of the Allies' manpower and the French people would not tolerate the return of wartime conditions without the stimulus of victory. He could not afford to repeat the defensive strategy he had employed so skillfully in 1814. Napoleon must attack, and the obvious target was the Low Countries, where Wellington and Blücher were gathered. They presented the most immediate threat leisurely preparations to concentrate his army, and even advised the Duchess of Richmond that she might hold her famous ball on 15 June. But during the 15th the French army crossed the border and by nightfall Napoleon's headquarters were at Charleroi, his army concentrated and already between the Allies.

It was at the ball that Wellington first appreciated the danger in which the Allies stood. First came the news that the Prussian advance guard had met the French at Fleurus and been repulsed; this was serious enough because Blücher was committed to a forward concentration at Sombreffe, less than five miles away. Then during supper Wellington learned from the Prince of Orange that French scouts had reached Quatre Bras, a vital crossroads on the army's route to join Blücher. The Duke had been caught completely wrong-footed for, fearing a flanking move around his right he had begun to assemble his army at Nivelles, away from Quatre Bras and Sombreffe. Fortunately the Dutch commander at Quatre Bras realized the significance of the crossroads and disobeyed his orders to concentrate at Nivelles; two brigades held this crucial point, nearly 30 miles from Brussels. Wellington might well tell the Duke of Richmond that:

'Napoleon has *humbugged* me, by God! he has gained twenty-four hours march on me!'

'What do you intend doing?'

'I have ordered the army to concentrate at Quatre Bras; but we shall not stop him there, and if so I must fight him *here*,' he said, indicating one of the long ridges across the Brussels—Quatre Bras road, south of the village of Waterloo.

Wellington's prophecies were soon justified. He was able to hold Quatre Bras for the whole of the 16th, largely by bluff. Ney, facing a slight slope up to the crossroads, assumed that although it seemed very thinly held, it in fact concealed the full strength of the Allied army. His Peninsular experiences made Ney unusually nervous of attacking Wellington in a prepared position. But on the same day, the Prussians, caught too far forward by Napoleon's speed, were being mauled at Ligny, although decisive victory avoided Napoleon because his *corps de reserve* was not committed on either flank but spent the day marching and counter-marching between the two wings. Nevertheless the Prussians were forced to withdraw, and the only question was which way they should move. The best roads led eastward, toward the Prussian base and General Gneisenau, Blücher's Chief-of-Staff, who considered that Wellington had failed in his promise to support his Allies, favored this route. Blücher had been rolled on by his wounded horse while leading a cavalry charge during the battle, but he was still full of fight. Trusting to doses of gin, rhubarb and garlic to cure his injuries, and possibly remembering that Wellington's promise had been conditional on his not being attacked himself, Blücher insisted on a more northerly withdrawal, to the town of Wavre, from where he could either support Wellington or still withdraw to the west if necessary.

Wellington did not know of Blücher's decision until nearly 0800 the following morning. It was clearly impossible to hold Quatre Bras any longer and Wellington immediately began moving off

his troops. Had Ney obeyed the Emperor's orders to resume his attack Wellington might have been too late, but the French troops were still foraging for their breakfast. Even Napoleon did not really grasp the urgency of the situation until the middle of the morning, when he moved to reinforce and hasten the dull-witted Ney. By 1400 Wellington had withdrawn all his infantry and only a screen of cavalry and light artillery remained to face the mass of French lancers, led by Napoleon himself, which was appearing over the southern slopes. The British horse batteries fired one round in greeting, then limbered up and galloped for the bottleneck of the one road through Genappe. Their shots were echoed by thunderclaps as a tremendous storm swept southward, drenching the fields and confining movement to the one major road. Dispiriting though the rain was, it saved the Allied army from serious loss. Confined to the roads Napoleon's cavalry could not come to grips with their enemies' rearguard and the pur-

Above: Marshal Ney, 'bravest of the brave', whose reckless daring was not enough to turn the tide of battle in favor of the French. He was executed for treason after Napoleon's exile to St Helena.

Right: William, Prince of Orange, at Waterloo, who had recently become William I, first King of the Netherlands, after the liberation which followed the Battle of Leipzig in 1813. His family had traditionally held the position of *stadhouder* of the Netherlands in the years of the Dutch Republic, which collapsed in 1795. **Center above:** Charge of the 1st Life Guards at Genappe on 17 June, the day before Waterloo. **Center below:** Wellington orders his men to charge during the last phase of the battle.

suit died out. Napoleon's great fear was that, having concentrated his main effort against Wellington, he would not be able to catch the Duke, and would thus lose the benefits of his initial move. It was therefore with great relief that Napoleon rode along his outpost line in the early hours of the 18th and saw a long line of bivouac fires, marking the position of the Allies along the ridge to the north. '*Je les tiens donc, ces Anglais*' ('I have those English now!'), he remarked.

Wellington had taken up a position along a low ridge just south of the hamlet of Mont-St Jean. Most of his army was posted on the reverse slope and could therefore, by lying down, protect themselves against the worst effects of the French artillery fire. On the forward slope was a strong skirmishing line, strengthened by the garrisons of a number of farms which Wellington had occupied to break the first force of the French attacks. The greatest weight was placed to the right of the Brussels road, which bisected the position. Wellington expected Napoleon to maneuver around

Left: Prince Blücher under his horse when the French cavalry pushed both aside. Blücher may have been down but was by no means out of the battle. **Below:** The Death of Frederick William of Brunswick at Quatre Bras on 16 June, 1815.

this flank rather than mount a frontal attack and in case the French should make a really broad sweep to the west, 17,000 men were placed at Hal, nearly ten miles away, thereby condemned to play no part in the coming battle. Wellington was content to accept weakness on his left flank because he expected to be supported there by the Prussians. He had told Blücher that he would march at dawn, supported by two more divisions. Wellington expected that they would make their presence felt by midday. Until then his own army had to hold off the French assaults unaided. Wellington had 67,661 men drawn from several nations under his command, composed of 49,608 infantry, 12,408 cavalry and 5645 artillerymen, with 156 guns. The backbone of the army were the British regiments, especially those which had served in Spain, and some experienced Hanoverian and King's German Legion units. However, most of his troops were untried in war and some of the Allied forces were decidedly unreliable. The first shots fired at the Duke of Wellington on the battlefield of Waterloo came from a battalion of Nassauers who panicked at the sight of the French troops deploying in front of them. To hold this heterogeneous force together required leadership of the highest quality and the ability to juggle reserves into danger spots with absolute precision.

On the other side of a slight valley Napoleon had 71,947 men: 48,950 infantry, 15,765 cavalry and 7232 artillerymen with 246 guns. They were generally much more experienced troops and Napoleon had no problems of international co-operation. In fighting the battle Napoleon intended to exploit his superiority in artillery and cavalry, and told brother Jerome:

'I shall have my artillery fire and my cavalry charge, so as to force the enemy to disclose his positions, and, when I am quite certain which positions the English troops have taken up, I shall march straight at them with my Old Guard.'

He was scathingly contemptuous of those on his staff who spoke well of the English Army and its commander: 'Just because you have been beaten by Wellington, you think he's a good general. I tell you, Wellington is a bad general, the English are bad troops, and this affair is nothing more than eating breakfast.'

The Emperor was also confident that he could deal with Wellington without any interference by the Prussians:

'The Prussians and English cannot possibly link up for another two days after such a battle.'

Two Crucial Decisions

In his sublime and unshakable assurance, Napoleon made two crucial decisions. He postponed the main attack from 0900 to 1300, to allow time for the ground to dry, which would permit the artillery to move more easily and improve the ricochet effect of their shots. Secondly, he neglected to send clear and early orders to Grouchy to advance to Wavre as quickly as possible, and to keep in touch with his own operations. It is clear from the wording of his despatch that Napoleon believed that only a fragment of the Prussian army was at Wavre, rather than its full strength. Grouchy followed orders only too closely and by refusing to use his initiative and move closer to Water-

loo, he ensured that nothing interfered with the Prussian corps which were marching to join Wellington.

Time is usually of vital importance in warfare and clearly the decisive moment in the battle of Waterloo would be the arrival of Blücher's Prussians. If Napoleon had not driven Wellington from the battlefield by then, he would inevitably face defeat and the loss, for the second time, of his Empire. Neither side knew exactly when the Prussians would appear and the suspense was increased when Bülow's corps, which had not been engaged on the 16th, was ordered to lead the advance. Its line of march lay across that of two other corps which were recovering from Ligny. By the time Bülow had emerged from the resulting confusion there was no possibility of his corps intervening before four in the afternoon.

While he waited for the ground to dry Napoleon deployed his army in parade array. Along the front of his position were the corps of General Reille, on the left, and of Count d'Erlon on the right. This thick line of infantry was supported by a great battery of 84 guns to its front, west of the Waterloo road. Behind it, along the same road, were General Lobau's corps and the Imperial Guard itself, and on either side of them were the cavalry under Kellermann and Milhaud.

As the two armies surveyed each other across the scant half mile of wheat which separated them Napoleon made his first move. Perhaps appreciating Wellington's concern about his right flank, he ordered a diversionary attack on the Château d'Hougoumont. Hougoumont was an ancient, partly fortified manor house, surrounded by a high wall and an orchard and wood. It was held by four light companies of the Guards, reinforced by 300 Hanoverian Jaegers and the same battalion of Nassauers who had so nearly shot the Duke. At 1150 the Château came under fire from the artillery of the French left wing and four regiments of Jerome Bonaparte's division advanced to the attack, preceded by a dense crowd of *tirailleurs*. Once the latter reached the southern edge of the woods, the Allied light infantry fell back to their prepared positions in the Château, its walled garden, and the orchard. The French could make no impression on these defenses and most of Jerome's division was soon milling about in the woods, under heavy shrapnel fire from Bull's howitzer battery, which Wellington brought to a position behind the Château over which the high-trajectory howitzers could safely fire. The French attack was checked by this fire and a sudden counterattack drove them from the woods altogether. This was no great matter, for the attack was only intended as a feint. However Jerome was so incensed that, instead of holding back and relying on his artillery to batter Hougoumont, he sent in his own infantry and troops from Foy's division. This attack was more successful, re-occupying the woods, entering the orchard, and then reaching the walls of the Château itself on the western side. However, Wellington was watching the struggle from the hill to the northeast and he sent forward a battalion of Coldstream Guards, in two bodies. Four companies retook the orchard and another four swept into the rear of the French troops who

Right: Napoleon was obliged to flee from the battlefield of Waterloo when the defenses of the Old Guard collapsed around him in the afternoon of 18 June. **Far right:** The Scots Greys stormed into the center of the French forces when Lord Uxbridge's heavy cavalry brigades attacked the exposed flank of d'Erlon's columns. **Below:** The *mêlée* at the center of the British position on the afternoon of the battle.

had just forced the northern door of the Château for the second time. Soon after this Wellington sent the 3rd Guards into the orchard, which meant that almost all of General Byng's Guards Brigade had been drawn down into the area of the Château. To support them Wellington brought up two brigades, du Plat's of the King's German Legion and then Halkett's Hanoverians, from the rear of his right flank. Although these troops were tied down for the rest of the day in the continuing fight for Hougoumont Wellington used only 3500 troops in all, as opposed to the 14,000 Frenchmen engaged in the struggle. Nearly all of Reille's corps was involved, but to no avail; as a diversion the attack on Hougoumont was a failure, for Wellington moved no troops from his center. Furthermore, by holding the Château, Wellington

confined the French attacks east of the Brussels road, which often came under enfilade fire. As many as 10,000 men were killed and wounded around Hougoumont, three-quarters of them French, and although the Château buildings caught fire at one stage the Guardsmen were not driven out. The only Frenchmen who entered the courtyard of Hougoumont were prisoners.

Although the fighting there continued throughout the day, it was soon obscured in the greater struggle about to commence. Just before Napoleon began the great bombardment which was to signal his attack on the center, movement was seen on his far right flank beyond the Bois de Paris. At first it was thought to be Grouchy, but a hussar soon brought the news that these were Prussian troops, in fact the leading elements of

Right: 'Scotland Forever', the charge of the Scots Greys. **Below:** The charge of the Life Guards at Waterloo.

The Battle of Waterloo, 1815

The Battle of Waterloo, 1815
When Napoleon escaped from Elba and
returned to France, the Congress
immediately massed five armies to
invade France. A combined force under
Wellington was in the Low Countries
with Blücher on his left flank. An
Austrian army was forming in the
Black Forest, with more Austrians and
Italians near the Riviera, and a Russian
army marching to the Rhine.

The Waterloo Campaign Maneuvers

During 15 June the French army crossed
the Franco-Belgian border and by
nightfall had made Charleroi its
headquarters. Wellington attempted to
hold Quatre Bras but was forced to
withdraw on the 17th. On the same day
Blücher was forced northwards to
Wavre, where he could either support
Wellington or withdraw to the west.

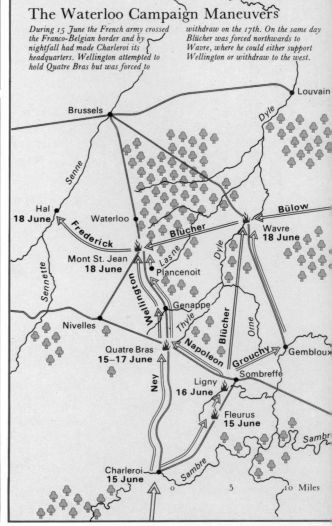

The situation at about 1600

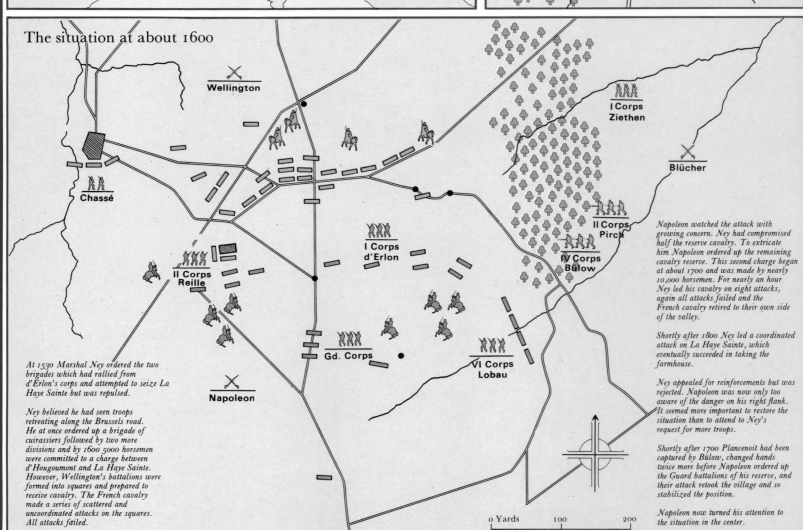

At 1530 Marshal Ney ordered the two
brigades which had rallied from
d'Erlon's corps and attempted to seize La
Haye Sainte but was repulsed.

Ney believed he had seen troops
retreating along the Brussels road.
He at once ordered up a brigade of
cuirassiers followed by two more
divisions and by 1600 5000 horsemen
were committed to a charge between
d'Hougoumont and La Haye Sainte.
However, Wellington's battalions were
formed into squares and prepared to
receive cavalry. The French cavalry
made a series of scattered and
uncoordinated attacks on the squares.
All attacks failed.

Napoleon watched the attack with
growing concern. Ney had compromised
half the reserve cavalry. To extricate
him Napoleon ordered up the remaining
cavalry reserve. This second charge began
at about 1700 and was made by nearly
10,000 horsemen. For nearly an hour
Ney led his cavalry on eight attacks,
again all attacks failed and the
French cavalry retired to their own side
of the valley.

Shortly after 1800 Ney led a coordinated
attack on La Haye Sainte, which
eventually succeeded in taking the
farmhouse.

Ney appealed for reinforcements but was
rejected. Napoleon was now only too
aware of the danger on his right flank.
It seemed more important to restore the
situation than to attend to Ney's
request for more troops.

Shortly after 1700 Plancenoit had been
captured by Bülow, changed hands
twice more before Napoleon ordered up
the Guard battalions of his reserve, and
their attack retook the village and so
stabilized the position.

Napoleon now turned his attention to
the situation in the center.

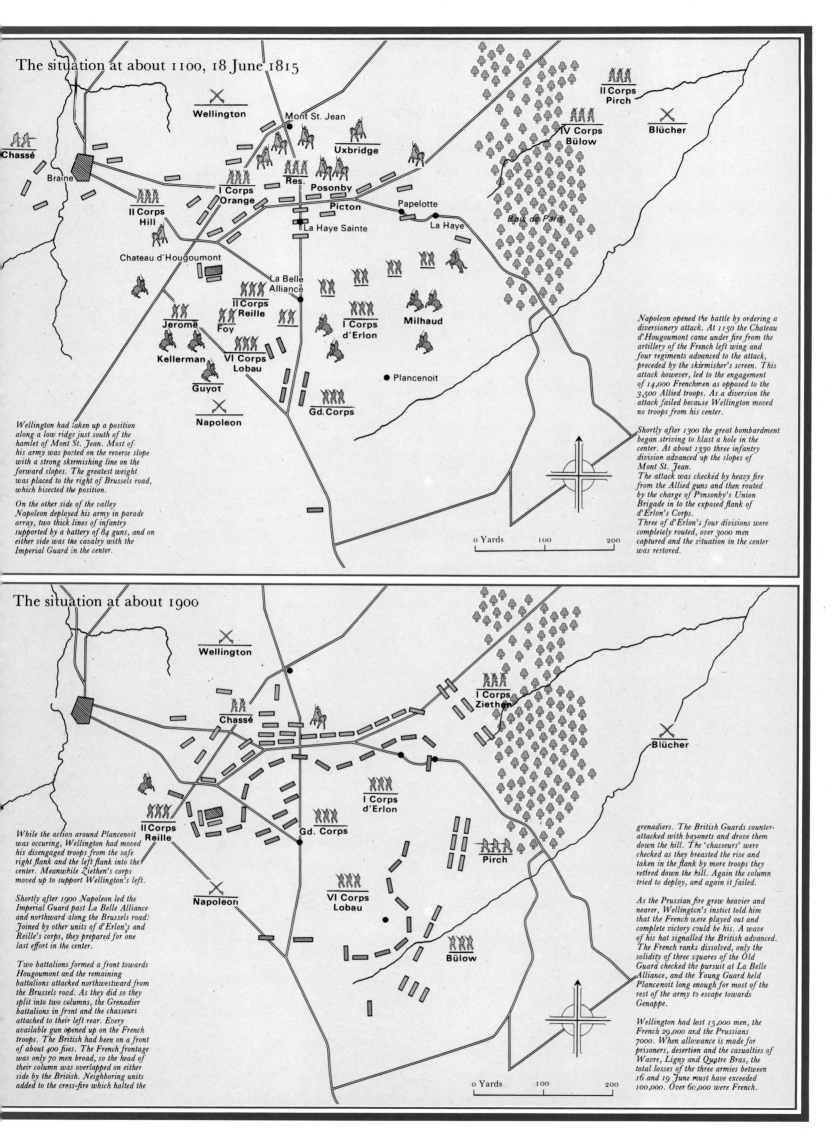

The situation at about 1100, 18 June 1815

Chassé

Braine

Wellington

Mont St. Jean

Uxbridge

II Corps
Pirch

IV Corps
Bülow

Blücher

II Corps
Hill

I Corps
Orange

Res.

Posonby

Picton

Papelotte

La Haye Sainte

La Haye

Bois de Paris

Chateau d'Hougoumont

La Belle
Alliance

II Corps
Reille

I Corps
d'Erlon

Milhaud

Jerome

Foy

Kellerman

VI Corps
Lobau

Plancenoit

Guyot

Napoleon

Gd. Corps

Wellington had taken up a position along a low ridge just south of the hamlet of Mont St. Jean. Most of his army was posted on the reverse slope with a strong skirmishing line on the forward slopes. The greatest weight was placed to the right of Brussels road, which bisected the position.

On the other side of the valley Napoleon deployed his army in parade array, two thick lines of infantry supported by a battery of 84 guns, and on either side was the cavalry with the Imperial Guard in the center.

Napoleon opened the battle by ordering a diversionary attack. At 1150 the Chateau d'Hougoumont came under fire from the artillery of the French left wing and four regiments advanced to the attack, preceded by the skirmisher's screen. This attack however, led to the engagement of 14,000 Frenchmen as opposed to the 3,500 Allied troops. As a diversion the attack failed because Wellington moved no troops from his center.

Shortly after 1300 the great bombardment began striving to blast a hole in the center. At about 1330 three infantry division advanced up the slopes of Mont St. Jean.
The attack was checked by heavy fire from the Allied guns and then routed by the charge of Ponsonby's Union Brigade in to the exposed flank of d'Erlon's Corps.
Three of d'Erlon's four divisions were completely routed, over 3000 men captured and the situation in the center was restored.

0 Yards 100 200

The situation at about 1900

Wellington

Chassé

I Corps
Ziethen

Blücher

II Corps
Reille

I Corps
d'Erlon

Gd. Corps

Pirch

Napoleon

VI Corps
Lobau

Bülow

While the action around Plancenoit was occurring, Wellington had moved his disengaged troops from the safe right flank and the left flank into the center. Meanwhile Ziethen's corps moved up to support Wellington's left.

Shortly after 1900 Napoleon led the Imperial Guard past La Belle Alliance and northward along the Brussels road. Joined by other units of d'Erlon's and Reille's corps, they prepared for one last effort in the center.

Two battalions formed a front towards Hougoumont and the remaining battalions attacked northwestward from the Brussels road. As they did so they split into two columns, the Grenadier battalions in front and the chasseurs attached to their left rear. Every available gun opened up on the French troops. The British had been on a front of about 400 files. The French frontage was only 70 men broad, so the head of their column was overlapped on either side by the British. Neighboring units added to the cross-fire which halted the

grenadiers. The British Guards counter-attacked with bayonets and drove them down the hill. The 'chasseurs' were checked as they breasted the rise and taken in the flank by more troops they retired down the hill. Again the column tried to deploy, and again it failed.

As the Prussian fire grew heavier and nearer, Wellington's instict told him that the French were played out and complete victory could be his. A wave of his hat signalled the British advanced. The French ranks dissolved, only the solidity of three squares of the Old Guard checked the pursuit at La Belle Alliance, and the Young Guard held Plancenoit long enough for most of the rest of the army to escape towards Genappe.

Wellington had lost 15,000 men, the French 29,000 and the Prussians 7000. When allowance is made for prisoners, desertion and the casualties of Wavre, Ligny and Quatre Bras, the total losses of the three armies between 16 and 19 June must have exceeded 100,000. Over 60,000 were French.

0 Yards 100 200

Bülow's corps. Napoleon was not yet committed to the main assault on Wellington's position and he could have waited for Grouchy before beginning the attack, but once again his overwhelming confidence drove him on. 'This morning we had ninety chances in our favor. Even now we have sixty chances, and only forty against', he assured Soult. He did send a new order to Grouchy, instructing him to march directly towards the main body, but by the time that he received this order it was too late for Grouchy to affect the issue. Napoleon also moved the cavalry of his central reserve to meet the Prussians and sent Lobau's 6th Corps after them. Lobau took up a position in advance of the village of Plancenoit, at right angles to the main line, and waited for Bülow to emerge from the Bois de Paris.

Having taken these precautions, Napoleon finally cast the die. Shortly after 1300 the great bombardment opened, striving to blast a hole in the center of the Allied position through which d'Erlon's infantry could advance and ensure a quick victory. However, the only target facing the French artillery was General Bylandt's brigade, standing rather in advance of the rest of the line, and a few scattered guns. Bylandt's brigade was shaken and withdrew to the line of the other Allied brigades, but otherwise the French gunners did almost nothing to prepare for the advance of d'Erlon's men, which began at about 1330. Three of d'Erlon's divisions adopted an unusual formation for their attack. Each battalion was deployed in a three-deep line, and the battalions formed one behind another in a vast column up to 200 files broad and 24 or 27 ranks deep. His-

torians have criticized the choice of this formation, rather than one of the more usual combinations of battalion columns or lines, for although it had depth, it lacked flexibility and the rear units had little chance to maneuver. However, French units often adopted this formation when massing in reserve or moving up in support and it may be that d'Erlon, overestimating the effect of the preliminary barrage and underestimating the steadiness of the troops before him, imagined that he had only to walk through an already shattered enemy.

If this was the case, d'Erlon was soon to be disillusioned. As the blocks of blue-coated figures began to ascend the slopes of Mont-St Jean, the Allied guns tore long and bloody lanes through them. Only Bylandt's brigade did not wait for their approach, falling back in a more or less orderly fashion to the woods in the rear, where they sat out the battle, smoking and drinking coffee. But the rest of Picton's division lay in wait as the French mass lapped around the farm of La Haye Sainte and into the farms of Papelotte and La Haye. As the French lines reached the forward edge of the crest, the gunners at last abandoned their pieces, but instead of retiring to the shelter of the infantry battalions many streamed to the rear. It seemed that the French battalions had only to rally their lines, disordered in crossing the fields and by the artillery fire, to complete the rout of the center. However, the Allied line at this point was under the command of Lieutenant-General Sir Thomas Picton, a Peninsular veteran who thoroughly understood the business in hand. His division rose from the ground and poured a

Below: Highland troops between La Haye and La Belle Alliance close in for the kill on the afternoon of Waterloo.

tremendous volley into the startled French. Pack's brigade of Highlanders flung themselves on the staggering column, followed by Kempt's brigade led by Picton himself. As Picton urged his troops on, one French bullet found its mark in his temple, killing him instantly, and although his valiant troops mangled the first lines of French infantry, they could not cut their way through all the twenty-odd ranks which faced them. They might yet have been overborne by sheer weight of numbers. Moreover, the center of the whole Allied line was threatened by a charge by French *cuirassiers* on d'Erlon's left flank. However Wellington, having overseen Picton's attack, had moved back to the center and was ready with the right riposte. The German infantry battalions west of the Brussels road moved into square and through the intervals thus formed Lieutenant-General Lord Uxbridge, commander of the cavalry, led Somerset's Household Brigade and Ponsonby's Union Brigade. These were both composed of heavy cavalry, and men and horses were perfectly fresh. The *cuirassiers* had not rested properly during the previous night and were now blown by the uphill charge. They were swept contemptuously aside and the British heavies crashed into the exposed flank of d'Erlon's corps. Almost simultaneously the Household Brigade struck the westernmost division and the Union Brigade carved into the two center divisions. As the Scots Greys passed through the ranks of the Gordons, many Highlanders hung on to their stirrups, and shrieking 'Scotland for ever' cavalry and infantry hurtled forward together. Even if there had been time, the clumsy French columns could not have deployed into squares, but as it was they were taken completely by surprise. Instead of presenting a solid front to their enemies the infantry had to rely on their individual efforts; a survivor described the result thus:

'In vain our poor fellows stood up and stretched out their arms; they could not reach far enough to bayonet those cavalrymen mounted on powerful horses, and the few shots fired into this chaotic *mêlée* were just as fatal to our own men as to the English. And so we found ourselves defenseless against a relentless enemy who, in the intoxication of battle, sabred even our drummers and fifers without mercy. That is where our eagle was captured; and that is where I saw death close at hand, for my best friends fell around me and I was expecting the same fate, all the while wielding my sword mechanically.'

Three of d'Erlon's four divisions were completely routed; over 3000 men were captured and the situation in the center was completely restored. But the British cavalry were drunk with their success. In the exhilaration of the charge they believed themselves invincible. 'At this moment,' wrote one Scots Grey, 'Colonel Hamilton rode up to us crying, "Charge! Charge the guns!" and went off like the wind up the hill towards the terrible battery that had made such deadly work among the Highlanders. It was the last we saw of our colonel, poor fellow! His body was found with both arms cut off... Then we got amongst the guns, and we had our revenge. Such slaughtering! We sabred the gunners, lamed the horses, and cut their traces and harness. I can hear the Frenchmen yet crying "*Diable!*" when I struck at them, and the long-drawn hiss through their teeth as my sword went home... The artillery drivers sat on their horses weeping aloud as we went among them; they were mere boys, we thought.'

By now the British cavalrymen were exhausted and surrounded on all sides by the French army. As they struggled to recross the valley they were particularly harassed by the lancers of General Jacquinot's brigade which attacked from the east, and scarcely half the troopers returned unharmed. The British cavalry had always been difficult to control, but never was its dash and strength more tragically wasted. An important part of Wellington's reserve had been dispersed and his ability to counterattack future French assaults had been drastically reduced.

However, this rash charge consumed more time, and it was 1530 before Marshal Ney led the next attack forward. With the only two brigades which had rallied from d'Erlon's corps he attempted to seize La Haye Sainte and was repulsed after some stiff fighting around the farmhouse. But Ney believed that he had seen troops retreating along the Brussels road. In fact these were only columns of wounded and transport but Ney was sufficiently deceived to order up a brigade of *cuirassiers* to hurry the apparent retreat. Two more divisions of cavalry followed, more or less on their own initiative and by 1600 hours 5000 horsemen were committed to a charge between Hougoumont and La Haye Sainte. Cramped into a front considerably less than a thousand yards wide the French cavalry were an ideal target for Wellington's artillery, which once again he had ordered to keep firing as long as possible, leaving their guns only at the last moment for the protection of the infantry squares behind them. Captain Mercer's 'G' Troop, Royal Horse Artillery, scorned even this precaution, distrusting the steadiness of the Brunswickers in their rear, and by the tempest of their fire they kept their front clear. Everywhere the infantry held firm, despite 'the awful grandeur of that charge. You perceived at a distance what appeared to be an overwhelming, long moving line, which, ever advancing, glittered like a stormy wave of the sea when it catches the sunlight. On came the mounted host until they got near enough, while the very earth seemed to vibrate beneath their thundering tramp'. However, the *cuirassiers* had no support except from a long range artillery bombardment, which had to cease as they approached the Allied line. D'Erlon's troops had been surprised by cavalry in an unsuitable formation and cut to pieces, but Wellington's battalions were formed in squares and 'prepared to receive cavalry'. As soon as the first impact of their charge was broken by the rolling volleys of musketry the French were split into small groups of squadrons which attempted scattered and uncoordinated attacks on the squares until at last the mass of them were forced into the bottom of the valley. Here they reformed and returned to the charge. However, their horses were so tired that they could only walk forward, and this attack was broken up by artillery fire before it reached the top of the hill.

Napoleon watched the attack with growing

concern. Bülow was clear of the Bois de Paris and, forcing Napoleon's right flank back toward Plancenoit, threatened the rear of the whole French line. Yet there was no sign that Wellington was on the verge of defeat and Ney had compromised half the reserve cavalry. To extricate him Napoleon ordered forward General Kellermann's wing of the cavalry which had been waiting west of the Brussels road. Kellermann would have queried the wisdom of this order, but his divisional generals would not wait for an answer. As they advanced General Guyot followed with the Empress's Dragoons and the Horse Grenadiers, Napoleon's last reserve of cavalry. This second great charge began at about 1700 and was made by nearly 10,000 horsemen, on a front of 500 yards. Again the first charge failed, but for nearly an hour Ney led the French cavalry in charge after charge. At least seven or eight attacks were made and Ney had his fourth horse killed under him. At one stage he was seen hacking at a British gun with his sword as rage and frustration overpowered him.

The scene inside the squares was almost indescribable. Around them, at twenty or thirty yards distance, was a rampart of dead or wounded men

and horses, which increasingly impeded French efforts to charge home. 'Inside them we were nearly suffocated by the smoke and smell from burnt cartridges' wrote Ensign Gronow of the 1st Foot Guards. 'It was impossible to move a yard without treading upon wounded comrades, or upon the bodies of the dead; and the loud groans of the wounded and dying was most appalling.' Above the groans came the volleys of musketry and the sounds of bullets striking steel *cuirassiers*, like 'the noise of a violent hailstorm beating upon panes of glass'. The 40th Regiment was greatly amused by the gesticulations and grimaces with which the *cuirassiers* faced the barrier of casualties

Opposite: La Belle Alliance, the farmhouse used by Napoleon as his headquarters during the battle. Waterloo is often called the battle of La Belle Alliance by the French for this reason. **Left:** The 3rd Regiment of Foot Guards repulses the final charge of Napoleon's Old Guard during the closing stages of battle.

Below: A British 9-pounder gun and limber first introduced during the Peninsular Campaign and used by Wellington at Waterloo. Although its range at ground level was only 400 yards, the range could be increased to 2,400 yards if the gun was elevated to ten degrees. It required a crew of seven.

Above: Wellington on his horse Copenhagen rides past his advancing troops. His horse, which he acquired at Copenhagen in 1807, nearly killed him after the battle was over.

and the storm of fire. Ordering their men to 'Prepare to receive cavalry' the officers added 'Now, men, make faces!' As the baffled *cuirassiers* fell back to prepare for yet another charge the Allied infantry came under fire from a battery of horse artillery at point blank range, which swept away whole files. To the diminishing squares, the cavalry charges were a welcome relief, giving them a chance to hand out punishment as well as take it. But despite the casualties the squares stood firm, apparently rooted to the spot. Among them rode Wellington, strengthening the infantry's resolve by a word, or ordering a counter-charge by his own weakened cavalry. 'We had a notion that while he was there nothing could go wrong', wrote one of his staff afterwards. In the end it was the French whose willpower gave way and the exhausted cavalry retired to their own side of the valley.

Ney's thoughts again turned to the infantry. A division and a half of Reille's corps had not been embroiled in the Hougoumont, and by 1800 Ney was leading them up slopes strewn with the bloody evidence of his previous failures. This attack, although supported by horse and guns, was no more successful. The area was now thickly held by Wellington's artillery and infantry and he was there himself to see the advance checked in front by Maitland's Guards Brigade and to order Adam's to a position on the flank of the French columns. For ten minutes the French stood in this killing ground, losing 1500 men out of 6000. Then they too turned their backs on the Allied line.

Napoleon saw this, but still he did not despair. He recognized the importance of La Haye Sainte, standing in easy range of the Allied center, and sent Ney categorical orders to capture it. Ney managed to scrape together a force of all arms,

chiefly from the remnants of d'Erlon's divisions, and soon had the farmhouse surrounded. The 2nd Light Battalion of the King's German Legion under Major Baring had held the farm against all comers throughout the day, but ammunition for their rifles was becoming scarce. A rash attempt to assist the garrison met with disaster when French cavalry emerged from the dead ground and caught half a brigade in line. Shortly after 1800 the defenders' ammunition gave out, and after holding their position with the bayonet for some minutes, Baring and 42 other survivors out of a garrison of 376 broke out of the doomed farm. At last Ney could report success to his Emperor. Artillery and *tirailleurs* pressed forward and the whole center of Wellington's line came under their fire. The rallied elements of d'Erlon's corps were pressing forward again, but to be sure of victory Ney needed fresh troops. Now was the time for Napoleon to throw in his last reserve, the Imperial Guard itself.

Ney's Appeals Rejected

But the Emperor rejected Ney's appeals: '*Des troupes! Où voulez-vous que j'en prenne? Voulez-vous que j'en fasse?*' ('Troops! Where do you expect me to get them from? Do you want me to make some?'). Having ignored or underestimated the Prussian threat all day, Napoleon was now only too aware of the danger. Plancenoit had been captured by Bülow shortly after 1700. Napoleon had ordered up the Young Guard Division of his reserve and their attack drove the Prussians back beyond the village, but Bülow was soon reinforced by Pirch's corps and the Young Guard was over-borne and forced out of Plancenoit again. Prussian artillery brought the Brussels road under fire. It seemed more important to Napoleon to restore the

situation on his right flank than to attend to Ney's request for troops. Of the fourteen Guard battalions available to him, Napoleon put eleven in a lines of squares east of the Brussels road. One battalion remained to guard the Emperor's person, and the remaining two stormed into Plancenoit and retook the village with the bayonet. Although they were unable to drive the Prussians further back the position had been stabilized and Napoleon could turn his attention to Mont-St Jean and the center of Wellington's army.

But he had once again underestimated his opponent. No one who knew Wellington's capabilities as a general would have allowed him even a moment to recover his balance. As soon as he heard the news of the fall of La Haye Sainte, Wellington moved to the point of greatest danger. At 1600 he decided that his extreme right flank was safe and had moved Chassé's Dutch-Belgian Division from there to a more central position on the Nivelles road behind the main line. His foresight was now justified, as he could bring them into the front line at the critical point. There were then twice as many brigades in the area immediately west of the Brussels road as there had been at the beginning of the battle, but the reliability of some of these units was doubtful. To strengthen them Wellington sent for every available gun and formed Vivian's and Vandeleur's brigades of light cavalry in a continuous line behind the infantry. They were there not just to support the front line but also to block any possible retreat to Brussels. To the west of this section of the line were Maitland's Guards brigades and Adam's brigade of light infantry, almost all Peninsular veterans. Beyond them was the still defiant bastion of Hougoumont. But undoubtedly the greatest strength in this grouping was the presence of Wellington

himself, restraining troops who jibbed at standing under fire without being able to reply and encouraging all to 'Standfast! . . . . we must not be beat —what will they say in England?'

Meanwhile Prussian assistance was approaching rapidly, as the first troops of General Graf von Ziethen's corps, led by General Müffling, moved up to reinforce Wellington's left. Ziethen had left Wavre for Mont-St Jean about 1400, but at 1800, as he approached Ohain, a junior officer told him that Wellington was in retreat. (He had, like Ney, been deceived by the sight of transports moving the wounded to the rear.) Ziethen decided to turn south to aid Bülow at Plancenoit, but Müffling had appeared in the nick of time and persuaded him to carry out his original orders.

It was shortly after 1900 when Napoleon led the Imperial Guard past his command post at La Belle Alliance and northward along the Brussels road. Authorities disagree about the number and composition of this column but it was probably made up of nine battalions of the Old and Middle Guards. About 600 yards short of the Allied line Napoleon handed over command to Ney; as he watched the Guard march past him he was saluted with cheers and cries of '*Vive l' Empereur!*' In the wake of the 'Immortals' other units of d' Erlon's and Reille's corps prepared for one last effort, encouraged by the Emperor's assurance that the ominous masses appearing in the northeast were not Prussians but Grouchy's long-awaited corps. But this elation did not last very long; a cannonade from the right flank and the rear of the advance announced that the approaching troops were in fact Prussian, whatever the Emperor might say. In the general hesitation only the Guard continued to move forward; the rest of the army waited to see whether they could ensure victory in the same way that they had completed many of Napoleon's greatest triumphs.

The details of the actual assault are far from certain. Two battalions formed a front toward Hougoumont and the remaining battalions attacked north-westward from the Brussels road. As they did so they split into two columns, the grenadier battalions in front and the *chasseurs* echeloned to their left rear. This move may have been intentional, or it may have been caused by the uneven ground and the tendency of the leading battalions to step faster than those behind when they came under fire. Wellington was with Maitland's Guards Brigade as they waited, lying down, for the leading column. Every available gun, double-shotted or with canister, opened up on the French troops, but ignoring this curtain of fire they pressed on at the *pas de charge*. There was no move from the British line as the French came to within forty yards of them. Then, above the drums, came the Duke's order 'Now, Maitland! Now is your time!—Stand up Guards! Make ready! Fire!' The Guards had been on a front of about 400 files. The French frontage was only 70

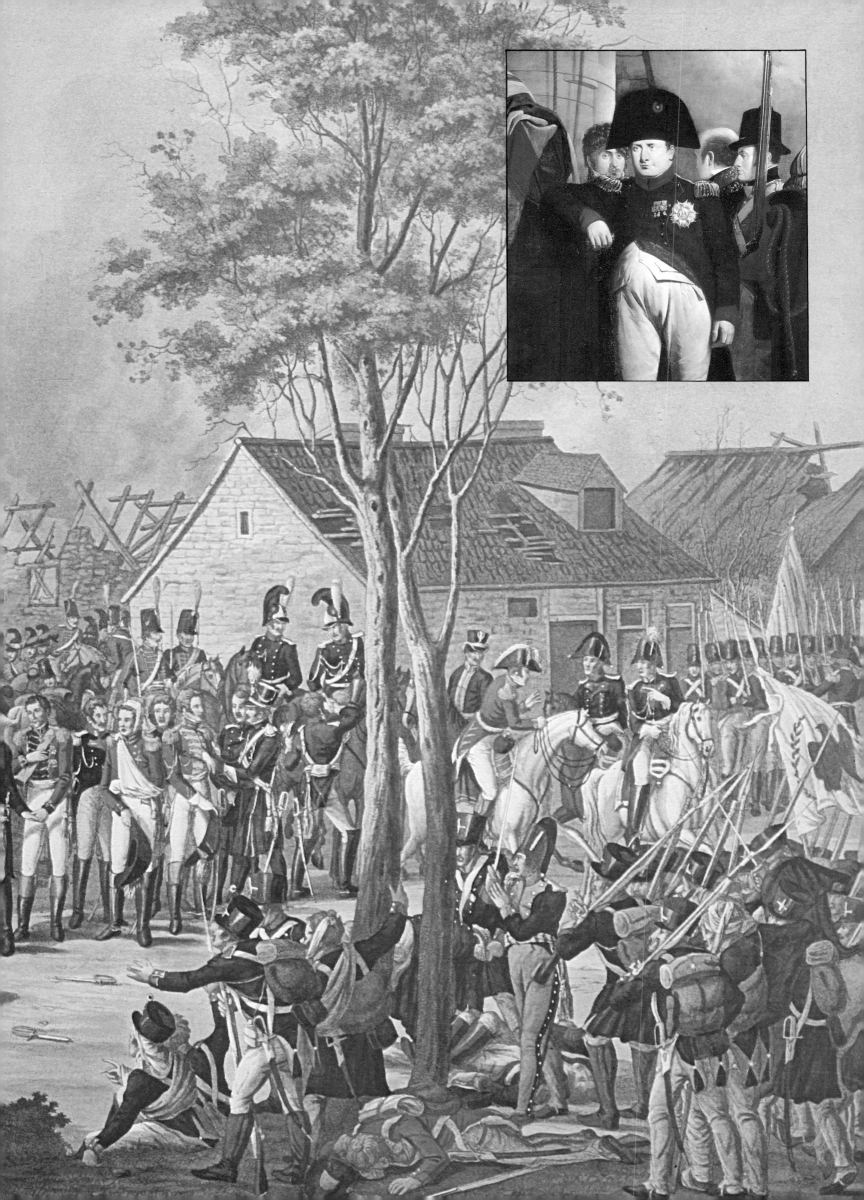

the Allied army turned on him, he saw that the French right wing was crumbling, but that the main body of the enemy had not yet broken. However, instinct told him that the French were played out and complete victory could be his. A wave of his hat signaled his decision to the army; cheering, the long-tried regiments swept forward.

The Imperial Army fell apart; 'Sauve qui peut' was now the cry and as the French ranks dissolved the British and Prussian light cavalry rushed upon them. Only the solidity of three squares of the Old Guard checked the pursuit at La Belle Alliance and the Young Guard held Plancenoit long enough for most of the rest of the army to escape towards Genappe. But Napoleon's attempt to rally the survivors there or at Quatre Bras failed, and it was only at Phillipeville, across the French border, that the rabble began to coalesce into an army again.

The Price of Victory

On the battlefield itself over 40,000 men lay dead or wounded, beside an untold number of horses. Wellington had lost 15,000 men, the French 29,000 and the Prussians 7000. When allowance is made for prisoners, desertion and the casualties of Wavre, Ligny and Quatre Bras, the total losses of the three armies between 16 and 19 June must have exceeded 100,000. Over 60,000 of these casualties were French, yet in numerical terms their army had not been destroyed. There were 117,000 troops available between Belgium and Paris, excluding fortress troops and conscripts; the Allied armies were scarcely more numerous than this field force. Politically, however, Waterloo had sealed the Emperor's fate. On returning to Paris he found little support in the Chamber of Deputies and on 22 June he abdicated in favor of his son. In exile he blamed subordinates such as Soult, Grouchy and Ney for his defeat, but he had chosen these men himself, after having known them for many years. What Napoleon could not bring himself to admit was that, after his initial success, he had been mastered by overwhelming self-confidence, so that he was no longer capable of seeing any flaws in his own appreciation of the situation and his own plans. The rest of his army were seized by the same failing; so great was their confidence in the Emperor that they attempted the impossible, and continued the struggle to the limit of human endurance. In the words of one English officer 'By God! Those fellows deserve Bonaparte, they fight so nobly for him'. The most serious error Napoleon made was to despise Wellington. The 'Iron Duke's' army had little chance of achieving total victory on its own, and the appearance of a growing mass of Prussian troops in the northeast certainly tipped the balance in the Allies' favor, but there would have been no victory waiting when they finally reached the battlefield had it not been for Wellington. As Harry Smith of the 95th said of Waterloo, every moment was a crisis, and without Wellington's knack of being ready with the right answer at every critical point, the result might have been completely different. Wellington's judgement was always reliable and as he immodestly put it: 'By God! I don't think it would have done if I had not been there'.

Opposite: Napoleon on the quarterdeck of the *Bellerophon* contemplates his defeat and exile. A few members of his staff were allowed to accompany him as far as England.

men broad and so the head of their column was overlapped on either side by the British. Neighboring units added to the crossfire which halted the Grenadiers; then the cheering British Guards were on them with the bayonet, driving them down the hill. As the western column breasted the rise they were met and checked by Adam's Brigade. Colonel Sir John Colborne wheeled the 1st/52nd until they stood parallel to the *chasseurs*' left flank. Again the column tried to deploy under a withering cross-fire and again it failed. The advance of the 52nd completed the defeat of the Imperial Guard.

The impossible had happened, and as the Prussian fire grew heavier and nearer the spirit of the French army began to waver. Wellington sensed this and moved to a mound beside the Brussels road, from which he could survey the battlefield and could be seen by his own army. As all eyes in

Left: The departure of Napoleon for St Helena, an obscure island in the South Atlantic, where he was to die in 1821. He boarded the brig *L'Épervier* which carried him to the waiting British ship *Bellerophon*. Far left: The *Bellerophon*, which carried Napoleon into his final exile.

Vicksburg
1863

The American Civil War was the greatest blood-letting between Waterloo and the outbreak of the First World War. More Americans died in the War Between the States than in either of the two world wars. But the eventual outcome was in considerable doubt during the first two years of the war. The British gave overt and covert assistance to the Confederacy in various forms; the Union blockade was run by British ships which brought military supplies to the South; ships built in England flew the Confederate flag and harassed American commerce. But British support for the Confederacy melted away during the first week of July 1863. In that week the South suffered two cruel blows from which it never recovered. The Battle of Vicksburg split the South; the Battle of Gettysburg forced the South into a permanent defensive posture. The loss of these two epic battles convinced Britain and any other potential ally of the South that the war could only be won by the Union.

In November 1860 the Republican candidate, Abraham Lincoln, was elected President of the United States of America. His election came at

a crucial time. For years public opinion in the Northern States had been offended by the survival of slavery in any part of their country. Conversely, the Southern States had resented attacks on a system held to be essential to their prosperity, and integral to their whole culture. Far from appreciating that their slave-holding civilization was fast failing in economic terms, and that its effects were almost as degrading to the whites as to their black slaves, the protagonists of the South built up an ideal picture of its way of life. In this idyll, every Southerner was an honorable, chivalrous, Christian gentleman. Those who owned slaves were careful of their property, kind and humane if only from motives of self-interest. Those who did not were freed from the depressing tasks of society, from the hewing of wood, and the drawing of water. The Northerners, or 'Yankees', were regarded as mere mechanicals, social inferiors, lacking the civilized graces of the South, and concerned only with vulgar practices such as trading or making money. These 'barbarians', seeking to exclude the extension of slavery to the newly occupied Federal Territories, and advocating its abolition throughout the Union, were at best dangerous radicals, at worst apostles of a black insurrection that would spread murder, arson, rape and pillage throughout the South.

On the Northern side an equally powerful stereotype was created. The practice of duelling, still existing in parts of Southern society, was no better than murder, and its hot-tempered practitioners tainted the whole South as a community of partly-civilized bullies. The popularity of Harriet Beecher Stowe's novel 'Uncle Tom's Cabin' created a belief that all Southern plantation owners were cruel and brutal slave-drivers. Few Northerners had any high regard for the characters of the Negro slaves themselves, but most shared a feeling of loathing for the slave system

and detestation of slave owners. A series of 'Personal Liberty Laws' in the Northern States, passed by legislatures where the Republicans had a majority, did everything possible to hinder the return of fugitives, and were themselves contrary at least to the spirit of the US Constitution, which protected the property, including slaves, of every citizen. The Republican Party itself was formed after Southern pressure had forced the acceptance of slavery in some of the new Western states. When, in 1860, the coalition of Northern conservatives and Southern moderates forming the Democratic Party was defeated, most Southern leaders determined that, if slavery were to continue, the Union must come to an end.

Seven of the slave states withdrew from the Union between December 1860 and February 1861, claiming that as sovereign states they had the right to secede from an association they had once freely joined. Together they formed a new Confederacy, which proceeded to take possession of all government property and public buildings under its control. Lincoln, in his inaugural address, declared that all the ordinances of secession passed by the Southern state legislatures were invalid, and announced his intention of occupying and holding all places and property belonging to the Government of the United States. The Confederate Congress called for 100,000 volunteers to resist any invasion, and on 12 April their batteries opened fire on Fort Sumter, at the entrance to Charleston Harbor, South Carolina. On the 14th the small garrison of US troops there laid down its arms, but the following day Lincoln asked the States of the Union to call out their militia to provide him with 75,000 men, for the purpose of quelling insurrection.

Lincoln had said in 1858 that a house divided against itself could not stand; it must either be all slave or all free; the proponents of slavery must

extend the legality of that institution throughout the Union, or its opponents must ensure its total abolition. Now four of the remaining eight slave states left the Union, rather than send their militias to fight against their Southern neighbors. Taking their stand on the principle that the Union was made up of sovereign states, who having freely entered it could freely leave, they turned their back on Washington, and joined the Confederacy, with its new capital at Richmond, Virginia. Lincoln met this threat by doubling the size of the US Regular Army, and adding to the militia a force of 200,000 volunteers, newly formed and enlisted for three years full-time service.

Union troops then marched against Richmond,

but were thrown back at the First Battle of Bull Run (July 1861), and for a time Washington itself was threatened. For four more years two great armies operated in this eastern theater, with the rival capitals within 100 miles of each other. The South, hopelessly outmatched in industrial and financial resources, and with half the population of the Union, had either to defeat the Northern troops in battle and impose its peace terms on a defeated Union, or to prolong hostilities until the North grew tired of the profitless struggle. Nevertheless, if the Union could bring to bear its vastly superior economic strength, and if her diplomats kept European powers from intervening against her, then the Confederate cause was doomed, and could not be saved by the most desperate valor or the most noble sacrifice.

Yet in the early months of 1863 the Confederate Army was still in the field, still with a chance of securing victory in battle, and still buying time, with its soldiers' blood, for the life of the Confederacy. In the east General Robert E. Lee's Army of Northern Virginia was well led, adequately armed, and consisted of veterans of more than a year's hard fighting. The Yankees were still prevented from marching on Richmond, and Washington still had cause to fear the dreaded 'rebel yell'. On the western front the outlook was grimmer. At the mouth of the Mississippi, New Orleans, the South's strategic seaport and commercial capital, had been captured by the US Navy in April 1862, and Admiral David G. Farragut and his deep-sea squadron could ply the lower stretches of the river with impunity. The headwaters of this mighty river and its great tributaries, the Ohio and Missouri Rivers, were in the North, so that another armada was gradually fighting its way downstream. But the river was still not open to Northern commerce. The great citadel of Vicksburg, frowning above the river on

Above: A sketch made during the First Battle of Bull Run, where the South proved that the Union would have no easy victory.

Left: Admiral David Farragut, whose Union Navy blockaded Southern ports and whose river fleet attempted to cut the Confederacy in two by driving up the Mississippi.

The Battle of Vicksburg, 1863

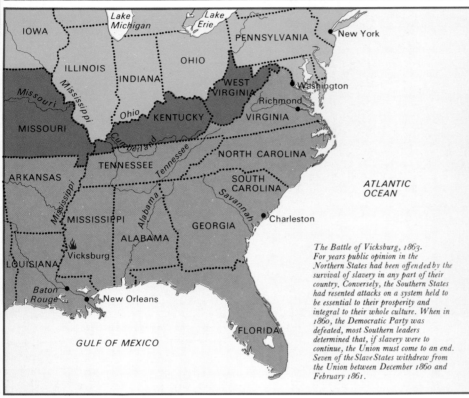

The Battle of Vicksburg, 1863. For years public opinion in the Northern States had been offended by the survival of slavery in any part of their country. Conversely, the Southern States had resented attacks on a system held to be essential to their prosperity and integral to their whole culture. When in 1860, the Democratic Party was defeated, most Southern leaders determined that, if slavery were to continue, the Union must come to an end. Seven of the Slave States withdrew from the Union between December 1860 and February 1861.

The maneuvers leading to the siege of Vicksburg

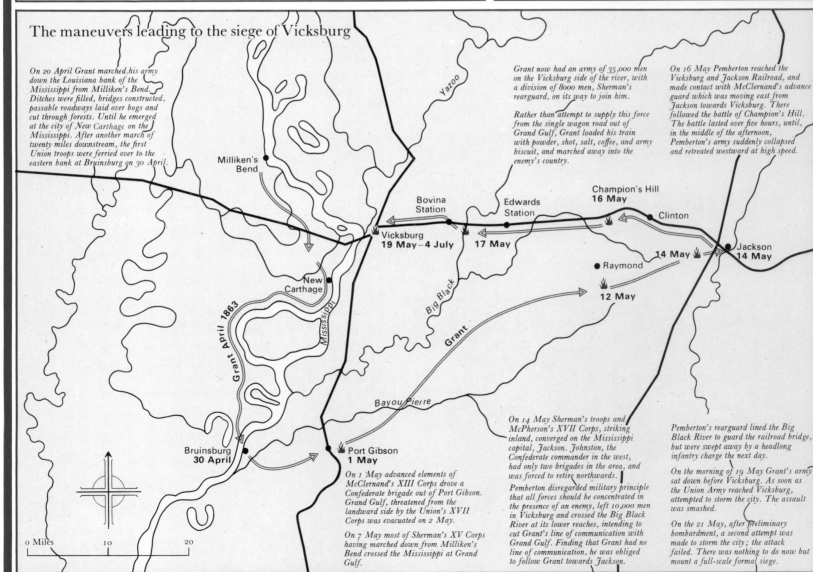

On 20 April Grant marched his army down the Louisiana bank of the Mississippi from Milliken's Bend. Ditches were filled, bridges constructed, passable roadways laid over bogs and cut through forests. Until he emerged at the city of New Carthage on the Mississippi. After another march of twenty miles downstream, the first Union troops were ferried over to the eastern bank at Bruinsburg on 30 April.

Grant now had an army of 35,000 men on the Vicksburg side of the river, with a division of 8000 men, Sherman's rearguard, on its way to join him.

Rather than attempt to supply this force from the single wagon road out of Grand Gulf, Grant loaded his train with powder, shot, salt, coffee, and army biscuit, and marched away into the enemy's country.

On 16 May Pemberton reached the Vicksburg and Jackson Railroad, and made contact with McClernand's advance guard which was moving east from Jackson towards Vicksburg. There followed the battle of Champion's Hill. The battle lasted over five hours, until, in the middle of the afternoon, Pemberton's army suddenly collapsed and retreated westward at high speed.

On 1 May advanced elements of McClernand's XIII Corps drove a Confederate brigade out of Port Gibson. Grand Gulf, threatened from the landward side by the Union's XVII Corps was evacuated on 2 May.

On 7 May most of Sherman's XV Corps having marched down from Milliken's Bend crossed the Mississippi at Grand Gulf.

On 14 May Sherman's troops and McPherson's XVII Corps, striking inland, converged on the Mississippi capital, Jackson. Johnston, the Confederate commander in the west, had only two brigades in the area, and was forced to retire northwards.

Pemberton disregarded military principle that all forces should be concentrated in the presence of an enemy, left 10,000 men in Vicksburg and crossed the Big Black River at its lower reaches, intending to cut Grant's line of communication with Grand Gulf. Finding that Grant had no line of communication, he was obliged to follow Grant towards Jackson.

Pemberton's rearguard lined the Big Black River to guard the railroad bridge, but were swept away by a headlong infantry charge the next day.

On the morning of 19 May Grant's army sat down before Vicksburg. As soon as the Union Army reached Vicksburg, attempted to storm the city. The assault was smashed.

On the 21 May, after preliminary bombardment, a second attempt was made to storm the city; the attack failed. There was nothing to do now but mount a full-scale formal siege.

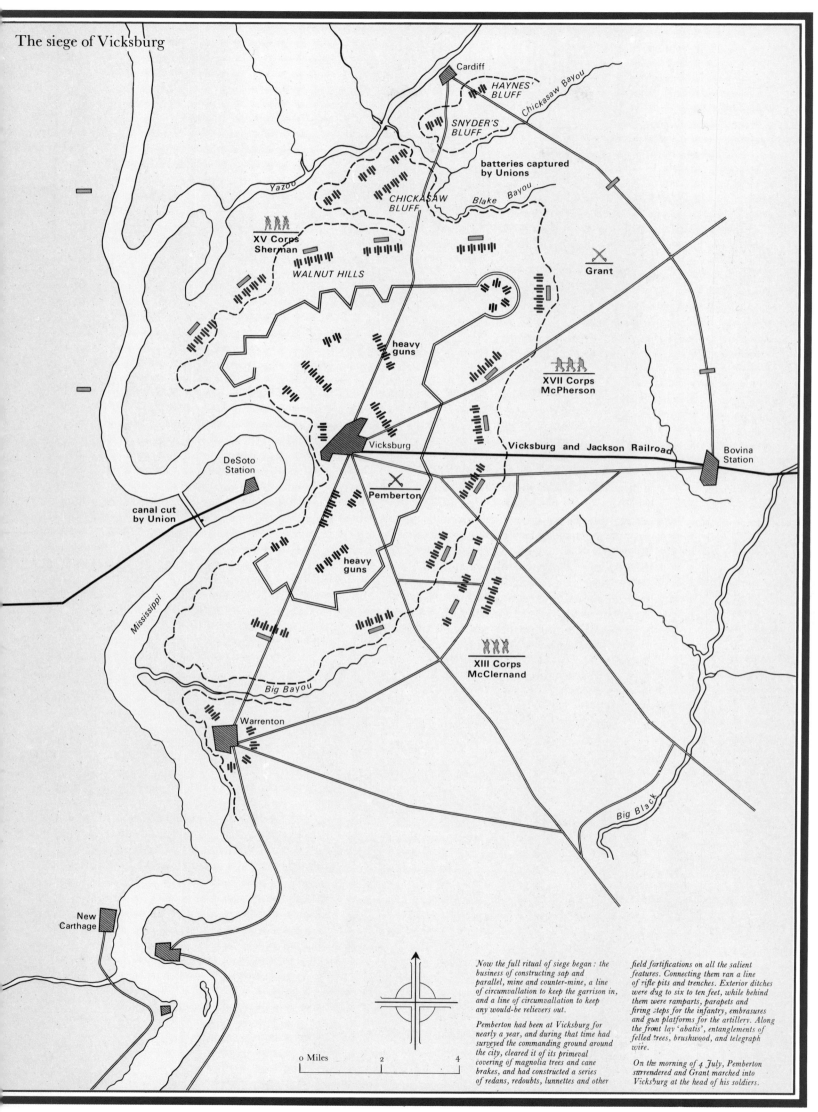

The siege of Vicksburg

Cardiff

HAYNES'
BLUFF

Chickasaw Bayou

SNYDER'S
BLUFF

batteries captured
by Unions

Yazoo

CHICKASAW
BLUFF

Blake Bayou

XV Corps
Sherman

Grant

WALNUT HILLS

heavy
guns

XVII Corps
McPherson

Vicksburg

Vicksburg and Jackson Railroad

Bovina
Station

DeSoto
Station

Pemberton

canal cut
by Union

Mississippi

heavy
guns

XIII Corps
McClernand

Big Bayou

Big Black

Warrenton

New
Carthage

o Miles   2   4

*Now the full ritual of siege began: the
business of constructing sap and
parallel, mine and counter-mine, a line
of circumvallation to keep the garrison in,
and a line of circumvallation to keep
any would-be relievers out.*

*Pemberton had been at Vicksburg for
nearly a year, and during that time had
surveyed the commanding ground around
the city, cleared it of its primeval
covering of magnolia trees and cane
brakes, and had constructed a series
of redans, redoubts, lunnettes and other*

*field fortifications on all the salient
features. Connecting them ran a line
of rifle pits and trenches. Exterior ditches
were dug to six to ten feet, while behind
them were ramparts, parapets and
firing steps for the infantry, embrasures
and gun platforms for the artillery. Along
the front lay 'abatis', entanglements of
felled trees, brushwood, and telegraph
wire.*

*On the morning of 4 July, Pemberton
surrendered and Grant marched into
Vicksburg at the head of his soldiers.*

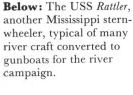

Above: The Federal gunboat *Cairo*, which drove up the Mississippi to Vicksburg. This ship was later sunk and her wreck was recently salvaged. **Above center:** A river steamer, the sternwheeler *Conestoga*, converted into a gunboat for use on the Mississippi.

Below: The USS *Rattler*, another Mississippi sternwheeler, typical of many river craft converted to gunboats for the river campaign.

its high bluffs, blocked the passage 400 miles from the sea. As long as it held out the Confederacy could still draw supplies, men and money from across the river.

At the same time the corn and wheat growers and meat producers of the Middle West were denied their traditional outlet to the sea. Their produce had now to go east by rail, or by steamboats and schooners on the Great Lakes. As the monopoly financiers who controlled these routes increased their freight rates, so the farmers and cattlemen of Illinois, Indiana and Ohio cooled in their ardor for the war. Peace party men began to win elections. There was talk of secession in the western states, of recognizing the Southerners' independence in return for their opening the river. The longer Vicksburg remained in Confederate hands, the greater the chance that the United States would be forced to give up the war. But if Vicksburg fell to the Union the Confederacy would be cut in two, the Mississippi would become a highway for the US Navy, and from it troops could push eastward to Alabama, Georgia, and the sea.

So far in the war, the descent of the Mississippi and Ohio Rivers had been achieved by gunboats

and troop transports operating on the river itself, while a powerful army marched parallel to it, but up to fifty or sixty miles inland. The same technique was used for the ascent of the Ohio's major tributaries, the Cumberland and the Tennessee, which flowed through rebel territory.

It was difficult for the Confederates to counter this strategy. On the one hand, they could concentrate their forces and march inland against the invader. But to do this meant leaving the river virtually defenseless against the Union flotillas, and risking the loss of those very towns and cities they were meant to be saving. On the other hand, they could throw strong garrisons into all the river towns, and man their defenses in strength. This, however, merely invited the Union forces on land to close up behind them, cut off their supplies and starve them into surrender. Thus the Confederates had been obliged to abandon a number of important centers on the river because they were outflanked by powerful armies operating in their hinterland.

At the end of November 1862 the Union troops moved to repeat the same technique against Vicksburg. Major-General Ulysses S. Grant, commanding the Union armies of the Tennessee and Mississippi, marched south, following the Mississippi Central Railroad from Grand Junction, where it joined the Memphis to Corinth line which ran along the Union front. His subordinate, Major-General William T. Sherman, steamed down the river from Memphis, to threaten Vicksburg's frontal defenses. As an added threat to the Confederates, Major-General Nathaniel P. Banks was to move upstream from New Orleans, supported by Admiral Farragut's warships, to threaten Port Hudson, most southerly of the Confederate river citadels, 250 miles (by river) below Vicksburg.

This time the plan failed. Two large-scale raids by the Confederate cavalry succeeded in cutting Grant's supply lines and even severing his communications with the outside world, so that he was forced to retrace his steps to Grand Junction. January 1863 found Grant back where

Above: The Confederate ram *Arkansas* runs through the Union fleet off Vicksburg. Fired by the example of the *Merrimack*, the Confederates built a number of ironclad rams in an attempt to counter Federal naval supremacy. **Left:** General Ulysses Simpson Grant in a sober moment.

he had begun. The New Orleans troops had not even started, and Sherman's river expedition had failed to make any impression on either the defenders or the defenses of Vicksburg.

The natural defenses of this city were of a completely different order from anything the Union forces in the west had previously met. The Mississippi River, here well into its mature stage, swings to and fro across its flood plain for hundreds of miles above and below the city. Both banks along virtually the whole stretch are lined with mudbanks, swamps, marshes and tangled underbrush, pierced by tributaries, channels, and innumerable watercourses, large and small. There was almost no place for an army to land, nor, having landed, any clear way for it to move. At Vicksburg there were a series of high bluffs, rising some 200 feet from the waterside. These allowed firm standing at the river's edge, which was why the first settlement had been made there and why it had developed into a thriving river port with docks, wharves, and railway yards. But to attempt to land troops in the teeth of the batteries and earthworks was impossible. The river, about a half-mile wide, curved sharply and

did not allow the gunboats either to outrange the shore batteries or to outmatch them in weight of metal. The slow, unarmored transports would be sitting targets as they ran in to put the troops ashore. Any that did land would be too few to resist the inevitable counterattack.

If Vicksburg were to fall, the assault had to be made from the landward side. Sherman tried to steam along the slow, muddy Yazoo River, a tributary entering the Mississippi five miles above Vicksburg itself. At Chickasaw Bayou, a few miles upstream, he landed and tried to climb out to the Walnut Hills, a ridge of high ground connected to the Vicksburg Bluffs. On 29 December he made his move. The Confederates manned the high ground with artillery and infantry. At the base of the hills, and on their slopes, more infantry concealed in rifle pits poured a deadly fire on the blue-clad attackers. Trapped in a tangle of swamps and thickets, the Union soldiers floundered helplessly toward their objective, then stopped. Sherman pulled them out, with the loss of more than 1700 men. The Confederates had lost 200 at the most, and were as secure as when they had started. They watched Sherman re-embark his

troops and steam away upstream, back to his moorings at Milliken's Bend twenty miles away, where he was joined by General Grant in his headquarters steamer, the *Magnolia*.

In theory, an army on one side of a river desiring to attack an enemy on the other has only to walk along the bank until the enemy's defenses have been passed, and then cross over. In fact this was just what Grant's men could not do in the winter of 1862–63. There was no point in crossing upstream of Vicksburg, since the Yazoo still lay between them and their prize. And if they crossed the higher reaches of the Yazoo, how were they to be supplied with that river blocked by Confederate batteries at Snyder's Bluff, at the Vicksburg end? Nor could they go downstream on the Louisiana bank, because the country was so low-lying that progress was impossible until the spring.

Yet if the river was high, then its waters might be put to use, and no less than four different schemes were evolved to this end. At the most, they would result in the army getting below Vicksburg in comfort and safety. At the least, they would keep the soldiers and sailors busy, and

Right: Blacks were used to dig a canal for Federal ships, which hoped to bypass Vicksburg.

Below: The fight in the crater of Fort Hill after the explosion of the mine, 25 June, 1863.

prevent them becoming demoralized while sickness increased and repeated stories magnified the impregnable nature of Vicksburg's defenses and the disastrous repulse of Sherman's expedition.

The first plan was the simplest. Vicksburg lay in the state of Mississippi, on the outside of a hairpin bend in the river. The Union army held the narrow promontory of Louisiana soil forming the inside of the hairpin. If a canal were cut across this, then riverboats could bypass the city and the mighty Mississippi might even change its course altogether, scouring out a new channel through the canal, and reducing Vicksburg to an inland town. Several weeks hard digging ensued, encouraged by the personal interest of President Lincoln himself. The design, however, was faulty. The defenses of Vicksburg would have been quite as strong behind a muddy slough as behind a river, perhaps stronger. Furthermore the Confederates, when they saw what was intended, simply built shore batteries at Warrenton, below

the canal's planned exit, blocking the river as effectively as before. The canal entrance joined the river in a backwater, so that there was no stream to deepen the canal. Eventually, in early March, the river rose, broke through the upper dam, and covered the whole peninsula, to the discomfort of Sherman and his XV Corps, who had been engaged on the work. Stores were lost, cattle drowned, camps flooded out, and men obliged to run for their lives or take to the trees for safety.

The next plan was more ambitious. The Louisiana side of the river was low-lying and contained numerous watercourses. Fifty miles above Vicksburg lay Lake Providence, separated from the Mississippi by a levee or embankment to prevent flooding. If this were cut, boats could float for 200 miles along tributaries of the Red River, which had its origins far to the west, but joined the Mississippi above Port Hudson. A steamboat was hauled overland into the lake, but after several days exploring reported that the waterways were impassable. The abnormally high rainfall had caused more problems than it solved for the sailors, since the main channels were lost in overflow swamps, with submerged tree stumps sticking up to hole the unwary. This project too was abandoned when it became clear there was no navigation for large steamers, since there were not enough shallow draft vessels to lift the army over such a distance.

Meanwhile there were plans to find a way on the eastern bank, into the Yazoo, and behind the Confederate forts which blocked the river at Snyder's Bluff. The Yazoo and its upper tributaries, the Tallahatchie and Coldwater, formed one long stream running roughly parallel to the Mississippi, and at one time linked to it, some 200 miles above Vicksburg, by a bayou known as

Yazoo Pass. This had been closed some years before the war by a levee. The plan now suggested by Rear-Admiral David D. Porter, commanding the Mississippi Flotilla, was to cut the levee and allow the mighty Mississippi to raise the level of the Yazoo and its headwaters. Then his ships could steam down through enemy country, take all the river defenses in the rear, capture the Confederate boatyards at Yazoo City, where several large vessels were under construction, and move down to land an army on the high ground upstream of Snyder's Bluff, thus bringing it at last within reach of Vicksburg.

On 3 February, 1863 the levee was blown up and the river poured in, down a drop of eight feet or so, cutting a passage 40 yards wide. Some days elapsed before the levels were matched and the torrent slackened enough for steamboats to navigate without the risk of damage. Scarcely had the little fleet begun its passage when it was

Above: Union gunboat fleet near Mound City, Illinois, where the Federal naval station directed operations south down the Mississippi.

stopped by the discovery that Confederate working parties had been that way before them. The Yazoo Pass was deep enough indeed, but it was narrow, and great trees had been felled across the waterway. It took another two weeks to clear it as far as the Coldwater River, at a time when speed was vital to the success of Union plans.

The gunboat fleet consisted of two ironclads, six shallow-draft, lightly armored 'tinclads', and two rams, with 4000 soldiers in transport steamers following close behind. The commodore, Lieutenant-Commander Watson Smith, although a brave and gallant officer, was ill-suited to this command. A professional deep-sea sailor, he hated operations where there was no room to swing, no water below his keel—indeed no keel, since he was now in flat-bottomed river boats. Moreover, he was becoming ill, and lacked both the spirit and the strength to urge on the expedition at the greatest pace. When they finally reached the junction of the Tallahatchie and the Yazoo on 10 March, it was found that the Confederates had made good use of the time. A fort of cotton bales and earth banks had been thrown up at one of the numberless hairpin bends through which the river meandered. Named Fort Pemberton in honor of the Confederate general, it was armed with field guns and three rifled cannon.

The same insoluble problem now faced Smith as faced Porter on the big river. The gunboats could not silence the batteries, and the troops could not get ashore into the flooded country above them. The two ironclads, attacking head-on, side by side down the narrow river, were riddled by the rifled guns of the fort. Smith, a dying man, handed over command to Lieutenant-Commander J. P. Foster, and went back upstream.

Foster, reinforced by another brigade of infantry, held on until 5 April, but finally had to steam back 200 miles the way he had come. He was only just in time, for the Confederates were moving troops to this river system in large numbers to cut off the entire expedition.

While these events were taking place, Admiral Porter conceived another plan. It was clear that even if Fort Pemberton fell, the Confederates were now fully aware of what was going on, and would be able to delay the advance on Yazoo City for months. Therefore he himself would take five stern-wheel ironclads, which had not gone with Smith, and try another route. This involved going up the Yazoo from the Mississippi, but, before reaching Snyder's Bluff, turning up a sluggish backwater called Steele's Bayou. An even narrower channel, Black Bayou, ran across from its higher reaches to join Deer Creek. This was a shallow and winding river, but if the fleet ascended this it could go through another bayou, Rolling Fork, and get into the Sunflower River. This flowed into the Yazoo above Snyder's Bluff, twenty miles as the crow flies from their starting point at Milliken's Bend, but two hundred miles by this river route. An infantry column led by General Sherman was ordered to march through the swamps along the banks, and the fleet started out on 14 March.

The difficulties of this route proved insurmountable even to Porter, despite his irrepressible sea-dog (or rather, river-dog) spirit. The watercourse wound in and out in tortuous serpentine bends, so that the five steamers, in line astern, at times found themselves apparently in line abreast, three going forward and two back, with narrow necks of land between them. The slightest error by the pilots, or delays by helmsmen, put them into the bank. There great trees overhung them, with branches to damage the smoke stacks, snag their guys and stays, or smash their wooden superstructures into splinters. When anxious officers reported increasing damage to their vessels' upper works, Porter told them all he required was an engine, guns, and a hull to float them. Birds' nests, fledglings, twigs and tree-rats fell from overhanging boughs in a ceaseless shower, and any sailor incautious enough to appear on deck risked being sniped at by Con-

federate marksmen or swept off by low branches. At one point, Porter's flagship with a 42-foot beam was going along a 46-foot wide waterway. Wooden bridges had to be rammed and carried away. Time after time, a gunboat would come to a halt, while her crew swarmed over the side with axes or ropes to free her. As the Union flotilla inched its way along, Confederate troops moved up to meet it, sending their pioneers ahead to fell more trees and prevent Porter from retracing his course. The forest seemed to be closing in on him, like the flesh around a healing wound.

Sherman and his men, still floundering through the swamps along Deer Creek could not come up in time to help, so Porter had to give up. He dropped back down river to the soldiers, unshipped his rudders, and let them haul him out stern first. Cutting through the new-felled trees, and overcoming numerous obstacles, the flotilla emerged safely into the broad waters of the Mississippi on 24 March. So far, the Confederates were still winning.

It must be remembered that the vessels forming Porter's Mississippi Flotilla were quite different from those of the West Gulf Squadron operating in the lower river under Farragut. The latter were seagoing warships, steam-engined, paddle-driven, but with a high freeboard, and fitted with masts and yards to carry sails. Although restricted to the deepest part of the navigable channel, they could make reasonable headway against the strong river current, and indeed in 1862 Farragut had steamed all the way up to Vicksburg with a brigade of troops before Confederate movements lower down forced him to go back. Porter's vessels were true river boats. With fore and aft decks just above the water line, and their vulnerable boilers, steam tubes, paddle wheels and gun batteries under a high, armored, central section, they well deserved their nickname 'Turtles'. But, driven only by the type of engine designed for peaceful river traffic, they lacked the power to move upstream at anything more than snail's pace. Thus any gunboat or transport going below Vicksburg would never get back up again as long as Confederate batteries remained in place.

Below: A rare photograph of Vicksburg under Union fire during an early stage of the siege.

Grant's decision to send seven gunboats, a ram, and three cargo steamers past Vicksburg on the night of 16 April, 1863 signaled that he was fully committed to an irrevocable plan. On the 20th his army began to march down the Louisiana bank from Milliken's Bend. The river had begun to fall, and the land, although still half-drowned, allowed his scouts to find a way along which to march. Ditches were filled, bridges constructed, passable roadways laid over bogs and cut through forests. For a week they struggled on, hauling guns, wagons, and horses through the mud, and at last emerged, triumphant, at the city of New Carthage on the Mississippi. More transports had run past Vicksburg to meet them and after another march of twenty miles downstream, the first Union troops were ferried over to the eastern bank at Bruinsburg on 30 April.

This landing took the Confederates by surprise. They were still expecting the main attack to come from the north, and had been confirmed in this view by a feint attack by Sherman against Snyder's Bluff on the 28th. Meanwhile, Farragut had run his flagship and another man-of-war up past the Confederate batteries at Port Hudson, and on the 29th joined with Porter in a bombardment of Grand Gulf, a well-fortified city some fifty miles below Vicksburg, but well upstream of Bruinsburg. At the same time, 100 miles inland, in one of the most successful cavalry

raids of the war, Colonel Benjamin Grierson rode south from La Grange, Tennessee, for 400 miles through Confederate territory until he came out before the Union lines at Baton Rouge. Brushing aside attempts by scratch Confederate forces to stop him, he spread alarm and confusion all the way, burning stores and contraband, and wrecking the Mobile and Ohio Railroad as he went.

The hope that Grant could be resupplied by vessels coming upstream from Baton Rouge came to nothing. Banks, fearing that Confederate forces from northwestern Louisiana might attempt to recapture New Orleans, had moved up the Red River to meet them. He could not return to march on Port Hudson, the lowest Confederate stronghold on the Mississippi, until the middle of May. And Port Hudson was strong enough to stop any cargo-boat, for it had stopped most of Farragut's deep-water warships, sinking one, and turning back all except his flagship and one other. No more supplies were coming down from Milliken's Bend, for the Vicksburg gunners had improved with practice, and several Union supply steamers and coal barges had by now been sunk or driven ashore.

But Grant was not to be stopped. The previous year his army had lived very well from commandeered supplies, as it retreated after the Confederate cavalry had cut its supply lines. Now, marching through the same type of well-stocked

countryside, it would do so as a deliberate act of policy. Moreover, the citizens of Mississippi would supply not only meat, poultry, vegetables and forage, but also vehicles and cattle for the army's train. An army living off the country needed few wagons to carry its food, but an army meaning to fight needed a great many to carry its munitions, and most of Grant's military train was still plowing its way along the Louisiana road to New Carthage, as working parties strove desperately to repair and improve the highway. To take its place, the bluecoat soldiers rounded up everything on wheels within their reach, from tumbrils and hay-carts to the finely-made sprung coaches of plantation owners. Teams of mules, oxen, draft and carriage horses were harnessed up with ropes or whatever tackle could be found, providing the army with the mobility it needed if it was to exploit the enemy's surprise.

On 1 May advanced elements of Major-General John A. McClernand's XIII Corps drove a Confederate brigade out of Port Gibson. Grand Gulf, threatened from the landward side by the Union's XVII Corps was evacuated on 2 May, and its defenders joined the Confederate forces sent from Vicksburg to hold the line of the Big Black River. On 7 May most of Sherman's XV Corps, having marched down from Milliken's Bend, crossed the river at Grand Gulf. Grant now had an army of 35,000 men on the Vicksburg side of the river, with a division of 8000 men, Sherman's rearguard, on its way to join him.

Rather than attempt to supply this force from the single wagon road out of Grand Gulf, Grant loaded his motley train with powder, shot, salt, coffee, and army biscuit, and marched away into the enemy's country. On 14 May Sherman's troops and Major-General James B. McPherson's XVII Corps, striking inland, converged on the Mississippi state capital, Jackson. General Joseph E. Johnston, the Confederate commander in the west, had only two brigades in the area, and was forced to retire northward. Nevertheless, Confederate reinforcements were on the way from the

east. Joe Johnston would have 15,000 men available in a few days, and another 9000 in a week. He sent word to Lieutenant-General John C. Pemberton, commanding the Confederate Military Department of Mississippi, to add the garrisons of Vicksburg and Port Hudson to his field army and march to form, with Johnston, a combined Confederate force of about 50,000 men. But Pemberton, although under Johnston's command, had orders from President Jefferson Davis that Vicksburg and Port Hudson were to be garrisoned at all times. Therefore, in disregard of the military principle that forces should be concentrated in the presence of an enemy, he left 10,000 men in Vicksburg, and crossed the Big Black River at its lower reaches, intending to cut Grant's lines of communication with Grand Gulf. Finding that Grant too had ignored military convention by having no lines of communication, he was obliged to follow Grant toward Jackson. On 16 May he reached the line of the Vicksburg and Jackson Railroad, and made contact with McClernand's advance guard which was moving east from Jackson toward Vicksburg. There followed the battle of Champion's Hill, one of the most hard-fought conflicts of this campaign. The tide of battle swayed to and fro for more than five hours, until suddenly, in the middle of the afternoon, Pemberton's army collapsed and retreated westward at high speed. The Confederates lost 6000 men, killed, wounded or captured, out of 23,000, and 27 guns out of 60. Grant had suffered severe losses too, amounting to more than 400 killed, and nearly 2000 wounded.

Grant Held the Field

But Grant held the battlefield. Pemberton succumbed to the temptation to retire behind his defenses, rather than escape northward and join Joe Johnston. His rearguard lined the Big Black River to guard the railroad bridge, but were swept away by a headlong infantry charge the next day, losing another 1700 men and eighteen guns captured. On the morning of 19 May Grant's Army

Left: The USS *Indianola* runs the gauntlet of Confederate batteries at Vicksburg in February 1863 to join the *Queen of the West.*

sat down before Vicksburg. Sherman led his men up the abandoned landward slopes of the hills he had attempted to take from Chickasaw Bayou the previous December. Snyder's Bluff and the adjacent strong-point, Haynes' Bluff, fell after a short engagement. Porter's supply vessels steamed up the Yazoo to reconnect the army with its base. Grant's risky but calculated gamble had paid off handsomely.

Indeed, as Sherman told him, Grant would have scored a major victory even if Vicksburg held out. Within twenty days of crossing at Bruinsburg his army had captured the state capital, destroyed vast quantities of strategic supplies, and had marched about for 180 miles in enemy territory, in a countryside so cut up by ravines, thickets, and canebrakes as to make it perfect for defense. It had fought five major engagements, had captured 61 fieldpieces and 27 heavier guns, and taken prisoner more than 6000 enemy soldiers. It had done all this on five days' official rations, and at a loss of only 2000 killed or missing and 7400 wounded, out of the 43,000 men who crossed the river. And now this army was in reach of Vicksburg.

It was in no mood to hesitate. The Union army had seen its opponents fleeing in panic before it and as soon as it reached Vicksburg, attempted to follow them into the defenses and take the place by storm. Grant soon realized he had misjudged the defenders' morale. Ten thousand of them had not been involved in the recent fighting, and were determined to show that they would not be panicked. The Federal assault was smashed. Grant paused to reconsider. Two days later, after a preliminary bombardment, he tried again, only to be driven back with heavier casualties. Pemberton's men had obviously regained their nerve. Grant had suffered 1000 casualties in the first assault, and 3000 in the second.

There was nothing to do now but mount a full-scale formal siege. Grant's soldiers did not welcome the prospect; they had spent a winter digging canals, and with the joyous dash across the river had felt they had at last exchanged the pick and shovel for the rifle. Now the realization came that all three implements had their proper place in the soldier's armory. The failure of the two assaults proved to the men that they were, despite their recent success, not invincible, and that a determined, well-defended enemy had to be treated with proper caution.

Now the full ritual of a siege began, as elaborate, predictable and formal in its procedures as the steps of a courtly dance: the business of constructing sap and parallel, mine and counter-mine, a line of circumvallation to keep the garrison in, and a line of countervallation to keep any would-be relievers out. As the pioneers and sappers sweated and dug, the infantry exchanged shots from rifle pits and trenches, or over parapets. Sometimes the two sides were near enough to throw hand grenades at each other. Sometimes, by a strange camaraderie in this sad war between brothers, men exchanged not bombs, but conversation, gibes, news, or even Confederate tobacco for Yankee 'hard-tack' biscuits.

The siege resolved itself into a duel between the skill and cunning of the opposing chief engineers, Captain F.E. Prime, succeeded by Captain Cyrus B. Comstock, United States Corps of Engineers, and Colonel H.S. Lockett, Confederate States Engineers. The Union forces, in fact, were short of trained military engineers. Some of Grant's troops came from the urban eastern seaboard. A few others came from the far western frontier, but the vast majority came from the Midwest agricultural area, the very region whose prosperity depended on the opening of the Mississippi and the fall of Vicksburg. Nearly all were wartime volunteer units, for the small US Regular Army

was either with the Army of the Potomac, or still in its peacetime location, deployed against the bands of Indians who threatened the outlying settlements. These volunteer soldiers brought with them ample skills from their peacetime occupations to meet all the needs Grant had for pioneers and field engineers, as their recent feats as road builders and canal cutters had proved. But what they lacked were the esoteric skills of the siege engineer. Grant, remembering his days as a cadet on the banks of the Hudson, recalled that West Point had taught future regular officers the rudiments of siege engineering, and therefore ordered every West Point graduate in his army to report to the four regular Engineer Corps officers, to act as assistant engineers.

During a truce called to bury the Union dead of 19 and 22 May, both chief engineers took the chance to view their enemy's works. Lockett was greeted by Sherman himself, who handed over some private letters to be delivered to Vicksburg addresses. After some courteous exchanges, Lockett found that Sherman detained him in conversation, each politely complimenting the other on their engineers' prowess. Sherman's unwonted civility served a useful military end, for the Confederate engineer complained in his memoirs that he was thus prevented from viewing a number of points he wished to see.

For all his Southern politeness, Lockett had prepared a vigorous reception for his Yankee visitors. He had been at Vicksburg for nearly a year, and during that time had surveyed the commanding ground around the city, cleared it of its primeval covering of magnolia trees and canebrakes and, using slaves to shift great quantities of earth, had constructed a series of redans, redoubts, lunnettes, and other field fortifications on all the salient features. A line of rifle pits and trenches connected them. When Pemberton and his field army were

driven in by Grant, fatigue parties were at once sent off to repair and strengthen the works. Exterior ditches were deepened to six or ten feet, while behind them were ramparts, parapets and firing steps for the infantry, embrasures and gun-platforms for the artillery. Along the front lay *abatis*, entanglements of felled trees, brushwood, and telegraph wire.

During the siege work went on behind the lines. Covered ways were built to foil the Union sharp-shooters. New traverses were constructed, damage repaired, guns shifted to fresh positions, retrenchments, or inner lines, thrown up, and every effort was made to foil the slow but steady approach of the besiegers' lines.

On the Union side, the conventional techniques of siege warfare were carefully employed. At dusk, sappers went out in a line pointing like a finger toward the heart of the enemy position. Each man, with pick, shovel, and wickerwork *gabion* for protection against snipers, stopped five feet from his neighbor, and then began to dig. Before daylight each had covered his own foxhole with the *gabion*, and burrowed through to link up with his neighbor. During the day other working parties, usually provided by the infantry, widened and deepened the new portion of the sap, and further improved the rear sections—some of which could accommodate men marching in columns of fours. The next night the whole process was repeated. To prevent the defenders shooting down the sap in enfilade, sap-rollers filled with cotton were pushed ahead. After Confederate exploding bullets had set fire to the cotton, care was taken to see it remained damp.

So the siege went on, lengthening from days to weeks. In the middle of June, the call went out in the Union lines for any men who had worked in coal mines. From the most experienced of these a detachment of 36 miners was formed, under Lieu-

Below: The Federal monitor *Ozark* on the Mississippi in 1864. The bare outline of the original *Monitor* has been cluttered with the superstructure and deck fittings of a conventional warship. By this time the Mississippi had been entirely cleared from source to mouth.

Above: The sidewheel gunboat USS *General Sterling Price* off Baton Rouge, Louisiana in January 1864, with the gunboat USS *Conestoga* in the background. By this time all effective contact between the eastern and western halves of the Confederacy had been stopped thanks to the seizure of Vicksburg.

tenant Russell of the 7th Missouri Infantry and Sergeant Morris of the 32nd Ohio. On the night of 22 June, the head of the flying-sap (the rapidly-dug night work) reached the wall of a redan held by the 3rd Louisiana Infantry. Confederate counter-mines were started to try and get under the sap, but the Union miners dug into the wall and sank a series of galleries into the earth below the fort. By the 25th the mine was fully dug. More than a ton of gunpowder was carried on the miners' backs, in 25-pound grain sacks, run across the open space between the sap head and the mine entrance, and then packed away below, tamped down with earth from the diggings.

The mine was exploded, blowing up the redan and leaving a breach into which poured men of the 31st and 45th Illinois Infantry. The 3rd Louisiana rushed to plug the gap, and 30 men in the storming parties went down before a hail of musketry. Nevertheless enough ground was held for another mine to be dug, and a further explosion of equal power, on 1 July, demolished the rest of the redan. This time the Union troops did not attack, but poured in such a storm of missiles that the Confederate pioneers found that as fast as they shovelled in earth from either side, it was blasted out again by Yankee fire power. Lockett himself was on hand to supervise their work, having narrowly escaped death in the explosion, as he had just been inspecting the Confederate mines.

These countermines, so close to the Union galleries that men could hear the orders and conversation of their foes through the earth, were collapsed by the concussion, or blown into the air. One black man was carried upwards by the blast and, incredibly, survived, coming down unhurt inside the Union lines. At length Lockett sent for tents and canvas wagon covers, had them filled with earth under cover, and gradually pushed the giant 'sausages' across to seal the gap. But nearly 100 Confederates had been killed or wounded by the explosion or the subsequent firing, and the Federal hold drew tighter around Vicksburg.

That other branch of siege warfare, the artillery, required as much improvization as the engineers. Grant's siege train consisted of six 32-pounders, and there was not another siege gun to

be had in the whole of the West. However, the Navy supplied a heavy battery manned by sailors, and the army's field guns were pressed into service, despite their lack of range and accuracy, so that by 30 June there were 220 guns in position against the city. The flat trajectory of the field pieces prevented full use being made of their power. Shells either flew over the parapets to burst inside the defenses, which were built of the thick red clay of which the Vicksburg Bluffs consisted, or else dropped short, to the annoyance of the Union infantry in their trenches. To drop bombs just inside the ramparts, mortars were made, by selecting logs of suitable length and diameter, boring out a tube, binding them with iron hoops, and then using a reduced charge to lob six- or twelve-pound shells into the enemy's positions.

The Confederate artillery had its own problems. Field and garrison guns together numbered 102, but, like most armies under siege, ammunition was limited and could not be replenished. Either in order to conserve ammunition against an assault, or because they had been dismounted by Union bombardment, the Confederate guns fell silent for long periods, allowing the besiegers to dominate the ground before them.

The river batteries, stripped of their land-service guns, but still well armed with coastal artillery pieces, continued a stout resistance. Union bomb schooners, each mounting a thirteen-inch mortar throwing a 200-pound projectile, kept up an incessant fire, day and night, joined from time to time by gun-boats from the flotilla. Good shooting by the Confederates sank the ironclad *Cincinnati*, but heavy naval guns mounted in scows established themselves opposite Vicksburg, enfilading part of the defense line and causing it to be abandoned.

Other gun-boats, accompanied by an infantry division, went up the Yazoo, past the abandoned defenses where the ironclad *Cairo* had gone down the previous November, and so on up to Yazoo City. There, Union soldiers burned anything left unscorched by its retreating garrison, while the gun-boats chased Confederate vessels up the narrow channels and backwaters where the expeditions had failed during the winter.

Within the walls of Vicksburg, men began to realize that there was no prospect of relief. Johnston had been able to scrape together a bare 30,000 men. Southern railroads had been somewhat inadequate even before the war. Now, with spares and raw materials cut off by the Union blockade, they could not cope with the wear and tear of ordinary traffic, increased as it was by military requirements. Far less could they repair the damage caused by Union raiders. Sherman's men, before evacuating Jackson, had devastated tracks, rolling stock, and railroad installations of every kind, rendering it useless to the Confederates as a communications center. Lee had refused to march west to help, and had told Davis frankly that he must risk losing either Mississippi or Virginia. Early in June, therefore, Confederate soldiers were marching not west, but north, where they would find their enemy at Gettysburg. Grant, on the other hand, was receiving massive reinforcements. From 43,000 at the end of May, his army grew to 72,000 by the middle of June. He even spoke of letting Johnston through into Vicksburg and increasing the number of future prisoners by 30,000. The only attempt by the Confederates to interfere on the Louisiana side was made on 7 June, when 3000 of them attacked the small garrison left at Milliken's Bend, but they were soon driven off.

Trench Warfare

Outside Vicksburg, Grant's men suffered the discomforts and boredom of trench warfare. All winter they had been frozen or wet through, up the river. Now they were baked in the 20,000 yards of dusty trenches, parched with thirst, unable to wash, and enduring the lot of anyone rash enough to fight in the Southern summer.

Inside, the situation was far worse. The besiegers, amply supplied, poured in musketry and artillery fire without a break. The defenders, husbanding their ammunition, made little reply. Food ran short. Mule stew, roast rat and cane shoots became desirable delicacies. Coffee gave out and was replaced by an ersatz brew of yams and blackberry leaves. As a substitute for flour, ground peas and cornmeal were issued. Soldiers became too weak to do more than man their positions. Union saps had reached the walls in a dozen places, and soon the numerical superiority of the attackers would enable them to swarm over in irresistible strength. Expedients such as the preparation of fougasses or the rolling down of fused artillery shells could only delay the inevitable.

On the night of 2 July Pemberton called a council of war. He told the officers present that there was no hope of relief, nor any hope that the garrison could cut its way out. The question was—surrender or not. Beginning with the junior officer present, according to military custom, the vote was taken. All except two voted to surrender while there was still a chance of making terms. Pemberton accepted the verdict. At 1000 on 3 July white flags were run up in the Confederate lines and a party went out under a flag of truce to parley.

At first Grant would offer nothing but his famous formula 'unconditional surrender', promising only that the garrison would receive the conventional respect due to prisoners of war who had fought bravely and endured much. At 1500 Pemberton came out, and the opposing commanders met face to face. They had little to say to each other, but their staff kept the talks going, and it was eventually agreed that Grant would send in his final terms in a letter at 2200. Meanwhile the ceasefire extended all along the front, and men on both sides had left their lines to gossip with their opponents. Both armies had recruited units from Missouri, a state claimed by North and South alike. Here was literally a case where families had been divided by the Civil War, but for a time several brothers and numerous cousins, Blue and Grey, met each other without rancor.

Grant eventually offered a concession. If Vicksburg surrendered, the garrison would be disarmed and released on parole, not to fight again in the war unless duly exchanged for a Union prisoner of war. Officers would be allowed to keep their side-arms, and mounted officers their horses. Personal baggage, rations, and clothing could be retained, but nothing else. Civilians would be protected, but no guarantee could be given about their property, including slaves. Thus he set the pattern for another surrender that he would take at Appomattox Court House. Years afterwards he wrote of Vicksburg, 'The men had fought so well that I did not want to humiliate them. I believed that consideration for their feelings would make them less dangerous foes during the continuance of hostilities, and better citizens after the war was over'.

So, on the morning of 4 July, Pemberton surrendered and Grant marched into Vicksburg at the head of his victorious soldiers. There was no cheering, no victory parade, merely the business-like work of taking over strongpoints, stores, and munitions. The defenders gave up 172 pieces of artillery and 60,000 small-arms, most of the latter being new Enfield muzzle-loading rifles, brought in by blockade-runners. These were better arms than many of Grant's regiments carried, and he authorized all colonels of units equipped with old US or Belgian muskets, or more modern, but non-standard calibre pieces, to exchange them for the captured weapons.

Southern apologists have tried to minimize the extent of the disaster. The Mississippi could still be crossed, for there was only one Union steamboat to patrol every ten miles of river, and only fifty places for them to be based. Confederate guerrillas, equipped with light artillery, could still harry passing traffic. The trans-Mississippi states had provided few supplies to the eastern states and were more of a liability than an asset.

Yet Jefferson Davis had tied his own prestige to the proposition that Vicksburg was impregnable. The propaganda effect of its fall was considerable. The South lost 30,000 men and arms it could ill afford. Port Hudson, which had been besieged by the Union troops from New Orleans since 26 May, surrendered on 9 July, on hearing the news of Vicksburg's fall. A week later the riverboat *Imperial* arrived at New Orleans, having steamed for a thousand miles from St Louis without hindrance. The Confederate stranglehold on the trade and traffic of the Mississippi had been broken. Lincoln, translating the river's Indian name, pronounced the epilogue: 'The Father of Waters again goes unvexed to the sea.'

Gettysburg

1863

Gettysburg, rightly termed 'the greatest battle ever fought on the American continent', was the climax of General Robert E. Lee's invasions of the North in the summer of 1863. It was also, in a sense, the climax of the American Civil War as a whole. In May the Confederate Army of Northern Virginia had defeated 'Fighting Joe' Hooker at Chancellorsville, a victory marred by the accidental death of Lee's ablest lieutenant, General 'Stonewall' Jackson. Within the next two months, however, the balance of the war was to swing against the Confederacy. In the west Major-General Ulysses S. Grant's successful attack on Vicksburg gave Union forces control of the Mississippi Valley. There were other Union successes further west, at Alexandria and Port Jackson, while in Tennessee the Confederates were forced back to Chattanooga. It was at Gettysburg,

though, that the major clash occurred, between Lee's Army of Northern Virginia and the main Union force, the Army of the Potomac.

Lee's army was reorganized into three corps following Chancellorsville. The methodical Lieutenant-General James Longstreet—Lee called him 'my old warhorse'—commanded I Corps, while the newly-promoted Lieutenant-Generals Richard Ewell and A.P. Hill led II and III Corps respectively. Ewell had lost a leg at Groveton nine months previously; suitably equipped with a wooden one, he remained cheery and popular. The red-bearded Hill was one of Lee's most pugnacious generals, with a good record as a divisional commander. Lee himself was a general of remarkable ability. A regular colonel on the outbreak of war, Lee had reluctantly accepted command of the forces of his native state, Virginia.

Far left: General Robert E. Lee, commander of Confederate forces at Gettysburg, who held off the Army of the Potomac for four years in Virginia and Maryland. **Left:** An early portrayal of Ulysses S. Grant, Lee's protagonist in the last stages of the war in Virginia, who was besieging Vicksburg at the time of the Gettysburg campaign.

Below: The slaughter at the Battle of Gettysburg, the most decisive conflict of the Civil War.

Above: Confederate winter quarters at Manassas, Virginia in March 1862. Manassas was the site of the First Battle of Bull Run, which gave the Union a healthy respect for Southern fighting skill and strength.

General Winfield Scott, who at the time commanded the Union armies, thought that the loss of Lee was equal to that of 50,000 veterans. In June 1861 Lee was appointed chief military adviser to the Confederate President Jefferson Davis, and a year later he took over command of the Army of Northern Virginia. The gentlemanly, courteous Lee had a record of almost uninterrupted success behind him when he moved north in June 1863. His 70,000 men, although fewer in number than their opponents, and in most respects miserably ill-equipped, were in excellent spirits, with no doubt of their ability to inflict yet another defeat upon the Army of the Potomac.

Lee's strategic aim was threefold. He sought to engage Hooker in a major battle, hoping that another defeat would weaken Union resolve to continue the war, and would increase the Confederacy's chance of recognition by foreign powers. Secondary motives for the invasion were the hopes of reducing Grant's pressure on Vicksburg, and of acquiring much-needed equipment and supplies in the North.

On 3 June Lee left his position on the south bank of the Rappahannock and set out for Culpepper. Once there he swung north, with Ewell's corps leading, followed by Longstreet and Hill. Ewell took Winchester on 15 June, after roughly handling a Union defending force. Hooker, meanwhile, was marching parallel to Lee, keeping his army between Lee and Washington.

Lee naturally intended to use his cavalry under the dashing Major-General J.E.B. Stuart to screen his advance, and ordered Stuart to cross the Potomac and station himself to Ewell's north and west. Stuart left two of his brigades to cover the passes through the Blue Ridge mountains to Lee's right rear, and set off with the remaining three, intending to ride right around Hooker's army, and then to move north to join Ewell. But Stuart found the going much harder than he had anticipated, and he was out of contact with Lee for eight days from 25 June onwards, thus depriving Lee of 'the eyes of his army'.

Ewell's corps was by now dispersed on a thirty-mile front, between Carlisle and York, gathering supplies. Hill was moving through the mountains in the Cashtown area, with Longstreet to his rear at Chambersburg. Lee had already ordered Ewell to cross the Susquehanna and take Harrisburg, when, on the evening of 25 June, he received some alarming news. One of Longstreet's scouts reported that the Union Army, after concentrating at Frederick, had moved rapidly northward on the front Emmitsburg-Westminster. Nor was this new energy accidental; Hooker, after yet another disagreement with President Lincoln, had been replaced by Major-General George Meade.

Lee at once set about driving his army west of Gettysburg. Unfortunately, with Stuart miles away to the east, he had no accurate intelligence of Meade's movements. On the evening of 30 July Hill's leading divisional commander, Heth, asked Hill for permission to march to Gettysburg next morning to obtain some shoes which he had heard were stored there. Hill cheerfully gave permission; there were some Union cavalry in the town, but he attached no particular significance to their

presence; Heth's infantry, he thought, should be able to dislodge them quickly enough.

The cavalry in question were, in fact, two brigades of Major-General John Buford's 1st Cavalry Division. Buford, a capable and experienced officer, realized that there were sizable Confederate forces in the area. On the night of 30 June/1 July he sent this intelligence back to Major-General John Reynolds, whose I Corps was encamped to the south. Reynolds relayed the information back to Meade, who responded by ordering Reynolds to move to Gettysburg at dawn to support Buford's cavalry.

At 0800 on 1 July Buford's scouts made contact with Heth's, in skirmishes on the Cashtown Road. Heth rapidly deployed two of his four brigades, sent forward some artillery, and attacked. Buford's cavalrymen, fighting dismounted, gave a good account of themselves, supported by one battery of guns. It was clear, however, that the cavalry could not hold on indefinitely in the face of growing Confederate pressure.

To Buford's rear was the small town of Gettysburg, from which roads radiated like the spokes of a wheel. On his immediate left was the Hagerstown Road, with the Emmitsburg Road to its south. Running into Gettysburg from due south was the Taneytown Road, with the Baltimore Pike on its right. The Carlisle and Harrisburg Roads ran north and northeast respectively, with the York and Hanover Roads running east. The main features of the terrain were two ridges, running more or less parallel, north to south. Seminary Ridge, so called from a Lutheran

Above: J.E.B. Stuart, the most daring cavalry commander of the Civil War, leads his men on a reconnaissance mission. **Left:** General James Longstreet, whom Lee called 'my old warhorse', commanded I Corps at Gettysburg.

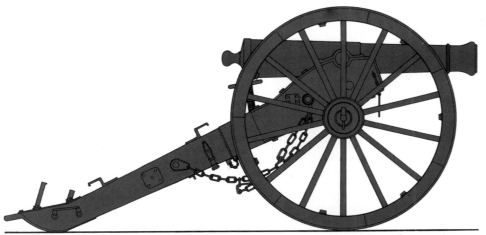

Above: 1849 pattern 6-pounder gun and carriage. Length: 116.6 inches; Weight: 900 pounds; Rate of fire: three rounds per minute maximum; Crew: seven.

Below: General Abner Doubleday, who fought at Cemetery Hill, is better known for having invented the game of baseball over two decades before in Cooperstown, New York than for his fighting skill.

seminary near the town, stood west of Gettysburg, immediately behind Buford's position. Due south of the town ran Cemetery Ridge, with Cemetery Hill at its northern end, and Culp's Hill to its northeast. At the southern end of Cemetery Ridge were two distinctive hills, Big and Little Round Tops. Just west of Little Round Top, in the valley of a small stream, Plum Run, was a rough, boulder-strewn area known as Devil's Den.

Gettysburg was thus amply provided with roads, and, on the morning of 1 July, the rival armies percolated down them into the fighting. Although both Lee and Meade were quite pre-

pared to fight, Gettysburg was in no sense a planned battle; once initial contact had been made both sides simply concentrated on Gettysburg as quickly as possible.

Reynolds was nearing Gettysburg at the head of his leading formation, Wadsworth's division, when he heard the sound of gunfire. Ordering Wadsworth to press on cross-country, he galloped forward, and conferred briefly with Buford at the seminary. Wadsworth's men checked the Confederate advance, and then briskly counterattacked, badly cutting up one of Heth's brigades. Reynolds himself was killed soon after this counterattack started, and fresh Confederate troops, Pender's division of Hill's corps, arrived, forcing Wadsworth onto the defensive. Doubleday's division of I Corps in turn came into action, soon followed by Major-General Oliver Howard's XI Corps. The Confederates were also being reinforced rapidly, with Rodes' division of Ewell's Corps advancing against Gettysburg from the northeast.

The battle was well under way before either Lee or Meade was fully aware of its significance. Lee arrived on the field while Heth's initial attack was in progress, but it took him some time to sanction the commitment of Pender's division. Meade was at Taneytown, a few miles south of Gettysburg. Deciding that he must remain there to concentrate his army, he sent Major-General Winfield Scott Hancock of II Corps forward, ordering him to take command of all Union troops engaged, and authorizing him to fight or withdraw as he thought fit. Hancock was well suited to this difficult task; he was tough, level-headed, and popular with the troops.

Lee sent Pender's division forward when he saw Rodes attack from the northeast. Howard's XI Corps managed to get into line at Doubleday's left, on the axis of the Carlisle road, in time to meet Rodes' attack, but at this point another of Ewell's divisions, under the vinegary Jubal Early, deployed down the Harrisburg road. Despite the hammering it had received at Chancellorsville, and its low reputation in the Army of the Potomac, XI Corps fought well, but it suffered heavily and was forced back through Gettysburg. The collapse of XI Corps necessitated the withdrawal of I Corps, and, accompanied by some very vicious fighting along the western slopes of Seminary Ridge, Doubleday fell back onto Cemetery Hill. As daylight faded the two battered Union corps reorganized on Cemetery Hill. Hancock decided to stay and fight, believing that a withdrawal would imply a Confederate victory, and knowing that reinforcements, in the shape of Major-General Henry Slocum's XII Corps and Major-General Daniel Sickles' III Corps, were close at hand.

On the Confederate side, Lee authorized Early to attack Cemetery Hill if he considered it practicable. Early eventually decided against an attack, and was supported in this view by Ewell, who arrived on the scene with his third division, Johnson's, shortly before nightfall. Early's failure to attack Cemetery Hill has been severely criticized. It is likely that an attack, launched at about 1600, could have succeeded; the loss of Cemetery Hill would have compromised I and

Sedan 1940: Breakthrough

The concept of breaking an enemy's front by direct assault has little to recommend it in terms of subtlety. It has, however, proved a useful means of attaining victory, though its successful employment has tended to depend upon the technical superiority of the attacker. In May 1940 the Germans used the tactics of blitzkrieg against the Allies who, beset by an essentially defensive strategy, spread their strength too widely. The main weight of the German blow was delivered by Rundstedt's Army Group A which, spearheaded by seven panzer divisions, crashed through the Ardennes and broke the Allied line at Sedan on the Meuse. A rapid Allied collapse followed as the panzers pressed on into France; reaching the Channel near Boulogne, they cut the Allied armies in half. The British, together with numerous French, were evacuated from Dunkirk, but France, paralyzed by the defeat, capitulated in mid-June. Blitzkrieg depended for its success upon the mobility and striking power of the panzers and *Luftwaffe*; it also relied upon the moral collapse of the defenders. It was used, again with considerable success, against Russia in the summer of 1941, but thereafter its results became less assured, and a German attempt to achieve an armored breakthrough at Kursk in July 1943 proved an expensive failure.

The tactics which won the 1940 campaign were revolutionary only in their technical ingredients, armor and air power. The concept of smashing the enemy's front is as old as warfare itself; indeed, the prime tactic of the armored horseman of medieval times was the charge *en masse*, usually directed at a weak point in the enemy's battle-line. Such a charge usually proved successful if the cavalry came to handstrokes with the opposing infantry, but the supremacy of the armored horseman was eroded by English longbowmen, Turkish horse-archers, Swiss pikemen and ultimately by the rise of firearms.

Many of the battles fought in the 17th and 18th centuries developed into mere slogging-matches in which lines of infantry exchanged murderous volleys while cavalry sought to find an opening for decisive action. Even the Duke of Marlborough's great victory at Blenheim (1704) exhibited little tactical sophistication. It was Napoleon who reintroduced conclusive means of breaking his enemy's front. He did so by concentrating his artillery against a selected point and smashing a breach through which his *masse de décision* would surge. Austerlitz was not the typical Napoleonic battle; Eylau, Wagram, Borodino and Waterloo, where the French artillery was massed in great batteries, and a tactical decision was sought by combined-arms assaults following preparation by the guns, are more indicative of the techniques which characterized the Emperor's battles. Such techniques were not always fruitful; at Borodino the bombardment proved less effective than had been expected, and the assault stuck fast in the face of staunch Russian resistance, while at Waterloo Wellington's skillfully-deployed forces offered a poor target for the French cannon, many of whose rounds were harmlessly absorbed by the damp ground.

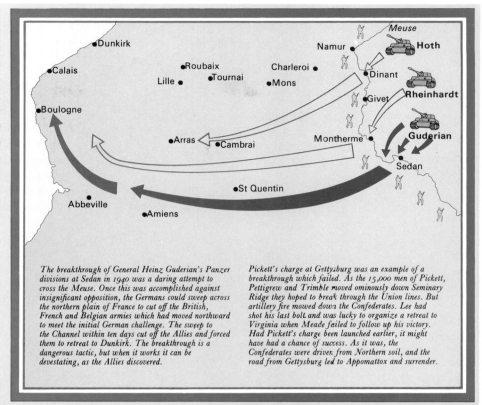

The breakthrough of General Heinz Guderian's Panzer divisions at Sedan in 1940 was a daring attempt to cross the Meuse. Once this was accomplished against insignificant opposition, the Germans could sweep across the northern plain of France to cut off the British, French and Belgian armies which had moved northward to meet the initial German challenge. The sweep to the Channel within ten days cut off the Allies and forced them to retreat to Dunkirk. The breakthrough is a dangerous tactic, but when it works it can be devestating, as the Allies discovered.

Pickett's charge at Gettysburg was an example of a breakthrough which failed. As the 15,000 men of Pickett, Pettigrew and Trimble moved ominously down Seminary Ridge they hoped to break through the Union lines. But artillery fire mowed down the Confederates. Lee had shot his last bolt and was lucky to organize a retreat to Virginia when Meade failed to follow up his victory. Had Pickett's charge been launched earlier, it might have had a chance of success. As it was, the Confederates were driven from Northern soil, and the road from Gettysburg led to Appomattox and surrender.

As the 19th century went on, so the increased power of artillery gave new hope to generals who sought to achieve breakthrough on the Napoleonic pattern, but, as the Confederates discovered at Gettysburg and the Prussians at Saint-Privat, infantry armed with rifled weapons could inflict frightful casualties upon an attacker unless the assault had been meticulously prepared by shellfire. Once infantry had realized that the spade was more important than the bayonet it became almost impossible for attackers to achieve a clean breakthrough, however powerful their artillery; the Battle of the Somme illustrated the strength of defense in depth against heavy bombardment and determined infantry assault. The German March Offensive of 1918 employed infiltration and a hurricane bombardment with considerable success, but it was the tank which provided the real answer to linear defense based upon barbed wire and trench-systems.

In the interwar years the Germans correctly assessed the importance of the tank supported by the dive bomber, and the breakthrough at Sedan in May 1940 was the price which the Allies paid for tactical obsolescence. There have, however, been suggestions that the postwar development of anti-tank weapons has rendered the tank itself obsolete. The major powers continue, nevertheless, to place great reliance upon armor; NATO forces in Germany face the specter of a Warsaw Pact blitzkrieg, supported by chemical and nuclear weapons, which could, so its authors believe, bring Soviet tanks to the channel coast within a week of its commencement. The concept of breakthrough, old though it may be, remains, in the opinion of many military authorities, viable. It remains to be seen, however, whether the tactical wheel has not once more come full circle and provided the defender with weapons which would enable him to halt an armored onslaught as firmly as the German machine guns checked British infantry on the Somme.

XI Corps, and made the eventual Union position untenable.

Lee conferred with Longstreet on Seminary Ridge after dark. The latter's troops were still on the march, but Longstreet himself was certain enough what they should do when they arrived. Lee announced his intention of attacking next morning, and proposed to move Ewell to the right to do so. Longstreet strongly disagreed, advocating instead a broad swing to the south, round the Union left flank and into the Union rear. Lee, however, had no idea of the whereabouts of the bulk of Meade's army, and such a move could end in disaster if it was itself outflanked by fresh troops. Once again, the absence of Stuart had a fatal influence on Confederate decision-making; supplied with accurate intelligence of Meade's movements, Lee would probably have carried out the plan suggested by Longstreet. The discussion ended with Lee gesturing towards Cemetery Ridge, stating forcefully that 'The enemy is there and I am going to attack him'. Longstreet rode back to his corps, dispirited; his dejection and irritation at Lee's decision were to have an important influence on the battle.

Ewell rode to Lee's headquarters later that night, with the news that Johnson's patrols had found Culp's Hill unoccupied. Ewell had been strangely indecisive during the latter part of 1 July, but by now he had recovered his composure. He suggested an attack on Culp's Hill, with the intention of placing artillery there to dominate Cemetery Hill and dislodge Union forces from it. Lee at once agreed. Such an attack, launched simultaneously with an assault against Cemetery Ridge from the west, seemed to offer a good chance of inflicting a decisive defeat on Meade. Unfortunately for Lee, Johnson's patrols were wrong. Culp's Hill was occupied in strength by XII Corps; its capture lay beyond Ewell's power.

Meade Arrives

Meade himself arrived on the field shortly after midnight. He confirmed Hancock's decision to stand and fight, aided by the knowledge that, with the exception of Major-General John Sedgewick's VI Corps, all his troops would be on the field by mid-morning. Sedgewick's men were on the march from Westminster, Maryland, some 37 miles away, and would not be up till well on into the afternoon. Meade spent the night putting his men into position. Slocum's XII Corps held Culp's Hill, with I Corps on its left, holding the ground west to Cemetery Hill, which was defended by the remnants of XI Corps. The Union line then ran south along Cemetery Ridge, held by Hancock's superb II Corps and Sickles' III Corps. Sykes' V Corps, an experienced formation, was in reserve on the reverse slope of the ridge. Meade himself set up his headquarters in a farmhouse behind II Corps.

The expected early-morning Confederate attack failed to materialize, and Meade ordered Slocum to prepare to attack Ewell. The former, though, advised that the terrain was unfavorable and that such an attack had little chance of success, and Meade concurred. Lee was also forced to modify his plans, in this case for an attack on

Culp's Hill. It had become apparent that Ewell's information was inaccurate, and the hill was strongly held. By now, however, it was too late to carry out Lee's original plan and move Ewell round to the right. Lee eventually ordered Ewell to attack if he saw a favorable opportunity, while Longstreet assaulted the southern end of Cemetery Ridge. Hill, in the center, was to assist Longstreet, and to attack if a suitable occasion arose.

Longstreet's attack could not be carried out until his corps was in position, and one of his divisions, Pickett's, was still well to the rear at Chambersburg. The remaining two were closer, but they still had some distance to cover. Longstreet was also preoccupied with the problem of getting his men to their concentration area unobserved, and he moved particularly slowly. There have been suggestions that he was sulking as a result of his disagreement with Lee the previous night, but the question remains unresolved. Whatever the reason, Longstreet's two leading divisions, commanded by Lafayette McLaws and John B. Hood, were not in position till mid-afternoon; by this time there had been a significant change in the Union dispositions.

Dan Sickles' III Corps had been posted on the southern end of the Union line, on Hancock's left. The corps was weak, containing only two divisions, and Sickles feared that he might be dislodged from his position. He had to hold the end of Cemetery Ridge, as well as the Round Tops on the extreme Union left. Furthermore, the ridge was nearly flat at its southern end, and Sickles considered that Confederate guns could engage it with success from the area of the Peach Orchard, on the Emmitsburg Road, half a mile to the west. Sickles informed Meade that he considered the Peach Orchard a better position for III Corps than the southern end of the ridge. Finally, when

his outposts reported Longstreet's advance, Sickles decided, on his own initiative, to move his corps forward into the Peach Orchard. This decision was to cost III Corps a severe mauling when Longstreet at last attacked.

While McLaws and Hood were forming up for their assault the latter noticed that the Round Tops were unoccupied, and requested permission to attack from the south and outflank the Union line. Longstreet, for reasons which remain unclear, refused, thereby missing an opportunity to turn Sickles incautious advance into a disaster.

By the time Meade learned of III Corps' move it was too late to countermand it, for Longstreet's attack, so long awaited, was at last ready. At about 1600 Hood and McLaws advanced against Sickles. Hood was wounded early in the action, but his men went on with the *élan* that could make charging Confederate infantry almost irresistible.

Above: Headquarters of General George Meade on Cemetery Ridge.

Below: Longstreet's attack on the center of the Union lines, in a sketch made at the time by A.R. Ward. **Overleaf:** Union forces fall on the Confederates who plunged into their lines during the afternoon of the second day of the Battle of Gettysburg.

McLaws crashed in against Sickles' right, and by about 1800 the Peach Orchard was lost and III Corps in retreat; Sickles himself was severely wounded, losing a leg. III Corps may have been roughly handled, but it was not routed, and its remnants were supported by V Corps and one of Hancock's divisions, leading to a hideous *mêlée* in the area around the Wheatfield and the Devil's Den. Hood's men eventually fought their way through the Devil's Den, and emerged facing the undefended Little Round Top.

The situation was now critical, for the loss of this salient feature would have imperiled the entire Union position. Fortunately for Meade, his chief engineer, Major-General Gouverneur

The Battle of Gettysburg, 1863

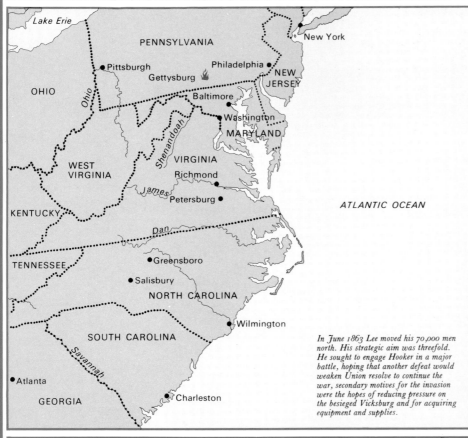

In June 1863 Lee moved his 70,000 men north. His strategic aim was threefold. He sought to engage Hooker in a major battle, hoping that another defeat would weaken Union resolve to continue the war; secondary motives for the invasion were the hopes of reducing pressure on the besieged Vicksburg and for acquiring equipment and supplies.

The maneuvers to Gettysburg

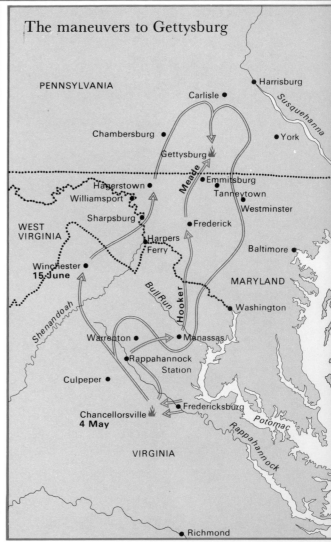

The situation on 2 July

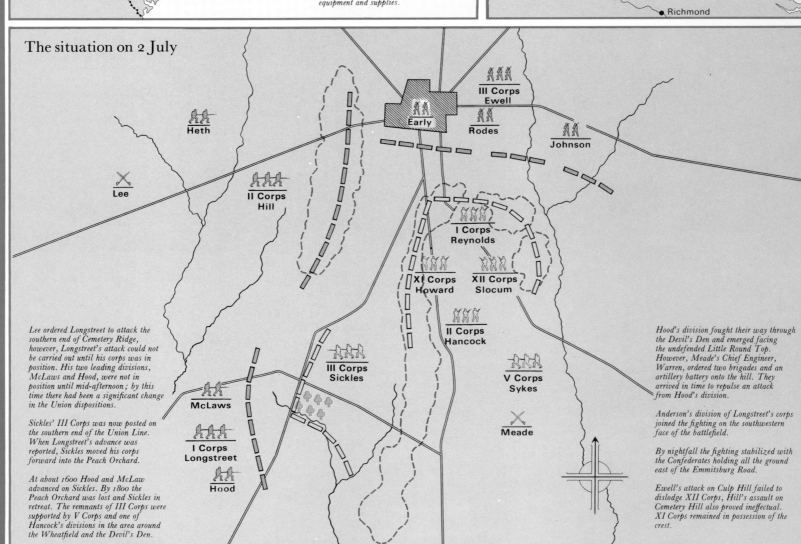

Lee ordered Longstreet to attack the southern end of Cemetery Ridge, however, Longstreet's attack could not be carried out until his corps was in position. His two leading divisions, McLaws and Hood, were not in position until mid-afternoon; by this time there had been a significant change in the Union dispositions.

Sickles' III Corps was now posted on the southern end of the Union Line. When Longstreet's advance was reported, Sickles moved his corps forward into the Peach Orchard.

At about 1600 Hood and McLaw advanced on Sickles. By 1800 the Peach Orchard was lost and Sickles in retreat. The remnants of III Corps were supported by V Corps and one of Hancock's divisions in the area around the Wheatfield and the Devil's Den.

Hood's division fought their way through the Devil's Den and emerged facing the undefended Little Round Top. However, Meade's Chief Engineer, Warren, ordered two brigades and an artillery battery onto the hill. They arrived in time to repulse an attack from Hood's division.

Anderson's division of Longstreet's corps joined the fighting on the southwestern face of the battlefield.

By nightfall the fighting stabilized with the Confederates holding all the ground east of the Emmitsburg Road.

Ewell's attack on Culp Hill failed to dislodge XII Corps, Hill's assault on Cemetery Hill also proved ineffectual. XI Corps remained in possession of the crest.

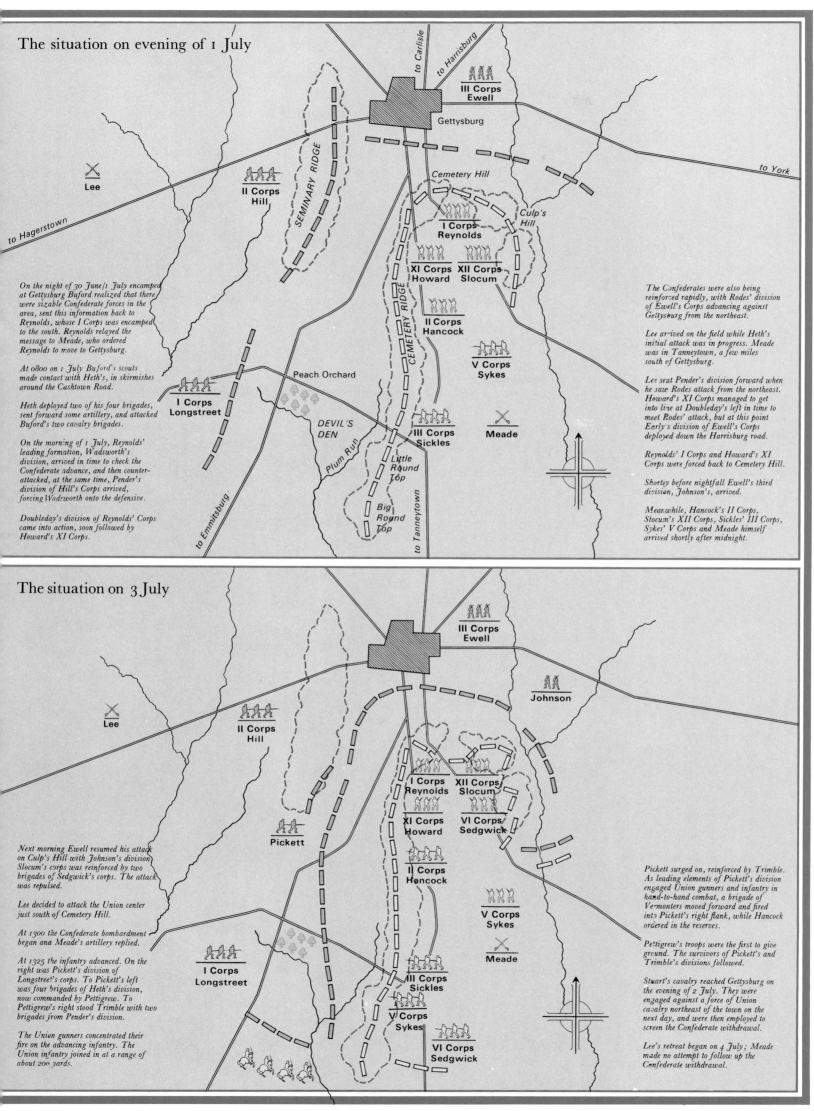

The situation on evening of 1 July

On the night of 30 June/1 July encamped at Gettysburg Buford realized that there were sizable Confederate forces in the area, sent this information back to Reynolds, whose I Corps was encamped to the south. Reynolds relayed the message to Meade, who ordered Reynolds to move to Gettysburg.

At 0800 on 1 July Buford's scouts made contact with Heth's, in skirmishes around the Cashtown Road.

Heth deployed two of his four brigades, sent forward some artillery, and attacked Buford's two cavalry brigades.

On the morning of 1 July, Reynolds' leading formation, Wadsworth's division, arrived in time to check the Confederate advance, and then counter-attacked, at the same time, Pender's division of Hill's Corps arrived, forcing Wadsworth onto the defensive.

Doubleday's division of Reynolds' Corps came into action, soon followed by Howard's XI Corps.

The Confederates were also being reinforced rapidly, with Rodes' division of Ewell's Corps advancing against Gettysburg from the northeast.

Lee arrived on the field while Heth's initial attack was in progress. Meade was in Tanneytown, a few miles south of Gettysburg.

Lee sent Pender's division forward when he saw Rodes attack from the northeast. Howard's XI Corps managed to get into line at Doubleday's left in time to meet Rodes' attack, but at this point Early's division of Ewell's Corps deployed down the Harrisburg road.

Reynolds' I Corps and Howard's XI Corps were forced back to Cemetery Hill.

Shortly before nightfall Ewell's third division, Johnson's, arrived.

Meanwhile, Hancock's II Corps, Slocum's XII Corps, Sickles' III Corps, Sykes' V Corps and Meade himself arrived shortly after midnight.

Map labels (evening of 1 July): to Carlisle · to Harrisburg · III Corps Ewell · Gettysburg · to York · Lee · II Corps Hill · SEMINARY RIDGE · Cemetery Hill · Culp's Hill · I Corps Reynolds · XI Corps Howard · XII Corps Slocum · II Corps Hancock · CEMETERY RIDGE · V Corps Sykes · to Hagerstown · Peach Orchard · I Corps Longstreet · DEVIL'S DEN · Plum Run · III Corps Sickles · Meade · Little Round Top · Big Round Top · to Emmitsburg · to Tanneytown

The situation on 3 July

Next morning Ewell resumed his attack on Culp's Hill with Johnson's division. Slocum's corps was reinforced by two brigades of Sedgwick's corps. The attack was repulsed.

Lee decided to attack the Union center just south of Cemetery Hill.

At 1300 the Confederate bombardment began and Meade's artillery replied.

At 1325 the infantry advanced. On the right was Pickett's division of Longstreet's corps. To Pickett's left was four brigades of Heth's division, now commanded by Pettigrew. To Pettigrew's right stood Trimble with two brigades from Pender's division.

The Union gunners concentrated their fire on the advancing infantry. The Union infantry joined in at a range of about 200 yards.

Pickett surged on, reinforced by Trimble. As leading elements of Pickett's division engaged Union gunners and infantry in hand-to-hand combat, a brigade of Vermonters moved forward and fired into Pickett's right flank, while Hancock ordered in the reserves.

Pettigrew's troops were the first to give ground. The survivors of Pickett's and Trimble's divisions followed.

Stuart's cavalry reached Gettysburg on the evening of 2 July. They were engaged against a force of Union cavalry northeast of the town on the next day, and were then employed to screen the Confederate withdrawal.

Lee's retreat began on 4 July; Meade made no attempt to follow up the Confederate withdrawal.

Map labels (3 July): III Corps Ewell · Johnson · Lee · II Corps Hill · I Corps Reynolds · XII Corps Slocum · XI Corps Howard · VI Corps Sedgwick · Pickett · II Corps Hancock · V Corps Sykes · Meade · I Corps Longstreet · III Corps Sickles · V Corps Sykes · VI Corps Sedgwick

K. Warren, was on the spot, and he at once appreciated the significance of Little Round Top. Galloping over to Sykes' corps, he ordered two brigades and a battery of artillery onto the hill. They arrived just in time, and were greeted by a vigorous attack from Hood's division, which was just—but only just—repulsed. Meanwhile, across the whole southwestern face of the battlefield, bitter fighting went on, with Anderson's division of Longstreet's corps joining in.

The Union artillery, under the capable Major-General Henry J. Hunt, had provided the infantry with superb close support throughout the attack in the area of the Peach Orchard, though it had lost some guns. Hunt also used his artillery in an effective if somewhat unconventional manner along the 'Plum Run Line' where there was a gap unheld by Union infantry. Hunt pushed a solid mass of 25 guns into the gap, and held the line unsupported. One Confederate regiment, the 21st Mississippi, actually got in among the guns as they were withdrawing, receiving and inflicting heavy casualties. By nightfall the fighting stabilized with the Union forces holding the Round Tops, the Plum Run Line, and Cemetery Ridge; the Devil's Den and much of the ground east of the Emmitsburg Road were in Confederate hands.

To the north, things went less well for Lee's army. Ewell had begun to bombard the area of Cemetery Hill and Culp's Hill when he heard Longstreet's guns announce that Hood and McLaws were going in. On Culp's Hill, XII Corps had been weakened by sending reinforcements to the southern end of the line, and when Ewell sent in Johnson's division it found only one brigade in position. Nevertheless, this formation put up a stiff resistance, aided by some troops sent over from I Corps. Johnson's men eventually managed to seize the lower part of the hill and some entrenchments, but XII Corps remained in possession of the crest.

Cemetery Hill was assaulted by Jubal Early, whose charge was warmly received by a particularly well-posted battery of I Corps artillery and by the massed guns of XI Corps. Despite some hand-to-hand fighting in the Union gun-line, Early's attack proved fruitless. Rodes, on Early's left, had been ordered to attack if he considered it feasible, but he decided against it; it was subsequently argued that had he supported Early, Cemetery Hill—as vital to the right of the Union line as was Little Round Top to its left—might have fallen. This must remain another of the unresolved problems of Gettysburg.

Both armies had suffered severely on 2 July. The dead and wounded lay in a broad swathe along the whole of the hook-shaped front, lying thickest in the Devil's Den—Wheatfield area, and in front of Cemetery Hill. The field hospitals on both sides were soon overloaded, and many of the wounded spent an agonizing night in the open. Meade held a conference of corps commanders at his headquarters. All agreed that retreat was out of the question, and that the army should stand and fight for at least another day before moving, if possible, onto the offensive.

Below left: A contemporary sketch by A. R. Ward of Cemetery Hill prior to Pickett's charge.
Bottom left: Pencil drawing of the battlefield taken from the junction of Gettysburg Pike and Taneytown Road on 3 July.
Below right: Major-General C.K. Warren, who attacked Little Round Top.
Bottom right: A.R. Ward sketching the Battle of Gettysburg, in a photograph taken by Matthew Brady, the greatest war photographer of the Civil War.

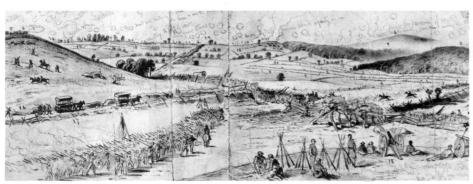

Meade announced that he suspected that Lee would attack the center of the Union position, in the area held by II Corps. He felt confident enough to repulse it; Sedgewick's VI Corps had arrived during the afternoon, and the Union artillery had adequate ammunition available—though Hunt had warned that there was none for 'idle cannonades, the besetting sin of some of our Commanders'.

Lee had less reason than Meade to feel satisfied with the result of 2 July. The opportunity opened by the ungarrisoned Little Round Top had been lost, and there had been little coordination behind the Confederate attacks. Had Longstreet and Ewell attacked simultaneously, and more promptly, things might well have gone differently.

Fighting flared up in the north early next morning. Johnson resumed his attack on Culp's Hill, to be met by the determined resistance of Slocum's corps, reinforced by two brigades of Sedgewick's. Despite a number of spirited attacks, Johnson's infantry could make no impression on the defenders, and were eventually forced to fall back. Over the remainder of the front things were relatively quiet. There were several minor exchanges of small arms and artillery fire, in one of which Pender was mortally wounded, but in the center and southern portions of the battlefield the Confederates were occupied in preparing for the assault which was to be the culminating point of the battle.

Pickett's Gallant Charge

Meade's prediction that Lee would attack the Union center proved correct. It was not, however, Lee's original intention. He hoped to use Longstreet's fresh division, under General George Pickett, to smash Meade's left in the Round Top area, but Longstreet pointed out that the confusion and close engagement in that vicinity made a set-piece attack difficult. Lee agreed, and decided instead to attack Meade's center just south of Cemetery Hill. The attack's objective was marked by a small clump of trees. One of Hill's brigades had reached the ridge top there on 2 July, but had been thrown back. Lee thought that Pickett's splendid division of fifteen Virginia regiments could punch through the Union line where a brigade had so nearly succeeded.

It was of paramount importance that the Union artillery should be as heavily engaged as possible before Pickett's attack went in. Hunt's gunners had been instrumental in repulsing Early's attack on Cemetery Hill on the previous day, and, given a chance, would inflict serious damage on Pickett as he crossed the open ground between the ridges. Early in the morning Lee told Longstreet's artillery commander, Colonel E.P. Alexander, of his plan, and Alexander set about concentrating his guns so as to be able to engage Cemetery Hill and the ground to its south. Alexander had 75 guns in line by 1000, while to his left Hill's corps had 63 more.

By 1300 an ominous silence reigned over the field. Alexander had moved into a suitable observation post at about midday. Once there, he received a note from Longstreet ordering him to advise Pickett not to attack if, in Alexander's opinion, the Confederate bombardment had not proved effective. Alexander, unwilling to take responsibility for such a decision, replied, warning Longstreet that ammunition was short, and that only one attack could be supported adequately. Even if this attack was successful it would, he predicted, be 'at a very bloody cost'. This opinion was shared by Brigadier-General A.R. Wright, whose Georgia Brigade had reached the ridge the previous day. 'It is not so hard to go there as it looks', he remarked to Alexander. 'The trouble is to stay there. The whole Yankee Army is there in a bunch.'

In fact, the Confederate attacking force was comfortably superior in numbers to the Union troops opposing it—perhaps 15,000 to 8000. Nevertheless, this superiority would be reduced as the advance progressed, first by the Union artillery and then by massed volleys of rifle fire. Meade also had reserves at his immediate disposal, to commit to the *mêlée* if Pickett actually reached the crest and, good though Pickett's Virginians were, Hancock's II Corps was in no way inferior. In the early part of the war Union infantry had shown a depressing tendency to break before a Confederate assault. By Gettysburg the overall quality of Union infantry was considerably high, and Hancock's men were among the best.

The assaulting units shook out into order west of Seminary Ridge. On the right was Pickett's division, with two brigades up and one in support. To Pickett's left stood four brigades of Heth's division, now commanded by Major-General J.J. Pettigrew who had taken over from the

Left: General George Pickett, whose heroic charge failed to break the Union forces. It was the most daring action of the battle and one of the most impressive infantry attacks in military history.

wounded Heth. Major-General Isaac Trimble, with two brigades from Pender's division, was to Pettigrew's right rear. Although the attack is usually known as Pickett's charge, Pickett himself had no authority over Pettigrew and Trimble.

At exactly 1300 two guns were fired by the Confederate Washington Artillery, signaling the beginning of the bombardment. The Confederate guns opened fire immediately, and Meade's artillery replied. For about half an hour the battle continued unabated, with clouds of dense smoke filling the depression between the ridges, and, in Alexander's words, 'missiles from every direction'. At 1325 Alexander was forced to advise Pickett to advance at once or not at all, otherwise ammunition would not permit him to give adequate support. No sooner had Alexander sent this note than the Union fire slackened as Hunt's guns withdrew from the Cemetery. Alexander sent a note to Pickett saying 'for God's sake, come quick'.

Pickett had, in fact, asked Longstreet whether he should advance when he received Alexander's

Far left: Union artillery fires at point-blank range into Confederate forces during the closing stages of the final day of the battle. **Left:** 'Furling the Flag'. All Southern hopes of retaining their independence and winning the war faded after Vicksburg and Gettysburg. **Below:** Union forces charge Confederate batteries.

reopened by Confederate guns. Those batteries with shells at hand fired with good effect as the infantry began to breast the rise, and were joined by the remaining batteries as the Confederates came within canister range. The Union infantry joined in at a range of about 200 yards. The effect on the advancing infantry was terrible. The Confederate ranks writhed like some hideous monster in agony, but continued to advance. Pettigrew's men were particularly hard hit, but Pickett surged on, reinforced by Trimble. With a low roar the leading elements of Pickett's division crashed into the Union lines, crossing a stone wall and engaging Union gunners and infantry in hand-to-hand combat. The fate of the battle, and, indeed of the war, hung in the balance. Hancock, however, had reserves at hand, and threw them in, while to his left a brigade of Vermonters moved forward and opened a brisk fire into Pickett's right flank, in an action similar to the British 52nd Regiment at Waterloo.

The gallant Confederate infantry could stand it no longer. Pettigrew's men, who had suffered heavily on 1 July, were the first to give ground. The survivors of Pickett's and Trimble's divisions followed. There were few enough of them; about half the attackers had been killed, wounded or captured. Pickett's division alone lost nearly 2900 men out of the 5000 who had initially moved over the crest of Seminary Ridge. Union losses, it is true, were not light. Hancock himself had been seriously wounded, his infantry were exhausted, and several of his batteries were crippled. Nevertheless, the Union line had held; Pickett's men had, despite their bravery and sacrifice, in the words of one Rebel, 'gained nothing but glory'.

Lee rode about the eastern slopes of Cemetery Hill alone, rallying the survivors of the charge. An English eyewitness described his conduct as 'perfectly sublime'. He rode slowly amongst the scattered groups of men, many of them wounded, and encouraged them to 'bind up their hurts and take up a musket'. The repulse, he told them, was his fault, not theirs, but they must rally now in case Meade counterattacked.

Meade considered his command in no condition to take the offensive. He had fresh troops available—part of VI Corps—but believed that a counterstroke was far too hazardous. His failure to turn the Confederate repulse into a rout was to cause Lincoln considerable dissatisfaction, but, under the circumstances, there was much logic behind Meade's refusal to compromise his victory.

There were many Confederates who hoped for a renewal of the action on 4 July, but Lee realized that he must withdraw to Virginia to reorganize. He ordered Ewell to fall back during the night to a position in line with Hill and Longstreet, in case of a Union counterattack. He then set about making arrangements for the transport of his wounded. Many of these could not be collected, and had to be left as a further burden on the already overworked Union medical services. Brigadier-General John Imboden, whose cavalry brigade had reached Gettysburg at noon on 3 July, was ordered to escort the column of wounded. Imboden moved out along the Chambersburg Pike, and then swung south to Williamsport, Maryland, where he crossed the Potomac.

first note. Longstreet, in an agony of indecision, could not bring himself to reply. Pickett saluted, galloped forward to his division, and began his advance. Longstreet rode over for an inconclusive conference with Alexander; while the two men were talking, Pickett's division emerged from cover. The Confederate guns ceased fire as the advancing troops passed through them and for some minutes a relative calm descended on the battlefield. There can have been few more impressive sights in the whole of military history than when the 15,000 men of Pickett, Pettigrew and Trimble marched down the slope of Seminary Ridge and into the valley beyond. They were in excellent order, with officers dressing the ranks as if on parade, colors fluttering overhead, and the July sun glinting off fixed bayonets.

The Union artillery opened up in earnest as the infantry reached the valley. Hunt's guns had, in fact, suffered surprisingly little. He had not intended to let them reply to the Confederate bombardment, but had been overruled by Hancock. The latter's batteries had expended most of their shells and roundshot but had canister available, a round with a devastating anti-personnel effect up to about 250 yards. The Union infantry, too, had suffered relatively few casualties from shellfire. Many of them were under cover and, on a ridgetop, they offered a difficult target; a good number of Confederate shells passed over the ridge to burst in the hollow to the east.

The Union gunners concentrated their fire on the advancing infantry, oblivious to the fire now

The plight of the wounded, riding, with the most rudimentary of medical attention, in unsprung wagons, was worsened by a blinding rainstorm which swept the field on the afternoon of 4 July. Imboden wrote that he learned more of the horrors of war in one night than he had in all the preceding two years.

Stuart's cavalry had at last reached Gettysburg on the evening of 2 July. They were engaged against a force of Union cavalry in an inconclusive action northeast of the town on the next day, and were then employed to screen the Confederate withdrawal. A Union cavalry brigade under Brigadier-General E.J. Farnsworth launched a fruitless attack on Longstreet's right rear late on 3 July; Farnsworth was killed and the attack speedily repulsed.

Lee's Retreat

Lee's retreat began on 4 July, the day that, away to the southwest, Vicksburg fell. Meade made no attempt to follow up the Confederate withdrawal. He moved off on 5 July, and marched to Emmitsburg before swinging down to the Potomac. The Confederates reached Williamsport only to discover that the river was unusually high, so the ford could not be used; moreover, Union cavalry had previously destroyed a pontoon bridge built by the Confederates in June. Lee deployed his army around Williamsport while his engineers worked desperately on a new bridge. Meade made contact with Lee's outposts on 11 July, but his corps commanders advised against an assault on the 13th. Meade proposed to attack the following day, but discovered that the main body of Lee's army had pulled back across the completed bridge during the night of 13–14 July.

The withdrawal of the Army of Northern Virginia across the Potomac effectively ended the Gettysburg campaign. It is a campaign which probably seems more decisive in retrospect than it did at the time. Satisfactory though the result was for the Union, Lincoln was disappointed in Meade's failure to pursue and make the victory conclusive. On the Confederate side, Gettysburg was seen as a defeat rather than a disaster. Lee made no attempt to avoid the blame, and wrote to Jefferson Davis offering to resign, an offer which Davis wisely declined. The battle had, however, been fought inside Northern territory, and Union as well as Confederate casualties had been heavy. Meade's army had lost 23,000 men, and the Confederates, according to their own figures, 27,500. This was a striking heavy overall percentage; about 30% of the participants in the battle had been killed, wounded or captured.

Gettysburg certainly did not make the defeat of the South inevitable. In outright strategic terms, it was probably less significant than the fall of Vicksburg, which cut the Confederacy in half. It was, for the Confederacy, the battle of lost opportunities. Lee, Longstreet, Stuart and Ewell have all been criticized for decisions at various stages of the action. Stuart's failure to maintain contact with the Army of Northern Virginia certainly placed Lee at an initial disadvantage. It is also difficult to view Longstreet's performance without questioning his judgement, particularly on the third day of the battle. Lack of coordination characterized the Confederate attacks; Pickett's charge, magnificent though it was, was launched too late, and with inadequate support.

The Union command, too, was by no means flawless. Sickle's advance to the Peach Orchard imperiled the entire Union right; the vital Round Tops were left ungarrisoned. Meade, although behaving with praiseworthy *sang-froid* during the battle, moved extremely slowly after it despite President Lincoln's impatience to follow Lee, and missed an opportunity of inflicting another, potentially more serious defeat on Lee at Williamsport. However, Meade should not be judged too harshly. He had taken over command of the Army of the Potomac only recently, and fought a difficult encounter battle against a determined enemy. He had, furthermore, held his army together in the face of pressure which, in previous actions, had invariably brought about its collapse.

It is profitless to speculate upon what might have happened at Gettysburg had events gone only slightly differently. What is certain is that the power of Lee's infantry had been sacrificed on the slopes of Cemetery Ridge, and that the Army of Northern Virginia, splendid fighting-machine though it remained, was never quite the same again. The war had come to Gettysburg because all the roads led there; after the battle, all the roads led to Appomattox.

Left: General Henry J. Hunt, who commanded the Union artillery superbly throughout the battle. His leadership kept the Round Tops and Cemetery Ridge in Union hands.

Königgrätz

1866

Few battles in history can equal Königgrätz as an instance of the way in which a day of fighting could transform the whole political complexion of Europe. Even as the dark-coated columns of Prince Frederick Charles' army bore down on the villages along the Bistritz River in the early hours of 3 July, 1866, and the Austrian batteries on the hills above Sadowa roared into life, Prussia was reckoned the weakest of the Great Powers. Ten hours later she was indisputably in the first rank. The near-universal expectation of an Austrian victory had been confounded, and the balance of power had been unhinged. Königgrätz was probably the most decisive clash of arms of modern times.

To understand the full significance of this event

it is important to realize that since medieval times Germany had been divided into a mass of small principalities. It was a political vacuum, an arena for constant attempts by France to extend her power and influence against that of the Habsburg monarchs of Austria. Only in the mid-18th century, with the accession of Frederick the Great to the throne of Prussia, did a third contender arise in the arena. But the rise of Prussia, though spectacular from the perspective of Prussia herself, was necessarily slow and painful in European terms. At the Battle of Jena in 1806, Prussia was shattered by Napoleon, and came close to being literally erased from the map. Even after her recovery during the final stages of the Napoleonic Wars, and the generous compensation she re-

Below: A clash of Austrian and Prussian cavalry at Königgrätz.

Below: A clash of Austrian and Prussian cavalry at Königgrätz.

ceived at the Congress of Vienna in 1815, Prussia was still far inferior to Austria in terms of size, population and apparent military strength. The kings of Prussia, though greedy to extend their power in Germany, found it hard to reconcile this ambition with the strong dynastic loyalty which they still felt towards the Habsburg emperors. They took refuge in inaction and awaited events.

And events were moving in Prussia's favor. In the first half of the 19th century her population grew from 9 to 18 million, and though Austria's was still double that, the Austrian empire had no national homogeneity. More importantly, Prussia's economic strength was already far greater. Since the 1830's Prussia had been building up a German free-trade area, the *Zollverein* (customs union), which broke down old internal customs barriers. Austria attempted to join the *Zollverein*, but her economy was too weak to tolerate its low external tariff. Nonetheless, all was not plain sailing for Prussia. The decade following the 1848 revolutions saw a considerable revival of Austrian power, while within Prussia repeated clashes between the king and the liberal opposition in the national parliament led to a severe constitutional crisis over the matter of army reform in the 1860's.

The year 1862 was a significant one for Prussia. On the economic front, her European position was cemented by a free-trade treaty with France, while on the political front the king took the first step towards solving the army reform crisis by appointing as his Minister President (first minister) the brilliant and outspoken Otto von Bismarck-Schönhausen. Bismarck's appointment was seen as an alternative to a royal *coup d'état* backed by the army, whose leaders detested constitutionalism and hankered after a return to absolute monarchy. Bismarck, who was to be at odds with the army for most of his long career,

believed that some sort of constitution was necessary to unite the nation's energies behind the government.

From 1862 to 1866 he pursued a course with the simple objective of securing Prussia's parity with Austria, which inevitably involved crushing Austria's pretensions to suzerainty in Germany. He carried through the army reform measures, against the opposition of the national parliament, by the expedient of ignoring it and gathering taxes by irregular methods to carry the scheme' out. The period of military service became longer, and Prussia's standing army increased in size. Bismarck counted on the success of his foreign policy to bring the liberals round in due course to endorsing his methods, and in this calculation he proved largely correct. But he had to deal with opposition not only from the left but also from the right wing, because conservatives saw the country singled out as Bismarck's adversary, Austria, as Prussia's natural ally against France.

Fortunately for Bismarck's plans, an issue existed which would cause the gradual and inexorable exacerbation of relations between the two great German Powers. This was the question of Schleswig and Holstein, two duchies which had been a bone of contention between the German Confederation and the Kingdom of Denmark since 1848. In 1864, following a dispute over the right of succession to the duchies, Austria and Prussia together went to war against Denmark on behalf of the German Confederation. The duchies were placed under their joint control —a certain recipe for friction. Bismarck made methodical preparations, securing an alliance with Italy to pin Austria in the south, and arranging for the neutrality of France. In June 1866 the Schleswig-Holstein issue finally caught fire, and Prussia occupied the whole area. The strength

of anti-Prussian feeling in Germany became clear as the whole Confederation sided with Austria and began to mobilize: Prussia's fate now depended on her military capability.

The Ghost of Radetzky

Few people outside Prussia suspected how great that capability would prove. Friedrich Engels, then a contributor on military affairs to the *Manchester Guardian*, regarded the Prussian army as a peacetime force of untried conscripts. The ghost of Radetzky threw a halo around Austrian arms, and the strength and discipline of the Austrian cavalry and artillery were internationally renowned. Austria's army was supposedly the largest outside Russia, consisting of ten conscript classes each of 83,000, serving for eight years with the colors, and yielding a strength (including reserves) of 850,000. However, this mighty national force took a long time to turn into flesh and blood. The Austrian mobilization in 1866 began on 21 April, while Prussia took no action until the third week of May. Nevertheless when hostilities commenced, Austria had been hard put to it to produce 320,000 effective troops, and one-third of these had to be deployed against Italy, while Prussia had mustered over 350,000, of whom some 250,000 could operate immediately against Austria.

Thus one of Austria's apparent advantages vanished at the outset. Another feature which had led Engels to his verdict of Austrian superiority was the Prussian command structure. The Prussian General Staff, which was to become the model for Europe after the wars of 1866 and 1870, had not yet reached the unchallenged position it later held. In particular, the Chief-of-Staff, Helmuth von Moltke, had not even been authorized to report direct to the Minister for War until

1859, and was not authorized to issue commands to fighting units until the very start of the Austrian war, on 2 June, 1866. The uncertainty of Moltke's position led Engels to assume that the king and the princes would be interfering with the efficient control of the army. He therefore gave Austria a 'decided superiority' in supreme command, in spite of the well-known aversion of the Austrian officer-corps to staff work of any sort.

The reason for his opinion was that the general

Above: The Austrian 64th Infantry Regiment defends itself against Prussian Uhlans at Biskupitz.

Left: Count Otto von Bismarck, 'the diplomatic genius whose cunning forced the Austrians into war at the time when the Prussians under von Moltke were at their peak of fighting readiness.

The Battle of Königgrätz, 1866

The German Confederation

Austria's leadership of the German Confederation was challenged when Bismarck attempted to unite Germany under Prussia, excluding Austria. After the Danish War, Prussia allowed Austria to jointly administer Schleswig-Holstein, and when Prussia threatened to annex both provinces in 1866, Austria was obliged to fight Prussia, playing into Bismarck's hands.

Moltke's military genius and a degree of luck won the battle and the war for Prussia. If Prussia had waited for Austria to fully mobilize, Austria could have threatened Berlin through the territory of Saxony, her ally. Instead Moltke chose to take the offensive, mobilizing his forces quickly and concentrating them in Bohemia. The blitzkrieg approach was a complete success, and with Austrian forces surrounded, they were forced to capitulate. From Königgrätz onward, Germany's fate was in Prussian hands.

Boundary of the Confederation

Kingdom of Prussia

Austrian Empire

The situation on 28 June, 1866

On 15 June Prussia struck at Austria's allies Hanover and Hesse. The campaign was short and brilliant. Within two days they took possession of both countries north of a line from Cologne to Eisenach.

On 16 June the Army of the Elbe invaded Saxony, and the Saxon army fell back into Bohemia to join the main Austrian force.

Benedek was having difficulty in achieving a concentration in northern Bohemia. He disposed seven army corps, but only I Corps was concentrated forward, in the extreme northwest. The remainder moved slowly northwards from Moravia in the direction of Josefstadt.

As the Saxons fell back towards Münchengrätz they were grouped with I Corps: no other force existed which was capable of disputing a Prussian advance into Bohemia.

On 22 June the Prussian forward movement was ordered. The First Army, to which the Army of the Elbe was attached, pursued the Saxon Army, while the Second Army advanced southwards through the mountain country along the Bohemian frontier to seek a juncture in the direction of Gitschin.

The Prussian Second Army crossed the mountains in three columns; I Corps in the north advancing on Trautenau, Guard Corps in the center advancing on Politz and Eypel, and V and VI Corps to the south advancing on Nachod and Skalitz. As a screen against this army, Benedek pushed two corps northwards.

On 27 June at Nachod, the Austrian VI Corps attacked the vanguard of V Corps and almost drove it back into the mountains. On the same day, X Corps assaulted the Prussian I Corps at Trautenau and succeeded in driving them back.

On 28 June von Gablenz' X Corps tried to repeat the operation against the Prussian Guard Corps at Prausnitz, he suffered an unmitigated defeat due to lack of support from IV Corps.

On 29 June the Prussian First Army assaulted the Saxon Army at Gitschin, forcing them to retire towards the main force, around the foothills northwest of Königgrätz. For two days Benedek regrouped his forces on the line of a small tributary of the Elbe, the Bistritz.

0 Miles 10

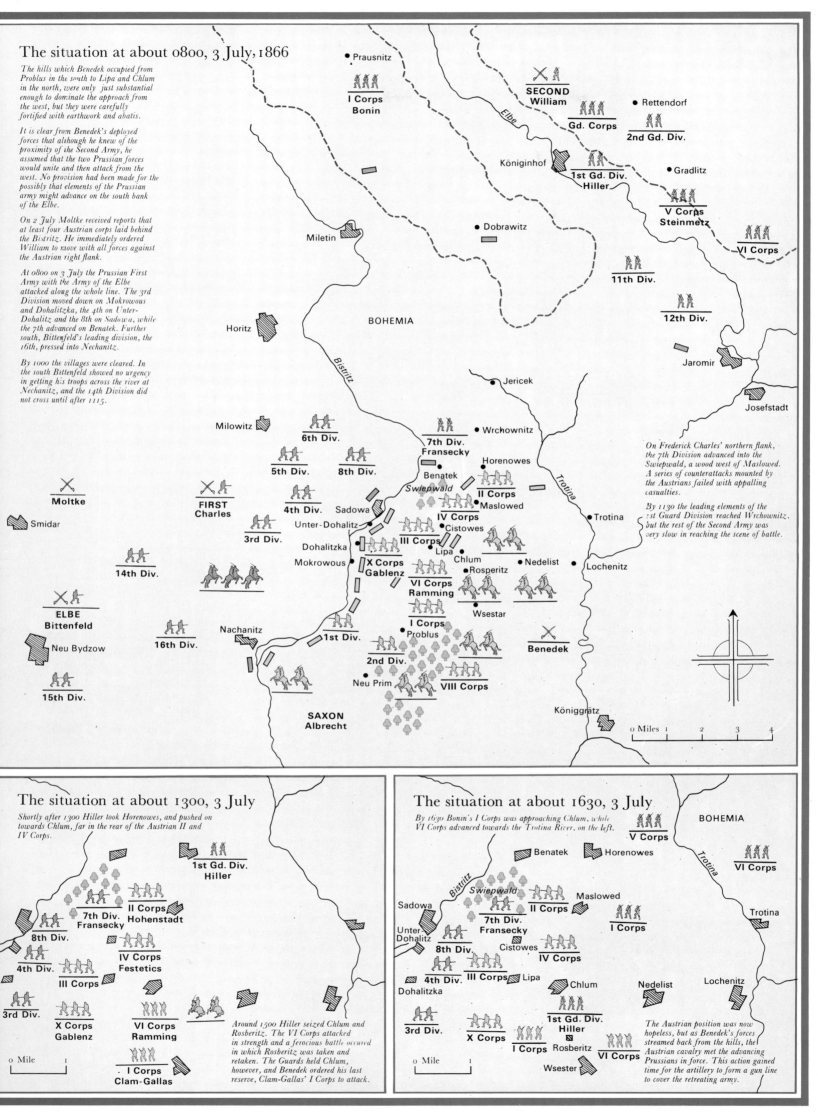

The situation at about 0800, 3 July, 1866

The hills which Benedek occupied from Problus in the south to Lipa and Chlum in the north, were only just substantial enough to dominate the approach from the west, but they were carefully fortified with earthwork and abatis.

It is clear from Benedek's deployed forces that although he knew of the proximity of the Second Army, he assumed that the two Prussian forces would unite and then attack from the west. No provision had been made for the possibly that elements of the Prussian army might advance on the south bank of the Elbe.

On 2 July Moltke received reports that at least four Austrian corps laid behind the Bistritz. He immediately ordered William to move with all forces against the Austrian right flank.

At 0800 on 3 July the Prussian First Army with the Army of the Elbe attacked along the whole line. The 3rd Division moved down on Mokrowous and Dohalitzka, the 4th on Unter-Dohalitz and the 8th on Sadowa, while the 7th advanced on Benatek. Further south, Bittenfeld's leading division, the 16th, pressed into Nechanitz.

By 1000 the villages were cleared. In the south Bittenfeld showed no urgency in getting his troops across the river at Nechanitz, and the 14th Division did not cross until after 1115.

On Frederick Charles' northern flank, the 7th Division advanced into the Swiepwald, a wood west of Maslowed. A series of counterattacks mounted by the Austrians failed with appalling casualties.

By 1130 the leading elements of the 1st Guard Division reached Wrchownitz, but the rest of the Second Army was very slow in reaching the scene of battle.

The situation at about 1300, 3 July

Shortly after 1300 Hiller took Horenowes, and pushed on towards Chlum, far in the rear of the Austrian II and IV Corps.

Around 1500 Hiller seized Chlum and Rosberitz. The VI Corps attacked in strength and a ferocious battle occured in which Rosberitz was taken and retaken. The Guards held Chlum, however, and Benedek ordered his last reserve, Clam-Gallas' I Corps to attack.

The situation at about 1630, 3 July

By 1630 Bonin's I Corps was approaching Chlum, while VI Corps advanced towards the Trotina River, on the left.

The Austrian position was now hopeless, but as Benedek's forces streamed back from the hills, the Austrian cavalry met the advancing Prussians in force. This action gained time for the artillery to form a gun line to cover the retreating army.

Far right: Wilhelm I, King of Prussia and future Kaiser of Germany. **Center:** Feldzeugmeister Ludwig August von Benedek, commander of Austria's Northern Army. **Bottom right:** Details of the famous Prussian needle-fire gun, invented by Johann Nikolaus Dreyse in 1827. This method of ignition relied on a needle or firing pin being thrust through the powder charge to a primer situated next to the bullet. The model shown is the Prussian bolt-action rifle. **Below:** General Helmuth von Moltke, who was in command of all Prussian armies, subject only to the authority of King Wilhelm himself. **Overleaf:** Prussian forces charge and break Austrian lines at Königgrätz.

appointed to command Austria's Northern Army, Feldzeugmeister Ludwig August von Benedek, was not a member of the Royal Family. Ironically enough, however, Austria's ablest high commander was a prince, Archduke Albrecht. Benedek was the most popular soldier since Radetzky, but he himself realized that he was not best suited to supreme command. Brave and energetic as a troop leader in close combat, he showed a strange lassitude in the strategic direction of a theater of war: in this respect he was curiously similar to Moltke's opponent in the war of 1870, Marshal Bazaine. Benedek had to cope with corps commanders brought up in the tradition of the Order of Maria Theresa, which encouraged heroism on the field at the expense of meticulous obedience to orders, and a command system which delivered him no less than three chiefs-of-staff for the decisive day of the campaign.

His troops also had to face the severe potential disadvantage of the Prussian infantry's capacity to dominate the battlefield with their breech-

loading rifle – the famous Dreyse 'needle gun'. Besides the sheer volume of fire which the needle-gun could deliver compared with the Austrian muzzle-loading Lorenz rifle, it enabled the Prussian infantry to develop a more dispersed tactical formation than had hitherto been possible except for sharpshooters. The Austrians, on the other hand, felt—perhaps wrongly—that they were compelled to stick to the old close formation and 'shock' tactics. In the event this compounded their ills by exposing large concentrations of troops to the rapid Prussian fire. Mass tactics might have succeeded if the short-service Prussian conscripts had lacked—as the Austrians and observers like Engels clearly expected that they would—the steadiness to stand against bayonet attacks put in with *élan*. Long before the day of Königgrätz, however, this expectation proved to be groundless.

The preliminary Prussian rail movements were complete by 6 June, but the campaign developed only hesitantly. Moltke was given direct control of the Prussian armies on 2 June, but his command was always subject to that of King Wilhelm, who remained Commander-in-Chief. It is impossible to establish precisely what Moltke's objectives were, or how far the eventual campaign accorded with his plans. For some time the Prussians assumed that the Austrians, assisted by their German allies, would take the offensive against either Berlin or Breslau, and this, together with the King's reluctance to initiate an invasion of Austria, led to a defensive concentration in two main areas, Lusatia and Silesia, covering these approaches. Meanwhile, on 15 June, secondary forces struck at Austria's allies Hanover and Hesse, about whom the king was less squeamish. The campaign was short and brilliant: as Engels reported in the *Manchester Guardian*, 'By rapid concentric moves, during which the troops showed a quite unexpected capability of supporting forced marches, they took possession in two days of all the country north of a line from Cologne to Eisenach'. On 16 June General Herwarth von Bittenfeld with three divisions, entitled the Army of the Elbe, invaded Saxony, and the Saxon army, under its capable commander Crown Prince Albrecht, began to fall back into Bohemia to join the main Austrian force.

Benedek, far from launching an invasion of Prussia, was having difficulty in even achieving a concentration in northern Bohemia. He disposed seven army corps, each normally consisting of four brigades and totaling 20–30,000 men; but only one of these, General von Clam-Gallas' I Corps, was concentrated forward, in the extreme northwest. The remainder moved slowly northward from Moravia in the direction of Josefstadt. As the Saxons fell back towards Münchengrätz they were grouped with I Corps under the overall command of the Saxon Crown Prince: no other force existed which was remotely capable of disputing a Prussian crossing into Bohemia.

The Prussian forward movement was not ordered until 22 June. As late as 18 June Moltke was writing to the Chief-of-Staff of the First Army, 'Day and night my thoughts turn to the question of how we can make both armies as strong as possible, no matter which of them the main Austrian army attacks'. The armies in question were the First, commanded by the King's nephew Prince Frederick Charles, to which the Army of the Elbe was attached, and the Second under the heir apparent, Crown Prince Frederick William. Both were of considerable strength, the First and Elbe having nine infantry divisions, one *Landwehr* division, and a cavalry corps (the strength of a Prussian division was 15,000), while the Second had eight divisions. But the two groups were separated by 70 miles of mountain country along the Bohemian frontier. Because of this, the order of 22 June that they should advance separately 'and seek a juncture in the direction of Gitschin' has been among the most heavily criticized in military history, for if the Austrians had moved swiftly each wing would have been exposed to the risk of meeting the whole Austrian army—a risk aggravated by the difficulty of crossing the mountains; until the evening of 2 July the Prussians had no knowledge of Benedek's whereabouts. Engels, who did not

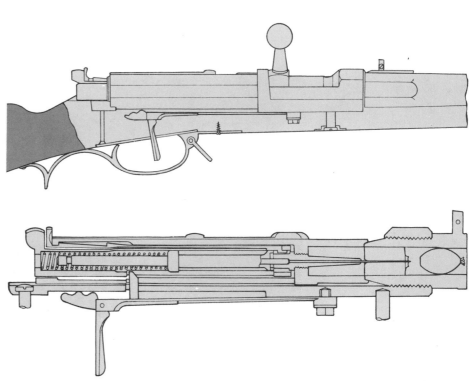

know that the order was Moltke's, was astounded. 'It would be completely inexplicable', he wrote, 'how such a plan could ever be discussed, much less adopted, by a body of such unquestionably capable officers as the Prussian general staff—if it was not for the fact of King William being in chief command.' He offered the Prussian soldiers only one hope: 'if they ever get out of the difficulties into which their generals so wantonly placed them they will have to thank the needle-gun for it'.

It is hard to dismiss such criticisms of the Prussian maneuver. One modern writer has pointed out in its defense that it would have been physically impossible to concentrate the whole Prussian army on a single line of advance: even as it was, the supply situation became critical within a few days of the invasion. It nonetheless remains true that Moltke's idea of 'forward concentration' was extremely ambitious, and rested on a number of as yet unproven assumptions about the Austrian reaction. As late as 29 June, for instance, when the Saxon Crown Prince's army was still holding Gitschin against Frederick Charles, Benedek's main force of six infantry and one cavalry corps was hovering over the four corps of the Prussian Second Army on the upper Elbe. Fortunately for the Prussian Crown Prince, Benedek had a fixed idea of marching to join the battle against Frederick Charles, and no amount of opportunity in the other direction could draw him away.

Benedek's intention was curious in view of the distance which Frederick Charles would have to cover in order to reach the theater of operations on the Elbe, and the slowness of his advance—for despite his overwhelming superiority to Crown Prince Albrecht's group he moved with almost exaggerated caution. His watchword was that 'There is no loftier or simpler law in strategy than to hold one's strength together'. In consequence his forces became piled up to a depth of over a day's march by 25 June, and supplies became almost impossible to obtain. Worse still, from a military point of view, nothing was done to find

out what enemy units might be ahead: the large cavalry corps stayed well back down the line of march. On 26 June, as the Second Army was moving across the mountains 50 miles away, Moltke wired that 'only a vigorous advance by the First Army could disengage the Second'. Frederick Charles remained unmoved, and took his time to organize a massive turning operation against the defenses on the River Iser between Münchengrätz and Podol on 28 June. Only when he was infuriated by finding nothing but the Saxon rearguard vanishing under his hammer-stroke did he really hasten his advance toward Gitschin.

Benedek, who in his intentions conformed exactly to Moltke's expectations, had planned to join Crown Prince Albrecht at Gitschin, and Albrecht thus prepared his first full-scale defense against Frederick Charles before that town. On 29 June, however, as this battle opened, Benedek was, as we remarked, still in the Josefstadt—Miletin area, and Albrecht was forced to extricate himself as best he could from a heavy engagement. Benedek's behavior at this point is difficult to fathom, especially his conclusion that the Crown Prince's army was moving northward and could safely be ignored. The border battles which had taken place against this army on 27 and 28 June had shown the daunting steadiness of the Prussian infantry, but they had also indicated how great an opportunity had been placed in the Austrian lap.

The Prussian Second Army crossed the mountains in three columns—I Corps in the north advancing on Trautenau, Guard Corps in the center advancing on Politz and Eypel, and V and VI Corps to the south advancing on Nachod and Skalitz. As a screen against this army, Benedek pushed two corps northward, and both mounted vigorous attacks upon the Prussians. At Nachod on 27 June, Lieutenant-Field-Marshal Freiherr von Ramming's VI Corps struck the vanguard of General von Steinmetz' V Corps and almost drove it back into the mountain defile, though Steinmetz' determination and the astonishing tenacity of his troops eventually broke the Austrian impetus. On the same day, Lieutenant-Field-Marshal von Gablenz' X Corps assaulted the Prussian I Corps so ferociously at Trautenau that the Prussians were thrown right back across the mountains and their commander, General von Bonin, never recovered his nerve. But this victory

Left: Frederick Charles, the Prussian Prince who worried von Moltke. He was prepared to move more quickly when the moment of victory was at hand.

was gained at heavy cost to the Austrians, who lost nearly 4800 officers and men killed and wounded, against a Prussian total of 1338. When von Gablenz tried to repeat the operation next day against the Guard Corps at Prausnitz, he suffered an unmitigated defeat due to lack of promised support from Lieutenant-Field-Marshal Count Festetics' IV Corps.

These border battles, coupled with the Austro-Saxon retreat from Gitschin, at last brought Benedek to realize—indeed to exaggerate—the seriousness of his position. On 30 June he telegraphed to the Emperor Franz Joseph that 'catastrophe for the army is unavoidable' and begged him to make peace at any price. The Emperor replied, not unnaturally, that this was impossible at this stage; while Benedek for his part grew more confident as he saw the possible strength of a defensive position in the hills northwest of Königgrätz.

For two days he regrouped his forces on the line of a small tributary of the River Elbe, the Bistritz. The hills which he occupied, from Problus in the south to Lipa and Chlum in the north, were only just substantial enough to dominate the approach from the west, but they were carefully fortified with earthwork and with *abatis* cut from the Holawald, a wood of some 1600 square yards

Left: The Prussian 14th Division crosses the Bistritz before Königgrätz.

127

Above: Four types of Austrian and Prussian weapons. (Top to bottom): Austrian Jägerstützen, cavalry carbine and 'extra-corps' gun, all three pre-dating the Prussian needle-gun (bottom), a model of 1862.

which lay between the Lipa Hill and the village of Sadowa on the Bistritz. The Austrian artillery, a superb arm of 770 guns, nearly all rifled, was positioned with careful regard to fields of fire, and fired measured ranges on the Lipa front. The troops which held the line can be divided into four groups. In the north-central (Chlum-Lipa) sector were III and X Corps, totaling 44,000 men and 134 guns. In the southern (Problus) sector, stood the Saxon Corps and VIII Corps with some 40,000 men and 140 guns. In the northeastern sector, between Chlum and Nedelist, were II and IV Corps with 55,000 men and 176 guns. Finally,

Right: Lieutenant-Field-Marshal Wilhelm Freiherr von Ramming, in charge of the Austrian VI Corps.

around Wsestar stood a large infantry reserve of I and VI Corps, some 47,000 men, with the cavalry corps of 11,435 and a massive reserve artillery of 320 guns.

A glance at the map will suffice to show that this position was unequivocally oriented toward the west. Its northern flank was dominated by the unoccupied Horenowes Hill, its northeastern flank in the Nedelist-Lochenitz area was open, and no provision had been made for the apparently unimagined possibility that elements of the Prussian Second Army might advance on the south bank of the Elbe. It is clear from Benedek's behavior that although he knew of the proximity of the Second Army, he assumed that the two Prussian armies would unite, perhaps in the Gitschin-Miletin area, and then attack his force on the front on which he himself wished to fight. His lax attitude to the fateful initiative of his northern corps commanders in moving their fronts around to bear westwards at the outset of the battle shows his refusal to think in terms of a threat from the north.

At Prussian headquarters on 2 July there was in fact some pressure to do what Benedek expected, but Moltke held out against uniting the armies. Owing to the atrocious failure of Prussian reconnaissance, nobody had any idea where the Austrians were. (It is significant that although the Second Army had been fighting two enemy corps on 27 and 28 June, contact had been so thoroughly lost that there was some doubt whether the Crown Prince would arrive at the Bistritz battle in time to assist Frederick Charles, who on 29 June had been 20 miles away from Benedek's army.) Moltke showed here the imperturbable flexibility which was the essence of his strategic method. When, during the evening of 2 July, patrols finally brought news that at least four enemy corps lay behind the Bistritz, his reaction was decisive. Exclaiming '*Gott sei dank!*' he sent orders to the Crown Prince to move 'with all forces against the right flank of the presumed enemy order of battle, attacking as soon as possible'.

Frederick Charles, now thoroughly aroused, was as anxious as Moltke to begin attacking the Austrians, and it was only with difficulty that he could be persuaded that his function was only to pin them frontally while his cousin made the decisive maneuver. His troops began to move forward at 0700 on 3 July, and when the King and Moltke arrived at his headquarters around 0800 an attack along the whole line was ordered. Frederick Charles was bitterly disappointed that he was not to be allowed to make the decisive attack, but he did his duty. Three of his divisions moved down on the villages on the Bistritz below Lipa—the 3rd Division on Mokrowous and Dohalitzka, the 4th on Unter-Dohalitz and the 8th on Sadowa—while the 7th Division moved on Benatek. Further south, Herwarth's leading division, the 16th, pressed into Nechanitz.

After a stubborn defense the Saxons and Austrians retired in good order to higher ground, pouring a destructive fire from cover into the smoke enveloping the Prussian columns, whose needle-guns could find few targets. By 1000 the villages were cleared, but the 3rd Division then came to a halt under punishing artillery fire. Under Lipa the 4th and 8th Divisions suffered still more, with only the scanty cover of the Holawald and the now blazing villages of Sadowa and Unter-Dohalitz to protect them from the fire of seventeen Austrian batteries using measured ranges, and reinforced during the morning to total 160 guns. In the south, Herwarth showed no urgency in getting his troops across the river at Nechanitz, and the 14th Division did not cross until after 1115. Although his smoke could be seen advancing toward the Prim-Problus position throughout the morning, around midday his movement halted for some two hours following a Saxon counterattack. Herwarth seems to have been fearful that Frederick Charles' center would give way, and so was unwilling to risk isolating himself by carrying out what might have proved to be a decisive movement on the exposed Austro-Saxon flank.

Herwarth's sluggishness with his large force made a sharp contrast with the situation on Frederick Charles' northern flank, where the issue of the battle was finally to hinge, and where a single Prussian division, the 7th, was to engage no

Above: Austrian infantry and cavalry charge Prussian squares at Königgrätz.

less than two Austrian corps. The Austrian right wing, consisting of Festetics' IV Corps and Count von Thun-Hohenstadt's II Corps, had originally been placed by Benedek under the Chlum bastion on a line with Nedelist and Lochenitz, but the two commanders, urged on by their chiefs-of-staff, had decided that their prepared positions were dominated by the hill of Horenowes to the north. They therefore moved out on to the line Maslowed—Horenowes, turning their front through 90 degrees to the west and leaving only one infantry brigade and a light cavalry division to cover the approaches from the north on Nedelist and Lochenitz. In the long run this astonishing oversight was to have catastrophic consequences for the Austrians, and even though in the short term it piled enormous pressure on the Prussian 7th Division, the latter's courageous advance caused a disproportionate number of enemy troops to be embroiled in an unnecessary battle.

When the general advance began at 0830 the vanguard of the 7th Division under Colonel von Zychlinski was already pressing through Benatek, and the divisional commander, Lieutenant General von Fransecky, decided to drive on into the Swiepwald, a wood west of Maslowed and north of Cistowes which measured some 2000 yards along the Austrian front and 1200 yards deep. Denser and more solid than the Holawald, the Swiepwald climbed a ridge running south from

Left: Austrians suffer casualties in the Swiepwald.

Benatek and rose up over a substantial hill of 920 feet (50 feet higher than the hill of Chlum). Zychlinski stormed into the wood supported by the 14th Brigade, led on by its commander Major-General von Gordon with the strange cry of 'Fresh fish! Good fish!', and succeeded in expelling its defenders, part of Brandenstein's brigade of IV Corps. A series of counterattacks mounted in ever-increasing strength by the Austrians failed with appalling casualties, and by mid-morning three of Festetics' brigades, those of Brandenstein, Poekh and Fleischhacker, had been broken, and Festetics himself had been wounded. His deputy, Mollinary, proved even more determined to hurl the Prussians out of the Swiepwald, and called on II Corps to supply further fresh troops. Fransecky's position was becoming desperate, and would have been hopeless if the Austrians had employed II Corps against his flank. But by this time the Austrian commitment was growing suicidal: around 1130 Benedek received his first intimation that the unthinkable was about to

occur—the Prussian Second Army might arrive on the battlefield at any moment.

In fact the leading units of the 1st Guards Division were already at Wrchownitz, having set out from Dobrawitz immediately on receiving a message, sent by Fransecky as he started his attack on the Swiepwald, urgently requesting support for his open left flank. But apart from this division, and the Guard Corps reserve artillery under the adventurous leadership of Prince Kraft zu Hohenlohe-Ingelfingen, the rest of the Second Army was very slow in reaching the scene of battle. Bonin's I Corps, still smarting from its experience at Trautenau, was especially hesitant. Moreover, in view of the fact that Moltke has often been thought to have planned a 'battle of encirclement' against the Austrians, the commander of the Second Army displayed an odd vagueness about his role. Prince Hohenlohe recorded that around 1130, while he was at Chotoborek preparing to attack the Austrian screening force at Jericek, the Crown Prince rode

awaiting his moment to go over to the offensive against Frederick Charles. Admittedly, prospects on the Bistritz line still seemed good: the defense was holding and the immobilized Prussians were becoming increasingly exhausted. At King Wilhelm's headquarters nerves were frayed, with only Moltke preserving an almost theatrical calm. When the King asked him about preparations for a possible retreat, Moltke replied 'Here there will be no retreat. Here the existence of Prussia is at stake', adding, with an optimism which others did not share, 'Your Majesty will today win not just the battle, but the campaign'. Moltke was right: Benedek took no action, even on the dangerously weak south flank where the Saxon defense was slowly crumbling in face of superior numbers. Around 1500, when a staff officer dashed into his headquarters with the news that the Prussians had seized Chlum, Moltke refused to believe him.

'A Terrible Moment'

A war correspondent watching the battle from Königgrätz gave a dramatic description of the scene as Hiller's troops hurled the Austrians—who were, incredibly, taken completely by surprise—out of Chlum and pressed down into Rosberitz.

'It is a terrible moment. The Prussians see their advantage, and enter at once into the very center of the position. In vain the Austrian staff officers fly to the reserves, and hasten to call back some of the artillery from the front. The dark blue regiments multiply on all sides, and from their edges roll perpetually sparkling musketry. Their guns hurry up, and from the slope take both the Austrian main body on the extreme right, and the reserves in flank. They spread away to the woods near the Prague road . . . The lines of dark blue which came in sight from the right teemed from the vales below, as if the earth yielded them.'

In fact, fortunately for the Austrians, the Prussians had not arrived in such numbers as this account would imply. In addition, tactical error was compounded by utter spinelessness, as Count Thun, who had extricated two untouched brigades from the Swiepwald combat, now marched them straight off the battlefield towards the Elbe. Major-General von Appiano, whose brigade had held Chlum itself, followed suit. Benedek at last awoke to the peril and began to show his fighting qualities. Ramming's VI Corps was moved up and, after a tremendous bombardment by the reserve artillery which reduced Chlum and Rosberitz to rubble, put in attack after attack against Hiller's division. A ferocious struggle developed in which Rosberitz was taken and re-taken, with terrible casualties on both sides. The Prussian Guards held Chlum, however, and eventually brought Ramming's assault to a standstill, at the same time fighting off a carefully planned attack by the Austrian III Corps from Lipa. Time after time the Austrian infantry, coming forward in close columns, was cut to pieces by withering needle-gun fire. Eventually Benedek withdrew Ramming and threw in his last reserve, Clam-Gallas' I Corps, to make possible the retreat of the remainder of his army. Once again the attack was pressed with suicidal courage: a quarter of the Austrian casualties at

up to assess the situation. Having previously assumed that Benedek was withdrawing across the Elbe, he now realized that the whole Austrian army was engaged against Frederick Charles, and that this was the decisive battle. 'I have two choices', he said. 'I can march to join him, but it's too far and I'd get there too late, or I can go straight ahead and take them in flank and rear. Take a look at that big tree—that's the Austrian right flank. Keep that on your right! And bang away, so that Fritz Karl will know I'm here!'

This decision to turn the advance slightly eastward toward Horenowes was a crucial one, but it is curious that the Crown Prince could have thought that any other course might be envisaged. The 1st Guard Division now began to press on under its thrustful commander, Freiherr Hiller von Gartringen, while the as yet unblooded VI Corps moved on the left toward the Trotina River. Shortly after 1300 Hiller took Horenowes and, calmly ignoring an order to stand fast until VI Corps had come up to forestall any possible Austrian flanking move, pushed on around Maslowed towards Chlum itself, far in the rear of the Austrian II and IV Corps.

It was now nearly two hours since Benedek had received warning of the Crown Prince's approach, but he behaved as though he was determined to shut his mind to the nightmare. No reconnaissance was made to follow the progress of the Prussian advance. He issued belated orders to IV Corps, which virtually disregarded them, to remain in line with III Corps, and he also ordered part of his reserve, VI Corps, to move up to the north-eastern flank. But the latter order was almost immediately countermanded, for he was still

Königgrätz were suffered by I Corps. The Prussian Guards' feat in holding Chlum—Rosberitz was even more astonishing than had been that of the 7th Division in the Swiepwald, but by 1630 the pressure was almost unbearable, and Hohenlohe's artillery was beginning to run out of ammunition. At this point Hiller at last heard that Bonin's I Corps was coming up behind him, seconds before he was killed by a shell-splinter.

Austria's Position Collapses

The Austrian position was now crumpling up, but thanks to the courage and discipline of his artillery and cavalry Benedek was able to stave off total disaster. As XI Corps, the battered III Corps and some remnants of II and IV Corps streamed back from the hills, protected in the south by the gallant Saxons, who maintained their discipline to the end, the Austrian cavalry cantered forward to meet the advancing enemy. In the face of punishing infantry fire, a total of $39\frac{1}{2}$ squadrons of the finest horse in Europe carried out a succession of charges, and persuaded the Prussians of the folly of attempting to pursue the retreating army. Besides dislocating the Prussian cavalry, this great mounted action also gained time for the Austrian reserve artillery under von Hofbauer to form a gun line to cover the withdrawal of the infantry. The artillery continued to rake the field to the end of the day with such coolness and precision, that, as the Prussian General Staff study later admitted, the victors had no idea of the extent of the Austrian collapse. True to the form he had shown throughout the day, General Herwarth did not press his victory on the Austro-Saxon left wing. Had he done so, it is hard to see how Benedek could have saved more than a small fraction of his command, especially in view of the chaos which reigned when the fleeing troops reached Königgrätz, where no preparations had been made to get them across the Elbe. As it was, however, the Prussians came to a thankful halt amidst the gathering dusk. Moltke's orders for pursuit the following day were half-hearted.

The Prussian army had lost 359 officers and 8794 men altogether, of whom 99 officers and 1830 men were killed. Austrian losses totaled 1313 officers and 41,499 men, of whom 330 officers and 5328 men were killed, 509 officers and 21,661 men captured, and 43 officers and 7367 men missing. The casualties of the Saxon corps were 55 officers and 1446 men, with 15 officers and 120 men dead. A sergeant from the famous Austrian 'Black and Yellow' Brigade told a German newspaper correspondent, 'We have surely done whatever may be expected from brave soldiers, but no man can stand against that rapid fire'. Still, as observers such as Engels conceded, one could not attribute the victory to a weapon alone. The battle was won largely because the ordinary Prussian soldier showed a courage and steadiness which no one had thought possible among short-service conscripts.

Thanks to the Prussian failure to pursue, the Austrian Royal and Imperial Army of the North remained in the field after 3 July, and when preliminary peace moves had no result, the Emperor Franz Joseph summoned troops from the victorious Army of the South (which, under the command of Archduke Albrecht, had defeated the Italians at Custoza) to join it. A junction was effected on 22 July near Vienna after a hectic retreat by Benedek; but the outcome of any future combat could scarcely be in doubt. Definitive peace preliminaries were signed on 26 July.

The military victory of Königgrätz—the battle was so named by the King of Prussia in his victory telegraph—encompassed a political revolution in Europe. Austria agreed to the dissolution of the German Confederation and the establishment of a new organization of Germany without the participation of the Austrian Imperial State. The dualism of Prussia and Austria in Germany was at an end; a new North German Confederation was set up in which Saxony was placed under Prussian tutelage, and Schleswig-Holstein, Hanover and Hesse were annexed to Prussia. The main hurdle in the way of German unification had been cleared, and the balance of power in Europe yawed alarmingly —most alarmingly from the point of view of the French, to whom the threat of the future was obvious. Four years later, Bismarck was to use war against France as the occasion for drawing the remaining southern states of Germany into a new German Empire—a 'Second Reich'—evoking echoes of the Middle Ages.

Equally significantly, Prussia's internal balance had shifted. Bismarck's policies were successful, and he reaped the rewards of success. The majority of liberals, amidst an excess of nationalist emotion, endorsed the illegal regime of 1862-66, and consented to the establishment of a constitution for the North German Confederation which was decidedly authoritarian in character. At the same time the army, most of whose chiefs resented the fact that there was any constitution at all, drew from its triumph in war an intense pride, mystique and arrogance which increasingly made it seem like a 'state within the state' with ambitions to control the development of national policy. Germany emerged on the European stage as a thoroughly disquieting political and military phenomenon.

Below: The fighting at Chlum proved the Prussians' tenacity in holding off a fierce Austrian assault.

Sedan

1870

If the dramatic Prussian victory at Königgrätz came as a shock to the Austrians, it was hardly less of a surprise for the French. The Second Empire of Napoleon III owed its prestige largely to its army, which had itself defeated the Austrians in 1859, and the implications of Königgrätz were, consequently, serious. Prussia had taken only six weeks to inflict a crushing defeat upon Austria, whereas in 1859 the French had taken considerably longer to win two infinitely less conclusive victories. The more perceptive French soldiers recognized the threat, and Königgrätz lent new urgency to their demands for military reform.

French diplomats and politicians, too, were nonplussed by Königgrätz and the subsequent creation of the North German Confederation. French demands for territorial cessions on the left bank of the Rhine were rejected by Bismarck, and France found herself without compensation for her non-intervention in the war. It was apparent to most Frenchmen that conflict with Prussia was, sooner or later, inevitable, but the growing liberalization of Napoleon's regime made harsh military service legislation impossible. The military reform of 1868 fell far short of the aims of its warmest advocate, the able Marshal Niel. More Frenchmen became liable for military service, but the reserve remained inadequately trained and the *Garde Mobile*, the French equivalent of the Prussian *Landwehr*, existed only on paper. The new law would not, moreover, take full effect for several years. Disaster might yet have been averted had French foreign policy reflected the temporary inferiority of French arms. Unfortunately the Imperialists, seeing their position at home weakened by the Liberal Empire, demanded, with increasing vigor, a hard line against Prussia. This policy led to a diplomatic clash over Luxembourg in 1867 and, in July 1870, to the confrontation which brought about the Franco-Prussian War.

One of the ironies of the situation was that, despite 1866, the French army appeared in many respects more than a match for the Prussians. It had considerable experience; French soldiers had fought in the Crimea, in Italy and in Mexico, but it was in Algeria that reputations had been made and new doctrines developed. The French invasion of Algeria in 1830 had been followed by years of intermittent fighting, and had witnessed the rise of a new style of commander and a new sort of tactics. Dash, drive and initiative were what mattered; the serried line of battle was replaced by the flying column, the European

concept of major war by a series of ambushes and skirmishes. Algeria produced troops to match its tactics; *Spahis* and *Turcos*, *Chasseurs d'Afrique* and *Zouaves* gave fresh opportunities to the military tailor and dazzled an infatuated France with new tales of martial prowess.

Useful though the Algerian experience was, it was all 'in the small change of war', and was not strictly relevant to European conflict. There was, indeed, much in the Army of the Second Empire which made it ill-suited for a continental war. Its organization and training emphasized quality at the expense of quantity; the French were to find themselves at a constant numerical disadvantage in 1870. In 1866 a new infantry rifle, the *Chassepot*, had been adopted, but the tactics upon which its successful use depended had not been fully developed. French artillery had remained muzzle-loading, and France's possession of a machine-gun, the *Mitrailleuse*, was to do little to remedy the inadequacy of her field-guns. There were also serious deficiencies in the training of

Right: General Helmuth von Moltke, who exceeded his own great reputation created at Königgrätz by his overwhelming victory over the French at Sedan.
Center right: Prince Frederick Charles of Prussia, whom Moltke ordered to attack Metz, the French fortress in Lorraine.
Opposite right: General Bourbaki, commander of the French Army of the East in 1870.

staff officers and senior commanders, while the commissariat, the *Intendance*, was not equipped to deal with the problems posed by a major war.

Although the Prussian army had less experience than the French, its recent history made it much better suited to overcoming the organizational and administrative difficulties entailed in a struggle against another major European power. Its command and staff had learned invaluable lessons from 1866, its commissariat was well organized and its mobilization procedure skillfully prepared. The needle-gun might be inferior to the *Chassepot*, but Prussian artillery was notably more effective than that of the French. Furthermore, in 1870 Prussia would not fight alone. The forces of the North German Confederation backed her as a matter of course and, to the surprise and dismay of the French, the South German states decided, albeit reluctantly, to take the field alongside their fellow-Germans.

The Prussian General Staff finalized its plans for the invasion of France in the winter of 1868–69. An offensive by four armies was envisaged, although in fact only three were employed in 1870. With the cooperation of the South German states, Moltke and his collaborators could expect to field 484,000 men, while the anticipated French strength was something in excess of 250,000. The First Army was to concentrate around Wittlich, the Second around Homburg and the Third, which was to include the South German contingents, around Landau. The Fourth Army was to be in reserve, but in 1870 this formation was merged with the Second Army.

French plans were less concise. There were several schemes in existence for the invasion of Germany; the favorite one laid down a three-army organization, with a projected offensive from the area of Strasbourg to sever North and South Germany, frightening the South Germans into neutrality before swinging north to deal with the Prussians. On the eve of war this plan was modified to permit cooperation with the Austrians who, it was hoped, would mobilize in support of France. This the Austrians failed to do, and furthermore, for reasons which remain obscure,

the French Order of Battle was changed during mobilization to one of eight corps operating under the command of Imperial Headquarters.

War came in July 1870 as a result of the Hohenzollern candidacy. Prince Leopold of Hohenzollern-Sigmaringen had been offered the throne of Spain, vacant since the expulsion of Queen Isabella in 1868. His acceptance produced such a howl of protest from France that the scheme was dropped, but King Wilhelm refused to give the French Ambassador a formal assurance that it would never be renewed. Bismarck, who hoped that the incident would lead to war, was dismayed, but edited the celebrated Ems Telegram in such a way that the Ambassador's demand was made to appear insolent, and its rejection irrevocable. This inflamed public opinion on both sides of the Rhine, and on the afternoon of 14 July orders went out initiating the French mobilization. Prussia mobilized the following day; the recall of reserves, issue of equipment and transport of units to their concentration areas went on with a well-oiled slickness for which the German military machine became justly famous.

A Botched Mobilization

The French mobilization went less well, largely because the Minister of War, Marshal Le Boeuf, had decided to combine mobilizations and concentration in an effort to save time. Units left for the frontier before their reservists had rejoined, and the resultant chaos may be easily imagined. The lack of permanently-organized divisions and brigades meant that formations had to be patched together in haste. The brigade commander who sent an angry telegram to the Minister announcing that he could find neither his divisional commander nor his regiments was by no means an exception. There was a general lack of equipment of all sorts, and problems of food distribution led to some early lapses of discipline.

By 18 July three French corps—General Ladmirault's 4th Corps, General Frossard's 2nd Corps and Marshal Bazaine's 3rd Corps, were deployed between Metz and the frontier. To the south Marshal MacMahon's 1st Corps, composed large-

ly of troops from Algeria, was forming at Strasbourg. General Failly's 5th Corps, based at Sarreguemines and Bitche, connected the forces at Metz with MacMahon's corps at Strasbourg, while General Bourbaki and the Imperial Guard moved from Paris to Nancy. General Felix Douay's 7th Corps concentrated at Belfort. On 23 July Le Boeuf, before leaving for the frontier to take up his post as Major General (Chief-of-Staff) to the Emperor, ordered a tighter concentration in the north; Failly edged to his left, and Bourbaki took the Guard to Metz. Away in the rear, at Châlons, the 6th Corps assembled under Marshal Canrobert.

Napoleon arrived at Metz to take command on 28 July. He was physically ill and was, as the 1859 campaign had shown, no military genius; he failed to provide his army with the firm and incisive leadership which alone could save it. On 2 August Frossard took Saarbrucken, an easy if pointless success which no effort was made to exploit. Four days later the French were to be overtaken by a disaster of alarming proportions.

While the French corps shuffled into position along the frontier, in a fashion, as one historian cruelly remarked, reminiscent of customs men, the German concentration went on. Bavaria and Baden had begun their mobilization on 16 July, and Württemberg had followed two days later; over a million men reported for duty, and 462,000 of them moved to the frontier. Prince Frederick Charles, with the six corps of the Second Army advanced via Kaiserslauten towards Saarbrucken. The obstinate General von Steinmetz, commanding the First Army, moved from Trier to the Saar, coming up on the right of Frederick Charles. The Third Army, consisting of two Prussian corps, two Bavarian corps, and a division each from Baden and Württemberg, was under the command of the Crown Prince of Prussia; it concentrated in the area of Landau, taking rather longer to do so than Moltke would have wished. Moltke's plan, in fact, was for the Third Army to attack the right flank of the French corps around Metz while Frederick Charles attacked them from the front. This is reminiscent of the plan

which had won Königgrätz, and its appeal is obvious; it would have brought about a battle of encirclement east of Metz in which the full weight of the German armies could be deployed.

Steinmetz, 'the Lion of Nachod', had facilitated Prussian victory in 1866, but he was to imperil it in 1870. With scant regard for Moltke's strategy, he pushed ahead toward Saarlouis, risking entanglement with the Second Army, and becoming involved in a dispute with Moltke, appealing, over the latter's head, to the King. Even after direct orders to the contrary, he sent two of his corps, VII and VIII, toward Saarbrucken on 5 August, a move which was to bring them into contact with Frossard's 2nd Corps, holding the heights west of the town. The Battle of Spicheren flared up on the afternoon of 6 August. Frossard's men repulsed the first German attacks but as the afternoon went on, increasing pressure, particularly against his flanks, endangered Frossard's position. Although Bazaine's corps was within easy marching distance, no help came, and by the late evening Frossard was forced to retreat. His men had given a good account of themselves, but the battle augured badly for the French. Their artillery had been seriously outclassed, and Bazaine's failure to support his colleague revealed the reluctance of French commanders to march toward the sound of gunfire.

While the cannon roared at Spicheren, MacMahon was brought to battle in Alsace. The Third Army had crossed the frontier on 4 August, lacerating an outlying French division, that of General Abel Douay, at Wissembourg the same morning. MacMahon, an officer of vast experience if limited capacity, was undismayed by Douay's defeat. He asked the Emperor for more troops, and planned to make a stand on the ridge of Froeschwiller. Napoleon put Failly's corps at

Left: Marshal Bazaine, whose 3rd Corps was deployed between Metz and the frontier at the start of hostilities.

Above: Marshal Mac-Mahon, who was wounded at Sedan.

Prince. The German artillery caused frightful casualties and, as more and more German troops came up to tip the scales against MacMahon, the situation worsened. The defense collapsed at about 1630, the division sent by Failly arriving only in time to cover the retreat. Failly heard of the disaster by telegraph, and fell back precipitately toward Phalsbourg, abandoning much of his equipment.

The battles of 6 August added a new air of gloom to the hesitation already prevailing at Imperial Headquarters. For the next few days the Emperor and his advisors struggled with the crucial problem of whether to concentrate on Metz or to fall back on Châlons. The catastrophic sequence of order, counterorder and disorder exercised its baleful influence on morale, which sank to a new ebb as the weather broke and turned the retreat into a nightmare.

On 9 August the French cabinet resigned, and a new one was formed by General Cousin de Montauban, Comte de Palikao, who was to act as both President of the Council and Minister of War. Energetic steps were taken to raise both troops and money; a state of siege was declared in Paris, and Marines, destined for northern Germany, were summoned to the capital.

The Retreat Goes On

In Alsace and in Lorraine the retreat went on. Bazaine suggested a concentration on Langres, but Napoleon at once vetoed the idea, since it presupposed the abandonment of the capital. What he failed to appreciate was that the defenses of Paris made it safe from a *coup de main*; his preoccupation with the city was undoubtedly more political than military. While the northern element of the French army lay at the mercy of its vacillating commanders, the southern portion— 1st and 7th Corps, and most of 5th Corps— struggled to Lunéville, and then moved by road and rail, on Châlons. The opportunity of joining the two wings of the French army on the Nancy-Metz axis was lost, and MacMahon's withdrawal left the northern corps dangerously exposed before Metz.

Moltke remained uncertain of MacMahon's line of retreat until 9 August, when he felt confident to issue a new directive, ordering the Third Army to move on Sarreunion, while the First and Second Armies marched on Boulay and St Avold respectively. Although the German forces were not victims of chaos on the French scale, there was considerable confusion to the rear of the marching armies, and friction between Moltke and Steinmetz imposed a further stress on operations. Furthermore, the German cavalry, although more enterprising than their adversaries, were far from perfect at their vital role of reconnaissance; the cavalry of the Third Army had contrived to lose contact altogether.

The Third Army, unopposed, reached Nancy on 14 August. On the same day the leading elements of the First Army engaged the French rearguard at Borny, just east of Metz. Napoleon, by now quite worn out, had handed over command of the Army to Bazaine, and the decision was at last taken to withdraw down the Verdun road to Châlons. The French lost valuable time on 14 and

his disposal, and MacMahon at once ordered him south. Failly's failure to support MacMahon was, like Bazaine's failure to aid Frossard, to be one of the *causes célèbres* of the war. Despite MacMahon's orders, he maintained that he could only produce one division immediately; the rest of the corps would move in its own good time.

On the morning of 6 August MacMahon, with just under 50,000 men, mostly of his own corps but including elements of the 7th Corps, was attacked by the Third Army. The Froeschwiller position, like that of Spicheren, was a strong one, and throughout a blazing August day Mac-Mahon's *turcos* and *zouaves* held off the Crown

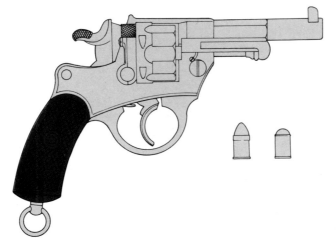

Right: A French revolver, 1869 model, used at Sedan. Caliber: 11 mm. Weight: 2.7 pounds. Capacity: six rounds. Length: 9½ inches.

15 August, much of it in forcing a way through the congested streets of Metz, and still more awaiting orders on the Gravelotte plateau. Bazaine, like Benedek, was personally brave, but totally unfitted by attitude, training or experience to command an army. He was mesmerized by the illusory security offered by Metz, and seemed reluctant to push on into open country.

On 16 August the Germans made Bazaine's decision for him. The Second Army had crossed the Moselle south of Metz on the 15th, and early the next day two German corps attacked the French advance guard at Mars-la-Tour. The Germans initially assumed that they had made contact with the French rearguard, but once the mistake was discovered they resolutely continued to attack, and as the remainder of the Second Army marched desperately to their assistance, Generals von Voigts Rhetz of X Corps and von Alvensleben of III Corps deceived Bazaine as to their real strength. A bitter day-long battle around Rezonville persuaded Bazaine that breakout to the west was impossible; he fell back onto the escarpment on the left bank of the Moselle, taking up a strong position running from St Privat in the north to Rozerieulles in the south. There, on 18 August, he was attacked in force. The Second Army bore the brunt of the battle, with the First intervening only against the extreme French left. The Prussian Guard, attacking the 6th Corps at St Privat, lost over 8000 men, but once again the German artillery proved decisive. Canrobert's men, after a brilliant defense, gave way at nightfall, laying bare Bazaine's right flank. The French fell back into Metz; they were never to leave it except as prisoners-of-war.

Napoleon had left Bazaine's army on the morning of 16 August, and had reached Châlons that evening. Châlons was, in peacetime, a huge military camp and Napoleon found it crammed with the troops making up his last army, the Army of Châlons. It included the three southern corps, 1st, 5th and 7th, parts of which were still arriving

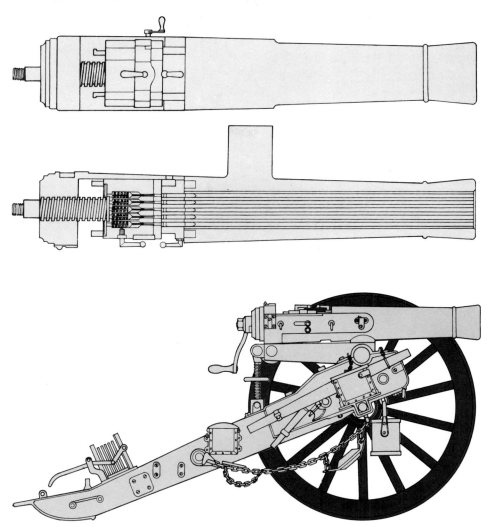

by rail. All three were badly depleted. One eyewitness pointed out that 5th Corps was in a sorry state without actually having been engaged: 'It had left one of its brigades at Sarreguemines, a part of its baggage at Bitche, its morale bit by bit on the road, and, without having fought, it was more disorganized than those which had seen the enemy'. These three corps were strengthened, if the term can properly be used in this context, by the addition of recruits of the class of 1868 who were, naturally, totally untrained.

Above: The French *Mitrailleuse*, Model 1866, used at Sedan. This 13-mm artillery piece, invented by a French Captain of Artillery, consisted of 25 barrels fired in five tiers of five bullets enveloped by a bronze cover. Its rate of fire was 130 rounds per minute with a range of 1200 yards. It weighed approximately 800 kilograms (about 1760 pounds) and required six horses to transport it.

Far left: Frederick William, Prussian Crown Prince, commanded the Third Army at Sedan.
Left: Prussian *Uhlans* enter a French town during the encirclement of Sedan.

Right: French and German cavalry engage at Mars-la-Tour, 16 August, 1870.
Below: Prussian Dragoons at Mars-la-Tour charge French infantry.

The newly-formed 12th Corps contained one division of such troops, one regular division, and a division of Marines who, although enthusiastic and bellicose, were unused to long marches.

The overall picture was uninspiring. One staff officer described the army as 'an inert crowd, vegetating rather than living'. Another witness likened Châlons to a beach with all manner of debris washed up on it. Discipline was poor; the breakdown of the *Intendance* during the retreat had made looting commonplace. Much vital equipment could not be provided; maps, guns and ambulances were all in short supply.

The army's fragile discipline was not reinforced by the presence at Châlons of eighteen battalions of Parisian *Garde Mobile*. These worthies had been close to mutiny ever since their arrival;

they loudly demanded to be sent back home, and their employment in the field was certainly open to question.

The use of the *Garde Mobile* was one of the issues discussed at a Council of War held on 17 August. It was attended by the Emperor's cousin, Prince Napoleon, MacMahon, General Trochu of the 12th Corps, his Chief of Staff, General Schmitz and General Berthaut, commander of the Parisian *Garde Mobile*. All present realized that the fate of the regime as well as that of the army hung upon their decisions. Prince Napoleon counseled an immediate return to Paris by Emperor and army, and the appointment of Trochu, a well-known liberal, as Governor of the city. It was eventually decided that Trochu would hand his corps over to General Lebrun, and depart immediately for

The Battle of Sedan, 1870

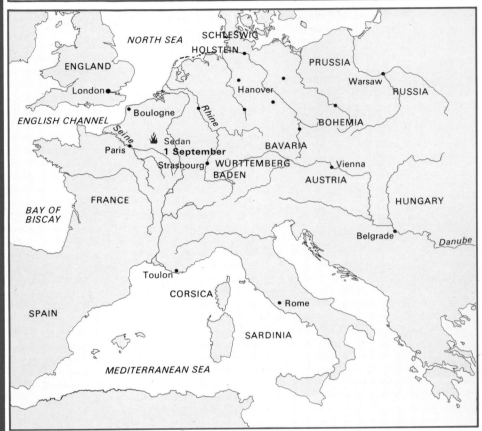

The situation on the 25 August

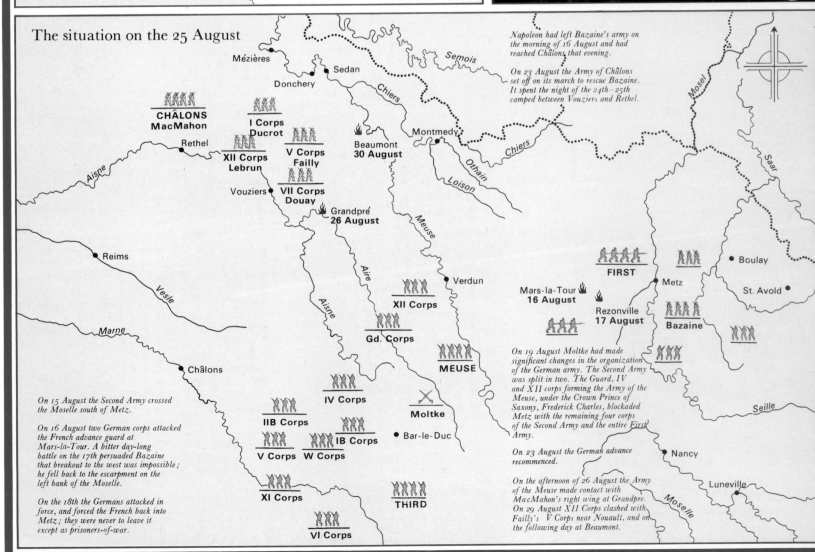

Napoleon had left Bazaine's army on the morning of 16 August and had reached Châlons that evening.

On 23 August the Army of Châlons set off on its march to rescue Bazaine. It spent the night of the 24th–25th camped between Vouziers and Rethel.

On 15 August the Second Army crossed the Moselle south of Metz.

On 16 August two German corps attacked the French advance guard at Mars-la-Tour. A bitter day-long battle on the 17th persuaded Bazaine that breakout to the west was impossible; he fell back to the escarpment on the left bank of the Moselle.

On the 18th the Germans attacked in force, and forced the French back into Metz; they were never to leave it except as prisoners-of-war.

On 19 August Moltke had made significant changes in the organization of the German army. The Second Army was split in two. The Guard, IV and XII corps forming the Army of the Meuse, under the Crown Prince of Saxony, Frederick Charles, blockaded Metz with the remaining four corps of the Second Army and the entire First Army.

On 23 August the German advance recommenced.

On the afternoon of 26 August the Army of the Meuse made contact with MacMahon's right wing at Grandpre. On 29 August XII Corps clashed with Failly's V Corps near Nouault, and on the following day at Beaumont.

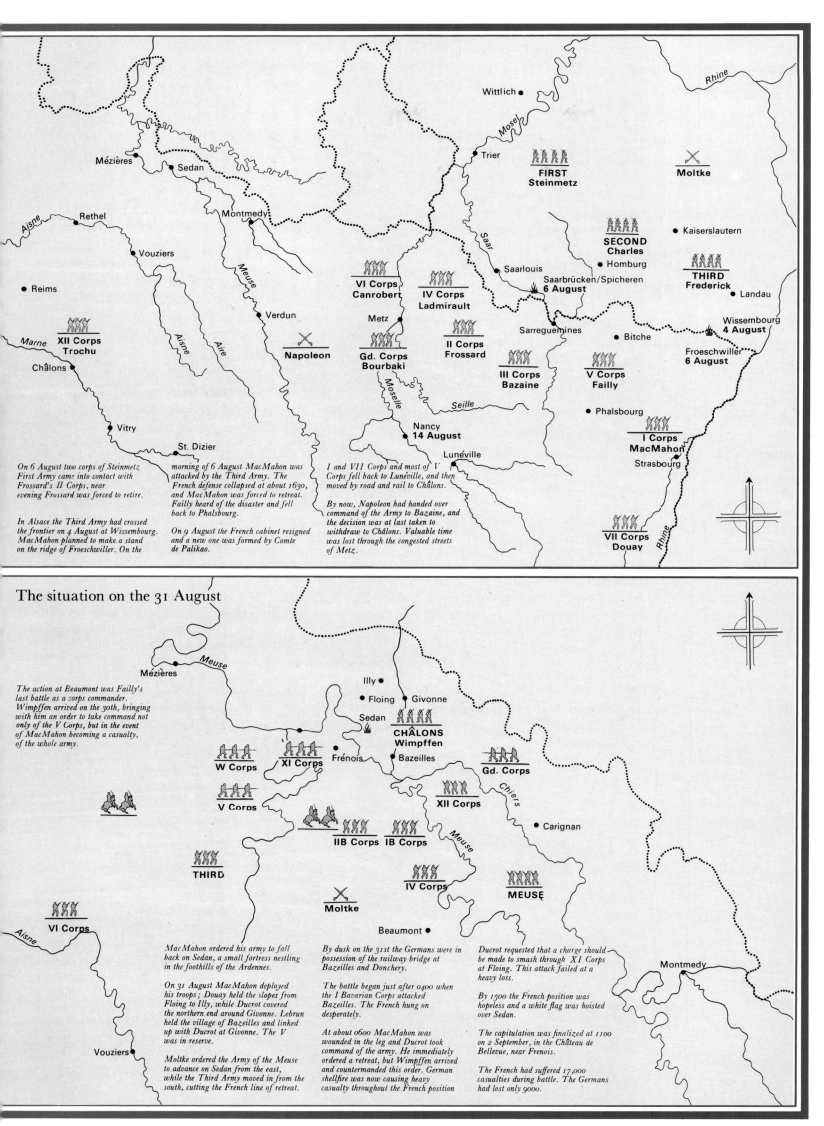

Wittlich •

Rhine

Mosel

• Trier

♟♟♟♟
FIRST
Steinmetz

⚔
Moltke

Mézières •

• Sedan

Aisne

• Rethel

Montmedy •

• Vouziers

• Kaiserslautern

♟♟♟♟
SECOND
Charles

Saar

Saarlouis •

• Homburg

♟♟♟♟
THIRD
Frederick

• Landau

• Reims

♟♟♟
VI Corps
Canrobert

♟♟♟
IV Corps
Ladmirault

Saarbrücken/Spicheren
6 August

• Verdun

Meuse

Aisne

Aire

Metz •

Sarreguemines •

• Bitche

Wissembourg
4 August

♟♟♟
XII Corps
Trochu

Marne

⚔
Napoleon

♟♟♟
Gd. Corps
Bourbaki

♟♟♟
II Corps
Frossard

Froeschwiller
6 August

Châlons •

♟♟♟
V Corps
Failly

Moselle

♟♟♟
III Corps
Bazaine

Seille

• Phalsbourg

• Vitry

• St. Dizier

Nancy
14 August

Lunéville •

♟♟♟
I Corps
MacMahon

Strasbourg •

On 6 August two corps of Steinmetz First Army came into contact with Frossard's II Corps, near evening Frossard was forced to retire.

In Alsace the Third Army had crossed the frontier on 4 August at Wissembourg. MacMahon planned to make a stand on the ridge of Froeschwiller. On the

morning of 6 August MacMahon was attacked by the Third Army. The French defense collapsed at about 1630, and MacMahon was forced to retreat. Failly heard of the disaster and fell back to Phalsbourg.

On 9 August the French cabinet resigned and a new one was formed by Comte de Palikao.

I and VII Corps and most of V Corps fell back to Lunéville, and then moved by road and rail to Châlons.

By now, Napoleon had handed over command of the Army to Bazaine, and the decision was at last taken to withdraw to Châlons. Valuable time was lost through the congested streets of Metz.

♟♟♟
VII Corps
Douay

Rhine

The situation on the 31 August

Meuse

Mézières •

Illy •

The action at Beaumont was Failly's last battle as a corps commander. Wimpffen arrived on the 30th, bringing with him an order to take command not only of the V Corps, but in the event of MacMahon becoming a casualty, of the whole army.

• Floing

Givonne •

Sedan 🔥

♟♟♟♟
CHÂLONS
Wimpffen

♟♟♟
W Corps

♟♟♟
XI Corps

• Frénois

• Bazeilles

♟♟♟
Gd. Corps

🐎🐎

♟♟♟
V Corps

♟♟♟
XII Corps

Chiers

• Carignan

🐎🐎

♟♟♟
IIB Corps

♟♟♟
IB Corps

Meuse

♟♟♟
THIRD

♟♟♟
IV Corps

♟♟♟
MEUSE

♟♟♟
VI Corps

Aisne

⚔
Moltke

Beaumont •

Montmedy

• Vouziers

MacMahon ordered his army to fall back on Sedan, a small fortress nestling in the foothills of the Ardennes.

On 31 August MacMahon deployed his troops; Douay held the slopes from Floing to Illy, while Ducrot covered the northern end around Givonne. Lebrun held the village of Bazeilles and linked up with Ducrot at Givonne. The V was in reserve.

Moltke ordered the Army of the Meuse to advance on Sedan from the east, while the Third Army moved in from the south, cutting the French line of retreat.

By dusk on the 31st the Germans were in possession of the railway bridge at Bazeilles and Donchery.

The battle began just after 0400 when the I Bavarian Corps attacked Bazeilles. The French hung on desperately.

At about 0600 MacMahon was wounded in the leg and Ducrot took command of the army. He immediately ordered a retreat, but Wimpffen arrived and countermanded this order. German shellfire was now causing heavy casualty throughout the French position

Ducrot requested that a charge should be made to smash through XI Corps at Floing. This attack failed at a heavy loss.

By 1500 the French position was hopeless and a white flag was hoisted over Sedan.

The capitulation was finalized at 1100 on 2 September, in the Château de Bellevue, near Frenois.

The French had suffered 17,000 casualties during battle. The Germans had lost only 9000.

Paris. The *Garde Mobile* were to accompany him.

All might yet have been well for the luckless Army of Châlons had Bazaine and Palikao not intervened. The former sent a telegram, arriving on the afternoon of the 17th, announcing that he had won a victory at Rezonville, but would have to regroup before continuing his march on Châlons. One of his *aides de camp* arrived at Châlons the following day with a note confirming this, suggesting that Bazaine would swing north to elude the Germans. Palikao, dismayed by the reappearance of the suspect Trochu and the dangerous *Mobiles*, warned the Emperor by telegram that a return to Paris would be fatal; it was essential, as much for the safety of the regime as for the success of the campaign, to rescue Bazaine.

MacMahon can have had few illusions. His army was not without value, but it was certainly incapable of a dash toward Metz in the teeth of the advancing Germans. His difficulties were increased by the presence of the Emperor, and by his nominal subordination to Bazaine who, on 18 August announced himself unable to give any instructions whatever, 'your operations lying at the moment entirely outside my zone of action'. Communications with Bazaine worsened after the telegraph line was cut, and dwindled to equivocal notes brought by couriers through German lines.

On 21 August Rouher, President of the Senate, met Napoleon, MacMahon and Courcelles, and stressed the importance of relieving Bazaine. Palikao re-emphasized the point by telegram the following day, warning that failure to aid Bazaine 'would have the most deplorable consequences in Paris'. Messages from Bazaine indicated that he

Below: Prussian cavalryman wounded at Gravelotte. Below right: Moltke meets King Wilhelm I at Gravelotte.

proposed to move via Montmédy, though Mac-Mahon was later to deny having received the most significant of these notes, dispatched on 20 August Pressure from the capital, added to indications that Bazaine was going to break out rather than wait lamely for aid, brought about a new and fatal change of plan, and on 23 August the Army of Châlons set off on its march to destruction.

The army moved slowly, its march made more difficult by heavy rain and muddy roads. It spent the night of the 24–25th camped between Vouziers and Rethel. Already MacMahon was deviating from his axis of advance toward Montmédy, since he was forced to remain close to the Reims-Mezières railway, to ensure supply. His two Reserve Cavalry Divisions, commanded by Generals Margueritte and de Bonnemains, had, by singular absence of logic, been ordered to screen the Rethel area, which was precisely that not threatened by the Germans.

Moltke had made significant alterations in the organization of the German armies. On 19 August he split the Second Army into two. The Crown Prince of Saxony was given three corps—the Guard, IV and XII Corps—forming the Army of the Meuse, with the task of pursuing Mac-Mahon. Frederick Charles, meanwhile, block-aded Metz with the remaining four corps of the Second Army and the entire First Army. The German advance recommenced on 23 August. The Third Army swung up toward Châlons, with the Army of the Meuse to its right. For several vital days, however, Moltke remained ignorant of MacMahon's intentions and, had the French fallen back on Paris, the elaborate German right-wheel would have come to naught. As it was, the

Above: French soldiers advance at Gravelotte. France's inability to take advantage of innumerable Prussian errors at Gravelotte cost them the only opportunity they had in the war to stop the Prussian advance and stave off total defeat.

Below left: The Prussian breakthrough at Gravelotte set the stage for the encirclement of French forces at Sedan. **Below:** Gravelotte showed that properly handled, the *mitrailleuse* machine-gun and the *chassepot* rifle were deadly weapons against the Prussian infantry.

PLATE 2.

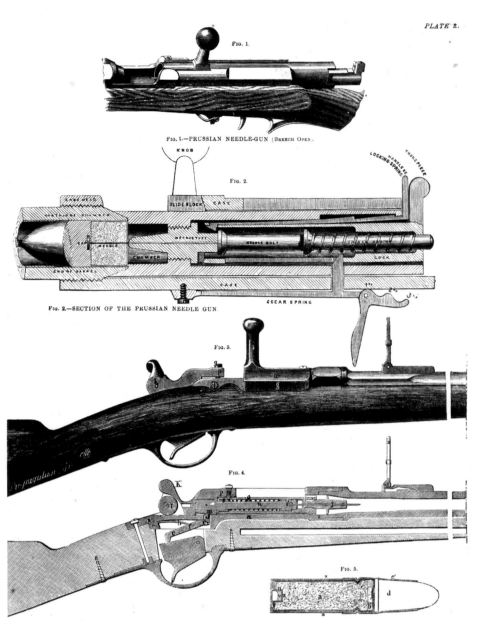

FIG. 1.—PRUSSIAN NEEDLE-GUN (BREECH OPEN).

FIG. 2.—SECTION OF THE PRUSSIAN NEEDLE GUN.

march on Montmédy played into Moltke's hands. He became increasingly certain that MacMahon was moving northeast, and on the afternoon of 26 August the cavalry of the Army of the Meuse made contact with MacMahon's right wing at Grandpré.

The Army of Châlons had struggled on, impeded by bad roads, appalling weather and dwindling supplies. On 26 August MacMahon realized that to continue was to risk encirclement, but his decision to fall back on Paris was greeted by a renewed protest from Palikao. The latter, never noted for his strategic prescience, maintained that MacMahon could easily brush aside the forces facing him, and that he was a clear 36 hours ahead of the Crown Prince. He ended by giving MacMahon an unequivocal order to press on. French movement, never particularly rapid, now became slower due to constant friction with hostile cavalry patrols. On 29 August there was a clash between 5th Corps and XII Corps near Noualt, and on the following day Failly was surprised at Beaumont.

The action at Beaumont cost the French well over 7000 men. It was Failly's last battle as a corps commander. It had already been decided to replace him, and his successor, General de Wimpffen, arrived on the evening of the 30th, bringing with him an order to take command not only of the 5th Corps, but, in the event of MacMahon becoming a casualty, of the whole army.

MacMahon, dismayed by the misfortunes of his right wing, ordered his army to fall back on Sedan, a small fortress nestling in the foothills of the Ardennes. He probably intended to halt there to reorganize before moving off once more, though in quite what direction he was uncertain. Sedan, like Spicheren and Froeschwiller, was not without

its attractions as a defensive position. The River Meuse wound south of the town swinging north from Torcy to form the Iges Peninsula before running northwest towards Mezières. Its valley was wide and marshy and, if the bridges were blown, the river offered an excellent barrier against attack from the south. North of the river the ground rose sharply. Above Sedan itself lay the Bois de la Garenne, with the Calvaire d'Illy at its northern point. A narrow valley, the Fond de Givonne, cut away south towards Bazeilles, while a re-entrant ran from Illy itself to Floing in the valley of the Meuse. South of the river, at Frenois and Wadelincourt, rose another range of hills.

On 31 August MacMahon deployed his exhausted army to take best advantage of the position. Douay's 7th Corps held the slopes from Floing to Illy, while General Ducrot put his 1st Corps into line covering the northern end of the Fond de Givonne. Lebrun pushed one division of 12th Corps into Bazeilles, while the other two held the Fond de Givonne to link up with Ducrot on their left. The 5th Corps was placed in reserve.

Moltke viewed the situation with enthusiasm. Unless MacMahon moved rapidly eastward along the north bank of the Meuse, there was every chance that he could be trapped with the Belgian frontier at his back and German armies at both flanks. Moltke ordered the Army of the Meuse to advance on Sedan from the east. The Third Army was to move in from the south, sending its left wing across the Meuse to cut the French line of retreat.

By dusk on the 31st the Germans were in possession of the railway bridges at Donchery and Bazeilles—neither, by a combination of confusion and ill-luck, had been blown by MacMahon's engineers. As night fell the peril of the Army of

Châlons was clearly marked by the broad arc of German campfires. Ducrot appreciated the full seriousness of the army's plight. '*Nous sommes dans un pot de chambre*', he remarked, '*et nous y serons emmerdés*' (We are in a chamber pot, and we are about to be covered in shit).

The battle began just after 0400, when troops of I Bavarian Corps attacked Lebrun's Marines in Bazeilles. The Marines were regulars, and fought hard from houses and barricades, aided by some of the inhabitants. Before long the village was on fire, but the French hung on desperately. MacMahon rode forward at about 0600, but was wounded in the leg by a shell-splinter almost immediately. He thought Ducrot the most competent of the corps commanders, and sent him a note ordering him to take over. It took nearly two hours for the message to reach Ducrot, and by then the situation had worsened.

The leading formation of the Army of the Meuse, XII Corps, came into action on the Bavarian right, taking La Moncelle at 0630. Within half an hour the Saxons had 72 guns in line above the village, but it took them three hours to force General de Lartigue's division of 1st Corps out of Daigny, where Ducrot had posted it at first light. As soon as Ducrot learnt that he had succeeded to MacMahon's command, he ordered an immediate retreat. Lebrun objected that his men were doing well in Bazeilles, and it was not until after 0800 that Ducrot felt certain enough to order him to fall back.

At this delicate juncture Wimpffen arrived to turn chaos into catastrophe. MacMahon had been unaware that Wimpffen held a dormant commission; he had told him nothing of any overall plan, which is hardly surprising since such a plan probably did not exist even in MacMahon's

Top: French cannon protect the defenses around Sedan. **Above:** General Ducrot, whom MacMahon considered to be the best of his corps commanders.

Opposite top: The Prussian needle-gun (above) and the French *chassepot*, two key weapons in the Franco-Prussian War. The *chassepot*, a breech-loader, was potentially as dangerous to the Prussian as the breech-loading needle-gun was to both Austrians and French in the 1866 and 1870 wars. The difference was the men who fired them and the men who led them. **Opposite bottom:** French horse artillery, exhausted from the battle, bring up the guns for a final defense of the fortress of Sedan.

Right: A Krupp 1000-pounder gun. The breech mechanism was a horizontal sliding block.

Below: The last stand by the hapless and exhausted defenders of Sedan.

mind. Wimpffen was, however, convinced that withdrawal was out of the question. He ordered Lebrun to remain in Bazeilles, and told Ducrot that 'We need a victory, not a retreat'.

It was by now doubtful if the army could have retreated even if it were given the order to do so. The left wing of the Third Army, V and XI Corps, had begun to cross the Meuse at Donchery at 0400, and cut the Mezières road at 0730. The II Bavarian Corps deployed its guns around Wadelincourt, shelling the ramparts of Sedan and the all too visible French positions around them, while V and XI Corps moved on Fleigneux and

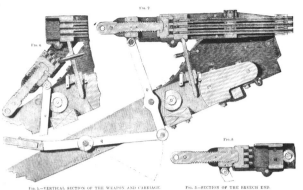

FIG. 2.—VERTICAL SECTION OF THE WEAPON AND CARRIAGE.   FIG. 3.—SECTION OF THE BREECH END.
FIG. 4.—SECTION OF THE BREECH WITH THE BLOCK OR CLOSER DRAWN DOWN).

FIG. 1.—MITRAILLEUSE IN ACTION.

Left: A French *mitrailleuse*, Napoleon III's secret weapon, which few French soldiers knew how to operate. It was the forerunner of the modern machine-gun.

Above: The capture of Napoleon III at Sedan also cost the French Army 80,000 men, who went into Prussian captivity. It was the end of the French Empire and the Napoleonic dynasty. **Above right:** Prussian infantry charge the French defenses as their encirclement of Napoleon's forces became complete.

XI on St Menges. Guns of both corps came into action against the 7th Corps, and under cover of their fire, infantry pressed forward toward the Floing-Illy road. General Bernis' brigade of the 5th Corps Cavalry Division tried to check this advance, but was warmly received. The divisional commander, General Brahaut, was captured, with many of his troopers. Still more were killed or wounded, but some, more fortunate, found their way through the thin German cordon into Belgium and internment. There was an equally abortive charge by General de Gallifet's brigade of Margueritte's cavalry division.

German shellfire was now causing heavy casualties throughout the French position. The artillery of the Guard, under command of the brilliant Prince Kraft zu Hohenlohe-Ingelfingen,

was deployed above the Fond de Givonne, mercilessly raking 1st Corps, while the guns of V and XI poured shells into Douay's exposed lines. Despite this fire, Douay felt confident that he could hold out as long as the Calvaire d'Illy remained in French hands. At about 1100 Wimpffen promised Douay reinforcements to hold this vital point, but within an hour was forced to ask him to send a division to aid 7th Corps, which was to spearhead the planned breakout towards Carignan. Douay tried to hold the Calvaire with a scratch force, but his corps became increasingly shaky under the hail of shells, and the German infantry pressed closer.

Wimpffen's breakout never really got under way. The chaos within his defensive perimeter was so great as to make a cohesive move im-

possible. But while he remained preoccupied with the southeastern sector, matters continued to deteriorate in the north. German infantry had reached the Calvaire at about 1400, and both Douay's right and Ducrot's left had been forced back into the Bois de la Garenne. Douay's left, above Floing, was also in danger, as German infantry filtered down the edge of the Meuse valley. General Lièbert's division, holding this area, was forced to give ground, and eventually fell back off Sedan, suffering frightfully from shellfire in the process.

Ducrot's growing despair was reflected by his next decision. Although Wimpffen remained deluded by the prospect of a breakout to the east, Ducrot was horribly certain that the army's last chance of safety lay to the west. His own troops,

like those of the 7th Corps, were exhausted, and the remnants of 5th Corps could no longer be depended upon. He turned, therefore, to Margueritte, whose division of *Chasseurs d'Afrique* was largely intact. Ducrot requested Margueritte to smash through XI Corps near Floing, opening a gap through which the infantry could follow. Margueritte rode forward to reconnoitre while his division shook out into order. His jaw was smashed by a bullet, but he struggled back to his *Chasseurs* and pointed down the slope at the Germans before collapsing. He died some days later. The charge of Margueritte's division was as gallant as it was useless. Some skirmishers were cut down, but the main attack was stopped dead by the rapid fire of the German infantry. With supreme gallantry, the shattered squadrons re-

Above left and right: Two reconstructed episodes from the Battle of Sedan, photographed in 1890.

Below: In another reconstructed episode from the battle, French artillery is dragged into position near Sedan.

grouped and came on again and again. King Wilhelm, watching the battle from the heights above Frenois, could not resist exclaiming 'Ah! The brave fellows!'

The failure of the last charge, and of the forlorn infantry rush that accompanied it, was followed by the almost total collapse of 7th Corps, which streamed off to the questionable safety of the Bois de la Garenne or Sedan. Even the *Africains* of 1st Corps were demoralized by the crippling fire to which they had been subjected all day. By 1500 the guard had penetrated the splintered trees of the Bois de la Garenne, and 1st Corps' position, like that of 7th Corps, was hopeless.

Napoleon had spent the day riding about with fatalistic resignation, indifferent to the heavy fire. One of his staff was cut in half beside him, and others were wounded. But death eluded him, and when approached by Lebrun, Ducrot and Douay, he agreed that the situation was hopeless, sending Lebrun to find Wimpffen in order to negotiate terms. Wimpffen still hoped to salvage something from the wreckage. He ordered Lebrun to help him gather troops for a last attempt to break out and together, at the head of a few hundred men from a mixture of units, they surged into Balan, taking the Bavarians by surprise and seizing the village. The assault got no further, and Wimpffen had, at last, to admit defeat. The white flag was hoisted over Sedan even before he reached it, and General Reille was sent to Wilhelm with a note announcing that, having failed to die among his troops, Napoleon placed his sword in the King's hands.

There was more to the capitulation than the exchange of civilities between monarchs. Wilhelm, in his reply, appointed Moltke his plenipotentiary for the conclusion of terms. On the French side, it was less easy to find a negotiator. Wimpffen refused and offered his resignation, but Ducrot emphasized that, as Wimpffen had taken command when there was 'some honor and profit' in it, he could scarcely avoid this last cruel

responsibility. Wimpffen, accompanied by General de Castelnau, met Moltke and Bismarck at Donchery. The French generals were unable to wring any useful concessions out of Moltke. There was a moment when Bismarck implied that, if the Emperor were seeking an end to the war rather than the capitulation of the Army of Châlons, things might be different. But Castelnau killed this fleeting possibility by stressing that Napoleon's own surrender did not include that of France, and the meeting ended with Moltke pointing out the hopelessness of the French position, and warning that, if no satisfactory answer were received by 0900 the following day, his batteries would open fire once more.

The capitulation was finalized at 1100 on 2 September, in the Château de Bellevue, near Frenois. Napoleon had endeavored to see Wilhelm personally in the hope of producing improved terms, but he had been politely interrupted by Bismarck, and nothing had been achieved. The final terms were uncompromising. The entire army, with all its equipment, was to become prisoner-of-war. Officers were permitted to go free if they undertook not to take up arms against Germany during the course of the current war. Relatively few took advantage of this concession.

The French had suffered 17,000 casualties during the battle, and had lost a further 21,000 prisoners. The capitulation gave the Germans 83,000 more, with 449 field guns, 139 fortress guns, and a rich booty of horses, rifles and vehicles. The Germans had lost only 9000 killed and wounded. A comparison between the casualty figures reveals the predominant role played by the German artillery. The lesson of St Privat had not been wasted. German commanders were now content to let their artillery do their work for them, and the German gunners showed themselves worthy of this new confidence.

The consequences of Sedan cannot be measured in purely material terms. As Napoleon III was driven off to captivity, Bismarck sagely remarked

THE ILLUSTRATED LONDON NEWS.

No. 1635.—VOL. LVIII.   SATURDAY, FEBRUARY 4, 1871.   PRICE FIVEPENCE

PROCLAIMING THE KING OF PRUSSIA AS GERMAN EMPEROR IN THE PALACE OF VERSAILLES.

Left: King Wilhelm I of Prussia is proclaimed German Kaiser in the Hall of Mirrors of the Palace of Versailles, 18 January, 1871. The German Empire, the Second Reich, was born out of the ashes of Sedan.

that a dynasty was on its way out. He was right; on 4 September the Regency in Paris fell, and was replaced by the Government of National Defense, an aggressively left-wing body pledged to continue the war. Its resistance was as remarkable as it was futile. Paris was beleaguered, and the provincial armies, one by one, were defeated. An armistice was concluded on 28 January, 1871, and in May the war was ended by the Treaty of Frankfurt. France lost Alsace and Lorraine, had to pay a substantial indemnity, and suffered three years of German occupation. The Treaty of Frankfurt, like that of Versailles nearly half a century later, brought peace but not forgiveness. The loss of Alsace-Lorraine was a source of continual bitterness to the French, while the new and aggressive German Empire, born as it was of military conquest, cast an alarming shadow over the future of Europe.

It is tempting to look upon French defeat in the Franco-Prussian War as inevitable. This is, however, to underestimate the fallibility of the German command, and the innate fighting qualities of the French soldier. What is certain, though, is that the defeat of the Army of Châlons was predictable and, at least until 23 August, avoidable. MacMahon's army was ruined as much by its own inadequacies as by the brilliance of its enemy. Impelled by political motives, and in defiance of military logic, it undertook a maneuver which would have taxed even a cohesive and well trained force. In the words of one French officer, MacMahon's success would have required a miracle; the age of miracles was over. As the German Empire was victoriously proclaimed in the Hall of Mirrors of the Palace of Versailles, Bismarck and Kaiser Wilhelm inaugurated a period of German hegemony in Continental Europe.

Opposite top: The Imperial Guard before their surrender at Sedan.
Opposite center: The French forces stampede as they enter Sedan in the closing phase of the action.
Opposite bottom: After the fall of Sedan, the Paris Commune took control of the capital, and Prussian forces surrounded Paris to begin their long siege of the city. Wounded were transported down the Seine to the Quai de la Megisserie.
Left: The capitulation of Bazaine and the Army of Metz, 27 October, 1870.

First Marne

The First World War began with all participants believing it could never take place, and once it started in earnest, they believed it had to be short. All over by Christmas was the universal misconception. The weapons would be too terrible, the loss of men too great for any nation to withstand. It lasted over four years. The losses of men and materiel were greater than anyone envisioned. It is remembered by this generation as a war of attrition rather than of movement, with millions dying along the Western Front whose trenches could not be breached by any offensive, however great, until one side or the other was morally, spiritually and materially exhausted. These reminiscences are in the main correct, but it was not meant to be that way. Count von Schlieffen, whose master plan for winning the war for Germany against the Franco-Russian alliance was polished and perfected by 1905, intended Germany to knock France out of the war within a few weeks, enabling the huge German military machine to turn eastward and deal with Russia, whose mobilization plans took six weeks to bring their full strength into battle. The Schlieffen Plan called for Germany to mobilize 7/8 of her army along the Belgian and French borders, to sweep away Belgian opposition easily, and then to turn at the English Channel southward in order to complete a grand encirclement of Paris which would force a capitulation as humiliating as that suffered in 1870–71 by the French. 'Keep the right wing strong' were Schlieffen's dying words. When the war broke out in August 1914 the Schlieffen Plan had become an article of faith for every German staff officer. Had it been adhered to strictly, the war might have been short. Germany might have retained her mastery of Europe. But it was not to be. The Battle of the Marne saved the French, but it plunged the world into a conflict from which Western Civilization has yet to recover.

The last few days of August 1914 saw the French armies and the British Expeditionary Force in northern France in full retreat following the massive German thrust through Belgium. Twenty-eight days before seven German field armies had marched into Belgium, Luxembourg and eastern France. Slowly, inexorably, following the Schlieffen Plan which had been meticulously elaborated by the German General Staff they moved through Belgium in a gigantic sweep towards the west. The French battle plan, 'Plan 17', had envisioned the possibility of a German violation of Belgian neutrality, but expected it to be limited to a thrust through the region northeast of the Ardennes rather than a wide sweep which would carry the Germans north of the Meuse. Analyzing the situation based on German moves in the direction of Liège, General Joffre, the French Commander-in-Chief, came to a fatal decision. Believing that the German right would remain south of the Meuse, he prepared for what he believed would be the decisive counterstroke. The French 3rd Army (General Ruffey) and 4th Army (General de Langle de Cary) were ordered to advance northeast into the Ardennes to attack the supposed rear flank of the German forces. At the same time the 5th Army (General Lanrezac) was to push northwest into the region between Givet and Charleroi. With the aid of the British Expeditionary Force on his left, Lanrezac was to clear the region north of the Meuse and join the 3rd and 4th Armies in a converging attack on the overextended Germans. Unfortunately for the Allies, the Germans, by placing their reserve units into the front line were able to extend their march to the west before turning south without weakening their center. So, rather than striking a weak flank, the French attacked the German center.

By 20 August the French deployment had ended and Joffre was ready for a general advance. He believed that seven or eight German corps and four cavalry divisions were moving southwest into the gap between Givet and Brussels. Judging the strength of the German right correctly, Joffre deduced that the center was necessarily weak. The idea of the Germans putting their reserve units into the line had been suggested to him, but he rejected it as being most unlikely.

Opposite: *Cuirassiers* move up to the front after the start of World War One in 1914. Enthusiasm was high in every country, and flowers were strewn in the paths of troops marching toward the destruction of Western Civilization.

Below: French soldiers at the Gare du Nord, Paris, on their way up to the front.

During 19 and 20 August the Germans had checked their advance and fortified their center in the expectation of a French attack. On the foggy morning of the 21st the French marched into the trap. Instead of crashing through a weakened German center, 3rd Army was literally massacred in futile attacks on strong German positions. Throughout the 21st and 22nd, the armies of the two nations were locked in a continuous battle from Lorraine to a line south of Brussels. It was a murderous engagement with heavy French losses. By the evening of the 23rd the evidence before General Joffre was irrefutable: a continuation of the offensive against the German center was no longer possible.

The Critical Left Flank

But it was to the west, on the Allied left flank, that the situation was the most critical. The Allied forces totaled thirteen divisions of the French 5th Army and the five divisions of the BEF. Opposed to them were three German armies; the *First* (von Kluck) and *Second* (von Bülow) were moving from the north, while the *Third* (von Hausen) advanced from the east. The failure of the attacks of the 3rd and 4th Armies on 21 August and the crossing of the Meuse by elements of the *Third Army* exposed the French left flank. The 5th Army and BEF were in serious danger of being crushed by the superior numbers of the German right wing. During the 22nd and the morning of the 23rd the 5th Army and the British were desperately—and unsuccessfully—trying to check the German advance. In and around Charleroi the French were forced, by sheer weight of numbers, to give way. By the evening of the 23rd the line of the Sambre had been abandoned and the French 5th Army was in full retreat toward the south.

While the French left was fiercely engaged in the region Charleroi-Namur, the British deployed in the area Mauberge-Mons on the evening of 21 August. On the 22nd, the British moved into positions on the line Condé-Binche immediately to the left of the 5th Army. The British expected—or assumed—that the 5th Army was containing the German advance and that one or two corps faced their front. The actual situation, however, was quite different. In the face of German pressure the 5th Army was forced to give ground. The *First Army* was directly in front of the British while the *Second Army* was moving toward the British right. The BEF was in imminent danger of being outflanked on both right and left. Attacked by the Germans before Mons the British were saved from destruction only by an unparalleled standard of accurate and sustained musketry. But, devoid of the support of the 5th Army, and in fear of being overwhelmed, Sir John French, the Commander-in-Chief of the BEF, was forced to order a general retirement for the morning of the 24th. It was the start of the Great Retreat.

In the midst of the collapse of the French position, on the 25th General Joffre issued a General Order calling for the strategic withdrawal of his center and left, anchored on the fortress of Verdun. Meanwhile, he proposed to use elements of the 4th and 5th Armies, the BEF

and newly arrived colonial troops to form a 6th Army which would take its place on the French left and push back the German right. The new army was to be assembled between 27 August and 2 September and to advance from the base St Pol-Arras, or Arras-Bapaume. In order to make it easier to start a new offensive, all efforts were made to coordinate the retreat and so prevent the withdrawing forces from separating and losing their coherence.

Meanwhile the German right continued to push southwest in an effort to outflank the Allied left. From 25 August to the end of the month the Anglo-French left stubbornly resisted the German advance. But the weight of the German right wing was crushing and it constantly pushed back the BEF and adjacent 5th Army. Its left wing bent, its center hard pressed, the rest of the Allied line was forced to withdraw in a line with its threatened left to prevent the whole line from snapping like a bent twig. On 26 August the *First Army* severely mauled the British 2 Corps at Le Cateau. Arriving in the region Amiens-Péronne, von Kluck's troops made the placement of the newly formed 6th Army, which was still only partially ready to move into the line, impossible. Joffre had no recourse but to continue to withdraw towards Paris and the Marne.

As the German right wing wheeled south to pursue the retreating Allied left, the campaign approached a crisis. Whereas the original German plan had called for von Kluck to pass to the west of the French capital, the new line of march pulled the *First Army*—the right flank of the German forces—to the east of Paris. This drastically changed the Schlieffen Plan and exposed the Germans to a French counteroffensive. The newly formed 6th Army (General Manoury) and the troops under the command of the military governor of Paris (General Galliéni) which had previously been in some danger of being outflanked, were now offered the opportunity of attacking the German right flank as it swung east of the capital. Much has been made of the German decision to modify the original plan which called for a considerably wider enveloping movement that would have brought the *First Army* across the Seine between Paris and

Above: German soldiers pass a burning house in northern France as their advance continues. The Germans hoped to take France in six weeks in order to turn their attention on the Russians, who were still mobilizing while Belgium was being overrun.

Opposite top: French officers inspect artillery pieces during a lull in the fighting. **Opposite bottom:** The British Expeditionary Force arriving in Le Havre, 14 August, 1914. The British presence on the collapsing Western front saved Paris from encirclement and the French army from defeat.

Above: French infantry dig in near the Marne. In the early days of the war trenches were not in evidence, as the war of movement was still employed by both sides. Only the French were moving backwards until they took a stand at the Marne. **Above right:** Headquarters of the British 2nd Cavalry Division on the Marne, September 1914.

Rouen. But the movement of von Kluck, while offering serious disadvantages to the right wing of the German armies did not in itself reverse the military situation. Coupled with the natural French desire to save Paris if they could, and the opportunity afforded by the river barrier of the Marne, von Kluck's march provided the opportunity for the Allies to strike at the German flank. It remained to be seen if the Allies could exploit a favorable situation on their left before

pressure on other sectors forced them to give way.

On 4 September the Allied front sprawled unevenly across northeastern France. On the far left, somewhat detached from the rest of the line, was the entrenched camp of Paris and the newly formed 6th Army. To the southwest stretched the five divisions of the British Army. Moving east, the 5th Army was on the line Dormans-Epernay, the 9th on the line Sézanne-Camp de Mailly-Sompius, and the 4th Army was astride the

Marne at Vitry-le-Francois. The line arched north to include the fortified region surrounding Verdun, held by the 3rd Army. Further to the east stood the 2nd Army, running across the Grand Couronne of Nancy and into Lorraine.

Except for the western edge of the battle line the German forces lay directly in front of the Allies. The *Sixth Army* was astride the Meurthe curving northwest to Pont-à-Mousson, opposite the 2nd Army. The *Seventh Army* covered the

fortified region of Verdun on its left and faced the 3rd Army across the Argonne on its right. Dipping southwest from Rivigny to Vitry-le-Francois the *Fourth Army* faced the 4th Army. The German right wing, composed of the *First, Second* and *Third Armies* was across the Marne. The *Third Army* had bridged the river near Epernay and had reached the area just north of the line Sompius-Fère Champenoise which was held by the 9th Army. Directly to the west, the *Second Army* was

Above left: A Belgian friar offers drinking water to the German troops sweeping through Flanders in August 1914. **Above:** The Germans move field artillery forward to face the British and French on the Marne. The Eiffel Tower could be seen on the horizon as the Germans moved within twenty miles of Paris. **Below:** When the French inaugurated Plan XVII, they invaded Alsace and Lorraine as the Germans swept through Belgium and northern France. But these provinces were not unprotected. Here Germans counterattack in Lorraine, preventing this area from being overrun and thus covering their left flank.

Above: The 59th Field Company of the BEF leaves its bivouac near Mons, from which the British were forced to retreat after having taken a stand on the Albert Canal.

in the marshes of St Gond close to Ville-en-Tardenois, across the front of the 5th and 9th Armies. Between the *Second* and *First Armies* lay a gap of some twelve to fifteen kilometers, the *First Army* being somewhat northwest of its neighbor. Von Kluck's right stretched to Beauvais and Senlis, and his center continued to move south; on 3 September it was on the line Creil-Senlis-Nanteuil, and by the 4th it was astride the Marne just east of Meaux.

On 4 September, General von Moltke, Chief of the German General Staff, and nephew of the hero of Sedan and Königgrätz, issued the orders which sent the German right wing to the east rather than to the west of Paris. The *First* and *Second Armies* were to move southeast and roll up the 'defeated' Allied left while the German left effected a breakthrough west of Verdun. While the danger of a French sortie from Paris was not excluded, it was assumed that the pressure of the main German thrusts would be heavy enough to prevent an effective countermove.

The French, however, had the as yet unused 6th Army which was temporarily under the jurisdiction of the military governor of Paris, General Galliéni. On 3 September Galliéni had received reports that the Creil-Nanteuil line was no longer being pressed by German troops. On the 4th the southwest march of the *First Army* was confirmed along the line Nanteuil-Lizy-sur l'Ourcq. Galliéni quickly grasped the opportunity that was offered to him, and ordered Manoury to prepare to attack the flank of the *First Army* as it passed in front of Paris on 5 September. Later in

the evening of the 4th, Galliéni was able to convince Joffre to halt the general retreat. Joffre issued orders which called for a resumption of the offensive on the morning of 6 September. Galliéni's action had provided the French with the conditions necessary to halt their retreat and to strike at the flank of the German right wing.

The day of 5 September was one of intense expectation punctuated by sharp local clashes and severe fighting between the 6th Army and flank elements of the *First Army*. As the weight of Manoury's troops was felt on the *First Army's* flank, von Kluck was compelled to shift *II Corps* to the northwest. It was to prove a fatal mistake, and one which would have serious consequences for the cohesion of the German battle-line. Had von Kluck pulled his flank closer to his main body he would have been able to maintain his forces in a tighter formation. As it was, a full half of the *First Army* was dangerously separated from the rest of the German forces.

On the morning of 6 September Joffre issued his celebrated Order of the Day:

At the moment when a battle, on which the welfare of the nation depends, is about to begin, I have to remind all ranks that the time for looking back is past. Every effort must be made to attack the ememy and hurl him back. Troops which find advance impossible must stand their ground at all costs and die rather than give way. This is the moment when no faltering will be tolerated.

Responding to orders sent out on the evening of 4 September, the 6th Army attacked the

German positions on the Ourcq, to the east of Meaux, early on the 6th, pressing the flank and rear of the *First Army*. The German *IV Reserve Corps* was dealt a shattering blow by the 6th Army's left along the line Marcilly-Acy en Multien. The Germans were pushed back toward the northeast, threatening to expose the rear of the *First Army* to the 6th Army. But the arrival of units from *II Corps* on the 6th Army front enabled the Germans to check the advance.

On the same day, the BEF ceased their southward march and started north for the first time since 23 August. Advancing from the line Jouy le Chatel-Farmoutiers-Villeneuve le Comte, the British encountered quite heavy resistance at first, but this decreased throughout the afternoon. The advance elements of the *First Army* were withdrawing in accordance with von Kluck's transfer of *II Corps*. The *IV Corps*, the advance guard of the *First Army*, abandoned the Grand Morin at Coulommiers, and withdrew in the direction of Rebais. By nightfall the heights of the Grand Morin were entirely in British hands.

After shifting to the line Courtacon-Esternay-Sézanne on 5 September, the 5th Army was ordered to attack in the direction of Montmirail on the 6th. The assault was to be delivered in echelon, with the western flank of 5th Army somewhat north of the rest of the attacking force. The left wing of the 5th Army was to link up with the advance of the 6th Army along the Ourcq and encircle the isolated *First Army*. The 5th, however, ran headlong into the *Second Army* and a desperate fight ensued. On the left, the 18th Corps was able to wrest Courtacon from the Germans, while on the center the *Second Army* was forced to evacuate Montceaux les Provins and Courgivaux, and 1st Corps, on the right wing of the 5th Army gained Catillon sur Morin. It was, however, a somewhat disappointing day for the 5th Army. It had advanced only slightly on its left and had not been able to push the *Second Army* far enough to the northeast to effectively isolate the *First Army* from the rest of the German line.

The 9th Army, holding the French center, faced the left wing of von Bülow's *Second Army* and the right wing of von Hausen's *Third Army*. The

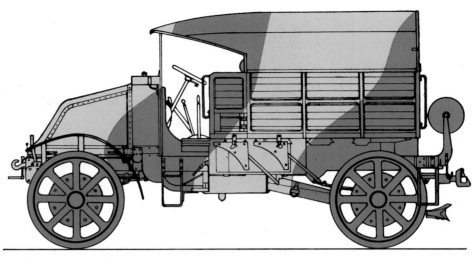

9th Army commander, General Foch, was ordered to support the advance of Franchet d'Esperey's 5th Army on his left, and to stand on the defensive with his center and right. Attacked, and under the heaviest pressure, Foch's left lost Tarlus to the *Second Army's X Corps* and was in danger of losing Charleville as well. The 9th Army's center was pushed south of the St Gond marshes by the *X* and *Guard Corps* of the *Second Army*. On the 9th Army's right, the 2nd Corps and its supporting 9th Cavalry Division were both forced to give ground to elements of the *XII Saxon Corps* of the *Third Army*. By the end of 6 September Foch's army was very hard-pressed, having made no gains and been forced back on both flanks.

On the right of the Allied line, the French were mainly on the defensive trying to repel the attacks of the *Fourth*, *Fifth* and *Sixth Armies*. Here the situation was quite the reverse of that on the left: the Germans were resolutely carrying out their attacks trying to break the French line. The 3rd Army under General Sarrail was barely holding the line Vassincourt-Villotte-Ville-sur-Cousances.

A critical question had been posed by the result of the first day's battle: could the 6th Army batter the German right wing and separate the *First Army* from the rest of the German line before the pressure of the *Third*, *Fourth* and *Fifth Armies* crumpled the French center? Aware that the temporary advantage on the extreme west of the battle line could not last indefinitely, Manoury

Above: French Renault artillery tractor. Towing capacity: 15 tons. Engine: six-cylinder, 60 bhp. Crew: four. Maximum speed: 42 mph.

Far left: General Galliéni, who commandeered the taxis of the Marne and moved his 6th Army forward in the 'Marne Maneuver' which turned the tide of battle in favor of France. **Left:** General Sir John French, Commander-in-Chief of the BEF.

pushed forward against the German right wing with every ounce of strength he possessed. Reinforced by 1st Cavalry Corps and the 61st Reserve Division on its left, 6th Army moved forward at dawn, only to grind to a halt. The German *IV Reserve Corps* had effected a tactical withdrawal late on the 6th and were now entrenched on the plateau of Trocy. The French line made little progress against the Germans, for von Kluck had placed the *II* and *IX Corps* in support of the *IV Reserve Corps*. Three of the four corps of the *First Army* had now shifted to face Manoury. Toward evening, *IX Corps* advanced against the 6th Army's left, threatening to outflank the French. The 6th Army had held its own against the Germans, but the original maneuver which had prompted the Battle of the Marne had been thwarted; von Kluck's change of front no longer offered the Allies the possibility of a flank attack. It remained to be seen if the Allies could hold in the center and right in these circumstances.

With only *III Corps* and cavalry of the *First Army* south of the Marne, British pressure was relatively minor on the second day of the battle, due to the skillful delaying action fought by the German cavalry under General von der Marwitz. Trying to maintain a bridgehead across the Marne at Coulommiers, von der Marwitz placed three cavalry divisions on the Grand Morin above the bridgehead, a position which was eventually taken by elements of the British 3rd Division. The three cavalry divisions (2nd, 9th and Guard) performed admirably, if not heroically, but were forced to withdraw by evening to the Petit Morin. By the end of the day's hostilities, the British were on the line La Haute Maison-Coulommiers-Jouy-sur-Morin.

To the right of the British, the 5th Army also benefited from German withdrawal north of the Marne. Moving into the vacuum, the 5th Army's left and center advanced with Montmirail as its goal, and achieved some ten kilometers in the face of relatively light resistance. The situation on 5th Army's right was considerably more difficult, as 1st and 10th Corps, on the right, were ordered to attack in a northeasterly direction to lessen pressure on the 9th Army. At the end of the day's fighting, 10th Corps had reached Charleville and was in effective contact with the left flank of the 9th Army.

The critical point in the Allied line was the frontage held by the 9th Army. Every effort was made by the Germans to break the French position and to relieve the pressure against their right. The 9th Army was heavily pressed throughout the day by the attacks of the *Second* and *Third Armies*. Foch ordered his left to maintain a defensive posture while his center and right held the line against the German assaults. Supported by an extremely heavy artillery preparation, *XII Corps* of *Third Army* repeatedly attacked the 2nd Corps on French right but made little progress. In the center the marshes of St Gond afforded a natural bastion for the 9th Corps and prevented

the Germans from seriously threatening the French position. The situation was altogether different on the French left. Although ordered by General Foch to attack in a northwesterly direction, two divisions on his left had to struggle hard to hold their ground against *X Corps* of the *Second Army*. Had it not been for the timely intervention of the 10th Corps (5th Army) operating on their left, the position might have collapsed.

Left: General von Moltke, nephew of the hero of Königgrätz and Sedan, who can be compared with his uncle in name only. He nearly suffered a nervous breakdown at the Marne and had to be relieved.
Below: French artillery returns German fire at the Marne, while a thinly protected observer directs the fire of his weapon.

The First Battle of the Marne, 1914

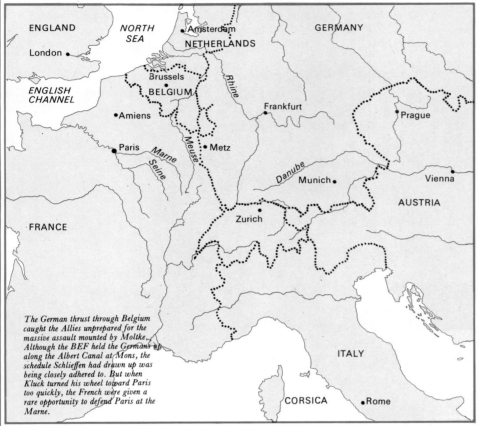

The German thrust through Belgium caught the Allies unprepared for the massive assault mounted by Moltke. Although the BEF held the Germans up along the Albert Canal at Mons, the schedule Schlieffen had drawn up was being closely adhered to. But when Kluck turned his wheel toward Paris too quickly, the French were given a rare opportunity to defend Paris at the Marne.

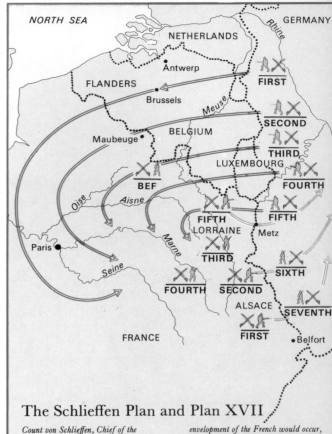

The Schlieffen Plan and Plan XVII

Count von Schlieffen, Chief of the German General Staff in 1905, perfected his plan to envelope the French by sweeping through Belgium and northern France, bringing his forces as far as the Channel to block the arrival of the BEF, and then encircling Paris, while the French sent the bulk of their forces to Alsace in Plan XVII. If the plan were carried out, a double envelopment of the French would occur, bringing the desired victory within six weeks. Then the Germans could send their main force against Russia, which took six weeks to mobilize. The plan took courage and precision to carry out. In 1914 the Germans deviated from the Schlieffen Plan, giving the Allies a chance to turn the German flank at the Marne.

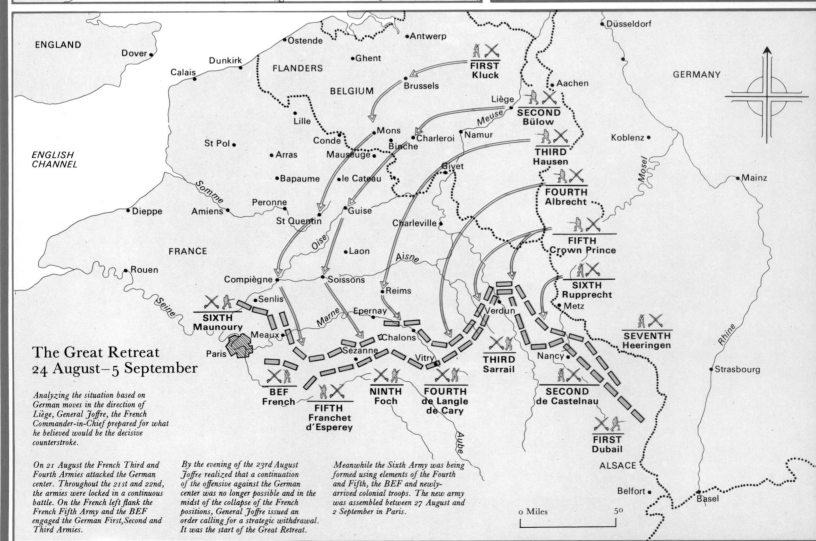

The Great Retreat
24 August – 5 September

Analyzing the situation based on German moves in the direction of Liège, General Joffre, the French Commander-in-Chief prepared for what he believed would be the decisive counterstroke.

On 21 August the French Third and Fourth Armies attacked the German center. Throughout the 21st and 22nd, the armies were locked in a continuous battle. On the French left flank the French Fifth Army and the BEF engaged the German First, Second and Third Armies.

By the evening of the 23rd August Joffre realized that a continuation of the offensive against the German center was no longer possible and in the midst of the collapse of the French positions, General Joffre issued an order calling for a strategic withdrawal. It was the start of the Great Retreat.

Meanwhile the Sixth Army was being formed using elements of the Fourth and Fifth, the BEF and newly-arrived colonial troops. The new army was assembled between 27 August and 2 September in Paris.

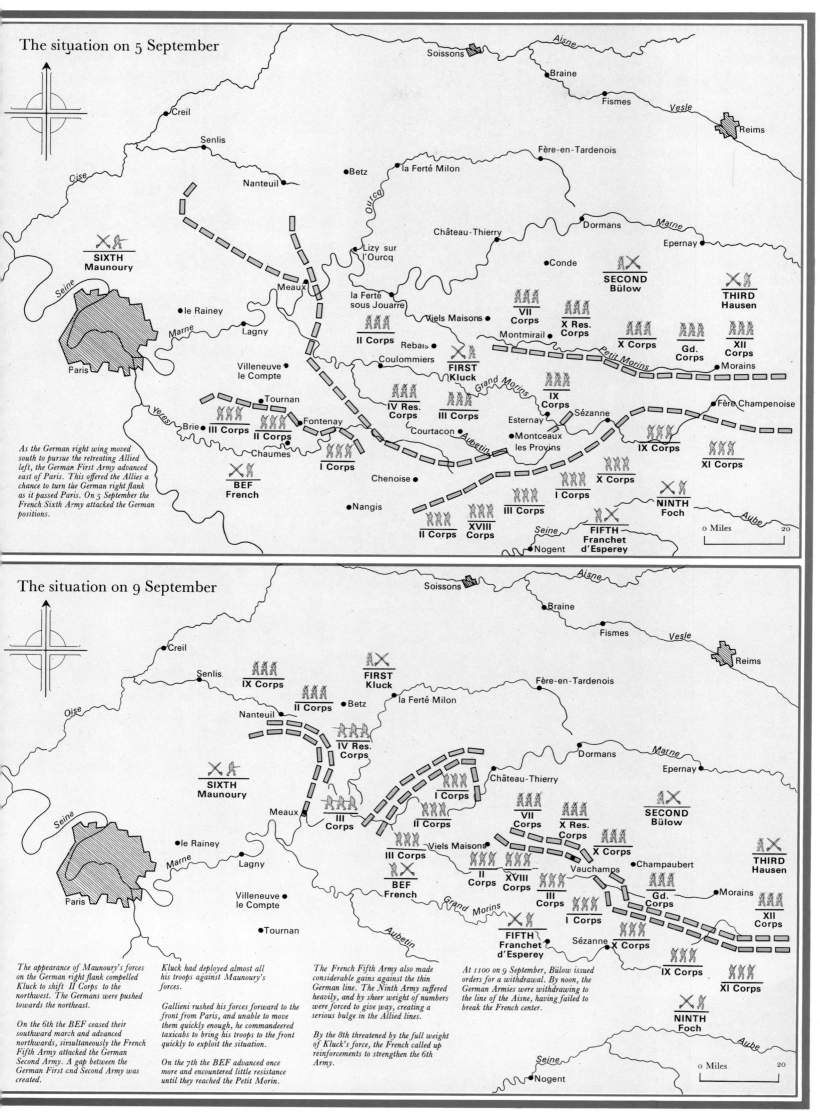

The situation on 5 September

As the German right wing moved south to pursue the retreating Allied left, the German First Army advanced east of Paris. This offered the Allies a chance to turn the German right flank as it passed Paris. On 5 September the French Sixth Army attacked the German positions.

Soissons
Braine
Fismes
Reims
Creil
Senlis
Nanteuil
Betz
la Ferté Milon
Fère-en-Tardenois
SIXTH Maunoury
Meaux
Lizy sur l'Ourcq
Château-Thierry
Dormans
Conde
Epernay
SECOND Bülow
THIRD Hausen
la Ferté sous Jouarre
VII Corps
X Res. Corps
le Rainey
II Corps
Viels Maisons
Montmirail
X Corps
Gd. Corps
XII Corps
Lagny
Rebais
Coulommiers
Petit Morins
Morains
FIRST Kluck
Villeneuve le Compte
Tournan
Fontenay
IX Corps
Sézanne
Fère Champenoise
Brie
III Corps
II Corps
Grand Morins
Esternay
III Corps
Chaumes
IV Res. Corps
III Corps
Montceaux les Provins
IX Corps
I Corps
Courtacon
Aubetin
XI Corps
BEF French
Chenoise
I Corps
X Corps
NINTH Foch
Nangis
III Corps
II Corps
XVIII Corps
Seine
FIFTH Franchet d'Esperey
Aube
Nogent

0 Miles 20

The situation on 9 September

The appearance of Maunoury's forces on the German right flank compelled Kluck to shift II Corps to the northwest. The Germans were pushed towards the northeast.

On the 6th the BEF ceased their southward march and advanced northwards, simultaneously the French Fifth Army attacked the German Second Army. A gap between the German First and Second Army was created.

Kluck had deployed almost all his troops against Maunoury's forces.

Gallieni rushed his forces forward to the front from Paris, and unable to move them quickly enough, he commandeered taxicabs to bring his troops to the front quickly to exploit the situation.

On the 7th the BEF advanced once more and encountered little resistance until they reached the Petit Morin.

The French Fifth Army also made considerable gains against the thin German line. The Ninth Army suffered heavily, and by sheer weight of numbers were forced to give way, creating a serious bulge in the Allied lines.

By the 8th threatened by the full weight of Kluck's force, the French called up reinforcements to strengthen the 6th Army.

At 1100 on 9 September, Bülow issued orders for a withdrawal. By noon, the German Armies were withdrawing to the line of the Aisne, having failed to break the French center.

Soissons
Braine
Fismes
Reims
Creil
Senlis
IX Corps
FIRST Kluck
Nanteuil
II Corps
Betz
la Ferté Milon
Fère-en-Tardenois
IV Res. Corps
SIXTH Maunoury
Château-Thierry
Dormans
Epernay
Meaux
I Corps
VII Corps
SECOND Bülow
le Rainey
III Corps
II Corps
X Res. Corps
X Corps
Lagny
Viels Maisons
Vauchamps
Champaubert
THIRD Hausen
III Corps
II Corps
XVIII Corps
Villeneuve le Compte
BEF French
III Corps
Morains
Tournan
Grand Morins
I Corps
Gd. Corps
XII Corps
Aubetin
FIFTH Franchet d'Esperey
Sézanne
X Corps
IX Corps
XI Corps
Seine
NINTH Foch
Nogent
Aube

0 Miles 20

165

Above: Rations are issued to the 1st Cameronians on 8 September during the Battle of the Marne.
Above right: The 1st Cameronians move forward toward the Aisne the following day as the German flank is turned. **Below:** German soldiers man their machine gun positions as they defend a line north of the Marne on the Aisne after they were forced to withdraw from the Marne.

By the end of the day, after frightful casualties on both sides, little ground had changed hands.

Further east, the 4th Army continued to be hard-pressed, although slightly less so than 9th Army on its left. The *XIX Corps*, supported by a division of the *XII Reserve Corps*, both of the *Third Army* thrust against the 4th Army's left at Sompius and nearly succeeded in breaking the French line. Although outnumbered in the center, the French 12th and Colonial Corps successfully resisted two corps of the *Fourth Army*, proving that firepower could be a fearsome defensive weapon when used by steady troops well-supported by field artillery. The French right performed notably less well than the center, and *XVIII Corps* and *XVIII Reserve Corps* succeeded in outflanking 2nd Corps of the French 4th Army and threatening the link between the 4th and 3rd Armies.

Oddly enough, there was no major action fought between the 3rd Army and its opponent the *Fifth Army*. Each side spent the day probing the other's defenses—which were exceptionally strong in both cases—and waiting for reinforcements which would permit a favorable resumption of the offensive. Toward evening General Sarrail received the 15th Corps from 2nd Army, but its arrival came too late in the day to support an attack of any importance. The German Crown Prince, commander of the *Fifth Army*, brought up elements of the *VI Reserve Corps*, but used them to strengthen his line rather than to launch an attack.

The second day of battle had ended less favorably for the Allies than the first. Kluck had largely succeeded in extricating the *First Army*, and the 6th Army's advance against the German right flank was seriously compromised. On the other hand, the Allied line held everywhere

and in some cases the Allies had gained ground. The French center, although hard-pressed, remained intact. The Germans, who had pursued a beaten foe for fourteen days, were unable to comprehend the ability of the French to turn and attack. The seeds of doubt were already being sown at German Supreme Headquarters as to the final issue of the battle. Moltke was losing his nerve.

On the extreme right of the German line the situation was far from ideal. The 6th Army occupied the position Betz-Etavigny-Puisieux-Marcilly-Chambry, and was faced by the four corps of the *First Army*. Opening the day with an attack by 45th Division against the German's center, Manoury hoped to use the 61st Reserve Division to outflank the German left. Amidst fighting of the fiercest intensity, the Germans counterattacked in the afternoon using *IV*

Corps to assault the French center between Puisieux and Etrepilly. On the 6th Army's right flank the French maintained a constant pressure in order to aid the decisive struggle on the left half of their line. The day ended with little gains on either side. Von Kluck's troops were now almost entirely north of the Marne astride the Ourcq. And although the *First Army* was no longer in danger of being overwhelmed by the French, the 6th Army was unlikely to be crushed by the weary Germans. It was a bloody stalemate, fought with an intensity that could not be long endured.

With von Kluck's troops engaged against Manoury's, the frontage along the Marne facing the BEF was only held by a rearguard of German cavalry. Advancing on the axis Nogent-Château-Thierry, the British encountered almost no resistance until they reached the Petit Morin

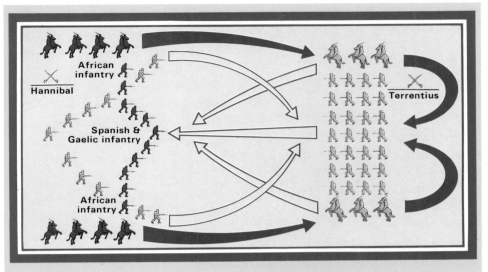

Cannae 216 BC: Double Envelopment

In August 216 BC a Carthaginian force under Hannibal defeated a Roman army well over twice its own size in what was to become known as the classic battle of envelopment. Hannibal drew up his army in a crescent, with Gauls and Spaniards in the center and the African veterans on both flanks 'refused'. His cavalry was stationed on the wings, and opened the battle by driving the Roman horse from the field. The Romans, ineptly led by the consul Terrentius Varro, attacked the Carthaginian center, which fell back steadily, permitting Hannibal's African troops to outflank them. Hannibal's victorious cavalry returned to complete the encirclement; the Roman army was 'swallowed up as if by an earthquake', and, according to one estimate, lost 70,000 of their 76,000 men.

The dream of Cannae has exercised an irresistible attraction on military minds for centuries. Count Alfred von Schlieffen, author of the celebrated 'Schlieffen Plan', sought to achieve a strategic Cannae by encircling the French armies in a battle of annihilation. The plan failed to achieve the results for which its author hoped, but, on the Eastern front, a Russian advance into East Prussia was smashed at the Battle of Tannenberg; the southern prong of the Russian attack—General Samsonov's Second Army—was itself counterattacked, encircled and destroyed by Hindenburg and Ludendorff in a battle of envelopment from which the Tsarist army was never to recover fully. Even today Cannae is still taught in Russian military academies as the apogee of the general's art; certainly, the tactics of 'double envelopment', when employed successfully, as at Cannae or Sedan, can lead to dramatic results.

A successful double envelopment depends as much upon the inflexibility of its intended victims as it does upon the skill of its executors. The Russian winter offensive of 1942–43 brought about the encirclement and destruction of the German Sixth Army at Stalingrad. Similarly, the envelopment of the French at Sedan in 1870 was due largely to the cumbersome nature of the Army of Châlons and to the slowness with which it marched. Finally, though the battle of envelopment is undeniably a concept of great value, it cannot guarantee victory; Hannibal won Cannae, but Rome ultimately won the war.

between La Ferté-sous-Jouarre and Sablonnières. After a stiff struggle in which the British made highly intelligent use of their field artillery they were able to crack the resistance of the German rearguard and cross the river. Making good progress through the day, they reached the line La Ferté-sous-Jouarre–Viels Maisons and were threatening Château Thierry.

General Franchet d'Esperey, commanding 5th Army, hoped to use this third day of battle to push the *Fourth Army* beyond Montmirail, thus relieving some of the pressure on the hard-pressed 9th Army. Advancing to the Petit Morin early in the morning almost as easily as the British on their left, the French met extremely heavy resistance in their attempts to cross that obstacle. The 18th Corps was able to force the river crossings but was soon held up in the region of Marchais-en-Brie. In the center, Montmirail fell to *III Corps* after an eight-hour battle which cost the Germans over 7000 casualties. On the right 1st Corps gained Vachamps and, more significantly, 10th Corps reached Charleville and then wheeled east to support 9th Army.

The center of the line held the key to the Allied success. With von Kluck engaged against the 6th Army, the British and 5th Army were able to make considerable progress against the thin German line in the sixty kilometer sector east and west of Château Thierry. Opposite 9th Army the situation was different. The Germans were making every possible effort to break the French line between Sézanne and Fère-Champenoise. The 9th Army's left was subjected to the severest punishment by the German X and *Guard Corps*, and by sheer weight of numbers the French were forced to give way, creating a serious bulge in the Allied line.

Immediately to the right of the 9th Army, the 4th Army was subjected to a pressure of almost equal intensity. His flanks threatened by the *Fourth Army*, de Langle de Cary was only able to

hold his position with the aid of the 3rd Army on his right. It was here, in the French center, that the battle reached its climax. The 9th Army was able to hold its ground with the greatest difficulty. Its neighbor to the right had visibly reached the point of rupture. A combined attack by the *Third* and *Fourth Armies* succeeded in the afternoon in enveloping both flanks of the 4th Army. All through the day the situation remained critical and it was only toward nightfall that the French were able to send the 21st Corps into the line to sustain the 4th Army.

The opposing armies had now been engaged for three days in a battle of the most desperate intensity. The question was not whether one side would effect a brilliant Napoleonic maneuver and sweep the other from the field. It was far more basic: which side would crack? The Battle of the Marne had become a question of will and nerve. It is perhaps indicative of the ultimate outcome of the battle that while Moltke was suffering a near nervous breakdown from the strain, Joffre was issuing his usual orders that under no circumstances was anyone to disturb his eight hours of unbroken sleep.

As the summer heat opened into severe rainstorm, the armies began the fourth day of of battle. The French 6th Army, while making some gains, was unable to cross the Ourcq and encircle the *First Army's* rear. Indeed, by the evening of the 8th, threatened with the whole weight of Kluck's force, the French were far from certain of being able to hold their positions. To

strengthen the 6th Army, General Galliéni ordered reinforcements to Senlis and Creil. Lacking transport, he created an instant legend by commandeering the 'taxicabs of the Marne'. Taxis packed with troops moved out to the field of battle from Paris as military transport proved insufficient. Whether or not the meters were running is anybody's guess. General Manoury ordered his retreating troops to turn and advance regardless of cost; he correctly appreciated that victory or defeat was now literally a matter of hours. It was the Germans who gave way first. Reacting to information that his exposed left flank—where a 'gap' of some thirty kilometers existed between the *First* and *Second Armies*—was being threatened by an advance of the BEF, Kluck ordered a withdrawal from the Ourcq, holding the line Nanteuil-Betz to delay the 6th Army should it attempt too rapid a pursuit.

Although the British were numerically small, their influence was conclusive. With little more

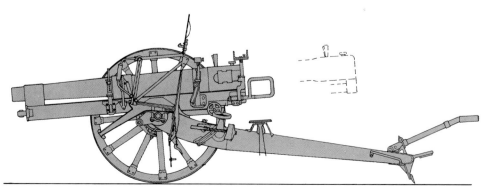

Above: Company D of the 1st Cameronians crosses a pontoon bridge over the Marne at La Ferté-sous-Jouarre on 10 September, 1914. **Top right:** the XI Hussars of the BEF pause at the Aisne. The crisis to defend Paris was behind them; the race to the Channel had begun. **Center right:** The long march back. German troops pass through a French village on their 'great retreat' after their failure to win on the Marne. **Right:** The French '75' in action.

than a cavalry division to oppose them they could, by a determined thrust, isolate the *First Army* from the rest of the German line. But three weeks of constant contact with the enemy had weakened Sir John French's resolution. Fearing to be caught alone and exposed in advance of the Allied line, French ordered an advance which minimized the risks. Pushing across the Marne at La Ferté-sous-Jouarre, Charly and Château-Thierry, the British were more significant for their presence rather than actual movements during this all-important day. Although the BEF had hesitantly nudged into the gap between the *First* and *Second Armies*, the Germans did not have the reserve to check the movement. By nightfall, the threat of a serious defeat hung over the German right.

Opposite the *Second Army*, the French 5th Army was ordered to push northeast to link up with the British on the Marne. Faced with little resistance, 5th Army was able to reach its objectives and increase the pressure on the Germans by threatening to push the *Second Army* northeast. The right of the 5th Army was, however, faced with a more difficult task: to aid the hard-pressed 9th Army by attacking the *Third Army*, which was slowly

pushing the 9th Army toward the marshes of St Gond. In this maneuver Franchet d'Esperey was equally successful and the Germans were forced to give way, all but eliminating the threat to the left flank of the 9th Army. Since the French center was holding its ground with increasing difficulty, the importance of the 5th Army's success cannot be overemphasized. If the 9th Army's front was not cracked by the evening of 9 September, the pressure on the German right would force von Kluck to continue his withdrawal, thus breaking the continuity of the whole German line.

The 9th Army's position was far from brilliant. On the 8th its left had barely held its own, whereas the right had lost substantial ground, perilously bending the French line. A further retreat could negate the success on the Allied left, and a German breakthrough would mean total disaster. Faced with this crisis, Foch responded in typical fashion, issuing an order of the day to attack which was brilliant in its ironic optimism.

Pivoting on his left, Foch used the 5th Army's support to strengthen his center and right. It was a maneuver which had the most important consequences. Three German corps, *Guard* of the *Second Army*, and *XII* and *XII Reserve* of the *Third*, pushed through the St Gond Marshes (near Fère-Champenoise) and forced the 9th Army's right to retire to Salon, forcing the center to fall back as well. But, pressed to breaking point, Foch managed to hold on for the extra day that was needed.

Foch's position was further aided by the 4th Army on his right which vigorously attacked the *Third Army* in order to lessen the pressure on the 9th Army. Pushing to within a mile of Sompius and moving laterally southwest of Humbauville, the 4th Army demonstrated a coordination with its neighbor which was notably lacking between the German army commanders.

But time had run out for the Germans. On 8 September Lieutenant-Colonel Hentsch was ordered by Moltke to visit each of the Army headquarters west of Verdun to assess the situation. In a move typical of the German Army, Hentsch, by virtue of his position as a General Staff Officer, was given full powers to 'coordinate the retreat, should rearward movements have to be initiated'. Moving from east to west, he became increasingly alarmed with each interview. Spending the night at *Second Army* headquarters, Henstsch found Bülow despairing of success. At 1100 on 9 September, Bülow issued orders for a a withdrawal. When Hentsch reached *First Army* headquarters at noon, orders had already been issued for a retreat. As Hentsch retraced his steps, he progressively ordered the *First, Second Third, Fourth* and *Fifth Armies* to the line of the Aisne. Having failed to break the French center, hard-pressed on their right, and lacking a firm hand to coordinate the army commanders in the the field, the Germans had no other choice. The Marne was a psychological rather than a physical victory for the Allies; it saved Paris, but ended with the Germans firmly ensconced on French soil. It was to take four more years of bloodletting through the stalemate of trench warfare to dislodge them.

Somme

1916

The German army which retreated from the Marne on 10 September, 1914 was far from a defeated force. Too much had happened too fast, and the Allied follow-up was fatally hampered by the confusion of near defeat. By the end of September, the Germans turned to face the Allied armies astride the Chemin des Dames ridge, and, following the inconclusive 'race to the sea', and the mutual exhaustion of both sides, field fortifications were constructed sporadically until they formed an almost continuous system stretching from Switzerland to the North Sea.

Local fraternization in Christmas 1914 could not conceal a situation which, to the generals of both sides, was serious in the extreme. To a military generation believing in movement, flank marches and decisive thrusts, the deadlock was

unacceptable. There were no flanks to turn, for the front ran from the North Sea to the Swiss border. There was only one possible solution: to break through the enemy's line and restore the war of movement.

A possible strategic alternative failed in 1915. Responding to Winston Churchill's suggestion, the British launched an attack against the Gallipoli Peninsula in late April, in an attempt to knock Turkey out of the war. But it was only in July that sufficient reinforcements were sent, and by then the Turks had heavily reinforced their own positions, significantly reducing the chances of British success. By the end of the year, the Dardanelles expedition had ended in dismal failure. Winston Churchill has convincingly argued that the Gallipoli campaign, if handled

Opposite: Human suffering on the Somme was horrendous. Mutilated men, some blinded by shellfire or gas attacks, were normal sights. The British lost 60,000 during the first hours of the months-long battle.

Below: Hopes were high in the British camp as the build-up for the Somme offensive continued. The Wiltshire Regiment marching to the trenches shared Haig's enthusiasm.

with sufficient determination and adequate force, could have succeeded. But his belief that it would have decisively changed the war is less credible. It was a long way from Istanbul to Berlin, even by way of Vienna, and there was no cheap way of beating Germany.

The British and French high command were largely unconvinced by Churchill's Eastern strategy. They believed that victory could only be won at the decisive point, where the German armies were concentrated—in northern France and Belgium. It was to this end that the Anglo-French armies in 1915 maintained a continuous initiative on the Western Front. On 10 March the British launched a limited attack at Neuve Chapelle. Supported by a brief but intense and effective artillery preparation, General Haig's First Army easily overwhelmed the German first line, but the narrowness of the frontage attacked, and the lethargic manner in which the initial success was exploited, gave the Germans enough time to close the gap. Yet the lesson of the battle glittered before the Allied eyes: given sufficient weight of fire, and adequate reserves, the German line could be broken.

The Allies, however, lacked both of these elements so essential to victory. Nor did they compensate by any particular astuteness in their tactics. In May the French were decisively checked between Lens and Arras at the same time as a British stroke at Aubers Ridge was repulsed. Too few reserves, too few heavy guns, too few men and unimaginative tactics. It was the formula for disaster. Between 15 and 27 May, the British continued their attacks on Festubert in conjunction with the equally fruitless French assaults around Lens. By the summer Allies' gains were negligible, at the cost of some 880,000 French and 183,000 British casualties in the period February-August. The Allies aimed at no less than a total breakthrough of the German lines. But, using a prolonged but relatively light preliminary bombardment which forfeited all surprise, they were successful nowhere. Often taking the first German positions relatively easily, the Allies were never able to successfully maintain the momentum of their initial assault. Furthermore, they were unable to find a tactical answer to the German use of machine guns in defense.

The 'New Armies'

The British 'New Armies' (volunteers) which appeared on the front in mid-1915, offered the British and French high commands a reserve which would enable them to break through the German lines and bring victory to the Allies. The New Armies would provide the manpower necessary for an assault which would 'compel the Germans to retreat beyond the Meuse and possibly end the war'. The 'big push' of 1915 was the idea of the French Commander-in-Chief, General Joffre. He envisaged a double stroke in Artois and Champagne to overwhelm the whole German line. General Sir Douglas Haig of the British First Army did not share Joffre's optimism, but was overruled by the C-in-C of the British armies in France, Sir John French. Despite his serious doubts, Haig agreed to an attack by six divisions of General Rawlinson's 4 Corps

and General Gough's 1 Corps. Following a four-day artillery bombardment which was badly hampered by lack of shells, the Allied attack was launched on 25 September. Impeded by a wind which prevented the effective use of gas, the British attack achieved only the most limited local gains, while the French in Champagne were equally unsuccessful. Although the assaults continued sporadically for two weeks, by 27 September the battle was an evident check for the Allies.

The twin Allied offensives of Autumn 1915 were a considerable improvement on those which took place in February and June. Planned with greater care, using more men and resources, they were a mechanical response to the problem posed by the deadlock. However, due to the military failures, Sir John French was replaced on 19 December 1915 by Haig. The problem which Haig faced in late 1915 was not really different from that which had existed twelve months previously. But he possessed more men and more matériel than Sir John French ever had at his disposal. With 36 British and Empire divisions in France by the end of the year, and the promise of significant increase in guns and shells, Haig had the two elements which he believed necessary to break the deadlock. Nothing could stop the assault of a half million men supported by a bombardment of a million shells. 1916 was to be the decisive year for the Allies, and for the British Army in particular.

Meeting at Chantilly on 5 December, 1915, the Allied commanders, under Joffre's influence, adopted the principle of a simultaneous offensive on the Eastern and Western fronts at a suitable date. Joffre claimed that, but for a lack of ammunition, the 'brilliant tactical results' of the September offensives would have produced a breakthrough. But the accumulation of sufficient stocks of ammunition was effected only slowly, and by February it was obvious that an offensive on the scale envisaged by Joffre could take place no earlier than the summer. Joffre pressed for an an attack over a 39-mile front, involving 40 French and 25 British divisions. It was an ambitious scheme which depended upon the Germans' remaining docile while the Allies methodically prepared for the assault. Unfortunately, the Germans were not to prove so helpful.

On 21 February, 1916, the French fortified zone at Verdun was subjected to a twelve-hour artillery bombardment of hitherto unparalleled intensity. That evening German troops moved forward into a battle of attrition which was designed to attract all the French army's reserves. The German attack seriously disrupted the Allied plans, reducing French participation from an original 40 divisions attacking over a 25-mile front to only five divisions over an eight-mile front.

The River Somme is a narrow stream, meandering through gently rolling hills. It is fine cavalry country, offering few natural obstacles to a horseman's progress. But what nature lacked, man had provided. Sir Douglas Haig said:

'During nearly two years preparation he (the enemy) had spared no pains to render these defenses impregnable. The first and second systems each consisted of

Opposite top: The 1st Lancashire Fusiliers fix bayonets prior to their assault on Beaumont Hamel in July 1916. **Opposite bottom:** Men of the Middlesex Regiment flee German gunfire after their failure to take Hawthorn Ridge on the first day of the battle. **Overleaf:** Bleak desolation and wanton destruction of human life and property was the legacy of the folly of the Somme.

several lines of deep trenches, well-provided with bomb-proof shelters and with numerous communication trenches connecting them. The first of the trenches in each system was protected by wire entanglements, many of them in two belts 40 yards broad . . . . .

'The numerous woods and villages in and between these systems of defense had been turned into veritable fortresses. The deep cellars usually to be found in the villages, and the numerous pits and quarries common to a chalk country, were used to provide cover for machine guns and trench mortars . . . . . The salients in the enemy's line, from which he could bring enfilade fire across his front, were made into self-contained forts and often protected by mine-fields; while strong redoubts and concrete machine-gun emplacements had been conducted in positions from which he could sweep his own trenches should these be taken . . . . .

'These various systems of defense, with the fortified localities and other supporting points between them, . . . formed, in short, not merely a series of successive lines, but one composite system of enormous depth and strength.'

The plan of attack called for a five-phase advance. First, the attackers were to achieve a breakthrough of the German front on the line Maricourt-Sens, and then to gain the heights between Bapaume and Ginchy before pushing northwest to Arras, and completing the break-through. This was to be followed by an advance north, aided by a secondary attack from the area of Arras, and by strategic exploitation to 'roll up' the German line.

The British Fourth Army (General Rawlinson) was to bear the brunt of the initial assault. Eleven divisions were to attack, with five in immediate reserve and two in army reserve. The Third Army was to commit two divisions to a diversionary assault toward Gommecourt. No hopes were placed on the achievement of strategic surprise. The scope of the preparations was too vast to hide from the Germans, who enjoyed the great advantage of holding the higher ground. To compensate for the lack of surprise, the generals planned to crush the Germans in their trenches by a bombardment of unparalleled ferocity and duration. Approximately 1500 guns, one to every twenty yards of front, were to prepare the assault.

On the morning of 24 June, 1916 the British bombardment began. It was planned according to a program which exemplified the ultimate in contemporary military science. Scheduled to last five days (coded U, V, W, X and Y) prior to the infantry assault (Z Day) the preparation was divided into two periods: on U and V days the guns were to concentrate on wire-cutting and registration. Some 350,000 shells were fired in two days. The second period of bombardment, on days W, X and Y, was aimed at destroying the enemy defenses and further damaging the wire. Gas shells were occasionally to be used to confuse the Germans, but the large-scale use of gas was confined to midnight on Y/Z Day. A total of 1,627,824 shells were fired between 24 June and 1 July, the date upon which the attack actually took place. The most notable disadvantage of the bombardment was that it gave the Germans ample warning; the moment it ceased,

they knew the infantry assault was imminent.

On 8 May General Headquarters issued an instruction for 'Training of Divisions for Offensive Action'. The infantry was to attack 'in successive waves or lines, each line adding impetus to the preceding one where this is checked, and carrying the whole forward to the objective'. Although Haig himself favored an advance by small groups, his views were strongly opposed by his army commanders at their conference on 15 June, and the use of waves was confirmed. An added factor to the rigidity of the British battle order was the amount of equipment which the assaulting troops carried. It totaled about 66 pounds—a weight which the *British Official History* notes ' . . . made it difficult to get out of a trench, impossible to move quicker than a slow walk, or to rise and lie down quickly'.

1 July 1916 was a day of blue skies and bright sun. The assault was set for 0730. It was expected to meet little initial resistance, coming as it did after 144 hours of continual bombardment. But the chalk of Artois proved ideal for deep dugouts:

'The garrisons of the first position remained below ground, close-packed, uncomfortable, short of food, depressed, but still alive and ready on their officers' orders when the barrage lifted, to issue forth with morale unbroken; . . .'

Nineteen Allied divisions, fourteen British and five French were ready to move into no-man's land. The Third Army, which held the line from Carency in the north to Hebuterne in the south sent two divisions, the 46th and 56th, to attack Gommecourt. The Fourth Army, which was the main assault force, was in position from Hebuterne to Maricourt, where it joined the French 8th Army. Rawlinson was ordered to send five corps forward on 1 July: 8, 10, 3, 15 and 13. With the 29th, 4th and 31st Divisions assaulting and 48th Division in reserve, 8 Corps was to attack in the area of Serre and Hamel, north of the Ancre. Further to the south, 10 Corps was to launch the 32nd, 36th and 49th Divisions south of the Ancre against Thiepval and Ovillers. In the center of the attacking line, 3 Corps was to take La Boisselle and press on to Contalmaison. Next in line, 15 Corps was to push two of its divisions

Opposite top: The Germans, prepared for the British attack, fire from their protected positions. Opposite bottom: A ration party of the Royal Irish Rifles pauses in a communications trench during the first day of the battle. Below: British soldiers assist two wounded German prisoners at La Boisselle during the third day of the offensive.

The Battle of the Somme, 1916

The Northwestern Front

Although the Germans had pushed the Russians well to the east, the battle lines which were drawn in the autumn of 1914 remained hard and fast along the trenches of the Western Front. The attempt to break through the wall of trenches from Switzerland to the Channel was the dream of Allied and German generals alike. The Somme was Haig's dream which ended as a nightmare for the Tommies.

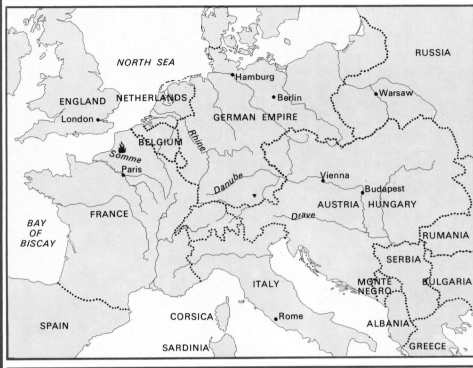

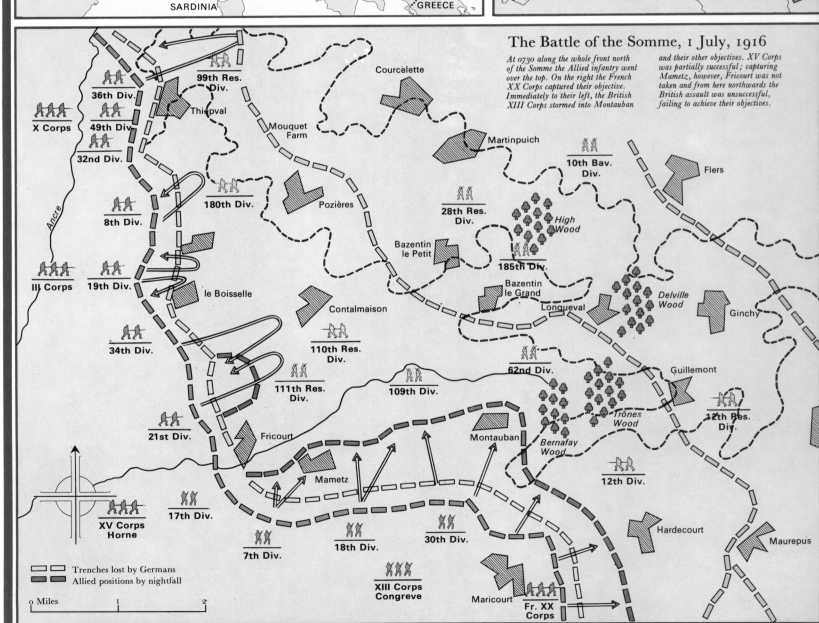

The Battle of the Somme, 1 July, 1916

At 0730 along the whole front north of the Somme the Allied infantry went over the top. On the right the French XX Corps captured their objective. Immediately to their left, the British XIII Corps stormed into Montauban and their other objectives. XV Corps was partially successful; capturing Mametz, however, Fricourt was not taken and from here northwards the British assault was unsuccessful, failing to achieve their objectives.

X Corps

36th Div.

49th Div.

32nd Div.

99th Res. Div.

Thiepval

Courcelette

Mouquet Farm

Martinpuich

10th Bav. Div.

Flers

8th Div.

180th Div.

Pozières

28th Res. Div.

High Wood

185th Div.

III Corps

19th Div.

le Boisselle

Contalmaison

Bazentin le Petit

Bazentin le Grand

Longueval

Delville Wood

Ginchy

34th Div.

110th Res. Div.

62nd Div.

Guillemont

21st Div.

111th Res. Div.

109th Div.

Trônes Wood

12th Res. Div.

Fricourt

Montauban

Bernafay Wood

12th Div.

XV Corps Horne

17th Div.

Mametz

Hardecourt

Maurepus

7th Div.

18th Div.

30th Div.

Trenches lost by Germans
Allied positions by nightfall

0 Miles   1   2

XIII Corps Congreve

Maricourt

Fr. XX Corps

NORTH SEA

Dunkirk

Bruges

Antwerp

Ghent

Ypres

Brussels

BELGIUM

Lille

Liège

Meuse

Arras

Bapaume

Charleroi

Sambre

Ourthe

Somme

Bastogne

Laon

Aisne

Semois

Montmedy

Oise

Reims

Marne

Verdun

FRANCE

Chateau-Thierry

Chalons

Paris

NORTH SEA

ENGLAND

NETHERLANDS

Hamburg

Berlin

Warsaw

RUSSIA

London

GERMAN EMPIRE

BELGIUM

Rhine

Somme

Paris

Danube

Vienna

Budapest

FRANCE

Drave

AUSTRIA HUNGARY

BAY OF BISCAY

RUMANIA

SERBIA

BULGARIA

SPAIN

ITALY

MONTE NEGRO

CORSICA

Rome

ALBANIA

SARDINIA

GREECE

Ancre

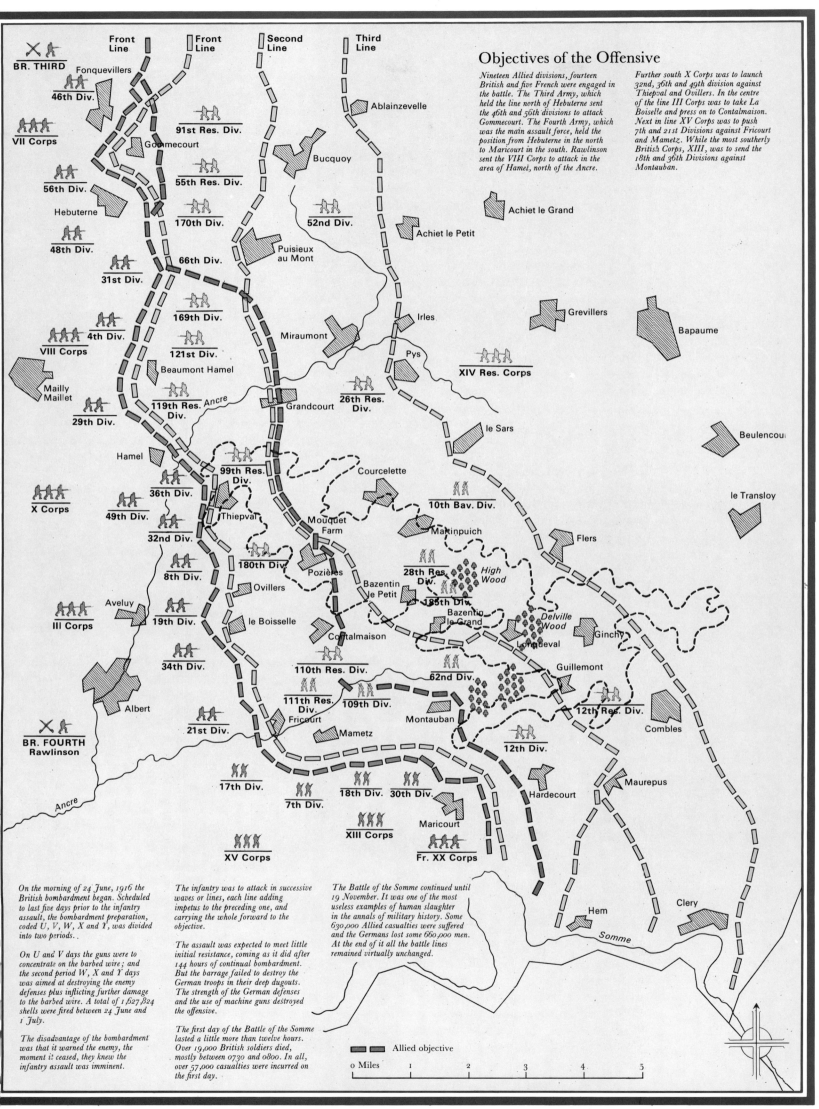

Objectives of the Offensive

Nineteen Allied divisions, fourteen British and five French were engaged in the battle. The Third Army, which held the line north of Hebuterne sent the 46th and 56th divisions to attack Gommecourt. The Fourth Army, which was the main assault force, held the position from Hebuterne in the north to Maricourt in the south. Rawlinson sent the VIII Corps to attack in the area of Hamel, north of the Ancre.

Further south X Corps was to launch 32nd, 36th and 49th division against Thiepval and Ovillers. In the centre of the line III Corps was to take La Boiselle and press on to Contalmaison. Next in line XV Corps was to push 7th and 21st Divisions against Fricourt and Mametz. While the most southerly British Corps, XIII, was to send the 18th and 36th Divisions against Montauban.

BR. THIRD
Fonquevillers
46th Div.
VII Corps
Gommecourt
56th Div.
Hebuterne
48th Div.
31st Div.
4th Div.
VIII Corps
Mailly Maillet
29th Div.
Hamel
36th Div.
X Corps
49th Div.
32nd Div.
Thiepval
8th Div.
Aveluy
III Corps
19th Div.
34th Div.
Albert
BR. FOURTH
Rawlinson

Front Line
91st Res. Div.
55th Res. Div.
170th Div.
66th Div.
Puisieux au Mont
169th Div.
121st Div.
Beaumont Hamel
119th Res. Div.
Ancre
Grandcourt
99th Res. Div.
Mouquet Farm
180th Div.
Pozières
Ovillers
le Boisselle
Contalmaison
110th Res. Div.
111th Res. Div.
Fricourt
109th Div.
Mametz
21st Div.
17th Div.
7th Div.
18th Div.
XV Corps
XIII Corps
30th Div.
Maricourt
Fr. XX Corps

Front Line
Second Line
Third Line
Ablainzevelle
Bucquoy
52nd Div.
Achiet le Petit
Miraumont
Irles
Pys
26th Res. Div.
le Sars
Courcelette
10th Bav. Div.
Martinpuich
28th Res. Div.
High Wood
185th Div.
Bazentin le Petit
Bazentin le Grand
Delville Wood
Longueval
Ginchy
62nd Div.
Montauban
Guillemont
12th Res. Div.
Combles
12th Div.
Hardecourt
Maurepus
Hem
Clery
Somme

Achiet le Grand
Grevillers
Bapaume
XIV Res. Corps
Beulencou
le Transloy
Flers

Ancre

On the morning of 24 June, 1916 the British bombardment began. Scheduled to last five days prior to the infantry assault, the bombardment preparation, coded U, V, W, X and Y, was divided into two periods.

On U and V days the guns were to concentrate on the barbed wire; and the second period W, X and Y days was aimed at destroying the enemy defenses plus inflicting further damage to the barbed wire. A total of 1,627,824 shells were fired between 24 June and 1 July.

The disadvantage of the bombardment was that it warned the enemy, the moment it ceased, they knew the infantry assault was imminent.

The infantry was to attack in successive waves or lines, each line adding impetus to the preceding one, and carrying the whole forward to the objective.

The assault was expected to meet little initial resistance, coming as it did after 144 hours of continual bombardment. But the barrage failed to destroy the German troops in their deep dugouts. The strength of the German defenses and the use of machine guns destroyed the offensive.

The first day of the Battle of the Somme lasted a little more than twelve hours. Over 19,000 British soldiers died, mostly between 0730 and 0800. In all, over 57,000 casualties were incurred on the first day.

The Battle of the Somme continued until 19 November. It was one of the most useless examples of human slaughter in the annals of military history. Some 630,000 Allied casualties were suffered and the Germans lost some 660,000 men. At the end of it all the battle lines remained virtually unchanged.

Allied objective

0 Miles 1 2 3 4 5

Right: Wounded German POWs are given water as they are taken back to British lines at La Boisselle, 3 July, 1916.

against Fricourt and Mametz, leaving one in reserve. The most southerly British corps, 13, was to throw two divisions into the line southeast of Mametz and drive for Montauban.

The 13 Corps had three distinct objectives. During the initial assault, on 1 July, Montauban was to be taken and a line established east of the village to gain contact with the French 20th Corps. The attack was to be pressed forward into Montauban itself and was to finish the day on the Montauban-Mametz Ridge, a total advance of some 2500–2700 yards. The German second line was not to be breached during the first day's assault, and its capture was in any case contingent upon the success of 15 Corps' attack north of Fricourt. This would secure the left flank and rear of 13 Corps, permitting it to wheel to the right and advance east to the German second position, in accord with the French south of the Somme.

In front of 13 Corps were nine battalions of the *12th, 28th Reserve* and *10th Bavarian Divisions*. The first position was strongly held and consisted of parallel trenches with a reserve line 700–1000 yards to the rear. Three thousand yards further was the second line, while away to the rear lay a partially constructed third position. The defense system was scattered with isolated strongpoints, and Montauban had been turned into a fortress.

144 Hours of Shellfire

Preceded by 144 hours of continual shellfire and eight minutes of 'hurricane bombardment' by six trench mortar batteries, 89th Brigade had the honor of being first into the 800-yard-wide no-man's land. The artillery preparation had done its work well; little difficulty was experienced in seizing the German front trenches. By 0830 Dublin Trench had been reached; abandoned by the Germans, it was immediately occupied. To the left of the 89th, 21st Brigade was equally successful, traversing no-man's land with a minimum of casualties, although the 18th King's suffered from machine gun fire on its left due to the inability of 18th Division to make similar progress. Once this obstacle was cleared, the advance continued and the first objectives were secured by 0835.

The 18th Division had the task of seizing Pommiers, a penetration of some 1500 yards, preparatory to the assault on Montauban. Exploding two mines, one of 5000 pounds and the other a mere 500 pounds at 0727, the 6th Royal Berkshires dashed across the 200-yard no-man's land. Held up by some persistent machine-gunners, the British were not able to reach the reserve line before it was heavily manned. By 0837, the Germans were still offering stubborn resistance, although the 30th Division finally forced the German reserve to abandon its line.

By 0900 the First Objectives had been reached and the attack had begun on the Second Objective, Montauban village. Leapfrogging the 21st Brigade of 30th Division, 90th Brigade moved forward at 0930 and, despite heavy resistance, assaulted the village. An hour later, Montauban and 30th Division's share of the Montauban-Mametz Ridge had been secured. Although hampered by German artillery fire, the 30th Division established itself in Montauban, extending its line south and southeast into La Briqueterie, a useful vantage

point. Fifteen hundred yards of German trench had been seized to a depth of 2000 yards. By noon, the advance stopped because the commander of 30th Division was ordered to await the advance of flanking formations.

On the left, the 18th Division was experiencing equal success, although at a somewhat higher cost. Its progress lagged slightly behind that of 30th Division due to the tenacious resistance of the German reserve trench, which was only partially cleared by 0930. The last redoubt blocking the advance was not subdued until about 1400. The 30th Division's right was now freed, and reached the Montauban-Mametz road an hour later. Two hours of heavy fighting lay ahead of 54th Brigade, but by 1700 it had reached the northern flank of Montauban Ridge.

The 30th Division had lost a total of 3011 casualties, while the 18th Division lost 3115. It was, on the whole, a successful day for 13 Corps. It must be emphasized, however, that in no place had the corps 'broken through'. The enemy's first position had been penetrated, but the second line remained. Only if equal success was achieved along the whole of the attacking frontage could a real breakthrough be effected, now that the initial bombardment had ended.

Facing 15 Corps, which occupied the line directly to the left of 13 Corps, was the Fricourt salient, a position of awesome strength. The first 1200 yards of the German lines were composed of an intricate maze of trenches. Fricourt itself had been turned into a fortress, and was extremely well-protected by machine guns. The garrison was ensconced in particularly deep dugouts. Fifteen hundred yards from the foremost position of the German defense was a second line (Fritz Trench-Railway Alley-Crucifix Trench), which was supported by a third line (White Trench-Wood Trench-Quadrangle Trench), 2000 yards behind the German front. Some 2500 yards further back stood the second German position and 6400 yards beyond this (9000 yards from the front) was the third position.

The 15 Corps was to send two of its three divisions (17th division remaining as Corps Reserve) forward to seize the high ground between Mametz and Fricourt. The corps was to push on into the third line of the first German position, effecting a penetration of 3500 yards, while maintaining contact with 13 Corps to the right and 3 Corps to the left. If the preliminary stage of the battle met with success, subsequent days were to see the seizure of Bazentin le Grand and Longueval in the German third position.

The attack of 15 Corps was meticulously prepared by artillery fire. At 0625 an intensive bombardment commenced, followed by the hurricane bombardment and the explosion at 0728 of seven mines totaling 59,000 pounds of high explosive. Rising from their trenches and following a somewhat imperfect creeping barrage, the British troops benefited from the artillery's efforts.

On the right, the 91st Brigade (7th Division) was to drive on Mametz and seize the line of Fritz Trench. The 20th Brigade was to mask Fricourt, maintaining parity with the 91st Brigade on its right, and was later to assault Fricourt in conjunction with the 22nd Brigade. Crossing no-man's land relatively easily, the 91st Brigade met with sporadic resistance as it moved through the forward trench system, but had gained some 700 yards by 0745. By 0800, the first objective was almost secured and resistance remained relatively light. In front of Mametz, however, the assault bogged down in front of fierce machine gun fire. Aided by renewed artillery support and the progress of 13 Corps, the 91st attacked again at 1300, finally entering Mametz by about 1340. The 20th Brigade had even more trouble, for it was called to effect an intricate wheel in front of Fricourt. The task was further complicated by the cratered terrain, the result of the British mines. Here the British had difficulty crossing no-man's land. The 9th Devons in the center suffered cruelly from small arms and machine gun fire, but were able to take the German first trench, although they only

gained a somewhat precarious hold. On the right, the 2nd Gordon Highlanders were able to progress some 300 yards during the morning, but were eventually pinned down. Only 2nd Border Regiment, on the left, made relatively satisfactory progress. By mid-morning, though, the assault of 20th Brigade had ground to a halt.

The 21st Division was to push into the German trenches to the right and left of Fricourt, using the 63rd and 64th Brigades to take the first reserve line (Crucifix Trench) and eventually moving into Quadrangle Trench, while the 50th Brigade was reserved for the assault on Fricourt. It was this last objective which was the key to 15 Corps' attack. The preliminary bombardment had not succeeded in sufficiently reducing the defenses of Fricourt, so that 50th Brigade suffered heavy casualties and were unable to reach the village. Further

Above: More Germans are captured at La Boisselle, and one gets a free ride.

Below: Machine-gunners, with their gas helmets on, fire into a German communications trench near Ovillers in July 1916.

to the left, the 63rd and 64th Brigades were cut to pieces by the machine guns in the German front line which had survived the bombardment. Finally reaching the front line trenches, the 63rd and 64th were forced to remain where they were and await support. Although the 64th Brigade eventually penetrated Crucifix Trench, it was at the cost of such frightful casualties as to temporarily bring the assault to a halt.

General Horne, commander of 15 Corps, upon receiving reports of success to both his right and left, ordered the 22nd, 62nd and 50th Brigades to assault Fricourt at 1430. Although the 1st Royal Welsh Fusiliers of 22nd Brigade actually reached the outskirts of the village, 50th Brigade was decimated and made no progress; 7th Green Howards lost 15 officers and 336 men in three minutes.

The 15 Corps had progressed on its flanks to an average distance of some 2000–2500 yards. By afternoon 7th Division had consolidated its position, aided by the success of the 18th Division of 13 Corps against Mametz. To the far left, 21st Division, having fallen far short of its goal of Mametz Wood, was nevertheless in possession of the German front line. But the key to the German

Opposite left: British soldiers time their next attack; each seemed to be more futile than the next.
Left: Field Marshal Sir Douglas Haig, architect of the carnage of the Somme.
Above: General Sir H. S. Horne, Commander of 15 Corps at the Somme.
Below: British and German wounded on their way to the dressing station near Bernafay Wood.

position, in 15 Corps' sector was Fricourt, and there the check was complete. For this, 7th Division lost 3380 men, 17th Division 1155 and 21st Division 4256; a heavy price for such small gains.

The front from Becourt to Authville, facing the heavily fortified villages of La Boisselle and Ovillers, belonged to 3 Corps. The high ground of the Fricourt, La Boisselle and Ovillers spurs provided a serious impediment to a successful advance. The Germans anchored their defense on three strong redoubts (Sausage, Scots and Schwaben) and the two fortified villages. A second line ran from Fricourt Farm to Ovillers, and a third lay in front of Contalmaison and Pozières. The second position ran from Bazentin Le Petit to Mouquet Farm with a third positon about 4500 yards behind it.

Two divisions, the 8th and 34th, were to assault, with 1st division as Corps Reserve. On the right, 34th Division was to push across the Fricourt spur and take La Boisselle, and then move to the line Contalmaison-Pozières, stopping 800 yards before the German second position. At the same time, the 8th Division was to take the western slope of Ovillers spur as well as the village before advancing to the line Pozières-Mouquet Farm.

The 34th Division launched a four-pronged attack. The two columns on the left were to attack the flanks of La Boisselle, thus isolating it, rather than attempting to seize it by direct assault. It was assumed that the preliminary bombardment would deal with the garrison of the village. The columns, three battalions deep, were expected to advance some 2000 yards and reach the fourth German trench, the last in their first line system, by 0818. The German intermediate line, in front of Contalmaison-Pozières, was to be seized by 0858, whereupon the 101st and 102nd Brigades would halt, and the 103rd Brigade would pass through them to seize Contalmaison and part of Pozières. This was to be accomplished by 1010. The assaulting battalions left their trenches at 0730, and within ten minutes 80% of their troops had fallen. Although some troops of the right hand column were able to reach and take the first German trench, further progress remained impossible amidst a storm of machine gun and rifle fire. The other columns made no progress. The *British Official History* notes that the success of the 102nd Brigade 'depended on the bombardment having obliterated the defenses near the two villages (Ovillers and La Boisselle), and upon the chance that the defenders, demoralized...would surrender freely'. Unfortunately, this was not the case; the two leading battalions went forward with great determination but were all but annihilated before they reached the German front line. Two of the four columns never reached the German lines at all; one had made only small gains, and the extreme right-hand column seized part of the line but was pinned down there. No further progress was made during the day.

To the left of the 24th Division, the 8th assaulted Ovillers Spur with a three-column advance north and south of the ridge. Although part of the 25th Brigade, 2nd Lincolnshire, actually reached the German trench, vigorous counterattacks by riflemen and bombers drove them from the position by 0900. The three battalions of the

25th Brigade lost over 50% of their strength and the 1st Royal Irish Rifles succeeded in getting only ten men across no-man's land. On the left, the first two waves of the 70th Brigade got across with little difficulty and reached the second German trench, but were stopped dead by heavy fire.

By 0900 the advance had died away all over 4th Division's front. In some places, particularly on the left, the German lines had been reached, but nowhere had penetration totaled more than two or three hundred yards. When requested by divisional headquarters to prepare a second assault, the commanders of the 23rd and 25th Brigades replied that it was not 'advisable', given the condition of the German defenses, and their own heavy casualties. A similar reply was made later in the day by the commander of 70th Brigade. An assault was subsequently planned for 56th Brigade of 19th Division, but this was postponed. Some isolated infantry continued to hold out in small sections of captured trench and in no-man's land, but after 1430 no sign of British troops appeared from the German lines.

Out of approximately 17,000 troops of 3 Corps who went into action that morning, 11,500 were casualties, mostly by 0800, and the German line remained unbroken. The seven-day bombardment, while making the German defenses unrecognizable, had not made them untenable, and 3 Corps paid a heavy price to discover this.

The task facing 10 Corps was no easier than that of its neighbors. As in 3 Corps' sector, the German position was dominated by a fortified village, in this case Thiepval. Overlooking the British trenches, Thiepval was a formidable obstacle. The commander of 132nd Division was confident, however, that the preliminary bombardment would knock out this keystone of the German defenses in the sector, and this in turn would entail the collapse of the whole edifice. No contingency plan had been drawn up for use if the bombardment failed in its purpose. The southern half of the sector's defense hinged on the Leipzig Redoubt. Behind these formidable obstacles, independent strongpoints mutually supported each other with enfilade fire.

The 10 Corps was expected to seize the Thiepval Spur and the plateau beyond as its first objectives, a task which totally depended upon the effectiveness of the preliminary bombardment. The 32nd Division was to assault the German line between the Leipzig Redoubt and Thiepval, including both strongpoints. Meanwhile, 36th Division was to seize the plateau between Thiepval and St Pierre Divion, taking the latter. These two divisions were to go on to the German intermediate line, a penetration of 1500–2000 yards, and then press forward to Grandcourt.

The two brigades of 32nd Division which made up the first wave of the assault, 97th and 96th, met with various misfortunes during the day. Although the 17th Highland Light Infantry of 97th Brigade were able, under cover of the bombardment, to rush the front of Leipzig Redoubt, they were unable to get much further. Despite devastating fire from other sections of the line, the British managed to consolidate their hold. The left of the 97th was not able to reach the German trenches owing to the fire from Thiepval, which had not been

Opposite top: British infantry prepare to advance yet again at Guillemont, September 1916. **Opposite center:** The Indian troops of the Deccan Horse at Bazentin Ridge in July. **Left:** German dead in a captured trench between Ginchy and Guillemont, August 1916. **Left center:** The remains of a German soldier outside his dugout at Beaumont Hamel, November 1916. **Bottom:** Men of the 16th Irish Division return for a well-deserved rest after helping to take Guillemont, September 1916.

Right: Assistance is given to a wounded Tommy in a trench converted into a makeshift field hospital. Danger was not far away.

subdued by the bombardment. The 96th Brigade suffered even more from machine gun fire and, although the Northumberland Fusiliers showed admirable courage by following 'a football drop-kicked by an eminent North Country player', they failed to cross no-man's land. At 0849, the 14th Brigade moved forward to assault the second German position. Not having been warned of the check to the 32nd, it was unprepared for the heavy fire it received, and could do little more than push some of its survivors into Leipzig Redoubt.

Perhaps surprisingly, 36th Division was able to seize a large part of its initial objectives. Leaving its trenches at 0715, and advancing to within one hundred yards of the German front line, 109th Brigade was able to reach the German trenches seconds before a firing line was established. They took the first trench and the advance was continued. By 0800 the German reserve trench was taken, as well as part of Schwaben Redoubt. Unfortunately 108th Brigade, to the left, was not able to seize St Pierre Divion, and its machine guns stood as a dyke preventing a rupture of the front. The failure of the 36th Division's left to break through north of the Ancre, which split the divisional frontage, necessarily limited the success further south. The failure of the 32nd Division to keep pace left the Ulstermen of the 36th in an exposed and uncomfortable position. At 0910 the 36th halted so as not to outpace its neighbors.

Meanwhile, through a lack of coordination, the 107th Brigade, not having received any counter-order, advanced past the halted 108th and 109th Brigades and attacked the Grandcourt line. Parts of the position were seized, although the garrison of Thiepval rendered it practically untenable by enfilade fire.

At 1445, 10 Corps Headquarters issued orders for an assault by the 146th Brigade of 49th Division, in reserve, against Thiepval, at 1600. Communications were difficult, and only a small fraction of the troops were able to move forward; the 1st/6th West Yorkshires lost half their strength in casualties in a gallant but vain assault. It was now the turn of the Germans, who opened a devastating trench-mortar barrage and began counter-attacking the isolated troops in Schwaben Redoubt; by 2230 the German 185th Regiment had retaken the position.

Before 8 Corps lay a series of spurs and valleys, which had been cleverly fortified to provide mutual support and enfilade fire. Beaumont Hamel, in the middle of the sector, was a fortress replete with machine guns and good protection for the soldiers who manned them. Four thousand yards behind the German front position a second line extended from Grandcourt to Puisieux, two fortified positions of great strength, while a third line lay another 4000 yards to the rear. The varied nature of the terrain was a serious disadvantage for the preliminary bombardment, as it was difficult for observers to check the fall of shot.

The 8 Corps hoped to precede its assault with a creeping barrage, which made no concessions to flexibility:

'At the commencement of each infantry attack the divisional artillery will lift 100 yards and continue lifting at the rate of 50 yards a minute...

'The rate of the infantry has been calculated at 50 yards a minute...

'The lines once settled cannot be altered. The infantry therefore must make their pace conform to the rate of the artillery lifts...'

The 29th Division pinned its hopes upon the devastating effect of a mine filled with 40,000 pounds of ammonal, fired at 0720 under a strong-point in the German line. This brought about a serious error, for the divisional artillery switched to the second trenches when the mine went up, and the Germans were able to maintain a position on the far edge of the crater, under little artillery

Below: British 6-inch, 26 cwt Mk I Howitzer. Maximum range: 11,400 yards. Weight: three tons, 12 cwt, 22 lbs. Crew: six. Shell weight: 100 lbs or 86 lbs.

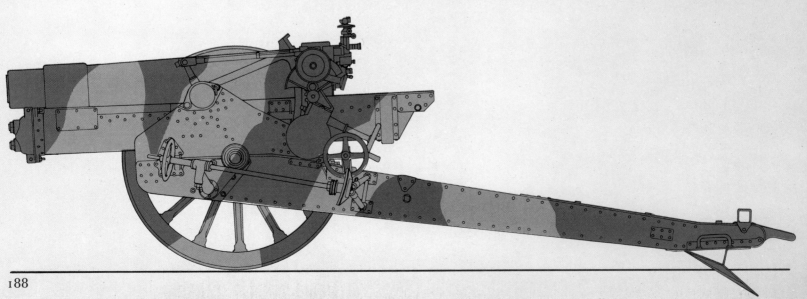

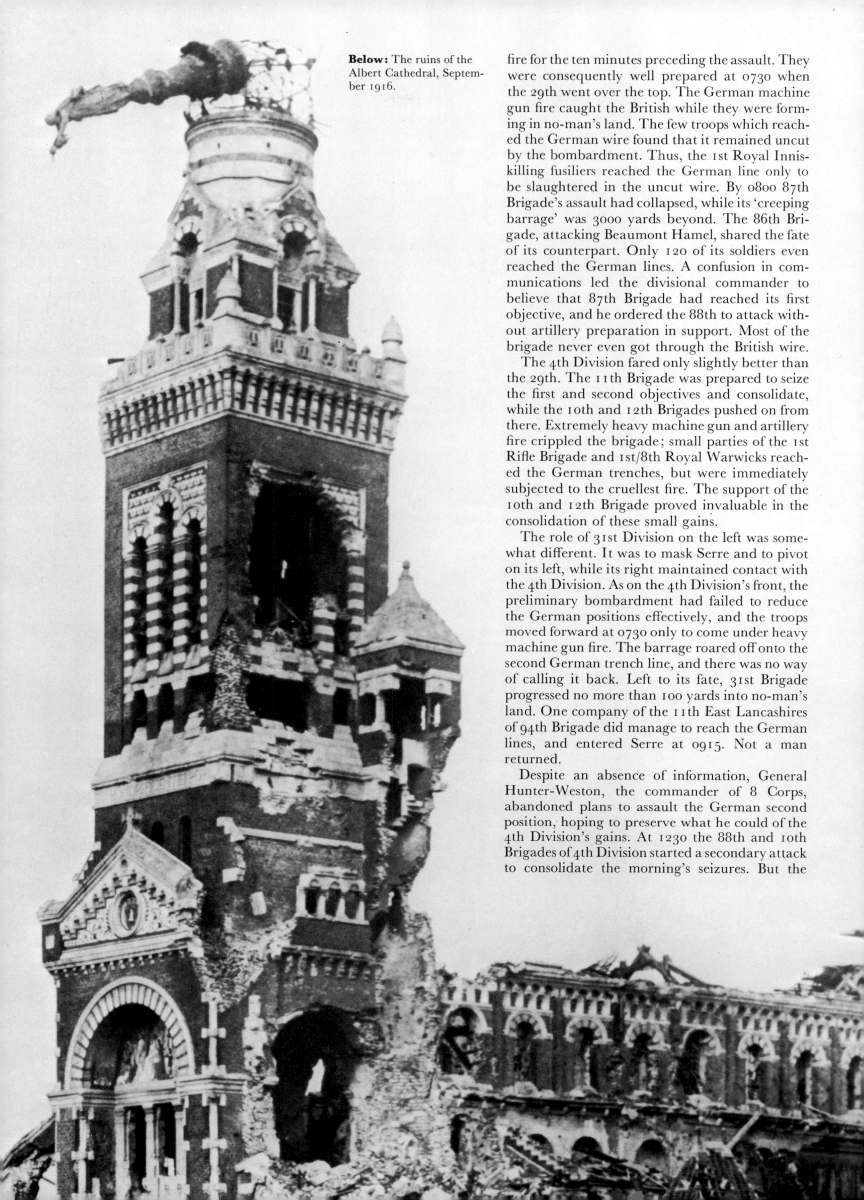

Below: The ruins of the Albert Cathedral, September 1916.

fire for the ten minutes preceding the assault. They were consequently well prepared at 0730 when the 29th went over the top. The German machine gun fire caught the British while they were forming in no-man's land. The few troops which reached the German wire found that it remained uncut by the bombardment. Thus, the 1st Royal Inniskilling fusiliers reached the German line only to be slaughtered in the uncut wire. By 0800 87th Brigade's assault had collapsed, while its 'creeping barrage' was 3000 yards beyond. The 86th Brigade, attacking Beaumont Hamel, shared the fate of its counterpart. Only 120 of its soldiers even reached the German lines. A confusion in communications led the divisional commander to believe that 87th Brigade had reached its first objective, and he ordered the 88th to attack without artillery preparation in support. Most of the brigade never even got through the British wire.

The 4th Division fared only slightly better than the 29th. The 11th Brigade was prepared to seize the first and second objectives and consolidate, while the 10th and 12th Brigades pushed on from there. Extremely heavy machine gun and artillery fire crippled the brigade; small parties of the 1st Rifle Brigade and 1st/8th Royal Warwicks reached the German trenches, but were immediately subjected to the cruellest fire. The support of the 10th and 12th Brigade proved invaluable in the consolidation of these small gains.

The role of 31st Division on the left was somewhat different. It was to mask Serre and to pivot on its left, while its right maintained contact with the 4th Division. As on the 4th Division's front, the preliminary bombardment had failed to reduce the German positions effectively, and the troops moved forward at 0730 only to come under heavy machine gun fire. The barrage roared off onto the second German trench line, and there was no way of calling it back. Left to its fate, 31st Brigade progressed no more than 100 yards into no-man's land. One company of the 11th East Lancashires of 94th Brigade did manage to reach the German lines, and entered Serre at 0915. Not a man returned.

Despite an absence of information, General Hunter-Weston, the commander of 8 Corps, abandoned plans to assault the German second position, hoping to preserve what he could of the 4th Division's gains. At 1230 the 88th and 10th Brigades of 4th Division started a secondary attack to consolidate the morning's seizures. But the front-line troops were short of ammunition, especially bombs, and were slowly driven back into the German front trenches. The attack had to be postponed in order to prevent further congestion. The reorganized German defenses on each side of the salient effectively checked any reinforcements, although it took the Germans some time to clear the British from the captured trenches.

The attack on Gommecourt by 7 Corps was considered by Haig to be a diversionary assault designed to increase the frontage under attack. It was separated from the main sector of operations by a two-mile gap which was to be left unattacked. The objective of the assault, the village of Gommecourt, was a position of the greatest strength. It was, in effect, a single fortified position, the fruit of almost two years of German labor. The 7 Corps' orders clearly stated that the attack was 'to assist in the operations of the Fourth Army by diverting against itself the fire of artillery and infantry which might otherwise be directed against the left flank of the main attack near Serre'. No reserves were allocated in case of a breakthrough, although it would not have been impossible to shift troops to 7 Corps if the situation warranted such action.

Resting on high ground, Gommecourt was perhaps the strongest point in the German line. It was well-protected by deep dugouts, which provided sufficient protection from any but the most heavy guns. The unenviable task of assaulting this for-midable position went to 56th and 46th Divisions.

The 56th went over the top at 0730 with the 168th and 169th Brigades up and the 167th in reserve. The two forward brigades were expected to reach the German third trench, and the 169th was subsequently to move left to link up with the 46th Division behind Gommecourt. Just beating the Germans to their trenches after the bombardment lifted, the forward brigades seized two trenches relatively easily, and one other with more difficulty. Further progress was hampered by the German artillery barrage, which isolated the British troops in the German forward trenches.

The 46th Division, attacking at the same time as the 56th, did not fare nearly as well. The muddy ground and extreme width of no-man's land was disastrous for 137th Brigade on the right, which was caught in the open by German machine gun and artillery fire. The 139th was able to reach the German first trench, but again the German artillery fire quickly isolated those who were lodged in the German lines, and machine gun fire prevented an advance into the second and third German positions. Throughout the morning the 139th remained trapped, while repeated attempts to support them failed. Of the men of the 1st/5th and 1st/7th Sherwood Foresters who reached the German trenches none returned.

With 46th Division stuck fast either in no-man's land or in the first German trench, the Germans

Below: Horses, up to their knees in mud, carry an ammunition limber forward along what once was the Lesboeufs Road, November 1916.

turned their attention to the 56th, which had been considerably more successful. The Germans concentrated some thirteen reserve companies against the 56th and counterattacked behind the cover of a brief but severe artillery bombardment. Effectively isolated, the British began to run out of bombs by noon, and the Germans were able to push them back into the second line. Four hours later the second line was in German hands, and by 0930 the last British troops abandoned the German lines.

The first day of the battle of the Somme lasted a little more than twelve hours. The formula of more men, more guns and more munitions as the key to breakthrough and victory had proved to be false. Some 1,627,824 shells were hurled into the German trenches in a 144-hour bombardment. The rigidity of the plans, the lack of effective tactical and artillery support for the infantry, the strength of the German defenses, and their skillful tactical use of machine guns and artillery doomed the attack before it began. Over 19,000 British soldiers died, mostly between 0730 and 0800. In all, over 57,000 casualties. And yet:

'No braver or more determined men ever faced an enemy than those sons of the British Empire who "went over the top" on 1 July, 1916. Never before had the ranks of a British Army on the field of battle contained the pick of all classes of the nation in physique, brains and education.

And they were volunteers, not conscripts. If a decisive victory was to be won, it was expected now.'

The failure of the British assault on 1 July did not end the battle. The offensive continued, with interruptions, until November, but British inability to achieve a clean breakthrough early on made it a long and bloody slogging-match. Newly arrived tanks were used in mid-September and achieved local success, but were too few in number to exercise a decisive influence upon the battle. The results of the battle remain a question of debate. Haig's expected breakthrough had failed to materialize, and the territorial gains of the Allies remained meager. The Germans had, however, sustained very heavy casualties—approximately 600,000 in all, roughly equal to the Allies' losses—and were in no position to replace them. One author has pointed out that Haig 'weakened the German Army in the west in much the same way as the Russian Army weakened Hitler's at Stalingrad'. He did so at the cost of frightful casualties, largely the result of tactical misappreciation and defective generalship. Yet it is, perhaps, too easy to make Haig the scapegoat for the bloodbath of the Somme. The Allies would not possess the means of breaking through the German lines in strength until the arrival of large numbers of tanks. Haig tried to apply the tactical lessons of 1914 and 1915, and his failure must be shared by the majority of British commanders at all levels.

El Alamein 1942

Opposite: General, later Field Marshal, Erwin Rommel, the Desert Fox of the *Afrika Korps* whose tactical skill made up for the inadequacy of men and matériel at his disposal.

The German blitzkrieg of 1939–40 which opened the Second World War was a complete success. Poland, Denmark, Norway, the Low Countries and France had quickly fallen to Hitler's Wehrmacht. Although total victory was not yet achieved thanks to 'the few' of the RAF who saved Britain from invasion, it looked all but over in Europe toward the end of 1940. Yet on the desert coast of North Africa the war of movement continued. Italy, already in possession of Libya, and backed by Nazi-influenced Vichy French North Africa, had only to plunge into British-held Egypt to take the Suez Canal and cut off Britain's lifeline of Empire and communication with India and the Far East. But the fortunes of war proved more than usually fickle in the Western Desert between 1940 and 1942. An Italian advance into Egypt in September 1940 was hurled back at Sidi Barrani in December, but German intervention in early 1941 brought about a rapid reversal of the situation. Lieutenant-General Erwin Rommel, an infantryman with a rare feel for the use of armor, struck back hard, driving the overextended British toward the Egyptian frontier. The ensuing lull saw both armies reinforced. The British Eighth Army was split into two corps, 8 and 30, with the latter containing most of the available armor. General Sir Claude Auchinleck was sent to take command of British forces in the Middle East, while General Sir Alan Cunningham took over the Eighth Army. Air Vice-Marshal Arthur Coningham commanded Air Headquarters Western Desert, soon to become the Desert Air Force, which provided Eighth Army with air support.

Rommel's command had also been expanded. It now contained three German divisions, *15th* and *21st Panzer*, and *90th Light*. The Italians fielded one good armored division, *Ariete*, a motorized division, *Trieste*, and four infantry divisions of less certain quality. Rommel had been promoted to general, and was in overall command of the entire Axis force, now known as *Panzergruppe Afrika*. The German element, the *Deutsche Afrika Korps*, was commanded by Lt-General Crüwell.

Rommel feared that the continued British build-up would eventually crush *Panzergruppe Afrika* by sheer weight of numbers. He therefore sought permission to attack before British preparations were complete. Rommel's stroke was, however, pre-empted by a British offensive, 'Operation Crusader', which was launched on 18 November. After a bitter see-saw struggle, during which Auchinleck replaced the exhausted Cunningham with Lieutenant-General N.M. Ritchie, Rommel fell back westward, and mid-January 1942 saw him at Mersa Brega near El Agheila. Rommel, typically, refused to remain on the defensive, and on 21 January he jabbed forward once more. Benghazi fell on 29 January and Ritchie disengaged, falling back to a strong position just west of Tobruk, running from Gazala on the coast to Bir Hacheim in the desert.

Ritchie's withdrawal was followed by a four-month lull during which the Eighth Army was again reorganized, largely in an effort to produce better cooperation between infantry and armor. The new American Grant tank began to arrive; mounting a 75mm gun, it was a much more effective weapon than either the Stuart light tank or the Crusader medium tank, which it replaced.

The Panzer Mark III

The mainstay of Rommel's Panzer divisions was the Panzer Mark III mounting the short 50mm gun. The armor on many of these had been reinforced, and they were particularly resistant to the British two-pounder antitank round. The *Afrika Korps* was also receiving a trickle of Mark III specials with the long 50mm gun and a few Mark IVs with a 75mm gun. Italian tanks, mainly the Mark 13/30 and the improved Mark 14/41, were considerably inferior to the Germans'.

The adversaries were far from evenly matched in terms of antitank weapons. The British two-pounder was unable to cope with face-hardened armor, and its replacement, the six-pounder, though more effective, was soon to be outclassed by German tank development. Moreover, only 112 six-pounders were available to the Eighth Army in mid-1942. Although German antitank guns, properly speaking, were no more satisfactory than their British equivalents, the Germans possessed an important asset; the 88mm anti-aircraft gun used in the antitank role. Although the 88 had some tactical disadvantages,

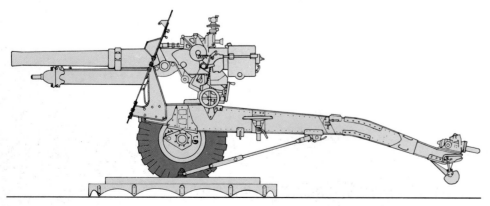

Below: British 25-pounder gun, used during the Desert campaign. Weight: three tons, five cwt. Length: 19 feet 3 inches. Range: 13,400 yards. Crew: six.

Above: British 25-pounder guns firing at night during the summer of 1942, when the Germans were advancing to within 60 miles of Alexandria.

it had an extremely flat trajectory and a high degree of penetrating power. Properly deployed, a few 88s could hold off large numbers of tanks; Rommel habitually employed a screen of 88s to cover his own armor when threatened by attack.

Churchill's Visit

The Gazala battles in late May and early June exemplified the strengths and weaknesses of the contending armies. Rommel launched an attack which was bold to the point of rashness, but his adversaries, although fighting doggedly, reacted slowly. The eventual British counterattack met with a bloody repulse, and by 12 June Ritchie had decided to disengage. Tobruk, isolated and ill-prepared, fell on 22 June, and the Eighth Army continued its headlong retreat. Ritchie was relieved of his command by Auchinleck, who flew forward from Cairo to take over personally. His intervention failed to stem the tide; the Mersa Matruh position collapsed, and the British stumbled back to El Alamein, where work was in progress on a new defensive line.

El Alamein was a small station on the railway between Alexandria and Mersa Matruh. It was, in itself, a place of no importance. What gave El Alamein its great strategic significance was that forty miles to the south began the Qattara Depression, a huge salt marsh with a sharp escarpment running along its northern edge. The escarpment ended near Siwa, but south of Siwa stretched the Great Sand Sea, running south and east toward the Oasis of Kuffa. The potential of the Alamein position had been visible to British commanders for some time. One of Auchinleck's first acts had been to order the construction of defenses in the area, but these, planned on the now discredited 'box' concept, were far from perfect. They could only guarantee the security of the ground which they held physically or could cover with their fire, and several avenues of approach were left unguarded. In any event, the viability of the planned position was never put to the test, since two of the projected 'boxes' were overrun before they could be garrisoned.

On 2 July Rommel launched what he hoped

would be his final attack on the Eighth Army. Auchinleck fought the battle with commendable skill. *Ariete* was roughly handled by the New Zealanders on 3 July, and Auchinleck counterattacked two days later. Although Rommel was crucially short of armor, he managed to contain the counterstroke, but the battle ended with the British in firm possession of the vital ground of Ruweisat Ridge and Tel el Eisa.

Rommel had, for the time at least, been thwarted before Alamein, but Axis fortunes seemed in the ascendent in all other theaters of war. On 28 June Field Marshal von Bock opened his offensive in southern Russia. The initially modest strategic aim of this offensive had become inflated into a drive for the oilfields of the Caucasus. Bock's attack was to be exploited by a thrust through Rostov to the oilfield at Maikop and on to Baku on the Caspian Sea. Rommel, ironically, was only 550 miles from Haifa and its oil pipelines, while Bock was nearly a thousand from Baku. It is a measure of the low strategic priority given to the Western Desert by the German High Command that Rommel remained desperately ill-equipped. Men and *matériel* which would have brought about German victory in the desert could be squandered in a day's fighting in Russia.

Rommel Attacks

News of the defeat at Gazala and the fall of Tobruk was badly received in England. Churchill himself was particularly irritated by the latter, and decided to visit Cairo on his way out to meet Stalin at Tehran. Auchinleck, meanwhile, was planning to mount a powerful offensive in September, but suspected that Rommel would attack before then, probably against the Eighth Army's left rear. Rommel himself was ill and tired. He was pitifully short of tanks and fuel; his attack could not be launched until mid-August. Its direction was that anticipated by Auchinleck; it was to swing around the British southern flank, but in doing so would be met by the full force of Auchinleck's defensive preparations.

Churchill was preceded to Cairo by the Chief of

Above left: Lt-Gen. (later
Field Marshal) Bernard
Montgomery addresses his
troops after he took com-
mand of the Eighth Army.
Above: Italian prisoners
taken at El Alamein eat
rations of bully-beef after
their arrival in POW camp.

the Imperial General Staff, General Sir Alan
Brooke. Brooke had hoped to do the groundwork
for the inevitable command reshuffle before
Churchill arrived, but, in the event, the two men
landed in Cairo within a few hours of each other.
Churchill came with certain preconceived ideas.
Firstly, the forthcoming Anglo-American invasion
of North Africa—'Operation Torch'—loomed
large in his mind; he was eager that Rommel
should be defeated in August or early September
in order to have 'a decisive effect upon the attitude
of the French in North Africa when "Torch"
begins'. Secondly, he was opposed to any reinforcement of Persia and Iraq by troops from
Egypt. The War Cabinet had been seriously
worried by the possibility that the Germans would
break through in the Caucasus and strike for the
oil of the Middle East. By early August, however,
it was apparent that the Russians would fight
hard on the Caucasus front; the danger of a
German thrust into Persia and Iraq was thus
diminished.

The next few days saw a crucial sequence of
decisions. Churchill and Brooke eventually agreed
that Lieutenant-General W.H.E. Gott should take
over the Eighth Army, while General Sir Harold

Alexander was appointed to the newly-created
Near East Command. This project, the result of
much hard bargaining, rapidly became obsolete.
Gott, flying back to Cairo from the desert on 7
August, was killed when his aircraft was attacked
by German fighters. Brooke persuaded Churchill
to replace him with Lieutenant-General B.L.
Montgomery—Brooke's choice for the post in the
first place. Auchinleck declined the proferred
Middle East Command, which went instead to
General Maitland Wilson. Auchinleck thus dis-
appeared from the scene. He had, perhaps, been
unfairly blamed for the Eighth Army's failures.
Even his adversary Rommel pointed out that he
was 'a very good leader', and paid tribute to his
'deliberation and noteworthy courage'.

Churchill left Cairo on 7 August. Before
departing, he gave Alexander his overall directive
for the campaign, stressing that 'your prime and
main duty will be to take or destroy at the earliest
opportunity the German-Italian Army commanded by Field-Marshal Rommel...' This, he
added, 'must be considered paramount in His
Majesty's interests'.

When Montgomery arrived in Egypt on 12
August, Auchinleck had not yet formally handed

Left: Soldiers of the *Afrika
Korps* trudge forward
during the first battle of El
Alamein.

over to Alexander. However, when Montgomery drove forward to the Eighth Army's headquarters on the morning of 13 August, he was so unimpressed by the gloomy air of the place that he decided, despite orders to the contrary, to take command immediately. Having done this, he canceled all orders for withdrawal, and announced to the assembled staff his firm intention of staying put in the Alamein position. Retreat was out of the question. Although an immediate attack by Rommel might be difficult to repulse, he felt confident that this would not be the case in a week's time. Finally, he announced the appointment of Brigadier F.W. de Guingand as his Chief-of-Staff, and emphasized that de Guingand was to have full authority over his headquarters and staff.

It seemed probable to Montgomery that Rommel would launch an attack fairly soon. From Rommel's disposition, and particularly from strenuous mining activities in the north, it was likely that he would try to repeat his former success with a 'right hook' around the southern end of the British position. Full moon was on 26 August, and this seemed the most likely time for an attack. Plans were already in existence to meet such a threat; it is, indeed, a moot point as to how far Montgomery was able to profit by his predecessor's planning in this respect. What is certain is that Montgomery at once took steps to instill into commanders at all levels the belief that there would be no retreat. He disputed the

Far left: Australian artillerymen in action in the autumn of 1942. **Right:** 'Monty' with his famous hat covered with badges of the units which served under him in a photograph taken at the time of Alamein. **Below:** A German Mark III tank which was put out of action near Tel-el-Eissa Station in August 1942.

Right: Rommel discusses tactics with German and Italian officers near Alamein in September 1942.

system of defensive 'boxes', and made forceful representations to General Headquarters, demanding that recently-arrived troops be sent forward sooner than the staff at Cairo had intended. These efforts produced the 44th (Home Counties) Division, most of which was sent to Alam Halfa Ridge. Further reinforcements also arrived, and with them came Lieutenant-General B.G. Horrocks to take command of 13 Corps.

By 26 August, the anticipated date of the attack, the Eighth Army was in a position to resist the expected onslaught. In the north, the 9th Australian and 1st South African Divisions held the El Alamein area. The 5th Indian division was strongly posted on Ruweisat Ridge with the 2nd New Zealand Division to its south, on Bare Ridge. To thwart a turning movement by Rommel, the 44th Division held Alam Halfa Ridge, with two armored brigades to its west and one to its south. Montgomery intended 'to stand firm in the Alamein position, hold the Ruweisat and Alam Halfa Ridges securely, and let him (Rommel) beat up against them'. The armor was not to rush forward to take on Rommel's tanks; it was to fight from hull-down positions at the western end of Alam Halfa Ridge. A substantial deception plan was also undertaken, with the hope of persuading Rommel that the southern flank was stronger than it in fact was.

Rommel was hampered by more than his worsening health. Although a grateful Führer had promoted him to the rank of Field-Marshal after the fall of Tobruk, he continued to be beset by contradictory orders emanating from a tangled chain of command; he was subordinate both to the Italian *Commando Supremo* and to Field-Marshal von Kesselring, German Commander of the Mediterranean theater. The problem of supply became more serious. British naval and air forces took a heavy toll of Axis convoys. General Bayerlein, the *Afrika Korps'* Chief-of-Staff, maintained that by mid-1942 only one-fifth of Rommel's supply requirements were arriving in North Africa. Even when *matériel* had been landed, it remained vulnerable. Most of the supplies came ashore at Benghazi and had to be moved eastward by truck under the watchful eyes of the Desert Air Force.

The whole question of supply was partially a consequence of a clash of operational priorities. The situation could have been improved by diverting all available air power to strike at Malta, the base from which many of the attacks on Axis shipping originated. This, however, would denude *Panzerarmee Afrika* of its air cover. In fact, both the *Commando Supremo* and Kesselring had favored calling a halt after the fall of Tobruk, in order to deal with Malta. Rommel, however, was backed by Hitler who authorized his drive to the Nile. It may, therefore, be argued that Rommel's advance from Tobruk was a strategic error, and that he himself was primarily to blame for the shortage of supplies which so imperiled his position in mid-1942.

Rommel launched his attack on the night of 30/31 August. The Desert Air Force hammered his troops as they advanced, and on 1 September the main armored attack broke against the Alam Halfa Ridge. Rommel called off the offensive on 3 September, though fighting went on for some days afterwards. The battle had cost Rommel 50 tanks; the British had lost slightly more, but, remaining in possession of the battlefield, were able to salvage some of these. The Battle of Alam Halfa—sometimes known as the first Battle of Alamein—was a sharp rebuff for Rommel, and it gave a useful fillip to the morale of the Eighth Army.

Below: Rommel and other German officers help extricate their vehicle which is being hauled out of a tight spot.

Montgomery began preparations for his offensive as soon as the Battle of Alam Halfa was over. Churchill continued to demand that it should be launched in September, but Montgomery and Alexander agreed that this was impossible, and 23 October was eventually selected as the target date. Montgomery emphasized three fundamental points during this pre-battle phase; leadership, equipment and training. Furthermore, steps had to be taken to ensure the continued security of the line. This was aided by extending the minefields to the south of the position. The other essentials were less easily tackled. The questions of training and leadership were closely interrelated. Montgomery's new mobile formation, 10 Corps, was commanded by Lieutenant-General Herbert Lumsden, formely of 1st Armored Division. He was not Montgomery's choice for the post, and was in open disagreement with his army commander over the plan for the forthcoming battle. Early in September, 10 Corps began to organize and train. It comprised three armored divisions; 1st, 8th and 10th, and was the Eighth Army's most powerful striking force.

Horrocks' 13 Corps

Lieutenant-General Horrocks' 13 Corps contained 7th Armored Division, newly reorganized and commanded by Major General John Harding, and two infantry divisions, 44th and 50th. Two Free French Brigade groups operated under command of the 7th. A major problem in both 10 and 13 Corps was the provision of adequate motorized infantry for the armored divisions. This eventually resulted in the 8th Armored Division being broken up; one of its brigades went to 10th Armored, the divisional troops formed the composite 'Hammerforce' in 10 Corps reserve, and the divisional headquarters were used for radio deception purposes. This complex reorganization required nearly a month, and 10 Corps was not fully concentrated until the end of September.

Lieutenant-General Sir Oliver Leese's 30 Corps, although a somewhat multinational force, found reorganization easier. It included the newly-arrived 51st Highland and 4th Indian Divisions; the latter relieved 5th Indian in early September. The corps was completed by Major-General

Freyberg's 2nd New Zealand Division which contained one armored and two infantry brigades, as well as the 1st South African and 9th Australian Divisions.

This extensive reorganization would in itself have proved difficult enough. It was complicated by the arrival of large quantities of new equipment, so that many units were forced to simultaneously reorganize, re-equip and retrain. The Eighth Army's tank strength rose, by the beginning of the battle, to 1029. Of these, 252 were new Shermans, mounting 75mm guns, more than a match for any of Rommel's tanks, even his few Mark IV specials. There were also 78 Crusader Mark IIIs, mounting six-pounder guns instead of the inadequate two-pounders carried by previous models. Unfortunately, neither tank was immune from mechanical failure; the Crusaders proved somewhat unreliable, and there were teething troubles with the Shermans.

Self-propelled artillery had also arrived, giving the armored divisions mobile fire support. Two types of guns were in use, the British 'Bishop', a 25-pounder mounted on the chassis of a Valentine tank, and the more reliable American 'Priest', with a 105-mm gun on a Grant chassis. Neither weapon had, however, arrived in sufficient quantity to replace the towed 25-pounder as the mainstay of British field artillery. Of the 1403 anti-tank

Above: Axis troops move forward in the desert sands.

Below: German soldiers laden with their field kits move up to the Alamein front.

guns available, 849 were six-pounders, a few of which, known as 'Deacons', were mounted on an armored chassis. Each infantry battalion now had eight two-pounders, while motor battalions each had sixteen six-pounders. Almost all the antitank regiments were equipped with the latter weapon.

The Desert Air Force, organized in two fighter groups and two light bomber wings, used the pre-battle period to rest and retrain, but kept up operations against Rommel's lines of communication. By 23 October Coningham had 750 aircraft available, of which 530 were serviceable.

Montgomery had considerable numerical superiority in all respects, though by no means the three-to-one ratio believed necessary for a set-piece attack. Rommel had only 104,000 infantry, just over half of them Italian, to Montgomery's 195,000. He was even more heavily outmatched in armor, with 489 tanks, of which 211 were German, mainly Mark IIIs. Only 30 Mark IV specials were available. In the air, too, Rommel was at a disadvantage; he had 675 aircraft in all, of which 350 were serviceable for the battle.

Rommel had decided, following his reverse at Alam Halfa, to dig in where he stood rather than to fall back to a position where the ground was better and supply easier. His engineers set to work creating a formidable series of defense works. The entire front of the Axis position was covered by minefields, or, as the Germans called them, 'Devil's Gardens'. These were not merely uniform expanses of mine-sown desert. They comprised several belts of mines running parallel to the front, with transverse sections to limit exploitation. Irregular strips on both sides of the main field strengthened weak points or shepherded attackers onto concealed positions. The mines were covered by fire from 'battle outposts' in the minefields themselves. Although in terms of sheer size the Axis position at Alamein was less impressive than the Russian defenses at Kursk, the planning of the minefields was certainly cunning in the extreme. Care was taken with concealment—although this was difficult in the desert, where the wind often

blew away the sand that covered the mines—and with the use of booby-traps and similar devices.

Behind the minefields and 'battle outposts' ran a line of positions designed around dug-in tanks and anti-tank guns. These positions followed the minefields from Sidi Abd El Rahman on the coast to Qarat El Himeimat in the desert. Rommel himself had been ordered home to rest, but, before handing over command to General Stumme, he deployed *Panzerarmee Afrika* behind its increasingly strong defenses. The *15th Panzer Division* was in the north, south of Sidi Abd El Rahman, and *21st Panzer* was in the south northwest of Gebel Kalakh. As part of his policy of interleaving Italian and German formations, Rommel split up the Italian *XX Corps*, sending the *Littorio Division* to join *15th Panzer*, while the battered *Ariete* joined *21st Panzer*. *Trieste* and *90th Light Divisions* were in reserve in the north.

General Navarrini's *XXI Corps* held the forward positions in the northern sector, opposite the British 30 Corps. In the extreme north were two battalions of General Ramcke's parachute brigade, with some Bersaglieri. The Kidney Ridge area was the responsibility of *164th Division*. The *Trento Division* held Miteiriya Ridge, and the *Bologna Division* covered the western end of Ruweisat Ridge; both these formations were stiffened with German parachutists.

General Orsi's *X Corps* held the front south of Ruweisat Ridge. The *Brescia Division* was in the area of Bab El Qattara, with the *Folgore Parachute Division* to its southeast. The *Pavia Division* held the Axis right, toward Qarat El Himeimat, and curled round onto the Taqa Plateau. The flank was screened by German reconnaissance units.

The defensive concepts which underlay the planning of the Axis position had much in common with those prevailing on the Western Front in 1917–18. The essence of both was depth; Rommel anticipated that the minefields and 'battle outposts' would absorb much of the initial impetus of the attack, just as wire and machine guns had done 25 years previously. Should the

British armor attempt to move through its own infantry, it would collide with the antitank guns in the defensive positions, while its infantry and artillery support remained stuck in the minefield.

Rommel left Africa on 23 September, handing over to Stumme who had arrived less than a week previously. Stumme was handicapped not only by his inexperience of desert war, but also by the fact that several of his senior staff officers were sick. Furthermore, all but two of his German divisions had had changes of command over the previous weeks, and the *Africa Korps* itself was now in the hands of General Ritter von Thoma.

Montgomery briefed his divisional commanders and their chiefs of staff for 'Operation Lightfoot' on 15 September. His intention was to attack both flanks of the Axis position. The main weight would fall in the north, where 30 Corps was to force a gap to permit the armor of 10 Corps to move through and into the enemy rear. To the south, 13 Corps was to attack with the intention of distracting forces which might otherwise be employed against the northern attack. The assault was to go in under cover of darkness; the mine-

fields would be breached and lanes cleared to enable the armor to move up at dawn. Once through the minefield, 10 Corps was to swing across the Axis supply routes and await the enemy reaction. Moonlight was essential for the first phase; this was largely responsible for the timing of the attack for 23 October, the night before the full moon.

Much thought was devoted to the important problem of mine-clearing. Some 'Scorpion' flail tanks were available, but these were distrusted and were not widely used. An electronic mine-detector had been recently developed, but only 500 were in the hands of the Eighth Army; many mines would have to be discovered by the more primitive method of prodding with a bayonet. A drill for minefield clearance was devised, and a school was set up at Burg El Arab to teach it. The expected rate of progress was 200 yards per hour using the mine detector, and considerably more if prodding was employed. The 24-foot gaps, once cleared, were to be marked by lights and wire to enable tanks and other vehicles to move safely through.

Above: German and Italian prisoners taken on the afternoon of 23 October.

Below: Italian infantry on the attack in October 1942.

Both 13 and 30 Corps were hampered in their training by the fact that they also had to hold the line. Although 10 Corps had no such responsibility, it was beset by problems of organization and re-equipment; some of its new tanks did not arrive until the day of the battle. Montgomery realized early in October that the army, and particularly 10 Corps, would not reach the required standard of training in time for the attack. He therefore decided to modify his plan. The breakthrough by 10 Corps was to be replaced by a 'crumbling' process by which the Axis infantry in the front line were to be destroyed while the British armor prevented any interference from Stumme's tanks. This was a sound concept; Field Marshal Model employed it at Kursk the following year, but lacking Montgomery's superiority in armor, he failed to achieve success.

The main blow was still to fall in the north, where 30 Corps, attacking on a front of four divisions, was to seize objective 'Oxalic', well inside the Axis position, and then open up two lanes in the minefield to permit 10 Corps to move through. Having passed through the infantry, 10 Corps was to hold the line 'Pierson', just west of 'Oxalic' to contain the enemy armor while 30 Corps 'crumbled' the infantry. Finally, once the 'crumbling' was complete, 10 Corps was to move forward against the Axis armor. Meanwhile, 13 Corps was to launch two attacks, one against Qarat El Himeimat and the Taqa Plateau, and the other towards Gebel Kalakh. It was hoped that these would draw some armor south, and would, furthermore, result in the mauling of *Folgore* and *Pavia*. The assault was to be prepared by a short but heavy artillery bombardment, concentrating first on the enemy guns before switching to the infantry.

Efforts at Tactical Surprise

Great efforts were taken to achieve tactical surprise. A complex deception plan was implemented, with emphasis being placed on the camouflage of real installations and concentrations, and the construction of dummy ones. Raids, both real and feint, were also employed in the weeks leading up to the offensive and on the night of 23 October itself, with the specific intention of tying down enemy reserves.

Although preparations for the offensive went well, all was far from serene among the British commanders. Lumsden disliked the role allocated to his corps; he would have preferred to give his armor more of a free rein. He also questioned the wisdom of the change of plan, arguing that it would be impossible for 10 Corps to break through unless 30 Corps had successfully cleared the minefields. Leese's three Dominion divisional commanders made the same point, claiming that they would require longer to carry out the 'break-in' phase. Montgomery, when approached by Leese, emphasized that there was to be no deviation from the plan; 10 Corps *would* move through 30 at dawn on the first day of the attack, come what may.

Battalion commanders were briefed by Montgomery on 19 and 20 October. He warned them that there would be no quick victory; they were to expect a long, hard slogging-match, lasting for perhaps twelve days. Nevertheless, he declared, *Panzerarmee Afrika* was doomed; it would be unable to sustain a long battle and, providing the plan was adhered to, British victory was certain. Junior officers and men were briefed by their commanding officers on 21 October, and on the night of the 22nd the infantry of 30 Corps moved up to their forward positions. On the following morning Montgomery drove to his tactical headquarters on the coast, close to the advanced headquarters of 10 Corps, 30 Corps and the Desert Air Force. Telephone lines had been well-buried, and all vehicles were dug in. Montgomery's order of the day was read out to the waiting troops, concluding 'Let us all pray that "the Lord mighty in battle" will give us the victory'. The assaulting units continued their deployment undetected, and at 2140 the artillery of the Eighth army opened up on the Axis battery positions.

The flashes of over 1000 British guns lit the night sky as the infantry began their advance. To help them keep direction, Bofors anti-aircraft guns fired tracers on fixed lines, and searchlights crossed in the overhead. At 2200 the guns switched to the Axis forward positions, and the barrage buzzed and roared ahead of the advancing infantry. The Australians on the right of 30 Corps made good progress, but were finally brought to a halt about 1000 yards short of their objective. The Highland Division went forward to the sound of pipes, meeting with a brisk fire as it passed the minefield. The Highlanders spent a confusing and bloody night, and dawn broke to find them short of their final objective. Furthermore, the gaps through the minefield had not been fully opened, and the 1st Armored Division, trying to move forward, became involved in a scene of growing chaos. Freyberg's New Zealanders were more successful, seizing Miteiriya Ridge, though Brigadier Currie's 8th Armored Brigade, moving forward in the early hours of the morning, ran into minefields and was unable to get any further forward. The South Africans, the southernmost formation of 30 Corps, also made good progress, getting onto the southern end of Miteiriya Ridge by dawn.

While 30 Corps' attack had, despite some confusion and numerous casualties, generally reached its objectives, 10 Corps had had a less satisfactory night. Most of its units were delayed by difficulties in clearing lanes through the minefield, and soon much of the corps was spread out behind 30 Corps, with considerable congestion in some areas. Montgomery spoke to Lumsden and Leese at 0330 on 24 October, making it quite clear that, despite the slow progress, there would be no change of plan; the armor, he emphasized, had to get through. By dawn the situation had improved somewhat, though most of 10 Corps had been unable to get ahead of the forward elements of 30 Corps.

In the south, 13 Corps' plan of attack leaned heavily on Harding's 7th Armored Division, which, assisted by General Koenig's 1st Free French Brigade, attacked through Qarat El Himeimat towards the Taqa Plateau. The 44th Division put in a smaller attack further to the north, but lost heavily in the process. Harding's attack made little progress. His division experi-

Above: A German tank and its crew are taken in the desert.

enced the same minefield problems as its counterparts in the north, and the French, after an initial success, were driven back, with the loss of the popular and gallant Colonel Amilakvari of the Foreign Legion. Horrocks decided to hold on to the ground that had been gained, and to resume the attack the following night.

The first that General Stumme knew of the offensive was the crash of the bombardment which heralded it. He did not immediately order his guns to reply, and the Axis counter-bombardment, by design or accident, took some time to get under way. Stumme was perplexed by the conflicting reports which arrived at his headquarters, and decided to go forward to investigate personally. While on this mission his car was shot at and Stumme himself, hanging onto the outside as his driver sped off, had a heart attack. His body was not found for 24 hours, and, though the capable Thoma took over, *Panzerarmee Afrika* was leaderless at a crucial stage in the action.

During the morning of 24 October 10 Corps tried to move forward through 30 Corps, in obedience to Montgomery's repeated urging, while the New Zealanders 'crumbled' to the south. By noon Montgomery had decided that the latter maneuver was likely to prove slow and costly, and he decided to switch the axis of the attack further north, where the Australians were to start 'crumbling'. The remainder of 30 Corps was to hold Miteiriya Ridge, while 10 Corps' main effort was to be directed toward Kidney Ridge. The Australians were to start their attack that night.

The same evening 13 Corps resumed their attack, while the 7th Armored Division and its supporting infantry spent another messy and fruitless night trying to force a way through the minefield. Early on the morning of 25 October

Horrocks and Montgomery agreed that the plan should be changed; instead, 50th Division was to attack the western end of Munassib, supported by a brigade of the 7th Armored Division. This attack was also unsuccessful.

While Harding's tanks burned in the minefields, the Australians in the north began to 'crumble', and successfully attacked the *125th Panzer Grenadier Regiment* in the area of the coast road. The Highlanders on their left made more limited gains, and once again the armor spent a frustrating night, still unable to get clear of 30 Corps positions.

It was now clear to Montgomery that reappraisal was essential. Casualties in 30 Corps numbered over 4500, the Highlanders having suffered nearly half this total. Although 13 Corps had lost 1000 men it had failed to gain any ground at all, and while 10 Corps had suffered lightly, it had accomplished relatively little. The situation was, however, far from hopeful for the Germans. Rommel returned to his army on the evening of the 25th, and was not encouraged to hear that petrol stocks were dangerously low, precluding major movement. The infantry had suffered severely from British artillery fire and air attacks, and *15th Panzer*, used in a series of local counterattacks, now had only 31 tanks in action. Rommel concluded that the greatest threat to his position lay in the salient at Kidney Ridge, and ordered *15th Panzer* and *Littorio* to counterattack at dawn on the 26th. He went forward to watch the attack, and was depressed to observe the fierceness of British artillery fire and air strikes. He soon committed *90th Light* to the battle, but a day's furious fighting saw no conclusive result.

Montgomery had, meanwhile, finalized his new plan and issued orders accordingly. The Highlanders were to consolidate their position, and the Australians were to resume 'crumbling' on the night of the 28th, while 30 Corps was given time to recover; apart from this no other major moves were to be undertaken. Ten Corps was to nudge forward in the area of Kidney Ridge, at the same time preventing enemy armor from interfering with 30 Corps. Finally, Harding was to prepare to move north if required to do so.

Lumsden ordered Brigadier Bosvile's 7th Motor Brigade to attack points 'Snipe' and 'Woodcock' near Kidney Ridge at 2300 that night, and to form an anti-tank screen through which two armored brigades would advance the following morning. 'Woodcock' was taken but proved untenable. 'Snipe' was duly seized by 2nd Battalion, The Rifle Brigade, but the armor which should have moved through failed to do so. The Rifle Brigade was heavily attacked by German and Italian armor throughout the day, but in a brilliant defense, beat off these assaults, knocking out 37 tanks and self-propelled guns in the process. Thrusts toward 'Woodcock' gained little ground, and at about 1600 Rommel unleashed a major counterattack, using both his Panzer divisions, together with *Littorio* and elements of *Ariete*. The attack made no headway, and its failure profoundly disturbed Rommel. 'No one can conceive the burden that lies on me', he wrote to his wife, warning her that defeat was likely.

At 0800 on 28 October, Montgomery met Leese, Lumsden and their chief of staff. He informed them that 1st Armored Division, battered in four days hard fighting, was to be withdrawn to regroup, and the Kidney Ridge area was, for the time at least, to become a defensive front. The Australians were to attack, as planned, that night, and Lumsden was to be prepared to move westwards. Radio interceptions confirmed that *21st Panzer* had moved north, and orders were later issued for Harding to move up toward the coast, leaving one of his brigades in the south.

The New Zealanders had been pulled back into reserve on the 26th, and Montgomery informed Freyberg that he was to take over the Australian sector on the night of the 29th, with a view to launching an attack the following night, supported by infantry from 13 and 30 Corps. The Australian attack on the night of the 28th did not meet with the expected success, due largely to the problems of mines and night navigation.

There were by now growing doubts about Montgomery's wisdom. Churchill was increasingly dissatisfied with the conduct of the battle, forcing Brooke to defend Alexander and Montgomery against accusations of weakness and inactivity. On the 29th Montgomery was visited by Alexander, his Chief-of-Staff, Lieutenant-General McCreery and Minister of State Casey. Montgomery, radiating confidence as usual, stressed that all was well, and reminded his listeners that he had predicted a long fight. Nevertheless, neither McCreery nor Montgomery's own staff were altogether happy with the planned breakout, codenamed 'Operation Supercharge'. They felt that an attack along the coast by the New Zealanders would encounter Rommel's main strength, since this sector was vital for the safety of his supply dumps and lines of communication. De Guingand, backed by his senior intelligence

Above: Germans inspect a captured British tank.
Left: General von Arnim is taken into captivity after the collapse of the Axis effort in North Africa in 1943, when some 250,000 Axis forces remaining in Tunisia surrendered to the Allies. Alamein was the first step in the long road back from Egypt to Tunis.

officer, pointed this out to Montgomery, who wisely decided to change the axis of the attack. The Australians were to attack northward on the night of the 30th but the New Zealanders, instead of moving through them, would attack further south, just north of Kidney Ridge, on the night of the 31st. They would be reinforced with one armored and two infantry brigades, and liberally supported by artillery and air strikes.

The Australian attack in the Thompson's Post area on the night of the 30th made useful gains. Rommel declined to withdraw his threatened units in this sector, and instead ordered counter-attacks for the next day. This proved an error; Rommel's attention remained fixed on the coast while the real threat developed further south.

The last details of 'Supercharge' were arranged at a conference early on the morning of 1 November. The attack was to go in at 0105 on the 2nd, with two infantry brigades assaulting on a 4000 yard front. These brigades, one each from the 50th and 51st Divisions, were under the operational command of the New Zealand Division. They were to be followed by the armor, which, as in the original 'Lightfoot' plan, was to pass through the infantry once the latter's objectives were secure.

The infantry objective lay just east of the Rahman Track, while the objective of the 8th Armored Brigade was just beyond it, across the strongly-held Aqqaqir Ridge. Once 8th Armored were in possession of the ridge, 10 Corps was to take over the battle from 30 Corps, and the 1st

Opposite: A German Panzer halts to survey the action at Alamein. **Left:** Italian troops move forward in one of their last assaults of the action at Alamein. **Below:** Thousands of German prisoners are rounded up by the 1st Household Cavalry Regiment at the start of the Nazis' long retreat across the rim of North Africa.

Armored Division would move through the 8th Armored Brigade. The attack was to be supported by the guns of five divisions, strengthened by three extra artillery regiments.

The infantry attack went well. Its objectives were taken well before dawn, and just after 0600 Currie's 8th Armored Brigade moved up. The brigade had lost several of its tanks in the approach march, but swept forward with great *élan*, suffering heavily from the 88s and dug-in tanks on Aqqaqir Ridge. The Royal Wiltshire Yeomanry lost almost all its tanks; the brigade as a whole lost 87 in this attack. Nevertheless, the leading brigade of the 1st Armored Division moved forward as planned, only to be heavily engaged by German armor, and a fierce battle developed between the infantry line and the Rahman Track.

While this action was in progress some armored cars of the Royal Dragoons discovered that the southwestern edge of the salient was weakly held, and pushed forward into open country, doing considerable damage in the Axis rear. An attack by the 7th Motor Brigade on Tel El Aqqaqir failed that night, and the armor was unable to make any progress the following morning. Montgomery decided to press his attack through the southern portion of the salient, using the Highland Division and an Indian brigade, in an effort to break through the defensive crust and enable the armor to fan out.

Rommel had decided that the battle was hopeless on 2 November. The *Afrika Korps* ended the day with only 35 tanks, largely as a result of the fighting around Kidney Ridge; petrol and ammunition were both dangerously low. Rommel decided to pull back to Fuka, withdrawing his troops from the southern sector that night,

Above: German forces in full retreat toward Cyrenaica after Alamein.
Opposite left: A German half-track drags an artillery piece back into Cyrenaica as the retreat continues.

The Battle of El Alamein, 1942

Objectives of 'Operation Lightfoot'

The main blow was to fall in the north, where XXX Corps was to seize objective 'Oxalic', well inside the Axis positions, and then open up two lanes in the minefield to permit the armor of X Corps to move through. Having passed through the infantry, X Corps was to hold the line 'Pierson' to contain the enemy armor. Finally, once the Axis defenses were broken down, X Corps was to move against the Axis armor at 'skinflint'.

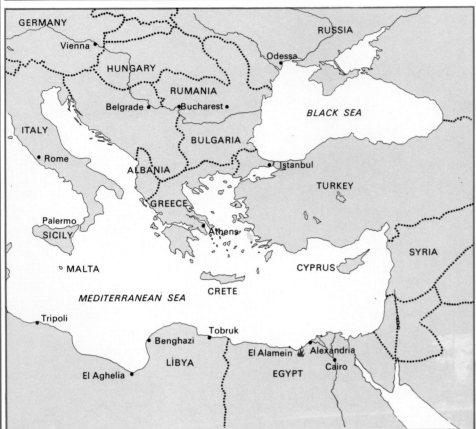

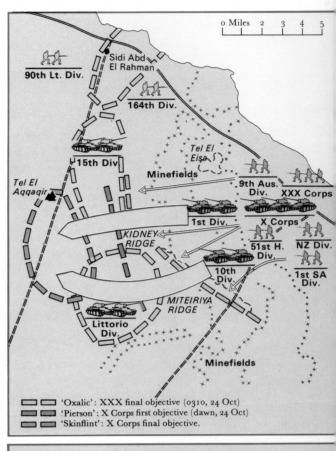

☐☐ 'Oxalic': XXX final objective (0310, 24 Oct)
☐☐ 'Pierson': X Corps first objective (dawn, 24 Oct)
☐☐ 'Skinflint': X Corps final objective.

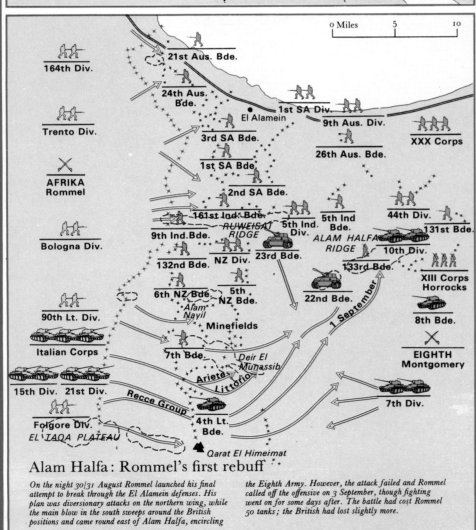

Alam Halfa: Rommel's first rebuff

On the night 30/31 August Rommel launched his final attempt to break through the El Alamein defenses. His plan was diversionary attacks on the northern wing, while the main blow in the south sweeps around the British positions and came round east of Alam Halfa, encircling the Eighth Army. However, the attack failed and Rommel called off the offensive on 3 September, though fighting went on for some days after. The battle had cost Rommel 50 tanks; the British had lost slightly more.

The Balance of Forces at El Alamein

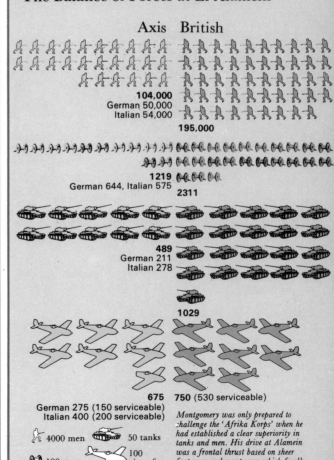

Axis   British

104,000
German 50,000
Italian 54,000

195,000

1219
German 644, Italian 575

2311

489
German 211
Italian 278

1029

675   **750** (530 serviceable)

German 275 (150 serviceable)
Italian 400 (200 serviceable)

🚶 4000 men   🚗 50 tanks

🔫 100 guns   ✈ 100 aircraft

Montgomery was only prepared to challenge the 'Afrika Korps' when he had established a clear superiority in tanks and men. His drive at Alamein was a frontal thrust based on sheer firepower and manpower which finally forced Rommel to retreat.

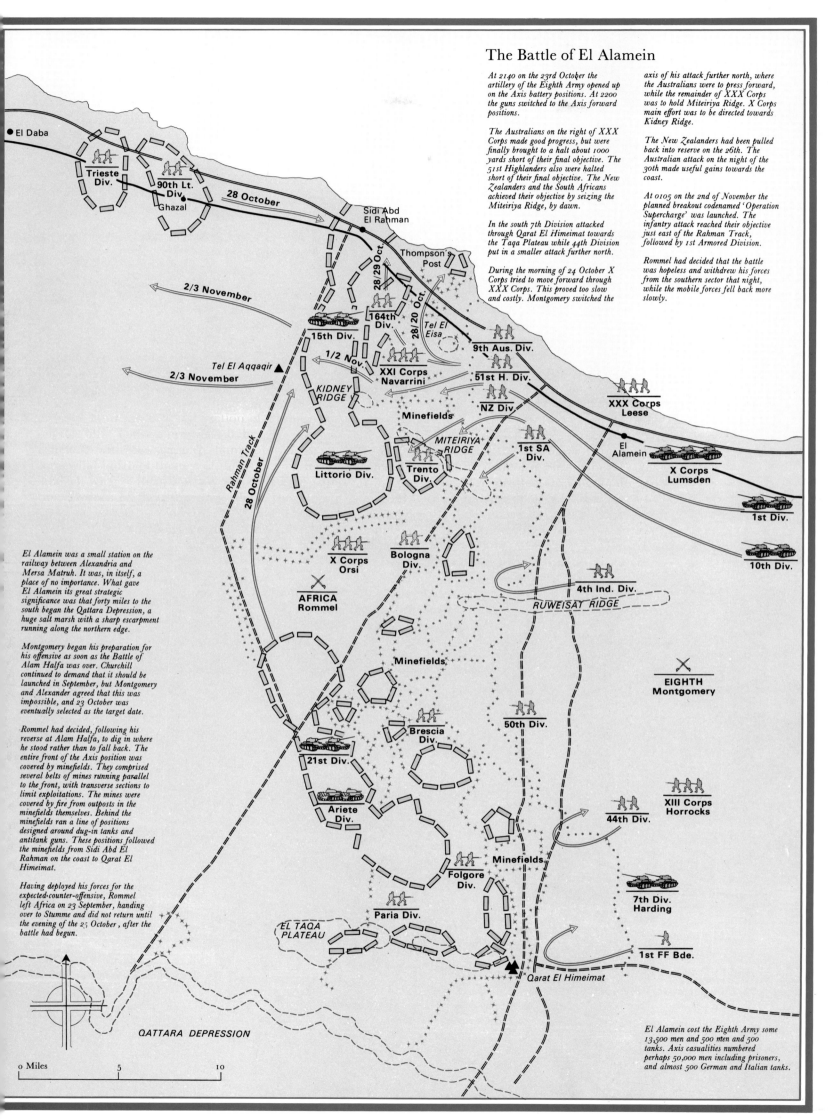

The Battle of El Alamein

At 2140 on the 23rd October the artillery of the Eighth Army opened up on the Axis battery positions. At 2200 the guns switched to the Axis forward positions.

The Australians on the right of XXX Corps made good progress, but were finally brought to a halt about 1000 yards short of their final objective. The 51st Highlanders also were halted short of their final objective. The New Zealanders and the South Africans achieved their objective by seizing the Miteiriya Ridge, by dawn.

In the south 7th Division attacked through Qarat El Himeimat towards the Taqa Plateau while 44th Division put in a smaller attack further north.

During the morning of 24 October X Corps tried to move forward through XXX Corps. This proved too slow and costly. Montgomery switched the axis of his attack further north, where the Australians were to press forward, while the remainder of XXX Corps was to hold Miteiriya Ridge. X Corps main effort was to be directed towards Kidney Ridge.

The New Zealanders had been pulled back into reserve on the 26th. The Australian attack on the night of the 30th made useful gains towards the coast.

At 0105 on the 2nd of November the planned breakout codenamed 'Operation Supercharge' was launched. The infantry attack reached their objective just east of the Rahman Track, followed by 1st Armored Division.

Rommel had decided that the battle was hopeless and withdrew his forces from the southern sector that night, while the mobile forces fell back more slowly.

El Alamein was a small station on the railway between Alexandria and Mersa Matruh. It was, in itself, a place of no importance. What gave El Alamein its great strategic significance was that forty miles to the south began the Qattara Depression, a huge salt marsh with a sharp escarpment running along the northern edge.

Montgomery began his preparation for his offensive as soon as the Battle of Alam Halfa was over. Churchill continued to demand that it should be launched in September, but Montgomery and Alexander agreed that this was impossible, and 23 October was eventually selected as the target date.

Rommel had decided, following his reverse at Alam Halfa, to dig in where he stood rather than to fall back. The entire front of the Axis position was covered by minefields. They comprised several belts of mines running parallel to the front, with transverse sections to limit exploitations. The mines were covered by fire from outposts in the minefields themselves. Behind the minefields ran a line of positions designed around dug-in tanks and antitank guns. These positions followed the minefields from Sidi Abd El Rahman on the coast to Qarat El Himeimat.

Having deployed his forces for the expected counter-offensive, Rommel left Africa on 23 September, handing over to Stumme and did not return until the evening of the 25 October, after the battle had begun.

El Alamein cost the Eighth Army some 13,500 men and 500 men and 500 tanks. Axis casualties numbered perhaps 50,000 men including prisoners, and almost 500 German and Italian tanks.

El Daba
Trieste Div.
90th Lt. Div.
Ghazal
28 October
Sidi Abd El Rahman
Thompson's Post
2/3 November
28/29 Oct.
28/20 Oct.
15th Div.
164th Div.
Tel El Eisa
Tel El Aqqaqir
1/2 Nov.
2/3 November
9th Aus. Div.
XXI Corps Navarrini
51st H. Div.
KIDNEY RIDGE
Minefields
NZ Div.
XXX Corps Leese
Rahman Track
28 October
Littorio Div.
Trento Div.
MITEIRIYA RIDGE
1st SA Div.
El Alamein
X Corps Lumsden
1st Div.
X Corps Orsi
Bologna Div.
4th Ind. Div.
10th Div.
AFRICA Rommel
RUWEISAT RIDGE
Minefields
EIGHTH Montgomery
Brescia Div.
50th Div.
21st Div.
XIII Corps Horrocks
44th Div.
Ariete Div.
Minefields
Folgore Div.
7th Div. Harding
Paria Div.
EL TAQA PLATEAU
1st FF Bde.
Qarat El Himeimat
QATTARA DEPRESSION

0 Miles   5   10

Above: A German soldier who fell at Alamein. **Left:** The race across the desert was on after Alamein. The battle decided the desert campaign, which ended only six months after the British breakthrough.

while the mobile forces in the north fell back more slowly. The fuel problem was so serious that many of the infantry would have no transport; their retirement would thus be a perilous affair. Rommel sent his ADC, Lieutenant Berndt, to explain the reasons for the withdrawal to Hitler, but before Berndt left the Führer sent an order countermanding the retreat. This proved difficult to execute, since units in the south had already begun to fall back.

The night of 3 November saw confused fighting around Tel El Aqqaqir, which fell at first light on the 4th. Two armored divisions, 1st and 7th, pushed through the gap. *Ariete*, fighting hard, was surrounded and overwhelmed, but a clean break-through was delayed as much by the chaos behind the British front as by Axis resistance. By late afternoon Rommel realized that disengagement was essential if he was to avoid encirclement. The orderly withdrawal of his earlier plan was replaced by a general retreat. The coast road was crammed with vehicles, but the Desert Air Force, possibly due to a preference for bombing rather than strafing, failed to cause as much damage as Montgomery and his staff hoped.

Montgomery intended to cut off at least part of the retreating Axis Army by a series of left hooks through the desert. These achieved little, due partially to a number of particularly heavy storms which turned large areas of the desert into a quagmire and bogged down the pursuers. Montgomery has been criticized for the slowness of his follow-up, though it is likely that but for the rain Rommel would have been caught at Mersa Matruh on 6 November. As it was, the remnants of Rommel's mobile forces got away, but most of the helpless Italian infantry, isolated and without transport, were captured.

On 8 November the Allies landed in North Africa, and the Western Desert became a front of diminished importance. German reinforcements which, if delivered six months earlier, would have had a decisive effect, were rushed into Tripoli, but to no avail. Tripoli fell on 23 January, 1943; Montgomery forced the Mareth Line in late March, and on 13 May the last Axis forces in North Africa surrendered.

Alamein cost the Eighth Army some 13,500 men and 500 tanks. Most of the latter were, however, capable of repair. Axis casualties numbered perhaps 50,000, of whom 30,000 were prisoners. Rommel's tank losses were most significant; about 500 German and Italian tanks were either destroyed in the battle or captured subsequently.

Alamein's effect upon Allied morale was probably more important than its long-term influence upon the course of the war. While less significant in strategic terms than Stalingrad or Kursk, Alamein marked a watershed in Allied fortunes. Montgomery was criticized by some at the time, and has been criticized by many since, for his conduct of the battle. His plan has been condemned as pedestrian and his man-management as theatrical. Nevertheless, the fact remains that Alamein was the Eighth Army's first conclusive victory. It had had numerical superiority in the past, but had squandered it in indecision and discord. Montgomery brought a new drive and persistence to the Desert Army, and planned a set-piece battle in which its quantitative superiority could, for once, be fully employed. He achieved a victory when victories were few and far between. Churchill put it, with characteristic exaggeration, 'Before Alamein we never had a victory. After Alamein we never had a defeat'.

Kursk

It is deceptively easy for British and Americans to think of the Second World War largely in terms of theaters in which their own troops were engaged. This, however, tends to obscure the fact that, as Alan Clark has pointed out, to the Germans the war meant the war in the East. It was on the Eastern Front that the bulk of Germany's forces were deployed; North Africa, for instance, was little more than a sideshow. In the opinion of Field Marshal Erich von Manstein, probably the *Wehrmacht's* ablest strategist, the German defeat at Kursk in July 1943 marked a turning point in the war in the East, with the initiative passing into the hands of the Russians. The summer of 1943 can, indeed, be seen as a turning point in a wider sense.

Until that time the Germans, who had for the most part held the strategic initiative over the battlefields of Europe, had a reasonable hope of avoiding defeat in the war they had precipitated in 1939. True, their difficulties were increasing. Germany's mastery of Europe failed to conceal the restlessness and despair of the subjected populations who faced exploitation and often extermination. Germany, too, lacked the manpower, the industrial production, the oil and the transport facilities needed to capitalize on her gains and to totally defeat her enemies. The United States, moving into top gear on the production front, was flexing her muscles in Europe for the first time. But the European war was essentially decided in the East—on the Russian steppes where the German army was bled white in one of the most barbarous campaigns in history. Success in the East in 1943 might have enabled the Germans to deploy and successfully counter Anglo-American assaults in the West; it might still have been possible to fight to a standstill. After Kursk-Orel the war was lost for Germany, though there was no immediate end to it in sight. The battle banished any lingering doubts concerning the survival of the Soviet Union and opened the way for the Soviet drive that was to bring much of Eastern and Central Europe under Stalin's sway. In conjunction with the Allied victory in the Atlantic—the prerequisite for successful operations on the European mainland by the British and Americans—the battle ensured the victory of the Allies over Germany. It also heralded the emergence of the Soviet Union not simply as Europe's greatest power, but as a state that could only be compared in strength to the United States, with all the implications that contained for the future of Europe and the world.

Kursk-Orel was the last major offensive undertaken by the Germans on the Eastern Front. By that time they had been fought very largely to a standstill; thereafter their stance in the East was increasingly defensive. Driving deeply into the Soviet Union in 1941, the *Wehrmacht* had inflicted losses on the Soviet Army that by any normal standards should have been fatal, but the Russians had held at Leningrad and thrown back the last attacks on Moscow in December. Despite their local successes in the Moscow region during the winter, the Russians had been unable to substantially improve their strategic position and the German Army was able to launch a summer offensive in 1942 in southern Russia. Seeking to secure the granaries and mineral wealth of the Ukraine and the oilfields of the Caucasian approaches, the Germans crushed the weak Russian forces that opposed them but were drawn into battle at Stalingrad where, in vicious street fighting, their superiority in equipment and training were nullified. With the winter came a Soviet counter-attack that encircled German forces in the Stalingrad area and ultimately resulted in the destruction of the 230,000-strong German *Sixth Army*. But in trying to exploit their victory the Russians overextended themselves; their armored thrusts were crushed around Kharkov in March, and the front stabilized on a line dictated by exhaustion and the spring thaw. The *Wehrmacht* had lost many of its best men and much of its equipment, but it had proved itself to be at least a tactical match for the Russians. German resilience was great, but was matched by that of the Russians, and as spring gave way to summer it became obvious that neither army could enforce its will upon its adversary.

For the Germans the spring of 1943 was a time of reappraisal and indecision. Despite two massive offensives they had failed to break the most formidable of their enemies, and they were faced with the prospect of Anglo-American action against southern Europe from North Africa where German and Italian forces stood on the edge of destruction at Tunis. In the Atlantic the U-boats had failed to starve Britain into submission and were suffering such losses that the outcome of the battle was no longer in any doubt. Politically, Italy was in deep trouble with Mussolini's credibility weakening with every defeat. Rumania, Hungary and Bulgaria had hardly been impressed by their German ally's defeat on the Volga, and there was a need to secure a victory that would put fresh heart into these countries and to forestall any Russian move that would bring the war closer to the Balkans.

Opposite: German tanks in action near the Kursk salient in the summer of 1943. Despite the introduction of the Panther and Tiger, two new German tanks, most of the tanks used by the *Wehrmacht* and *Waffen SS* were Pzkw IVs.

Only a victory in the East could stabilize the deteriorating situation, and it was becoming increasingly essential because of the Russians' increased industrial production. Throughout the war the Russians had enjoyed—and usually dissipated—an overall superiority of men, armor, artillery and aircraft but this had been offset by superior German tactics. By the spring of 1943, however, quality was being grafted onto an ever-increasing quantity that the Germans could not hope to match. It had therefore become essential for the Germans to bring the bulk of the Soviet Army to battle and to cripple it, in order to permit the redeployment of German forces in other theaters of war.

Preparations for the Offensive
Given that they were committed to make an attack in the East—a presumption that Colonel-General Heinz Guderian resisted—the Germans were faced with the twin problems of where, and with what forces, the attack should be made. Behind the enemy front there were no immediate objectives of strategic importance, in defense of which the Russians would be forced to commit their armies if attacked by the Germans. Leningrad, partially relieved in September 1942, offered a target, but room to maneuver was limited. Despite inflicting appalling losses on the Russians in November 1942 around Rzhev the Germans had been forced to abandon this salient and shorten their line the following March—with the result that thereafter Moscow was too far away for any successful attack to be considered. In the south, however, the front had stabilized in a manner that seemed more promising for a German attack. In the Bryansk-Orel-Kursk-Kharkov region the front had formed into a Russian-held salient sixty miles wide with the German Army Group Center holding the northern flank, and Army Group South the southern sector around Kharkov. From this salient the Russians threatened the entire German position in the Ukraine, since a breakout to the southwest might trap a major part of Army Group South against the Sea of Azov. The Russians had,

indeed, attempted this unsuccessfully, in February and March. Field Marshal Erich von Manstein, C-in-C Army Group South, anticipated such a Russian move and planned to lure any such attack toward the lower Dnieper and then strike it in the flank from Kharkov. This backhand battle of riposte was nevertheless rejected; there was no certainty as to where the Russians might attack and, much to Hitler's displeasure, such a technique would involve the temporary abandonment of ground. Instead, the Germans considered short but sharp thrusts on each side of the salient in May when the ground had dried. But here the Germans came up against an insoluble problem. In order to overwhelm the Russians in the salient—before they had time to shore up its defenses and possibly launch an attack of their own on the northern part of the Orel re-entrant—time was of the essence. The offensive had to be carried out as soon as possible after the ground had dried, but the Germans themselves were no better prepared in this sector than were the Russians. In January 1943 their eighteen Panzer divisions could muster between them only 495 battleworthy tanks and production was simply inadequate. Monthly production of the Pzkw IV—a tank not superior to the Russian T-34—only exceeded the hundred mark for the first time in October 1942, and the two new tanks, the Tiger and the Panther, were experiencing the teething problems inherent in any new equipment. Nevertheless, from April onwards German preparations for an offensive began, but by the beginning of May the first doubts began to grow in the minds of some of the field commanders.

Russia's Intelligence Network
The Russians, aided by an extremely efficient Intelligence network within the German Army High Command, had no illusions as to German intentions. They were thus able to choose between an offensive of their own to pre-empt the German blow, and a defensive battle in prepared positions, followed by a counterattack. Their experience of mobile operations convinced the Soviet High Command that the latter course of action was preferable. In open warfare, moving away from their supply dumps across a razed countryside, the Russians had been consistently outfought and outmaneuvered in the past; they lacked the experience and the means to maintain deep penetrations while the Germans still possessed mobile reserves. In defense, however, the ordinary Russian soldier had exhibited qualities of stoicism, bravery and self-sacrifice that made him a match for his German counterpart. Accordingly, the Soviet Command, playing to its strengths and not its weaknesses, prepared for a defensive battle, followed by heavy counterattacks once the main German assaults had been halted. Men, armor, artillery, aircraft and engineering equipment were moved to the area in profusion. By this time Soviet tank production was running at 2000 per month and the balance of manpower, equal in 1942, had swung in favor of the Russians.

Divided into three fronts—the Central, Voronezh and Steppe (Reserve)—the Kursk salient witnessed elaborate Russian preparations. Defenses were sited in depth, based on clusters of

Right: Field Marshal Erich von Manstein, C-in-C Army Group South, who helped plan the Kursk offensive. He was one of Germany's ablest strategists throughout the war.

anti-tank positions and minefields. Each of these small positions included three to five 76mm anti-tank guns, about five antitank rifles, and up to five mortars with infantry and engineer support. Because of the limited ability of the 76mm gun to destroy Tigers, strong points were mutually supporting and centrally controlled, and were covered by minefields in order to channel the German tanks into killing zones where they could be overwhelmed by sheer weight of numbers. By the time the battle opened the defensive systems were up to 110 miles deep, and consisted of six main belts within the salient alone. Behind it was a further defensive network that stretched back to the Don River. On the Central Front 3100 miles of trenches were dug.

Naturally, preparations on such a scale did not go unnoticed. The Germans soon became aware of the buildup, and many German generals believed that the Russians were simply too strong to be attacked at Kursk-Orel with any reasonable hope of success. On the other hand a battle would result in the commitment of the great majority of Russian reserves of manpower and armor, the very elements of the Soviet Army that the Germans sought to bring to battle. On balance, German planners believed that the task lay within their army's capabilities. The Russians had never withstood the opening of a blitzkrieg attack; difficulties in Russia had begun as the German tanks had fanned out on the limitless steppe. For this offensive, the attacking pincers had to travel only 60 miles—an apparently feasible task.

Nevertheless, the realization that the battle was assuming the nature of a head-on collision, a decisive trial of strength, did not recommend itself to the more perceptive German generals. Hitler himself was genuinely undecided whether or not to order the offensive, but with most of the Army High Command enthusiastic for the battle and no alternative offensive operation planned, the attack on the Kursk salient, 'Operation Citadel', was sanctioned scheduled for 4 July.

Despite the activities of the Russian partisans against the lines of communication (according to the Germans' own figures the partisans carried out 1092 attacks in June and 1460 in July behind the battle area) the Germans were able to concentrate a formidable striking force around the salient for the start of the battle. This force of 900,000 men, 10,000 artillery and 2700 tanks and assault guns enjoyed the support of 2500 aircraft. The main attacks were be handled in the north by *Ninth Army*, under the command of Field Marshal Walter Model, and in the south by *Fourth Panzer Army* and *Operational Group Kempf*, under the overall direction of von Manstein. Realization of the strength of the Russian defenses dictated a change of tactics. Instead of the usual opening attack in which the panzers streaked ahead of the infantry, Model proposed to use his infantry and artillery to drive a wedge through the Russian defenses into which the tanks would be fed. These had been the tactics used by Montgomery at Alamein in October 1942—but with one vital difference. Montgomery had enjoyed overwhelming superiority of numbers and equipment; and even then the attack had only just succeeded. Model, faced with greater in-depth defenses than

Above: Manstein scans Russian positions in June 1943. The planning of the Kursk offensive was meticulous, but the Russians were equally prepared. **Left:** German paratroops drop behind Russian lines in mid-June, prior to the great offensive.

Right: Field Marshal von Kluge inspects the new German tank, the Tiger I, during the preparations for the Kursk offensive. The Tiger was first used at Kursk, but suffered some teething problems. **Center right:** A Russian T-34 in flames. The T-34 was by far the most superior tank at Kursk and, on balance, the best used by any side in the war. The presence of the versatile T-34/76 helped turn the tide of battle in favor of the USSR.

the British had encountered in the desert, had no marked numerical advantage. In the south Manstein concentrated eight of Germany's best armored divisions on a 30-mile front in order to implement the *panzerkeil* (armored wedge). By these tactics he intended to prise open the defenses by a series of thrusts in which the armor was concentrated along the cutting edge. The latest tanks, the Tigers, were concentrated at the tip, while in their wake were the lighter tanks, the Panthers and the Pzkw IVs, which would be backed up by the infantry. These would be followed by the artillery and mortar support. The Germans, in the south, intended to use the bludgeon rather than the rapier. In ordering the tanks not to stop to support disabled colleagues the German Command, anxious to maintain the momentum of the attack, effectively wrote off many of their tanks that were to be disabled. Damaged vehicles, often isolated from their own infantry, fell easy prey to untouched Soviet positions on the flanks of the thrusts.

The Soviets, on the other hand, were inferior in numbers along the axis of the German thrusts, but were superior in numbers and equipment in the salient area generally. Behind minefields with an average density of about 2200 antitank and 2500 anti-personnel mines per mile of front were some 1,337,000 soldiers, 20,220 artillery pieces and 3306 tanks—with one more Tank Army in reserve. Of the artillery 6000 pieces were 76mm antitank guns and 920 Katyusha multiple rocket-launchers. Only in the air did the Soviets lack any marked numerical advantage over the Germans, deploying about 2650 aircraft.

The Russians were confident in their ability to hold and defeat the German thrusts, despite the qualitative superiority of some of the latest German equipment. Months of preparation ensured that in the battle firepower and a tenacious defense would offset superior German technique, while in the critical opening stage mobility would be minimal. The Russians, bolstered by the knowledge that the Ural factories could more than easily replace their losses, were prepared to fight a gigantic battle of attrition, trading lives and equipment for the elimination of the German armor which had brought them close to defeat in 1941 and again in 1942.

Nevertheless, Helmuth von Moltke's adage that no plan ever survives the first contact of battle proved very accurate. Not only did the German plan go badly wrong, but Soviet deployment was also, in part at least, erroneous, and this was to lead to a critical situation which made the outcome of the battle an open question. The Russians were under the impression that the major German effort would be from the Orel salient against General Rokossovsky's Central Front with a smaller effort against General Vatutin's Veronezh Front in the south. The reverse proved to be the case, since Model deployed only three panzer divisions compared to Manstein's eight. The balance of Russian deployment essentially favored Rokossovsky, though this was redeemed by the deployment of reserves to help the southern sector. The German attack in the north was held relatively quickly. In the south, however, Russian losses were extremely heavy, German gains were more marked than in the north and the decision delayed. This was to mean the Russian plans for simultaneous counterattacks in the north and the south after the defensive battle lacked synchronization and failed to achieve either of the two super-encirclements planned.

The German attack was scheduled for 0330 on 5 July, but effectively the battle was under way by the afternoon of the 4th. In the south Manstein's forces undertook an artillery attack to make tactical gains in order to secure better start lines. On both fronts patrolling was undertaken and frequent clashes occurred, especially in the afternoon when the German engineers tried to clear their own wire and minefields ready for the attack. Prisoners and deserters gave the Russians the time of the attack and it was on this basis that the Russians began to bombard the German positions in the north at 0220. This disrupted German preparations and it was not until 0430 that the Luftwaffe and the German artillery mounted their reply. This provoked a second, far heavier, Russian counter-bombardment which was not particularly effective. Half-battalion strong tank probes began about 0530 in the north, but intense fire quickly drove them back. Two hours later the main assault opened with the armor, Tigers, Panthers and Ferdinand self-propelled guns moving forward. Because of their very thick front

Opposite: The movement of tanks on both sides continued throughout the action. Kursk was the greatest tank battle in history, with over 6000 of various types taking part.

armor the Tigers and Ferdinands were able to move through the first defense line, but it quickly became apparent that the one division used in this attack was not enough to overcome the resistance, which was far stronger than anticipated. By the afternoon all the armor had been committed, but with little return. On most of the front the Germans made no progress, though a $3\frac{1}{2}$-mile penetration was achieved against the 15th and 81st Rifle Divisions of Thirteenth Army. A three mile break-in was made near Gnilets against the 132nd and 280th Divisions of Seventieth Army, but already there were signs that things were going wrong for the Germans. More than 100 tanks had been lost in the minefields where they had attracted the unwelcome attention of the antitank guns and the Soviet Air Force. Small-arms fire had forced the German infantry to go to ground with the result that the armor became isolated and ensnared in the Russian defense lines. Despite intense fighting during the night, however, the Russians were unable to prevent the Germans from clearing most of the first line. By placing fresh tanks in hull-down positions the Russians ensured that their next-day's firepower was not reduced very much despite their losses, but this did not prevent Model making the same depth of penetration on the 6th. Unfortunately for the Germans their assault had been most successful on the right flank where it had eventually been halted in front of a low line of hills north of Olkhovata. No major progress had been made in the center or on the left flank that could give aid and protection to the right. And it was against the German left flank that Rokossovsky had concentrated his armored reserves, though he sent three tank corps to the threatened sectors. Their rapid counterattacks on the morning of the 6th were relatively easily stopped, however, and the failure led the Russians to dig in their tanks. For the next four days positions in the north hardly shifted despite frenzied close quarter battles and ferocious armored clashes. Russian forces had turned the Olkhovata ridge into a formidable strongpoint, but wave after wave of German assaults finally cleared the village and the heights on the 8th. Nevertheless such were their losses that the Germans could not consolidate and the ridge was

to change hands six times in all. On the eastern sector the Russians managed to contain the German thrust around Ponyri, after bitter street fighting. This meant that by the 10th the front in the northern section of the salient had been stabilized, and the Germans, for the moment, were halted and exhausted.

In the South, where the two sides were more evenly matched than in the north, Manstein's

Above left: Kreim, Kluge and Model discuss tactics as the offensive begins.
Above: Artillery of the exhausted *SS Grossdeutschland Division* fire at the advancing Russians. This division was one of the strongest the Germans employed during the offensive.

Right: German field artillery in action somewhere near the salient.

forces made greater headway. Russian preparations had been hampered by lack of knowledge of German intentions. With a concentration of five panzer divisions north of Belgorod and three to the east of the city, several options were open to the Germans, all of which had to be anticipated by the Russians. There was a risk that by attacking on the right flank with the three armored divisions, the *Kempf Group*, the Germans might be able to roll up the defenses from the east. But the greatest danger lay in the direct approach with the *Fourth Panzer Army* making the main effort against either Oboyan or Korocha. To meet these eventualities the Russians deployed Sixth Guard and Seventh Guard Armies on the left and center of the Voronezh front. Supporting Sixth Guard was the reinforced First Tank Army with some 1304 armored vehicles. Ahead of these dispositions, General Hoth, the commander of *Fourth Panzer Army*, intended to try to sidestep the defenses and engage the Russian reserves around Kursk and further east. To prevent these reserves being moved rapidly to the theater of operations, Hoth chose to strike midway between Oboyan and Korocha at Prokhorovka, a place where any Russian reserves would have to detrain. Thus the Russian defenses in the south were off-balance to some extent before the battle began.

Russian Miscalculations

For the Russians in the south things began to go badly as soon as the battle opened. They had carefully planned a pre-emptive air attack designed to catch the German aircraft on the ground, but this plan miscarried because the Germans had installed radar in the area. This gave the Germans enough time to get their aircraft in the air and meet the incoming attack. Soviet air losses were heavy—though the German claim of 400 kills is certainly too high—and this allowed the Germans to secure a local air supremacy on 5 July. Some 2000 sorties were flown in support of Manstein's attack which, unlike Model's, committed most of its armor from the outset. This plan proved quite successful and *XLVIII Panzer Corps* was able to break through 67th Guards Rifle Division and head for the Psel River crossings and Oboyan. To the east

the *SS Panzer Korps* broke through the defenses of 52nd Guards Rifle Division and began to move on Prokhorovka, but the *Kempf Group* faced tougher opposition in Seventh Guard Army and was only able to make slow progress towards Rzhavets, a situation that bared the right flank of the *SS Panzer Korps*.

For both sides the situation was critical. Except on the front of the *XLVIII Panzer Corps* the Germans had been unable to make continuous gains, since the three SS Panzer divisions which had punched separate holes through the Russian lines had been unable to link up. Furthermore Manstein's forces ran up against the same problems that were to face Model when the latter put in his attack—the tendency of the Panthers to break down and catch fire rather easily, and the danger of the armor and infantry becoming separated. For the Russians, the loss

Right: Members of the *SS Leibstandarte Adolf Hitler Division* withdraw after suffering heavy casualties.

of their forward positions combined with their faulty initial dispositions meant that the decision in the south—and hence the salient generally—was in the melting pot; the familiar exhortations to fight to the last gave credit to the seriousness of the situation.

After the early successes on the 4th Hoth decided to cross the stream in the Sawidowka-Ssyrzew at dawn on the 5th, the areas to the south of the stream having been cleared during the night. Unfortunately, heavy rains swelled the stream to a torrent and inundated the surrounding fields. This gave the Russians a chance to reform, and a combination of human and natural obstacles prevented any German success in the area on the 5th. Nevertheless, on the following day *XLVIII Panzer Corps* was able to resume its offensive; they penetrated to Syrtzewo on the 7th, though some time was lost when *3rd Panzer*

Division was forced to deal with a local Russian counterattack that regained part of Sawidowka. On the drying ground the Panzers were able to break almost to the main Russian artillery positions and attempts were made by *XLVIII Panzer Corps* to link-up with the SS Panzers who had managed to penetrate a further four miles on the right. By the 7th the Germans had pried the Russians out of most of their positions on the Pena. On the 8th German forces began to cross the river and successfully withstood a counterattack by T-34s from III Mechanized Corps in support of First Tank Army.

After five days of conflict the Germans had succeeded in breaking through the first two Russian defense lines, but only on the east flank of *XLVIII Panzer Corps* had the extremely strong *SS Grossdeutschland Division* managed to break into the third line. Russian resistance,

Left: Soviet anti-tank crew repulse a Panzer attack.

221

The Battle of Kursk, 1943

The Balance of Forces involved at Kursk

	🚶	🔫	🚜	✈
German	900,000	10,000	2700	2500
Russian	1,337,000	10,220	3306	2650

The German Offensive 4–12 July (southern front)

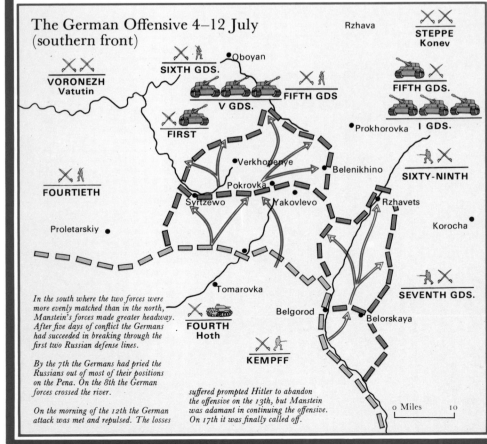

In the south where the two forces were more evenly matched than in the north, Manstein's forces made greater headway. After five days of conflict the Germans had succeeded in breaking through the first two Russian defense lines.

By the 7th the Germans had pried the Russians out of most of their positions on the Pena. On the 8th the German forces crossed the river.

On the morning of the 12th the German attack was met and repulsed. The losses suffered prompted Hitler to abandon the offensive on the 13th, but Manstein was adamant in continuing the offensive. On 17th it was finally called off.

0 Miles 10

'Operation Citadel' 4–12 July

The German attack was scheduled for 0330 on 5 July, but effectively the battle was under way by the afternoon of the 4th.

In the Bryanak-Orel-Kursk-Kharkov region the front line had formed into a Russian held salient 60 miles wide with the German Army Group Center holding the northern flank, and Army Group South the southern sector, around Kharkov. From this salient the Russians threatened the entire German position in the Ukraine. A Russian breakthrough would pierce the German front and open the road to Warsaw and eventual German defeat.

German High Command devised a plan to eliminate the salient. The plan, known as 'Operation Citadel', involved short but sharp thrusts on each side of the salient, intended to encircle the Russians within the bulge.

German preparations began in April. However, aided by an extremely efficient Intelligence network, the Russians were aware of the German intentions. Accordingly, the Soviet Command prepared for a defensive battle, followed by heavy counter attacks once the main German assaults had been halted. Men, armor, artillery, aircraft and engineering equipment were moved into the area. Defenses were sited in depth, based on clusters of antitank positions and mine fields. By the time the battle opened the defensive positions were up to 110 miles deep, and consisted of six main belts within the salient alone.

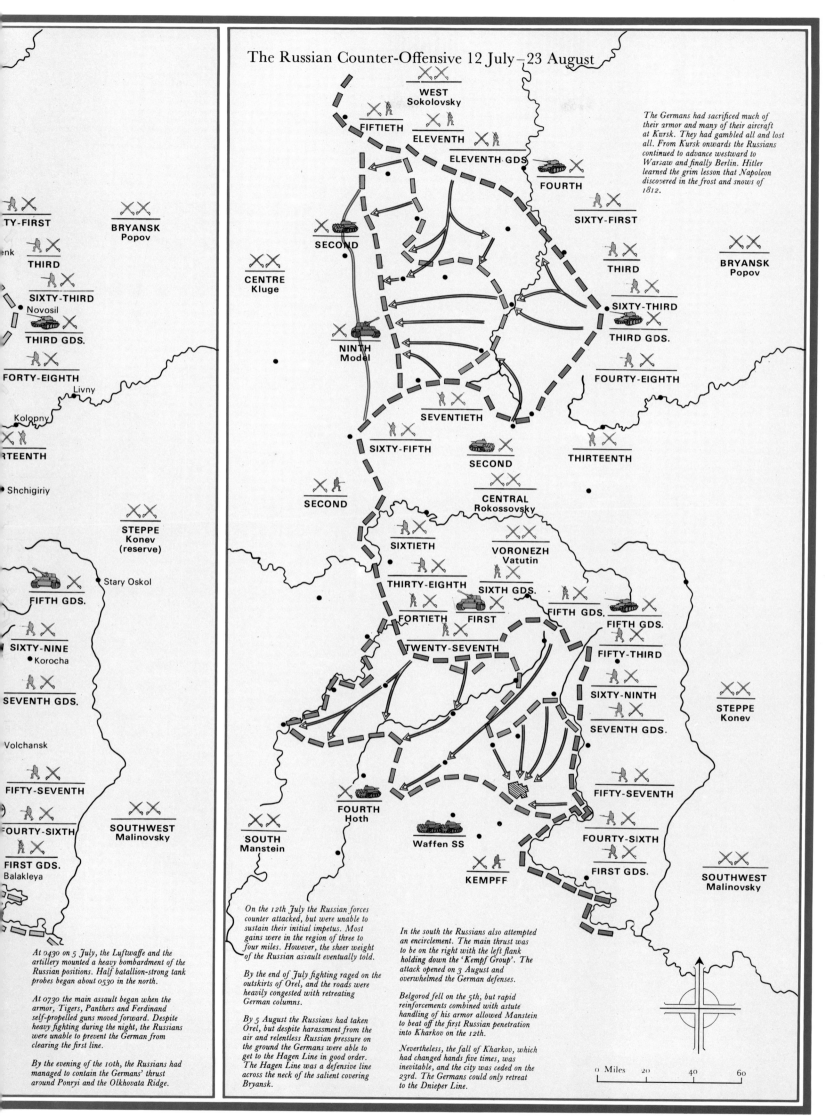

The Russian Counter-Offensive 12 July–23 August

WEST
Sokolovsky

FIFTIETH

ELEVENTH

ELEVENTH GDS.

FOURTH

SIXTY-FIRST

SECOND

CENTRE
Kluge

THIRD

SIXTY-THIRD

THIRD GDS.

NINTH
Model

FOURTY-EIGHT

SEVENTIETH

SIXTY-FIFTH

SECOND

THIRTEENTH

SECOND

CENTRAL
Rokossovsky

SIXTIETH

VORONEZH
Vatutin

THIRTY-EIGHTH

SIXTH GDS.

FIFTH GDS.

FORTIETH

FIRST

FIFTH GDS.

TWENTY-SEVENTH

FIFTY-THIRD

SIXTY-NINTH

SEVENTH GDS.

FIFTY-SEVENTH

FOURTH
Hoth

FOURTY-SIXTH

SOUTH
Manstein

Waffen SS

FIRST GDS.

KEMPFF

SOUTHWEST
Malinovsky

TY-FIRST

BRYANSK
Popov

nk

THIRD

SIXTY-THIRD

Novosil

THIRD GDS.

FORTY-EIGHTH

Livny

Kolopny

RTEENTH

Shchigiriy

STEPPE
Konev
(reserve)

Stary Oskol

FIFTH GDS.

SIXTY-NINE

Korocha

SEVENTH GDS.

Volchansk

FIFTY-SEVENTH

FOURTY-SIXTH

SOUTHWEST
Malinovsky

FIRST GDS.

Balakleya

BRYANSK
Popov

STEPPE
Konev

The Germans had sacrificed much of
their armor and many of their aircraft
at Kursk. They had gambled all and lost
all. From Kursk onwards the Russians
continued to advance westward to
Warsaw and finally Berlin. Hitler
learned the grim lesson that Napoleon
discovered in the frost and snows of
1812.

At 0430 on 5 July, the Luftwaffe and the
artillery mounted a heavy bombardment of the
Russian positions. Half battalion-strong tank
probes began about 0530 in the north.

At 0730 the main assault began when the
armor, Tigers, Panthers and Ferdinand
self-propelled guns moved forward. Despite
heavy fighting during the night, the Russians
were unable to prevent the German from
clearing the first line.

By the evening of the 10th, the Russians had
managed to contain the Germans' thrust
around Ponryi and the Olkhovata Ridge.

On the 12th July the Russian forces
counter attacked, but were unable to
sustain their initial impetus. Most
gains were in the region of three to
four miles. However, the sheer weight
of the Russian assault eventually told.

By the end of July fighting raged on the
outskirts of Orel, and the roads were
heavily congested with retreating
German columns.

By 5 August the Russians had taken
Orel, but despite harassment from the
air and relentless Russian pressure on
the ground the Germans were able to
get to the Hagen Line in good order.
The Hagen Line was a defensive line
across the neck of the salient covering
Bryansk.

In the south the Russians also attempted
an encirclement. The main thrust was
to be on the right with the left flank
holding down the 'Kempf Group'. The
attack opened on 3 August and
overwhelmed the German defenses.

Belgorod fell on the 5th, but rapid
reinforcements combined with astute
handling of his armor allowed Manstein
to beat off the first Russian penetration
into Kharkov on the 12th.

Nevertheless, the fall of Kharkov, which
had changed hands five times, was
inevitable, and the city was ceded on the
23rd. The Germans could only retreat
to the Dnieper Line.

0 Miles   20   40   60

Below: Germans inspect a
Russian T-34 destroyed
during the early stages of
the Kursk offensive. **Far
right:** A Pzkw IV moves
through burning grass as
the German offensive
continues.

despite a slackening on the Pena on the 8th, was
still fierce and the reserves—especially Fifth
Guard Tank Army—were still uncommitted.
Wheeling south from the Pena *6th Panzer Division*
was able to crush the encircled 71st Guards Rifle
Division by the 10th, securing the left flank, but
Hoth's intention was to regroup for an attack
toward Prokharovka to meet the Russian reserves. On the German right flank the *Kempf
Group* was still struggling to make headway against
Seventh Guard Army. Overall the result had been
poor for the Germans; about 130 square miles of
battered earth had changed hands and their
maximum penetration had only been ten miles.
Nevertheless the Russians had been forced to
send some of their reserves to their right flank and
this commitment was to weaken the forces they
had nursed for the counterattack. The Fifth
Guard Tank Army moved into the threatened

areas on the evening of the 9th after a 225-mile
move, but it was held back for two more days to organize and prepare while the Germans exhausted
themselves in clearing their flanks. For the
Russians the crisis had passed. They had halted
Model in the north and exhausted Manstein's
forces in the south. With fresh troops and unworn
equipment they were now ready to counterattack
on two fronts against an enemy strained by a
week of continuous heavy fighting.

In the south four armies, including the fresh
Fifth Guard and Fifth Guard Tank Armies, were
detailed to counter the anticipated German
assault on Prokhorovka by the *XLVIII* and *SS
Panzer Corps*. On the morning of the 12th about
700 German tanks moved out to attack, to be met
by about 850 Russian tanks, mostly T-34s. In
a head-on clash, as violent as it was unexpected,
numbers told, for the Russians were able to

Above: Troops and tanks of the *SS Totenkopf Division* move forward. The soldier in the center is carrying a *Panzerfaust*, the German equivalent of a bazooka, a close-range anti-tank weapon. **Above right:** German machine-gun post during the night fighting at Kursk.

Below: Panthers and Tigers, introduced for the first time at Kursk, pause during a lull in the fighting.

get in close where their guns could penetrate the Tigers and their shorter barrels very often gave them the first critical shot. In a grueling eight-hour battle fought under a blazing sun and a cloud of dust that prevented close air support, the two armored formations played a deadly game of hide and seek. By evening the battlefield was in Russian hands, together with its booty of disabled tanks and wounded crews. About 600 tanks had been lost, roughly equally divided between the two sides. But whereas the Russians still had at least 500 intact, *Fourth Panzer Army* had less than two full strength divisions left and the tired *Grossdeutschland Division* had to go back into action to help extricate *3rd Panzer Division*. Even the belated gains of the *Kempf Group*, which finally managed to capture Rzhavets, could not restore the balance.

In the north too the Germans were in trouble as the Russians attacked in the northern part of the Orel salient in an attempt to cut off Model's armor. In all, some 490,000 combat troops and 1000 tanks and assault guns were in danger of encirclement, but fortunately for the Germans Rokossovsky's attack was weaker than it should have been and Model's forces were able to disengage.

These two counterattacks, combined with the losses suffered, prompted Hitler to abandon the

offensive on the 13th. Three days earlier Anglo-American forces had landed in Sicily and first reports were not encouraging for the Germans. Italian morale and fighting ability was low and it was obvious to Hitler that only by cutting his losses at Kursk and sending armor from Russia could the situation be stabilized. Field Marshal Gunther von Kluge, Model's superior, concurred with this assessment, especially since it would mean the extrication of his threatened forces, but Manstein was adamant in trying to continue the offensive. Either he failed to realize that 20% of his force had been lost in the previous day's eight-hour battle, or he believed that Soviet losses had been so great that victory was within his grasp. In fact he later claimed that Russian losses were four times as heavy as his own. He certainly believed that the Russians had exhausted their reserves and were in no state to meet any further German assault. In this he was quite wrong. Though the Reserve Front had committed its two Guard Armies, three more were unused, while in the north four armies, including two tank armies, remained intact. Manstein was confident that the battle should be continued until the Russian armor already deployed was defeated and he was convinced this could be achieved. Hitler conceded part of the argument and allowed Manstein to continue in the south. Some partial success was achieved when the *Kempf Group* virtually encircled the battered Sixty-Ninth Army near Rzhavets. To hold this thrust the Russians had to commit all the reserves not already allocated to the counteroffensive. Of the eight armies that made up the strategic reserve only one remained. But the Russian commitment of their reserves, and checking of *Kempf*'s advance spelled the effective end of Citadel. On the 17th it was finally called off, though fighting continued in the south for another week.

The balance of forces and the initiative had swung heavily in favor of the Soviet Army, but its hope of twin encirclements, already thrown out of gear by Manstein's persistence, never materialized. Despite overwhelming numerical superiority in the northern salient—2:1 in men, 3:1 in artillery, 2.4:1 in tanks and 2:1 in aircraft—the Russians were unable to make the rapid progress necessary to catch Model's forces before

Left: German armor rolls forward across the Steppes. The two tanks closest to the camera have light plating protecting their tracks and turrets against bazooka fire. **Below:** A knocked-out Tiger is stopped, but the cost in Russian lives was dear.

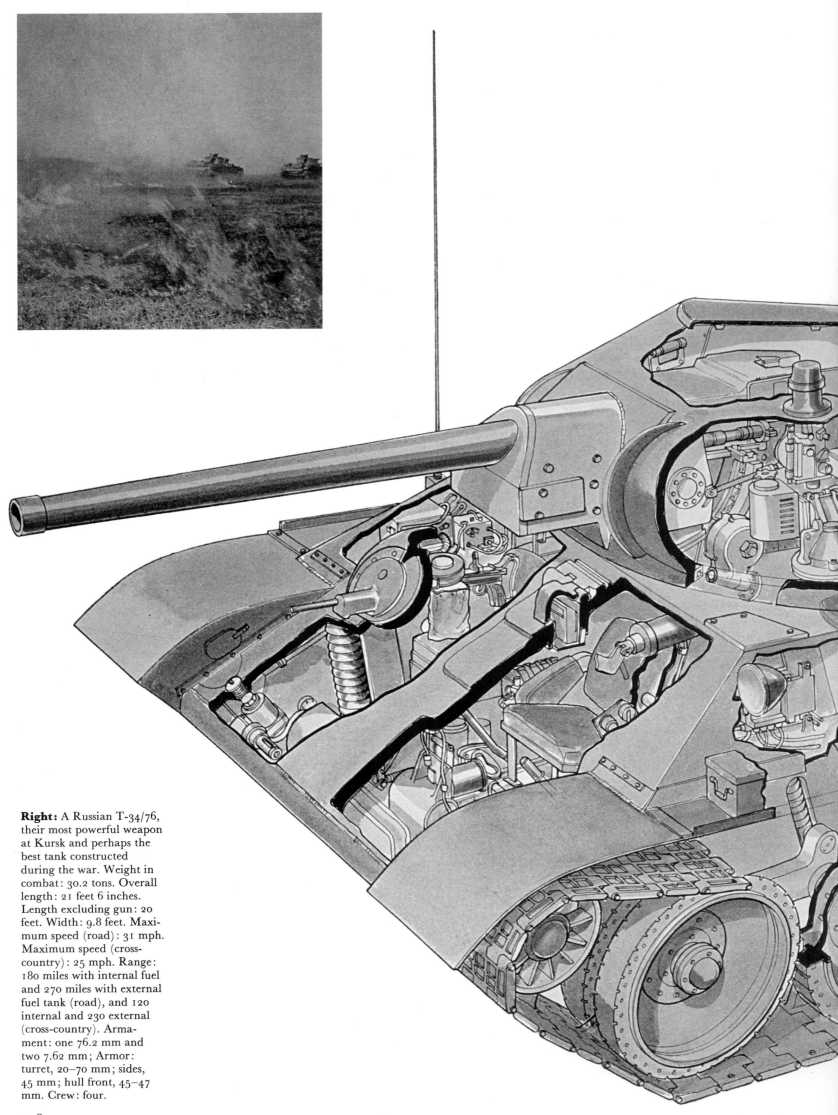

Right: A Russian T-34/76, their most powerful weapon at Kursk and perhaps the best tank constructed during the war. Weight in combat: 30.2 tons. Overall length: 21 feet 6 inches. Length excluding gun: 20 feet. Width: 9.8 feet. Maximum speed (road): 31 mph. Maximum speed (cross-country): 25 mph. Range: 180 miles with internal fuel and 270 miles with external fuel tank (road), and 120 internal and 230 external (cross-country). Armament: one 76.2 mm and two 7.62 mm; Armor: turret, 20–70 mm; sides, 45 mm; hull front, 45–47 mm. Crew: four.

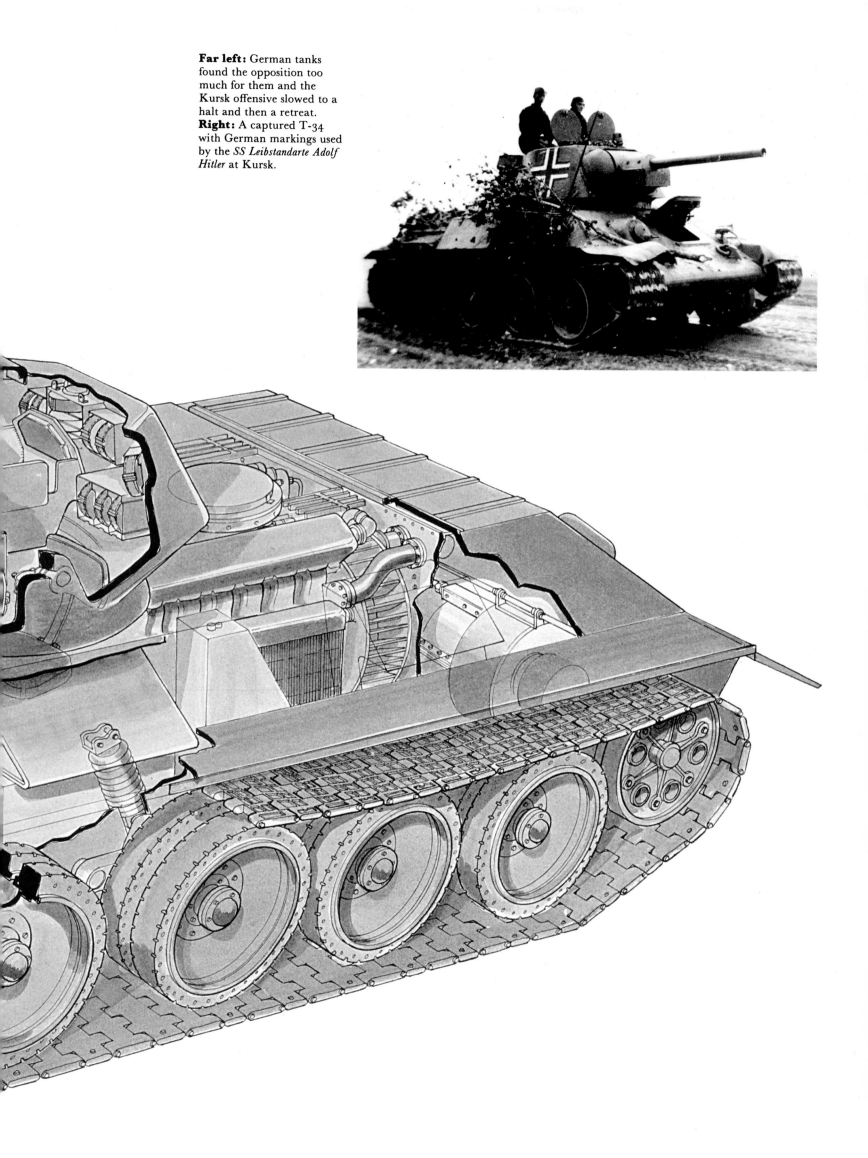

Far left: German tanks found the opposition too much for them and the Kursk offensive slowed to a halt and then a retreat.
Right: A captured T-34 with German markings used by the *SS Leibstandarte Adolf Hitler* at Kursk.

they reached the safety of the Hagen Line, a defensive line across the neck of the salient covering Bryansk. During the two years the area had been in German hands elaborate field fortifications had been built, and these slowed down a Soviet Army unused to this type of operation. Despite the frightening scale of artillery support—attacking infantry regiments had five artillery regiments in support and Eleventh Guard Army massed one artillery piece every five yards for fifteen miles—the Russians were unable to sustain their initial impetus. On 12 July Eleventh Guards penetrated sixteen miles, but this was exceptional. Most gains were in the region of three to four miles, and attempts to feed in reserves failed to secure a lasting advantage. The sheer weight of the Russian assault eventually told, however. By the end of July fighting raged on the outskirts of Orel, and the roads in the area were heavily congested by retreating German columns. By 5 August what was left of Orel, and it was not very much, was in Russian hands but losses in the area were to continue for months to come. Before they left the Germans had strewn the region with mines and skillfully concealed booty traps. Despite harassment from the air and relentless Russian pressure on the ground the Germans were able to get to the Hagen Line in good order. Though no encirclement had been achieved during the pursuit, the Russians had good reason to be pleased; *Army Group Center* had lost 20% of its strength. Fourteen of its divisions, including all its armor, had changed beyond all recognition, and the two armies that had spearheaded the attack, the *Ninth* and *Second Panzer*, were never to recover.

In the south the Russians also attempted an encirclement, but to the southeast of the battle zone. On the Russian left flank the Southwest, South and North Caucasus Fronts had remained passive, while the Kursk battle raged. With the issue by and large resolved on the 12th, North Caucasus Front attacked in the Taman Peninsula, south of the Don, but was repulsed with appalling losses, while attacks by the South and Southwest Fronts met with only partial success and again incurred heavy losses. Russian lack of armor and heavy artillery on these fronts, combined with the fact that, as in the Orel salient, the Germans had had two years to prepare defensive positions, meant that progress was slow. But the German defenses along the River Mius were broken on 19 July and this prevented the despatch of forces to help Manstein's thrust on Rzhavets. The Russian breakthrough on the Mius threatened the whole of the German position in the south, but Hitler was unwilling to evacuate the Donetz basin and ordered counterattacks to be launched. After some heated exchanges between Hitler and Manstein, the latter counterattacked and eliminated the Russian bridgehead, capturing 18,000 prisoners. Yet nothing could stop the steady disintegration of the German position in the south; the Russians were now preparing encircling attacks on Kharkov.

The Russians intended to use a massive infantry attack to beat in the German front, and to feed in their armor to exploit their gains.

With over 650,000 combat troops, 12,000 guns, 2400 tanks and 1200 aircraft the Russians had nearly a 4:1 superiority on the ground and a 4:3 advantage in the air. Narrow frontage and massed artillery characterized the Russian plan. The main thrust was to be on the right with the left flank holding down the *Kempf Group*.

The Attack Opens

The attack opened on 3 August and quickly threatened to overwhelm the German defenses. Belgorod fell on the 5th—its capture and that of Orel prompted the first of the numerous victory salutes that continued to the end of the war—and in places the Russians achieved a 62-mile advance in five days. The *19th Panzer* and three infantry divisions were shattered in the Grayvoron region and even greater danger seemed to threaten the six divisions around Kharkov, which Hitler was determined to hold. Rapid reinforcement combined with astute handling of his armor allowed von Manstein to beat off the first Russian penetration into Kharkov by the 12th, and a heavy counter-attack halted an advance from the east of the city by First Tank Army. Nevertheless, the fall of Kharkov, which had already changed hands five times, could only be postponed and not prevented; its smouldering ruins were ceded on the 23rd. Von Manstein had decided to abandon the city contrary to orders. With Russian offensives being conducted along the whole length of the Russian front, with fresh drafts of men and equipment meeting about 25% of their losses, the Germans in the south could only retreat, hounded all the way to the Dnieper Line. By the new year the eastern Ukraine had been liberated and the Germans had to face Russian offensives throughout the year, not just in the winter—a sure sign of the changing picture in the East.

Losses in the battle are difficult to assess with accuracy. During the whole of the operations around the Kursk-Orel salients German records admit to 907,000 casualties, but the greatest loss had been among the cherished, once all-conquering Panzer divisions. At the height of the battle about 3000 tanks had been on the move at the same time, and it seems likely that about that number were destroyed, perhaps a few hundred more, with the balance of loss being about 40:60 against the Russians. Although Russian losses were no less than the German, the former could make up their casualties, while the latter could not. Kursk-Orel was the swan song of German armor, and the Russian headlines 'The Tigers Are Burning' signified not only the funeral pyre of the Panzer arm but the pall that overhung Germany's New Order and her hopes of victory.

Opposite above: SS Grenadiers await fresh orders during a pause in the withdrawal from the Kursk salient. **Left:** Russian SU-76 self-propelled guns enter Kharkov as the German front is rolled westward after Kursk: 23 August, 1943.

231

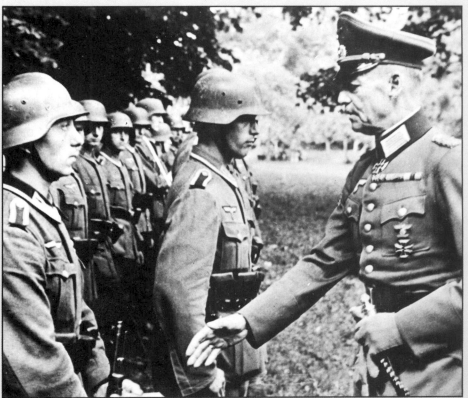

The Ardennes

1944

By the autumn of 1944 the once-powerful *Wehrmacht* had been forced onto the defensive on all fronts. North Africa was long since lost, most of France was in Allied hands, and the situation in the East deteriorated daily. After the mauling of the Panzers at Kursk, Germany's only hope on the Russian Front lay in fluid, mobile defense. Hitler's dismissal of Manstein, the leading practitioner of these tactics, only worsened the *Wehrmacht's* plight. June 1944 saw the crippling of *Army Group Center* which, despite substantial reinforcements which might more usefully have been employed in the West, was tumbled back to the Polish border.

The declining fortune of German arms was matched by growing discord within the Reich. The 20 July bomb plot was followed by a sharp increase in arrests and denunciations; suspicion and distrust between the army and the SS reached a new and dangerous level. However, in spite of the ferocity of Allied air attacks, German industrial production actually rose, and in August 1944 the record number of 869 tanks and 744 assault guns came off the assembly lines. But equipment was no use without soldiers to operate it; in a frenzied effort to get every available man

Opposite left: Field Marshal Gerd von Rundstedt, who was brought from retirement to direct the Ardennes offensive. He was forcibly retired by Hitler in 1944 after he advised him to surrender on the best terms possible when the Allies landed in Normandy. **Opposite right:** Rundstedt inspects troops in his capacity as C-in-C West. **Below:** An American 105-mm self-propelled howitzer crew takes on fresh ammunition as they prepare the counter-offensive in the Bulge.

Above: Walter Model, who was promoted to Field Marshal in 1944, commanded Army Group B in the Ardennes offensive.
Above right: General Hasso von Manteuffel, who commanded the Fifth Panzer Army in Hitler's last offensive.

into uniform the call-up age was lowered to 16½, and ruthless steps were taken to 'comb out' those in hitherto reserved occupations.

One of the consequences of the 20 July plot was the appointment of Heinrich Himmler, head of the SS, as commander of the 'Replacement Army'. Himmler added this office to his many others and, even without the Army-SS tension, it would have been difficult enough for any one man to cope. Himmler's new activities were indicative of the hostility between the agencies of the tottering Reich. The 'combing-out' process made thousands of men available; boys, businessmen, airmen without planes and sailors without ships. Instead of using them to reinforce weakened Army formations, Himmler posted them instead to new *Volksgrenadier* divisions, whose short training period was, in part at least, compensated for by very high *esprit de corps*. This was fostered by giving these divisions much of the new equipment. Most of the rest of it went to the SS, while for the battered Army divisions tanks, vehicles and guns were in short supply.

There was immediate employment at hand for the *Volksgrenadiers*. Hitler regarded the situation as far from hopeless. He was convinced that the Allies would soon be at each others' throats; the incongruous union between communist and capitalist could not survive for long. Germany could endure, she might yet triumph. The collapse of the alliance would, Hitler believed, be facilitated by striking a sudden and violent blow on one front. In August 1944 he had ordered that preparations should be made for an offensive on the Western Front in November. His generals maintained that troops would never be available in sufficient quantities, but the efforts of Himmler, Goebbels and the local *Gauleiters* proved them wrong.

But where were these new troops to be employed? An offensive against the Russians would be unlikely to achieve decisive results. In the West, however, things were different. The Allied

advance into Belgium had left the Ardennes—the hilly, wooded area where Belgium, Germany and Luxembourg meet—held by only six divisions. The events of 1940 had illustrated vividly that the area was passable to armor. To the undeniable tactical attraction of attacking a point where the enemy was weak, was added the historical appeal of staging a blitzkrieg on the very ground over which it had been so successful three and a half years before.

Desperate though the plight of the *Wehrmacht* was, there were certain factors favoring a limited offensive. The *Volksgrenadiers* would certainly enable the Germans to obtain local superiority. Of the 28 divisions available, eight were Panzer, and the Panther and Tiger tanks they contained were superior to the Shermans with which most British and American armored units were equipped. Surprise, an essential ingredient of blitzkrieg, was facilitated by the fact that the Allied commanders believed the Germans to be exhausted and quite incapable of a counter-offensive. On the other hand, there were two important factors militating against an attack. The first of these was Allied air superiority. The Luftwaffe, even by straining every nerve, could only hope to offset this on a local basis. Secondly, there was a critical shortage of fuel which was to severely limit movement on the ground.

The strategic aim of the Ardennes Offensive —often referred to as the Battle of the Bulge—was the capture of Antwerp and the encirclement of the four Allied armies north of the line Malmédy-Liège-Antwerp. This objective seemed unrealistic to the aged Field Marshal Gerd von Rundstedt, brought out of retirement to act as Commander-in-Chief West. 'Antwerp?' he inquired bitingly. 'If we reach the Meuse we should go down on our knees and thank God'. Von Rundstedt's command was little more than nominal; Hitler was to direct the battle personally. The three armies taking part in the offensive were to form *Army Group B* under Field Marshal Walter

Model, an excellent tactician who had shown his worth in the defensive battles in the East. Model's army commanders were an ill-assorted trio. SS General Joseph 'Sepp' Dietrich, a former regular NCO, led *Sixth SS Panzer Army*, which was to form the northern prong of the German trident. On his left was *Fifth Panzer Army* under General Hasso von Manteuffel who, at 47, had a brilliant record as a fighting general on the Russian Front. The less dramatic figure of General Erich Brandenburger commanded *Seventh Army* on the German left.

Planning the Operation

Rundstedt and Model discussed the operation with the three army commanders on 27 October. They reported in favor of a limited offensive with Liège as its target, but were overruled on 1 November by the arrival of an operations order which decreed that Antwerp should remain the objective. The attack was to be launched on an 85-mile front, between Monschau and Echternach. Dietrich was to cross the Meuse at Andenne and Huy, before thrusting straight for Antwerp. Manteuffel was to take Namur, Dinant and Brussels. Brandenburger was to cover Manteuffel's southern flank, an unspectacular but essential task. The advance was to be preceded by parachutists who were to seize major road junctions. SS Colonel Otto Skorzeny trained a special force which would wear American uniforms to sow confusion in the Allied rear.

Both Rundstedt and Model protested that the operation was too ambitious, and they were joined by Manteuffel, whose well-known tactical expertise persuaded Hitler to permit some small adjustments to the initial phase of the attack. The date for the launching of the offensive was initially to be 25 November. The concentration of the assaulting division took longer than expected, however, and the attack was steadily postponed, first to 7 December and finally to 16 December.

The Allied commanders, also were not without their problems. The rapid advance from the Normandy bridgeheads in August, and the subsequent liberation of Paris, could not conceal a serious difference of opinion between the Supreme Allied Commander, General Dwight D. Eisenhower, and his subordinate, Field Marshal Montgomery, commander of 21 Army Group. Montgomery wanted to push on north with his own army group and General Omar Bradley's 12 Army Group. This 'solid mass of 40 divisions' was to make for Brussels, and then for the Ruhr, thus crippling Germany's industry. Eisenhower envisaged a totally different approach. His plan was, in his own words, 'to push forward on a broad front with priority on the left'. Montgomery's plan might well have worked if implemented in August, but German resistance stiffened in September. 'Operation Market Garden', the seizure of the river crossings between Eindhoven and Arnhem, was only partially successful. This did not, however, curb Montgomery's enthusiasm. He continued to press for a drive into the Ruhr, but was eventually persuaded that the capture of Antwerp must be given first priority.

Antwerp fell on 4 September, although the port was not operational till 28 November. General George S. Patton's Third Army took Metz on 22 November, and the US Seventh Army entered Strasbourg the following day. Montgomery continued to argue, however, that the north was the crucial front, and stressed to Eisenhower that there should be a unified command of all forces north of the Ardennes. Eisenhower met Montgomery and Bradley at Maastricht in early December. It was decided to keep up pressure on the Germans in the north with a view to an attack on the Ruhr. For this purpose 21 Army Group would be reinforced with one American Army. The boundary between the two army groups was to be the Ruhr, not the Ardennes as Montgomery had wished.

The decision taken at Maastricht would un-

Center left: A Royal Tiger tank burns on a Belgian roadside as the German thrust to Antwerp is brought to a halt. **Near left:** General Dwight David Eisenhower, who was appointed as a Lieutenant General in 1942 to command American and Allied forces in Europe. After the success of 'Operation Torch', when this photograph was taken, he directed operations in Italy and France. His first major setback was suffered in the Ardennes. **Above:** Lieutenant General George S. Patton, commander of the American Third Army. 'Old Blood and Guts' was one of the most daring and controversial commanders in the US Army, who was tragically killed in a road accident soon after VE Day.

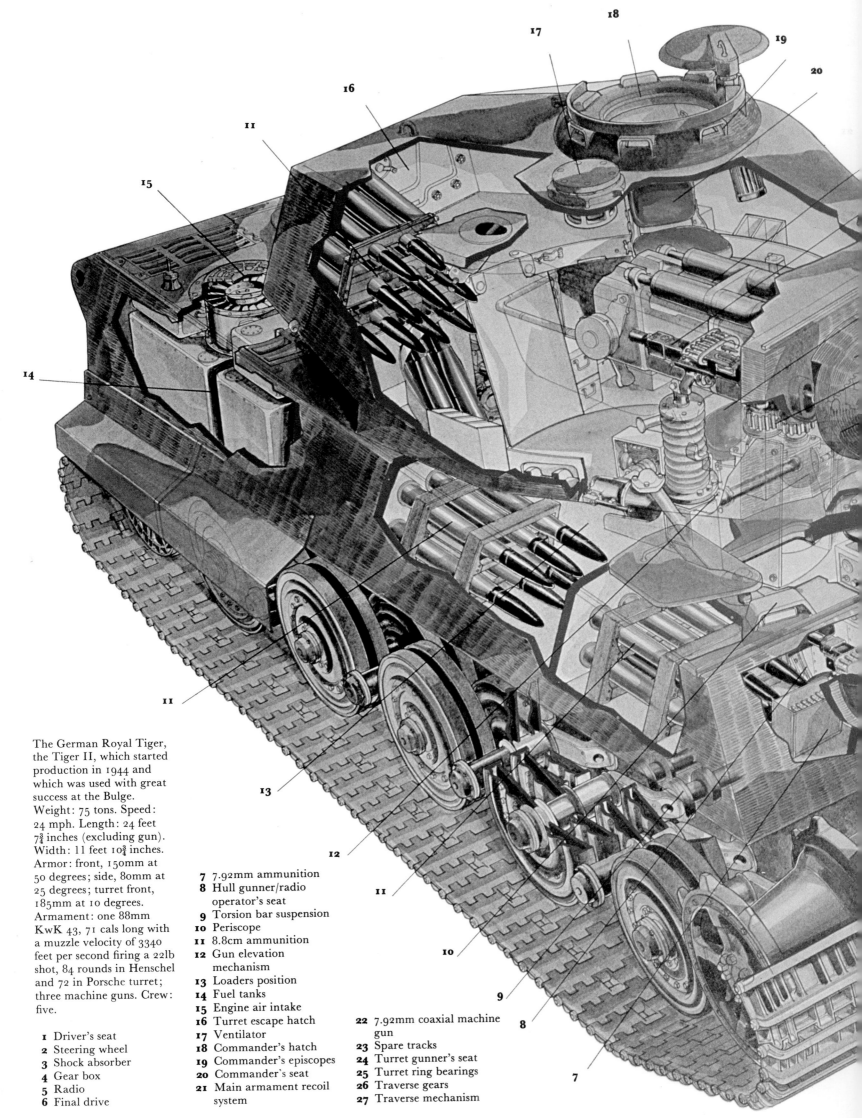

The German Royal Tiger,
the Tiger II, which started
production in 1944 and
which was used with great
success at the Bulge.
Weight: 75 tons. Speed:
24 mph. Length: 24 feet
7¾ inches (excluding gun).
Width: 11 feet 10¾ inches.
Armor: front, 150mm at
50 degrees; side, 80mm at
25 degrees; turret front,
185mm at 10 degrees.
Armament: one 88mm
KwK 43, 71 cals long with
a muzzle velocity of 3340
feet per second firing a 22lb
shot, 84 rounds in Henschel
and 72 in Porsche turret;
three machine guns. Crew:
five.

1 Driver's seat
2 Steering wheel
3 Shock absorber
4 Gear box
5 Radio
6 Final drive

7 7.92mm ammunition
8 Hull gunner/radio
   operator's seat
9 Torsion bar suspension
10 Periscope
11 8.8cm ammunition
12 Gun elevation
   mechanism
13 Loaders position
14 Fuel tanks
15 Engine air intake
16 Turret escape hatch
17 Ventilator
18 Commander's hatch
19 Commander's episcopes
20 Commander's seat
21 Main armament recoil
   system

22 7.92mm coaxial machine
   gun
23 Spare tracks
24 Turret gunner's seat
25 Turret ring bearings
26 Traverse gears
27 Traverse mechanism

236

doubtedly have been different had Allied intelligence fully appreciated the significance of *Sixth Panzer Army*. It had been detected early, but a SHAEF (Supreme Headquarters Allied Expeditionary Force) report of 12 November maintained that 'the Army's most obvious use is counterattack', pointing out that a lack of petrol precluded the launching of 'a true counteroffensive'. The move of *Sixth Panzer Army* to the area east of Aachen was seen as little more than an attempt by the Germans to buttress their crumbling front. Thus it was that, in mid-December, the Ardennes sector, irrelevant for the projected Allied thrust to the Ruhr, lay dangerously bare.

The threatened area was the responsibility of Lieutenant-General Courtney H. Hodges, US First Army. Most of the attack frontage was in the hands of Major General Troy H. Middleton's VIII Corps. On Middleton's left was the southernmost formation of V Corps, 99th Division, which had been in the line for only six weeks and was relatively inexperienced. This would have been serious enough. There was, however, an unguarded space of some two miles between the two corps. South of this lay the Losheim Gap, a classic avenue between Belgium and Germany, held only by 18th Cavalry Squadron, which had incomplete liaison with its right-hand neighbor, 106th Division. The 106th, holding the forward slopes of the Schnee Eifel Ridge, was totally inexperienced, and had arrived in its position only three days before the attack was launched. On its right stood the center formation of VIII Corps, 28th Division. This was, in contrast, a battle-tried division, but it had recently lost over 6000 men in the fierce fighting in the Hurtgen Forest, and was in the Ardennes to rest and reorganize. Hodges' only notable advantage was the presence of the excellent 2nd Division in the north. As part of Fifth Army's preparation for a thrust at the Koel Dams, this division had just launched a successful attack in the sector held by 99th Division. Its presence was to be of great value over the coming days.

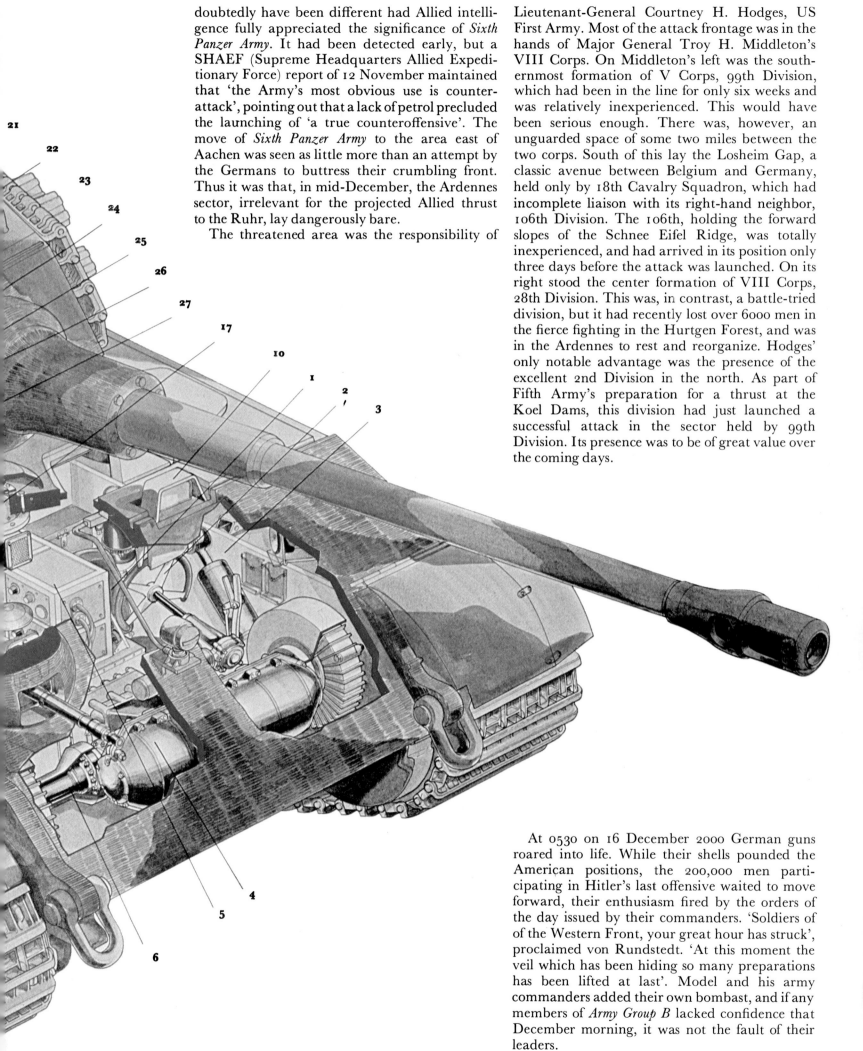

At 0530 on 16 December 2000 German guns roared into life. While their shells pounded the American positions, the 200,000 men participating in Hitler's last offensive waited to move forward, their enthusiasm fired by the orders of the day issued by their commanders. 'Soldiers of of the Western Front, your great hour has struck', proclaimed von Rundstedt. 'At this moment the veil which has been hiding so many preparations has been lifted at last'. Model and his army commanders added their own bombast, and if any members of *Army Group B* lacked confidence that December morning, it was not the fault of their leaders.

The surge of fire came as a rude shock to the American front line units, many of whose members had previously been concerned with

nothing more important than the possibility of Christmas leave. As the fire died away, the German infantry and armor advanced, aided by searchlights bounced off low cloud.

German successes on the first day were dramatic but uneven. In the north, *LXXII Corps* of *Sixth Panzer Army* was checked before Monschau. The American attack toward the Roer Dams had reduced the forces available in this sector and, despite the furious assaults of *326th Volksgrenadier Division*, gains were limited. In particular, *LXXII Corps* failed to seize the Monschau-Eupen Ridge, whose capture was essential to the German plan. 'Hard Shoulders' were to be set up to bolster both flanks of the attack, and the Monschau-Eupen line was to form the northern shoulder. On the southern edge of the attack front, Brandenburger had the task of setting up a 'hard shoulder' across the Sauer at Echternach. This called for a complex river-crossing by his left-hand corps, *LXXX*. Brandenburger's *Volksgrenadiers*, aided by an effective preparatory bombardment, got across the river and successfully penetrated the American defenses. The US 4th Division, holding the sector, fought back with creditable tenacity, aided by a small number of tanks from the US 10th Armored Division. The *Volksgrenadiers* were poorly supplied with anti-tank weapons, and an American counterthrust into the village of Lauerborn achieved local success. The artillery of 4th Division, meanwhile, wreaked havoc amongst Brandenburger's horse-drawn artillery and transport, and impeded German pioneers in their efforts to bridge the Sauer. By nightfall, although the Germans were across the river in strength, the southern 'hard shoulder' had not been established.

Brandenburger's right-hand corps, *LXXXV*, had the dual task of cooperating with Manteuffel and assisting *LXXX Corps* in its seizure of the 'hard shoulder'. It was faced by 28th Division, whose 109th Infantry Regiment, dug in on high

ground, assisted 60th Armored Infantry Battalion, to its south, to beat off *276th Volksgrenadier Division*. Thrusts by *352nd Volksgrenadier Division* against the 109th Infantry's left were also thwarted. The *5th Parachute Division*, Brandenburger's most northerly formation, made slightly better progress. The partial success of *Seventh Army's* right could not compensate for the failure of *LXXX Corps*. *Seventh Army* fell consistently short of its objectives in the subsequent days, and never provided *Fifth Panzer Army* with the necessary flank protection.

In the German center Manteuffel crashed through 18th Cavalry Squadron in the Losheim gap, and reached the St Vith road. On his left *XLVII Panzer Corps* crossed the Our, but was checked on the Clerf by the gallant 28th Division. To Manteuffel's right, Dietrich's men pressed forward rapidly. *Sixth Panzer Army's* main thrusts were delivered by *1st* and *12th SS Panzer Divisions*, both preceded by *Volksgrenadier* divisions who were to make the initial break, to permit the armor to funnel through the American position. The results of these tactics were not dissimilar to those of comparable plans at Kursk and Alamein. The *Volksgrenadiers* were very heavily shelled and were unable to get through the American line. The *12th SS Panzer Division* tried to move forward without infantry support, but was stopped dead; *1st SS Panzer* might have shared the same fate had its leading battlegroup not been commanded by a particularly ruthless and aggressive officer, SS Colonel Jochen Peiper.

Above: Gliders brought reinforcements to the beleaguered 101st Airborne Division trapped in Bastogne.

Panzer Army, Peiper's failure to seize the Stavelot dump with its two million gallons of petrol was itself of prime significance.

While the German armor and infantry assaulted the American front, Otto Skorzery's special forces and Colonel von der Heydte's parachutists were employed against the American rear. Skorzery's men were quite successful; they destroyed several installations, spread disquieting rumors and caused a wave of saboteurmania behind the lines. Large numbers of roadblocks were set up, and troops whose presence was urgently required in the firing-line wasted hours in elaborate identity-checks. The parachutists, on the other hand, were dogged by bad luck. They were dropped 24 hours late; few of the aircraft found the dropping zone, and those parachutists that landed did so only with heavy casualties. Von der Heydte eventually collected 350 or so, and remained in the area of Baraque Michel for two days before ordering his men to return to their own lines in small groups. Few managed to make their way back; the majority, including von der Heydte, were captured.

On the second day of the offensive Manteuffel renewed his pressure on 106th Division, two of whose regiments became isolated on the Schnee Eifel Ridge. When reinforcements sent by VIII Corps failed to arrive in time, after being held up by retreating troops, over 8000 men surrendered in the most serious reverse incurred by American troops in Europe.

Eisenhower had immediately realized that the Ardennes thrust was a full blooded counter-offensive. He ordered 7th Armored Division to St Vith from its rest area near Aachen, and sent a combat command of 10th Armored Division to Bastogne. To Bastogne, too, he sent the US 101st Airborne Division, which set out from Reims on the evening of 17 December and arrived at its destination early on the 19th.

It was toward Bastogne that Manteuffel's main attack now developed. His advance was spearheaded by *XLVII Panzer Corps*, containing two good divisions, *26th Volksgrenadier* and *2nd Panzer*. The élite *Panzer Lehr* division was initially in reserve. Their high quality notwithstanding,

Below: US infantrymen plunge forward through the wintry snows of the Ardennes.

Peiper led his panzers past the chaos of the abortive *Volksgrenadier* attack, broke through the American lines, and took Honsfeld at dawn the following day. Unwilling to be burdened with prisoners, Peiper's men shot several captured Americans, setting a grim precedent for their subsequent behavior. After refueling with captured petrol at Bullingen, Peiper's force drove on to the Malmédy crossroads, where 86 American prisoners were machine-gunned in the infamous 'Malmédy Massacre', for which Peiper was later to be tried for his life. Peiper's objective was the Meuse bridge at Huy and, on the afternoon of 17 December, he seemed likely to reach it. However, his advance guard halted just short of Stavelot, deterred, it seems, by the large numbers of American vehicles in the area. This was the moment at which Peiper's leadership might again have tipped the scales, but, somewhat surprisingly, he failed to come forward to examine the situation personally. It was just as well for the Americans that Peiper did not cast his incisive glance over Stavelot, for it was held only by engineers, with no heavy weapons. Most of the vehicles there were moving petrol from a large fuel dump nearby. Since lack of fuel was one of the major causes of the limited advance of *Sixth*

the attackers' task proved difficult in the extreme. The *26th Volksgrenadier* had to cross two rivers, the Our and the Clerf, in the face of determined resistance. Although the isolated American strongpoints were eventually overcome with the aid of *2nd Panzer*, the advance went much slower than Manteuffel had hoped. The spirited defense of the Clerf line gave the Americans valuable time in which to reinforce Bastogne, and it was against Bastogne that Manteuffel's strength was ultimately to break.

Panzer Lehr was within five miles of Bastogne by dusk on 18 December. Although the commander of *XLVII Panzer Corps* was aware of the vital importance of Bastogne, he failed to infect Lieutenant-General Bayerlein of *Panzer Lehr* with the essential sense of urgency. Bayerlein halted at Magaret, and the route to Bastogne was lost; 101st Airborne Division arrived early the following morning.

Other Allied reinforcements were on their way. Hodges had bolstered up the Elsenborn Ridge south of Monschau with troops from the First Army's northern sector. Lieutenant-General W. H. Simpson of the US Ninth Army sent two divisions south to aid Hodges, and Eisenhower sent the US 82nd Airborne Division to Werboment, with the aim of blunting Peiper's thrust. On 19 December Eisenhower in a conference at Verdun laid down broad policy for preventing a breakout. Bradley and Montgomery were authorized to carry out limited withdrawals, but the west bank of the Meuse was to be the limit of such maneuvers. Lieutenant-General J.L. Devers was to extend his Sixth Army Group to the north to permit the US Third Army to intervene against the German left. Simpson was to carry out a similar extension to the South, to free more of Hodges' troops. Finally, Eisenhower took the decision, controversial but undeniably correct, to place all troops north of the breakthrough under Montgomery's command, while Bradley commanded those in the south. Pained though Bradley must have been by the temporary use of his First and Ninth Armies, there was logic in Eisenhower's decision. It was difficult for Bradley, whose headquarters were in Luxembourg, to control

Above: Planes of the 9th Troop Carrier Command parachute supplies to the 'Battling Bastards of Bastogne', 23 December, 1944.

armies with which his telephone links had been cut. Furthermore, by placing Montgomery in command of the northern sector, Eisenhower ensured that British reserves would be used to contain the breakthrough in this area.

Montgomery's immediate intention was, in his own words, 'to get the show tidied up and to ensure absolute security before passing over the offensive action..'. His efforts to 'tidy up' brought him into conflict with Hodges, whose headquarters he visited on 20 December. Montgomery suggested abandoning St Vith and the Elsenborn Ridge, but dropped the idea in the face of American protests. He even went on to authorize an advance by 82nd Airborne to the Salm, which *Sixth Panzer Army* had, as yet, been unable to cross in strength. Finally, Montgomery ordered Hodges to pull Major General J.L. 'Lightning Joe' Collins' VII Corps out of the line near Aachen to be strengthened for subsequent use as a counterattack force.

Although substantial steps had been taken to limit the German exploitation, the crisis was far from over. The *116th Panzer Division* of *XLVIII Panzer Corps* advanced into the void between Bastogne and St Vith, taking Houffalize on the evening of 19 December. The reconnaissance of

Below: US infantrymen outside St Vith in January 1945, during the counter-offensive which effectively destroyed the remnants of the German Army in the West.

The Battle of the Ardennes, 1944

The German Offensive
16–24 December

At 0530 on 16 December 2000 German guns opened up on the American positions. As the fire died away, the German infantry and armor advanced.

German successes on the first day were dramatic but uneven. In the north 'LXXII Corps' was checked before Monschau. In the center Manteuffel advanced through the Losheim gap and reached the St Vith road. On his left 'XLVII Panzer Corps' crossed the Our, but was checked on the Clerf by the 28th Division. On the southern edge of the attack front, Brandenberger crossed the Sauer at Echternach in strength. Dietrich's men pressed forward rapidly, but only Peiper's battle-group of 1st SS Panzer Division broke through the American lines, took Honsfeld at dawn the following day and after refueling at Bullingen, drove on to the Malmédy crossroads, and on the afternoon of the 17th halted just short of Stavelot.

Objectives of the Offensive

The strategic aim of the Ardennes offensive was the capture of Antwerp and the encirclement of the four Allied armies north of the line Malmédy-Liège-Antwerp. Gerd von Rundstedt was to direct the battle. The three armies taking part in the offensive were to form 'Army Group B' under Model.

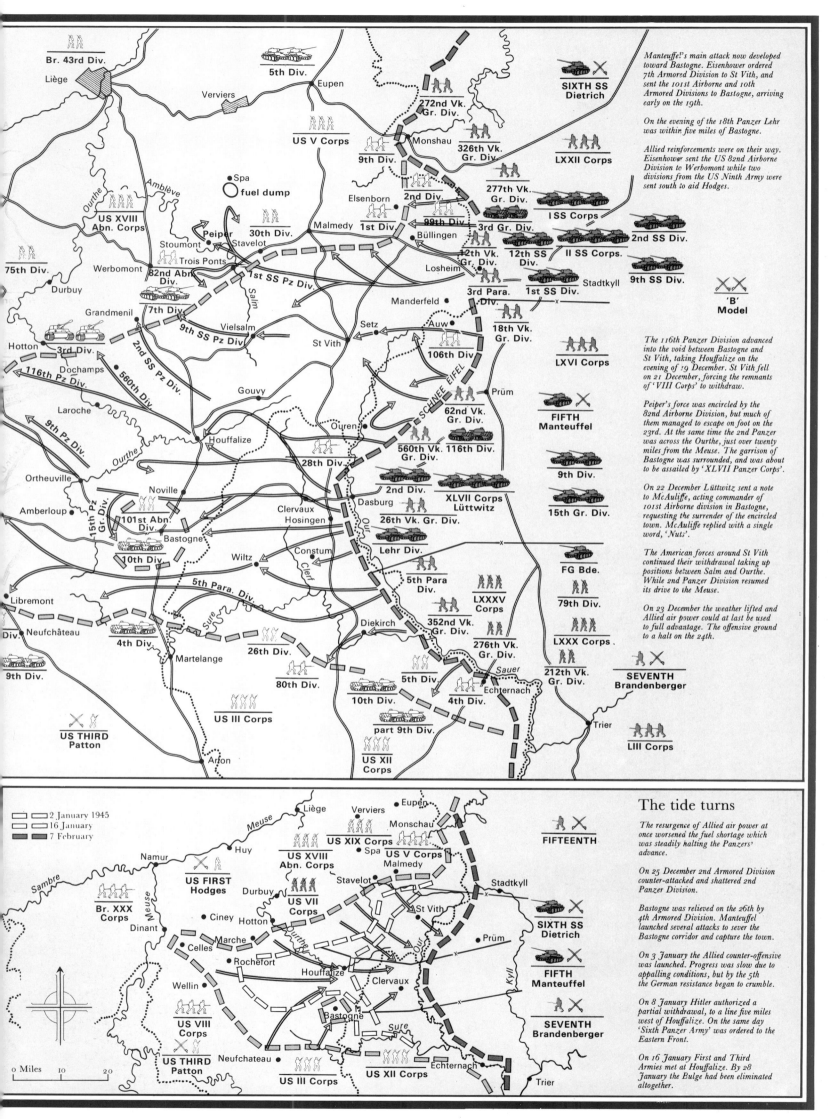

Br. 43rd Div.

Liège

Verviers

5th Div.

Eupen

SIXTH SS
Dietrich

272nd Vk.
Gr. Div.

Monshau

326th Vk.
Gr. Div.

LXXII Corps

US V Corps

9th Div.

Spa
fuel dump

Elsenborn

2nd Div.

277th Vk.
Gr. Div.

I SS Corps

Amblève

Ourthe

US XVIII
Abn. Corps

30th Div.

Malmedy

1st Div.

99th Div.

3rd Gr. Div.

2nd SS Div.

Peiper

Stoumont
Stavelot

Büllingen

II SS Corps.

75th Div.

Trois Ponts

Werbomont

82nd Abn.
Div.

Losheim

12th Vk.
Gr. Div.

12th SS

9th SS Div.

Durbuy

1st SS Pz Div.

Salm

3rd Para.
Div.

1st SS Div.

Stadtkyll

'B'
Model

Grandmenil

7th Div.

Manderfeld

18th Vk.
Gr. Div.

Hotton

3rd Div.

Dochamps

9th SS Pz Div

Vielsalm

Setz

Auw

LXVI Corps

The 116th Panzer Division advanced
into the void between Bastogne and
St Vith, taking Houffalize on the
evening of 19 December. St Vith fell
on 21 December, forcing the remnants
of 'VIII Corps' to withdraw.

116th Pz Div.

2nd SS Pz Div.

560th Div.

St Vith

106th
Div.

Laroche

Gouvy

Prüm

62nd Vk.
Gr. Div.

FIFTH
Manteuffel

9th Pz Div.

Ourthe

Houffalize

Ouren

560th Vk.
Gr. Div.

116th Div.

9th Div.

Peiper's force was encircled by the
82nd Airborne Division, but much of
them managed to escape on foot on the
23rd. At the same time the 2nd Panzer
was across the Ourthe, just over twenty
miles from the Meuse. The garrison of
Bastogne was surrounded, and was about
to be assailed by 'XLVII Panzer Corps'.

Ortheuville

28th Div.

2nd Div.

XLVII Corps
Lüttwitz

15th Gr. Div.

Noville

Dasburg

Amberloup

15th Pz
Gr. Div.

101st Abn.
Div.

Clervaux
Hosingen

26th Vk. Gr. Div.

Bastogne

10th Div.

Wiltz

Constum

Lehr Div.

On 22 December Lüttwitz sent a note
to McAuliffe, acting commander of
101st Airborne division in Bastogne,
requesting the surrender of the encircled
town. McAuliffe replied with a single
word, 'Nuts'.

Clerf

FG Bde.

5th Para.
Div.

79th Div.

The American forces around St Vith
continued their withdrawal taking up
positions between Salm and Ourthe.
While 2nd Panzer Division resumed
its drive to the Meuse.

Libremont

5th Para. Div.

Sure

LXXXV
Corps

Neufchâteau

4th Div.

26th Div.

Diekirch

352nd Vk.
Gr. Div.

276th Vk.
Gr. Div.

LXXX Corps.

On 23 December the weather lifted and
Allied air power could at last be used
to full advantage. The offensive ground
to a halt on the 24th.

9th Div.

Martelange

80th Div.

5th Div.

Sauer

Echternach

212th Vk.
Gr. Div.

SEVENTH
Brandenberger

US THIRD
Patton

Arlon

10th Div.

4th Div.

part 9th Div.

US XII
Corps

Trier

LIII Corps

SCHNEE EIFEL

Manteuffel's main attack now developed
toward Bastogne. Eisenhower ordered
7th Armored Division to St Vith, and
sent the 101st Airborne and 10th
Armored Divisions to Bastogne, arriving
early on the 19th.

On the evening of the 18th Panzer Lehr
was within five miles of Bastogne.

Allied reinforcements were on their way.
Eisenhower sent the US 82nd Airborne
Division to Werbomont while two
divisions from the US Ninth Army were
sent south to aid Hodges.

The tide turns

2 January 1945
16 January
7 February

Namur

Liège

Verviers

Eupen

Meuse

Monshau

FIFTEENTH

Huy

US XIX Corps

US V Corps

Spa
Malmedy

Stadtkyll

US FIRST
Hodges

US XVIII
Abn. Corps

SIXTH SS
Dietrich

Br. XXX
Corps

Durbuy

US VII
Corps

Stavelot

St Vith

Prüm

FIFTH
Manteuffel

Sambre

Meuse

Dinant

Ciney

Hotton

Ourthe

Marche

Celles

Rochefort

Houffalize

Clervaux

Kyll

Wellin

SEVENTH
Brandenberger

US VIII
Corps

Bastogne

Sure

Neufchâteau

Echternach

US THIRD
Patton

US III Corps

US XII Corps

Trier

The resurgence of Allied air power at
once worsened the fuel shortage which
was steadily halting the Panzers'
advance.

On 25 December 2nd Armored Division
counter-attacked and shattered 2nd
Panzer Division.

Bastogne was relieved on the 26th by
4th Armored Division. Manteuffel
launched several attacks to sever the
Bastogne corridor and capture the town.

On 3 January the Allied counter-offensive
was launched. Progress was slow due to
appalling conditions, but by the 5th
the German resistance began to crumble.

On 8 January Hitler authorized a
partial withdrawal, to a line five miles
west of Houffalize. On the same day
'Sixth Panzer Army' was ordered to the
Eastern Front.

On 16 January First and Third
Armies met at Houffalize. By 28
January the Bulge had been eliminated
altogether.

0 Miles   10   20

Right: German machine-gunners pause for a cigarette during the second day of the Ardennes offensive. **Far right:** American half-tracks and jeeps burn as the US forces are thrown back on the second day, 17 December, 1944. **Below:** US artillerymen are forced to manhandle a 57-mm anti-tank gun in mud reminiscent of the Belgian terrain fought over in World War One.

the division pressed on toward the western branch of the Ourthe, hoping to find it with the bridges intact. South of *116th Panzer, 2nd Panzer Division* of *XLVII Panzer Corps* was unable to help, since the Bastogne garrison blocked its path at Noville. By the time *116th Panzer* reached the river the bridges were blown and it thereupon fell back to Houffalize before resuming its advance northwest. Meanwhile, *2nd Panzer* forced its way through Noville, and managed to cross the Ourthe west of Bastogne.

St Vith fell on 21 December. The town's fall was a blow to the Americans; St Vith was an important communications center, and its loss made the withdrawal of the remnants of VIII Corps in the St Vith horseshoe inevitable. By this time 82nd Airborne Division was in position along the Salm, and could probably prevent a new breakout in that sector. Peiper's force was encircled, and on 23 December much of it escaped on foot, abandoning over 100 armored

vehicles. But *116th Panzer Division* was likely to resume its advance from Houffalize, and, worse still, *2nd Panzer* was safely across the Ourthe, just over twenty miles from the Meuse. The garrison of Bastogne was surrounded, and was about to be assailed by *XLVII Panzer Corps*.

On the credit side, American retention of the Elsenborn Ridge seriously constricted *Sixth Panzer Army's* line of advance. Furthermore, artillery fire from 1st Division compelled Dietrich to edge south, bringing about a series of traffic jams as the left wing of *Sixth Panzer Army* became enmeshed with the right wing of *Fifth Panzer Army* north of St Vith. Both Rundstedt and Model had been disappointed by the slowness of the advance. The former had advocated calling a halt as early as 19 December, but Model argued that the operation could still succeed if Manteuffel were given command of some of Dietrich's panzers. Hitler opposed this, not wishing to put SS formations under army command. On 21 December the

increasingly congested state of the roads around St Vith at last brought about the transfer of two SS Panzer divisions to Manteuffel.

On 22 December Lieutenant-General von Lüttwitz of *XLVII Panzer Corps* sent a courteous note to Brigadier-General Anthony McAuliffe, acting commander of 101st Airborne Division in Bastogne. 'There is only one possibility', said the note, 'of saving the availed USA troops from total annihilation; that is the honorable surrender of the encircled town'. The message went on to warn McAuliffe that failure to capitulate would result in the destruction of his forces. McAuliffe, undeterred by this threat, replied with the one unequivocal word, 'NUTS!'

Away to the south, in a blinding snowstorm, Patton began his counterattack. In other sectors, the battle hung in the balance. The defenders of the St Vith horseshoe continued their withdrawal, taking up new positions between the Salm and the Ourthe. On the following day *116th* and *2nd SS Panzer Divisions* attacked in this area, dragging part of Montgomery's counterattack force into the battle. While Dietrich, having at last ceased his futile battering at the Elsenborn Ridge, swung two SS Panzer divisions into the central sector, *2nd Panzer Division* resumed its drive to the Meuse.

Yet the tide was turning. On 23 December the weather lifted, and Allied air power could at last be employed to full advantage. The fog and snow which had obscured the skies since the beginning of the offensive had been an added bonus for the Germans, preventing the Allies from striking their advancing columns. Once the skies were clear, the Luftwaffe had no hope of gaining even temporary air superiority. Its aircraft were driven from the sky by Allied fighters, while fighter-bombers raked the roads and bombers attacked concentrations, supply dumps and communications in the rear. The Luftwaffe, it is true, was not quite finished, and on New Year's Day mounted a 700-flare attack on Allied airfields. However, as General Adolf Galland later admitted, the Ardennes battle ruined the Luftwaffe in the West.

The resurgence of Allied air power at once worsened the fuel shortage which was steadily throttling Model's Panzers. Petrol had been in short supply even at the start of the offensive, and no sizable stocks of it had been captured. Lack of fuel imposed a constant strain upon German movement. It delayed the southward move of Dietrich's Panzer divisions, and brought Peiper to a halt. It is a measure of the *Wehrmacht*'s petrol crisis that when the leading tanks of *2nd Panzer Division* stopped at Celles, only four miles from the Meuse, it was lack of fuel, not Allied pressure, which brought them to a halt.

Shortage of petrol was not the only problem besetting *2nd Panzer Division* on Christmas Day 1944. Montgomery was, as we have seen, opposed to piecemeal counterattacks. He could afford to be, since he had deployed 30 Corps along the Meuse downstream of Namur, and felt confident of dealing with any German forces that might struggle as far as the river. Hodges was less calm, owing partly to a natural reluctance to give up ground for which his men had fought hard. When

Above: Brigadier-General Anthony McAuliffe confused the Germans by his one-word reply to the German offer to surrender: 'Nuts!'
Right: Members of the 84th Division dig into snowy terrain after the German breakthrough; American lines held and the big push back began.
Center right: Three German soldiers, sent behind the lines by Skorzeny disguised as Americans and trained to learn American English down to slang expressions and GI jargon, are caught, court-martialed and sentenced to death by firing squad. These soldiers, Cpl. Wilhelm Schmidt (being tied), Officer Cadet Günther Billings and Sgt. Manfred Pernass, were caught when they failed to give the proper password while armed with American weapons and driving an American jeep. Their mission was to sabotage communications across the Meuse. **Far right:** Pernass is taken down after his execution. **Right:** German prisoners are marched to the rear during the Allied advance.

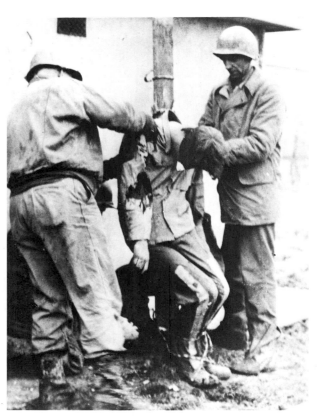

2nd Panzer reached Celles, the US 2nd Armored Division was within striking distance, and its commander, Major-General Ernest Harmon, asked his corps commander for permission to attack. The request was relayed to Hodges, who, on the evening of the 24th, tacitly authorized an attack. The next day 2nd Armored Division went forward, well supported by American aircraft, and shattered 2nd Panzer Division.

Nor was the defeat of 2nd Panzer an isolated occurrence. The 2nd SS Panzer Division, trying to force its way between the Salm and the Ourthe, was checked by the US 3rd Armored Division; 116th Panzer fared no better in the area of Marche, and Panzer Lehr was held up by VII Corps in the south. Bastogne, the ulcer on the German lines of communication, continued to hold out. Manteuffel launched a heavy attack on the town early on Christmas morning. His tanks were knocked out by well-sited American tank destroyers, and the infantry, denied armored support, were dealt with by McAuliffe's parachutists. At dusk on the following day the leading tanks of the US 4th Armored Division entered the town. Bastogne was relieved, and the southernmost prong of the German advance was in danger of being cut off.

There was a reappraisal on 28 December. The time seemed ripe for an Allied counterattack, but Montgomery and Bradley were unable to agree on this. Bradley favored immediate thrusts by the First Army in the north, and the Third Army in the south. Both armies were to be heavily rein-forced—the former with four of Montgomery's divisions. Montgomery preferred to wait. He suspected that the Germans would make one more major effort, and he was not, like the Americans, in the fortunate position of expecting constant reinforcement. Eisenhower eventually authorized Montgomery to delay his attack till 3 January. This decision did not please Bradley or Patton; nor did Montgomery's demands for a continuance of the centralized command arrangement which, the Field Marshal insisted, was essential if the forthcoming Ruhr offensive was to be successful.

The Germans, too, took stock of the situation. Rundstedt again warned Hitler that the objective of Antwerp was clearly unattainable. The best that could be achieved was what Hitler had earlier termed the 'Small Solution'; a thrust toward Liège and the encirclement of Aachen. By 28 December Rundstedt felt that the time for even this was past. He recommended instead the withdrawal of the two Panzer armies to a line east of Bastogne, to prepare for the inevitable Allied counterattack. Hitler rejected both solutions. German setbacks had, he maintained, been incurred because his plan had not been followed to the letter. He was prepared to sanction a change of emphasis by two Panzer armies, but this jab to the northwest was to be purely temporary. Antwerp remained their goal. Hitler also believed that Patton had now become so overextended that a German offensive in Alsace would compel him to disengage from the Ardennes to meet it.

The Alsace offensive was launched on New Year's Day 1945. The Germans committed ten divisions in all, and the threat to Strasbourg gave rise to another inter-Allied crisis. American suggestions that the line should be rationalized to lessen the danger of a German breakthrough were opposed by General Jean de Lattre de Tassigny of the French 1st Army, who, naturally, was backed by General Charles de Gaulle. De Gaulle protested to both Roosevelt and Churchill, and eventually, partially due to Churchill's intervention, Eisenhower decided against withdrawal. Strasbourg was held, and though the offensive made slight progress, it did so at the price of 25,000 German casualties; if the Allied troops used to check it could not be employed in the Ardennes, neither could the German forces be engaged; the Alsace offensive simply whittled away at the already thin German reserves.

The battle in the Ardennes was not yet over. Manteuffel had launched several attacks on the corridor to Bastogne, but on 2 January, worried that his forward elements would be cut off by an American attack, he asked for permission to fall back to take up a defensive line running through Houffalize. Hitler refused, and on 3 and 4 January Manteuffel renewed his efforts to sever the corridor and take Bastogne. The capture of Bastogne remained as vital as ever, for even if, as Hitler now realized, a drive to Antwerp was impossible, retention of the Ardennes pocket could significantly delay the Allied Ruhr offensive. And, if the bulge was to be held, Bastogne had to be taken.

The failure of Manteuffel's last thrusts at Bastogne became obscured by the Allied counter-

Far left: Wounded German soldier in winter gear awaits capture. **Center left:** Sgt. Joseph Holmes of Cumberland, Maryland was typical of the unshaven and exhausted GIs who fought in the Bastogne area. **Left:** Members of the 101st Airborne greet the liberators of the Bastogne pocket at their HQ.

offensive. On 3 January, despite frightful weather conditions which totally prevented air cover and which turned roads into lethal skating-rinks, Collins began to advance from the Ourthe toward Houffalize. Progress was painfully slow, largely due to the appalling conditions which made it easy for a few desperate men behind a roadblock to hold up the advance for hours. Things were no easier on the Third Army front, but on 5 January the crust weakened. Model withdrew one SS Panzer division to aid Dietrich in the north, and Manteuffel took another out of the line to form an operational reserve. On 8 January Hitler at last authorized a partial withdrawal, to a line five miles west of Houffalize.

The policy of limited withdrawal could not survive for long. The Eastern Front had remained virtually stationary from August 1944 until the end of the year, but on 12 January the Red Army launched a massive offensive. Guderian had aptly compared the Eastern Front to a house of cards, and the ferocious Russian pressure compelled Hitler to take all available steps to shore up the crumbling structure. Dietrich's Panzer divisions were ordered back to St Vith on 8 January, and on the 22nd *Sixth Panzer Army* was transferred to the Eastern Front.

The US First and Third Armies met at Houffalize on 16 January. On the following day Bradley resumed command of the First Army, although the Ninth Army remained under Montgomery for the Ruhr offensive. The German retirement from the pocket never became a rout. Here the Germans were once more helped by the weather, which in early January again restricted Allied mastery of the air. Also, the Allied decision to not attack the shoulders of the bulge with the aim of cutting it off, made an orderly withdrawal possible. Manteuffel was pushed back by frontal pressure, rather than

Far left: Members of the 83rd Infantry Division move through the main street of Bihain in Belgium to attack Nazi troops dug in the woods beyond the town. **Above left:** US combat engineers work in icy water to widen a bridge during the advance near Houffalize in January 1945. **Below left:** US Army transport moves into Bastogne after the town is relieved.

251

being compelled to fall back by threats to his flanks. His men, although demoralized by the failure of the offensive from which so much had been expected, retired with stubborn determination, aided by terrain and weather. On 22 January the skies cleared once more, and Allied aircraft hammered German columns on the Our crossings. By 28 January the bulge had been eliminated altogether.

The fighting had cost the Americans 81,000 men and considerable quantities of equipment. Yet while American losses could be quickly replaced, the 100,000 German casualties imposed a further strain upon dwindling German manpower. The same was true of equipment; German tank and aircraft losses could never be repaired.

It is too easy to see the Ardennes offensive as simply another of Hitler's strategic blunders. There was some logic behind it. An offensive would permit the *Wehrmacht* to seize the initiative and to employ its armor in what many German generals regarded as its prime role, the attack. It would also spoil the Allied offensive into the Ruhr, and might substantially weaken Allied unity. The fact that Hitler undertook the operation in defiance of the opinion of his professional military advisers is, in itself, no guarantee that Hitler was wrong. He had, after all, been right, in the face of serious military opposition and over the same ground, in 1940.

This logic, such as it was, rested upon false premises. Firstly, the Allies were by no means in such disarray as Hitler imagined. Although the Ardennes offensive did put stresses, both political and military, upon the Allies, it totally failed to induce defeatism in London or Washington. Far from weakening Allied resolve, the offensive strengthened it. Secondly, Hitler's desire to mount a new blitzkrieg was at variance with bald facts. The 1940 attack had succeeded because the Germans possessed air superiority over the Ardennes; their columns could use the narrow roads and bridges without danger of attack. To attempt the same task with the roads worsened by winter was dangerous enough; to attempt it in the face of Allied air power was fatal. The American retention of Bastogne, and the long defense of St Vith further reduced the roads available, compressing the German lines of supply into a dangerously narrow bottleneck. Shortage of petrol, too, placed growing stresses upon movement in and behind the battle area.

Finally, none of the senior German commanders believed that the offensive could succeed. As Dietrich put it, 'All I had to do was to cross the river, capture Brussels, and then go on to take the port of Antwerp. The snow was waist deep and there wasn't room to deploy four tanks abreast, let alone six armored divisions. It didn't get light till eight and was dark again at four, and my tanks can't fight at night. And all this at Christmas time'. Manteuffel, the most sanguine as well as the most capable of the German army commanders, said after the war that while the offensive was justifiable in strategic terms, the tactical and logistical problems it entailed were bound to bring about its failure.

Although the offensive had caused the Allied commanders considerable loss of sleep, it had never produced a climate similar to that of, for

Below: An example of how even the heaviest German tank could be wiped out by a direct hit. This Panther was knocked out near Bastogne on 3 January, 1945.

instance, March 1918, when the Germans threatened to break through on the Western Front. But the rifts in the Allied command were not easy to heal. Montgomery's cool, even clinical handling of the northern sector was praiseworthy, but his subsequent interviews with the press made implications which Bradley, in particular, found objectionable. Churchill took a less partisan view. Speaking in the House of Commons, he pointed out that there had been 30 or 40 times more Americans than British engaged, and 60 to 70 times more American casualties. It was, in his opinion, the greatest American battle of the war and an ever-famous American victory.

Conclusion

The twelve epic land battles described in this book noted the changes in weaponry from the pikes and swords of Yorktown to the planes and tanks of the Ardennes. Since World War Two far more terrifying and sophisticated weapons have been invented and used in war. But one point emerges clearly from these changes of style and emphasis over the past two centuries:

Over the past two centuries: weapons and tactics may change, but certain strategic concepts still remain valid. The Cannae principle of double encirclement still tantalizes military planners; the lust for territory and power is still evident. It was ever thus, and shall continue to be as long as human beings are prone to human error and weakness.

Index

Acknowledgments

Associated Press: 220 above, 251 centre; **Balzer/Trans Ocean:** 234 above left; **Bildarchiv Ost. Nationalbibliothek:** 123 left, 128, 129, 130; **Bundesarchiv:** 4–5, 195 below, 224–225 **Dorka:** 169; **Mary Evans Picture Library:** 96 above right; **Giraudon:** 30–31, 32, 33 above left, 35, 38, 39, 41, 42, 44 above, 44–45, 46–47, 48, 52, 53, 134, 138 above 148–9 below, 150 above left; **Robert Hunt Library:** 2–3, 34–35, 40, 56, 78 above, 80 above left, 92–93, 104–5, 118, 119, 122, 123 right, 124–7, 131 below, 132, 133, 135, 137 below, 139 below, 144 below, 145 below left, 146, 148 above, 149 above, 150 above right, 152 centre, 152 below, 153 above, 154–161, 162–3 below, 166 above left, 166–7 below, 167 above, 168, 170–1 below, 185 above right, 193,

195 above left 198, 199 below, 200–1 below, 203 above, 203 below, 205 above, 206 above, 207–9, 214, 217, 218, 219 above, 220 below, 221 above, 225 above right, 226–231, 232 above, 234 above centre, 240, 246 above left, 249, 250 above left, 251 below; **Illustrated London News:** 99; **Imperial War Museum:** 166 above right, 170, 171 above, 171 centre, 172–179, 182–4, 185 above left, 186–191, 194, 195 above right, 196–7, 201 above, 203 centre, 204, 212–3 above, 219 below right, 221 below, 232–3 below, 234–235, 235 centre right, 238 above, 238 centre right, 242 inset, 247 above, 248; **Independence National Park, Philadelphia:** 14 above; **Library of Congress:** 10 above left, 12, 13, 14–5 above, 19 below, 21 below, 25, 27 inset, 29, 74–5,

75 above, 76 above, 77 above, 81, 82–3 below, 85, 86 below right, 88–9 below, 89 above, 96 above left, 96–7 below, 98, 100, 102 above right, 102 below, 103, 106–7 below, 107 above, 110, 112–3, 113 above left, 115; **Magnum Photos:** 116–7, 131 above; **Mansell Collection:** 102 above left, 114; **Mariners' Museum Newport News, Virginia:** 20 below; **National Army Museum:** 50–1, 54 above, 54 centre right, 54–5, 55 above, 57, 59–66, 67 above, 68–70, 70–1; **National Maritime Museum:** 71 inset, 72 below left, 72–3 above; **New York Public Library:** 16; **Novosti Press Agency:** 43 below; **Pierpont Morgan Library:** 28; **Tennessee State Museum:** 10 left; **US Air Force:** 241 above; **US Army:** 26–7, 205 below, 235 above centre, 238–9

below, 241 below, 244–5, 246 above right, 246–7 below, 250 above right, 250 below, 251 above, 252–3; **US National Archives:** 17, 22–3, 216; **US National Park Service:** 18, 19 above right; **US Navy:** 19 below left, 77 below, 80 below, 80–1 above, 81 above right, 83 above, 84, 85, 85 centre left, 86–7 above, 87 below, 90–1, 94 above; **H. Roger Viollet:** 33 above right, 33 below, 43 above, 72 below right, 136 above, 137 above, 140 above, 140–1, 142, 144 above, 145 above, 145 below right, 147, 150–1, 151 above, 152 above, 152–3 below, 163 above; **Virginia State Museum:** 10–11 below; **West Point Museum Collection, US Military Academy:** 113 centre right; **Zennaro:** 199 above.